James L. Buchanan

Cases Decided in the Supreme Court of the Cape of Good Hope

with table of cases and alphabetical index, 1868-1869

James L. Buchanan

Cases Decided in the Supreme Court of the Cape of Good Hope
with table of cases and alphabetical index, 1868-1869

ISBN/EAN: 9783337091392

Printed in Europe, USA, Canada, Australia, Japan

Cover: Foto ©Suzi / pixelio.de

More available books at **www.hansebooks.com**

CASES

DECIDED

IN THE SUPREME COURT

OF THE

CAPE OF GOOD HOPE,

DURING THE YEAR

1868,

WITH TABLE OF CASES AND ALPHABETICAL INDEX.

BY

JAMES BUCHANAN,

ADVOCATE.

JUDGES OF THE SUPREME COURT

DURING THE YEAR

1868.

HODGES, C. J. : Died 17th August.

BELL, J. : Appointed Acting C.J. 18th August. Confirmed as C.J. December.

CONNOR, J. : Returned to Natal 1st August.

DENYSSEN, J. : Joined Supreme Court from Eastern Districts Court 1st September.

DWYER, J. : Arrived from England, *vice Connor, J.*, 14th August.

CASES REPORTED IN THIS VOLUME.

	PAGE
A. B., *in Re* Estate of..240,	250
Archer, *in Re* Insolvent Estate of..	105
Arnholz, Applicant ; Divisional Council of Tulbagh, Respondents......	37
Basson *vs.* Civil Commissioner, Paarl..	235
Blignaut's Trustee *vs.* Cilliers' Executors and Others.....................	206
Board of Executors, Applicants ; Stigling, Respondent...................	25
Brits *vs.* Brits (1842), *Appendix*...	312
Ceres, Municipal Commissioners of, *vs.* Arnholz	2
Ceres, Municipality, *in Re*..	234
Collison & Co. *vs.* Schmidt...	33
Collison & Co. *vs.* Wiese..	24
Dantu *vs.* Widow Hart's Executors..	168
Deare & Dietz, Applicants ; Honeyborne, Respondent.....................	107
Deare & Dietz *vs.* Korsten	17
De Kock's Estate, *in Re*	252
Denison, *in Re*	5
De Pass, Appellant ; Owners *Tigris* and *Eunomia*, Respondents......	26
De Pass & Co. *vs.* Trustees Frontier Fire & Life Insurance Company...	28
De Vos, Trustee of, Applicant ; Bourhill & Co., Respondents............	1
Dickson *vs.* Cape Town Council and McKenzie	13
Dreyer's Estate, *in Re*..	246
Esterhuysen's Executrix *vs.* Vermeulen.......................................	76
Fick and Karstel *vs.* Baartman...	240
Fleck *vs.* Möller	118
George Divisional Bank, *in Re*	241
Gowie & Co., Applicants ; Smith, Respondent	103
Graham, N. O., *vs.* Pocock & Co.......................................231,	'233
Hawkins, H., *in Re*..23,	285
Honeyborne, Appellant ; Tinley, Respondent.................................	34
Hofmeyr, Neethling's Executor, *vs.* De Wet (1853). *Appendix*.........	317
Jahre, *in Re*...	17
Jonker, *in Re*...	21
Joseph's Executor *vs.* Peacock..	247
Lamb Brothers *vs.* Rousseau...3,	139
Laubscher *vs.* Basson's Executor...	251
Lubbe and Others *vs.* Burton	7
Magistrates' Reviewed Cases..140,	309
Matthews' Trustees *vs.* Stewart...	251
McLeod & Co. *vs.* Dunell, Ebden & Co.	182
Meiring, G. H., *in Re*...	12
Mostert *vs.* S. A. Association..	286
Natal Land Company, *ex parte*..	4

	PAGE
Nicholson's Trustee vs. Coetzee	239
Oosthuysen vs. Oosthuysen	51
Pocock, Applicant, vs. Stoll, Respondent	115
Port Elizabeth Divisional Council, Appellants ; Uitenhage Divisional Council, Respondents 40,	221
Preuss & Seligmann, Applicants ; Bosman, Respondent	113
Prickett vs. Prickett	25
Queen vs. Swartz	13
Reed, Appellant ; Divisional Council of Port Elizabeth, Respondents	110
Rykie vs. Rykie	114
S. A. Loan and Investment Company vs. Widow Jacobs and Another	6
Saget, Applicant ; Bataillou, Respondent	32
Silberbauer vs. Ruthven	100
Smith & Another vs. Pinto	105
Smith, J. O., & Co., vs. Stewart	48
Smith, J. O., & Co., vs. Standard Bank	253
Southey, G., in Re	15
Truby's Trustee, Applicant; Swemmer & Coetzee, Respondents....218,	285
Truby's Trustee, Applicant ; Barrington, Respondent	219
Tucker, Appellant ; Austen's Trustee, Respondent	145
Uitenhage Divisional Council vs. Reed	126
Van der Byl & Co. vs. Widow Du Plessis	2
Van der Byl & Co. vs. Hoffman	14
Van Wyk vs. Van Wyk	252
Von Ludwig vs. Van Reenen	244
Vigors vs. Campbell	120
Walker & Co. vs. Beeton's Trustees	225
Waterman's Executors vs. Wolfrey	139
Wollaston vs. Wehmeyer	243
Wykham vs. Kingon	24

INDEX TO THE VOLUME.

ACT 15, 1856, § 5.—See Master and Servant.
—— 20, 1856, § 33.—See Appeal.
—— 20, 1856, § 35.—See Provisional Sentence.
—— 20, 1856, § 37.—See Enrolled Agent.
—— 20, 1856, § 45.—See Resident Magistrate.
—— 9, 1858, §§ 38, 39, 41.—See Public Roads Act.—Trustees.
—— 23, 1858, Schedule A.—See Ferry.
—— 4, 1861, § 8.—See Witness Expenses.
—— 6, 1861, § 5.—See Medical Charges.
—— 20, 1861, § 2.—See Telegraph.
—— 10, 1864.—See Main Roads.
—— 16, 1864, § 24.—See Eastern Districts Court.
—— 4, 1865, §§ 16, 75.—See Divisional Councils Consolidation.
—— 7, 1865.—See Land Beacons Consolidation.
—— 11, 1867.—See Public Bodies' Debts Act.
—— 17, 1867, §§ 7, 8.—See Receiving Stolen Goods.
—— 12, 1868.—See Joint-stock Companies' Winding-up.
—— Mutiny, § 85.—See Prisoners' Statements.
APPEAL—Leave to appeal from Resident Magistrate's judgment granted, after time for noting fixed by the Act 20, 1856, § 33, had expired. *Smith vs. Pinto* 105
—— See Enrolled Agent.
APPREHENSION—Warrant of, must be on sworn information............ 140
ARREST—*Personal, Civil.*]—Is an arrest effected in the back-yard of a dwelling-house legal ? *Pocock vs. Stoll*................................. 115
—— *Discharge of,* where at the time of the arrest the arresting deputy sheriff had not a copy of the writ in his possession, but acted solely on telegraphic message from the sheriff in Cape Town. *Silberbauer vs. Ruthven*.. 100
—— of part interest in a vessel at the suit of a co-part-owner in another vessel refused. *A. de Pass vs. Cwners " Tigris" and " Eunomia"* 26
—— *Discharge of. Saget vs. Bataillou*... 32
ASSIGNMENT.—See Sequestration.
ATTACHMENT—*Tenant—Rent.*]—Where an order was granted attaching a tenant's goods for arrear rent, but before it could be executed the tenant had removed the goods into another house, where she was not, however, a tenant for hire, the Court ordered the removal of the goods into the house from which they had been so taken away. *Board of Executors vs. Stigling*.. 25
AUCTIONEER.—See Warranty.
BAIL BOND—*Cancellation of*.. 32
BEACON.—See Land Beacons Consolidation Act.

BEQUEST—*Inofficious.*—See Legitimate Portion.
BOUNDARIES.—See Land Beacons Consolidation Act.
BROKER'S NOTE.—See Custom of Trade.
CHILDREN—*Custody of.*—See Marriage.
CIRCUIT COURT—*Costs, Taxation of.*—See Costs.
CIVIL COMMISSIONER.—See Divisional Councils Consolidation Act.
COLLUSION BY CREDITORS.—See Undue Preference.
COMMISSIONERS (*under Act* 7, 1865.)—See Land Beacons Consolidation Act.
CONJUGAL RIGHTS.—See Marriage.
CONTEMPT OF COURT.—See Resident Magistrate.
CONTRACT—Breach of. *Dropped defence. Fick and Karstel vs. Baartman* 240
—— Action for damages for breach of. *Smith vs. Standard Bank* 253
—— Specific Performance of. *Joseph vs. Peacock* 247
COSTS—*Taxation of.*]—The Supreme Court refused to allow the re-opening, for review in Cape Town, of a Circuit Bill of Costs taxed and allowed by the Registrar of Circuit; but gave liberty to apply before the next Circuit Court. *Truby's Trustee vs. Swemmer and Coetzee* 218
—— See Provisional Sentence.
—— See Retainer.—Divisional Councils Consolidation Act.—Master.
CURATOR BONIS.—*Appointment of.*]—*Re Henry Hawkins* 23
—— Where a mortgagor had left the Colony thirteen years ago, and was since unheard of, the Court, to save the expense of edictal citation, usually resorted to, held it sufficient to insert a special notice in the *Gazette*, and thereafter to appoint a *curator bonis* and decreed sequestration. *Executors Waterman vs. Wolfrey* 23, 139
CUSTOMS REGULATIONS.—*Ord.* 6, 1853, § 32.]—Where an entry was passed at the Custom-house for three carriages and a package of glassware, and on seizure of the carriages by the Custom-house authorities they were found to contain 3,350 gross of corks, the Court ordered the forfeiture of the corks and carriages, but not of the glassware. *Intent.*—The question of intent is immaterial under section 32 of the Ordinance. *Graham, N.O., vs. Pocock & Co.* 231
—— § 50.] In order to make out a case under § 50, it is essential to prove guilty knowledge and fraudulent intent .... *Ibid*, 233
CUSTOM OF TRADE.—*Sale and Purchase.—Broker's Note, interpretation of, by extrinsic evidence.*]—McLeod & Co, of Cape Town, sold to Dunell, Ebden & Co., of Port Elizabeth, 25 hhds. of Cape brandy, upon a broker's note which made the strength of the brandy to be "19°," without mention of a standard. The Court held, and it was indeed admitted, that, interpreted by extrinsic evidence, chiefly gathered from correspondence between the parties, the expression "19°" in the note meant 19° according to Cartier's hydrometer. It was proved that the brandy, when shipped, was of 19° strength, as tested, in the broker's presence, by a small glass Cartier, without scale or thermometer attached. Evidence was also led to show that, by the custom of trade in the Colony, brandy is bought and sold by such a test, and not by that of a true brass Cartier, with scale and thermometer attached; the only Cartier in the Colony of that superior description being in the possession of the defendants.

HELD: (by majority, CONNOR, J., *diss.*) That such a custom of trade as above stated had been proved to exist ; that it was a reasonably fair one ; and that there was evidence to show that the defendants must have been aware of its existence at the time of contract. *McLeod & Co. vs. Dunell, Ebden & Co.* 182

DEFAULT—*Action by.—Defective service in. Collison & Co. vs. Schmidt* 33

DEFENCE—*Dropped.*—See Contract.

DEPUTY-SHERIFF—See Arrest.

DIVISIONAL COUNCIL—*Action to recover subsidy*—See Main Roads Act.

DIVISIONAL COUNCIL CONSOLIDATION ACT (*No.* 4, 1865, § 16)—*Costs of abandoned motion under.*] SEMBLE. It is the duty of the Civil Commissioner of a Division to produce to registered voters the nomination list for candidates when application is made within the limits of time fixed by the Act. *Lubbe and others vs. Burton* 7

—— § 75—*Interpretation of.*] What is a Divisional Councillor's "direct or indirect interest" in a Council Contract, under § 75. *Arnholz vs. Tulbagh Divisional Council* 37

DIVORCE.—See Marriage.

EASTERN DISTRICTS COURT.—*Act* 16, 1864.—*Exception.*]—Where it appeared from the record that a case had been sent up to the Supreme Court by the Eastern Districts Court, under section 24 of Act 16, 1864 (there being a difference of opinion), but for the adjudication of one exception only, and not for the hearing of the whole case, the Supreme Court declined to hear arguments on the exception, and remitted the record to the Eastern Districts Court for amendment. *J. O. Smith & Co. vs. Stewart* 48

EVIDENCE.—*Inadmissible questions. Vigors vs. Campbell.* 120

—— Extrinsic.—See Custom of Trade.

ENDORSEMENT.—See Provisional Sentence.

ENROLLED AGENT.—*Appeal.—Act* 20, 1856, § 37.]—Where an enrolled agent in the Prince Albert Magistrate's Court appealed to the Supreme Court against an order that he should be struck off the roll, the Court set aside the order on account of the non-hearing of appellant's evidence. *Honeyborne vs. Tinley* 34

ENTRY.—See Customs Regulations.

ERROR OF LAW.—*Action to recover money paid under.*—See Main Roads Act.

EXCEPTIONS.—See Marine Insurance.—Eastern Districts Court.

EXECUTOR.—*Ord.* 104, § 21.]—Where the survivor and executor under a joint will becomes insane, the Court, if satisfied upon affidavit as to such incapacity, will, under section 21 of Ord. No. 104, direct a meeting for the election of a fresh executor. *Re Estate of G. Southey* 15

FALCIDIAN FOURTH--*Will, construction of. Liquidation Account, amendment of.*]—A testatrix first bequeathed £950 as a legacy between twelve persons, of whom J. W. D., the plaintiff, was one ; and then declared "further to nominate and appoint as the sole and universal heirs of all the residue and remainder of her estate and effects, S. V. H. and M. J. D., in equal shares and proportions," &c. The executors, on realizing the estate, found the proceeds £850 only, and made a *pro rata* distribution thereof among the legatees, awarding to each £134 1s. 6d., instead of £189 6s. 5d. ; the difference between these amounts being the *pro rata* contribution of each legatee towards the Falcidian Fourth, which the executors awarded to S. v. H. and M. J. D., regarding them as ordinary heirs, and entitled to such portion. The plaintiff brought an action to amend the liquidation account, on the ground that on his construction of the words of the will, S. v. H. and M. J. D., having been instituted heirs " of all the residue and remainder," &c., they were not heirs in the ordinary sense of the word, nor entitled to claim the Falcidian Fourth. And so the Court held. *Dantu vs. Wid. Hart's Executors* 168

FORFEITURE FOR COLLUSION.—See undue Preference.

FERRY.—*Right of.*—*Pleading : Non-joinder.*—*Act* 23, 1858, *Schedule A.*] *Uitenhage Divisional Council vs. Reed* 126

FIDEI-COMMISSUM.—See Legitimate Portion.

GRANT.—Is a quitrent grant a liquid document debt ? *Basson vs. Civil Commissioner, Paarl* 235

———. See Land Beacons Consolidation Act.

INFORMATIONS.—See Warrant.

INHERITANCE.—Where two co-heirs under a testator's will prevailed upon a third co-heir to sign a document during the testator's lifetime, but unknown to such testator, whereby the third co-heir surrendered or modified his right of inheritance to accrue under the will, SEMBLE. That such document or consent-paper is void, and cannot bind the party signing. *Blignaut's Trustee vs. Cilliers' Executors and others* 206

INSOLVENT ESTATES.—See Master.

INTENT.—The question of intent is immaterial under Sec. 32 of the Customs Ord. 6, 1853. *Graham, N. O., vs. Pocock*................231, 233

INTERDICT.—See Nuisance.

JOINT-STOCK COMPANY, *dissolved.*—*Receivers, Liquidators & Managers of.*]—Where a joint-stock company was formed for a limited time, and expired by the efflux of that time, but no provision had been made in the deed of incorporation for the winding up of the company, application was made to the Court for the appointment of receivers, liquidators and managers domiciled within the Colony, to make transfer, in the neighbouring Colony of Natal, of certain lands there enregistered in the name of the company ; but the application was refused on the ground that it had better be made to the Natal Court. *Trustees Natal Land Company, Ex parte*...... 4

JOINT-STOCK COMPANIES WINDING-UP ACT (12, 1868).—*First proceedings under.*—*Practice. In re George Div. Bank*........................ 241

LAND BEACONS CONSOLIDATION ACT (7 *of* 1865), *Construction of. Decision of Commissioners appointed under, reversed on appeal.*—" *Sale according to diagram,*" *effect of.*]—Original beacons, and occupation according to, prevail over diagram and grant where the dispute as to such diagram and grant is raised within thirty years after the passing of the Act. And where, upwards of seventeen years before the passing of the Act, Esterhuysen had commenced an action against respondent as to boundaries, but upon advice by counsel that according to the then state of the law, having purchased " according to diagram," he would be unsuccessful in the action ; and where, accordingly, he withdrew the action, and abandoned homestead and spring of water to respondent ; but after the passing of the Act of 1865, revived his former dispute, which was thereupon inquired into by the Commission, and decision given against him. HELD : That, notwithstanding the abandonment aforesaid, no vested right had accrued thereupon to respondent ; but that it was open to Esterhuysen, availing himself of the provisions of the Act, to have a fresh inquiry into the merits of the dispute. *Esterhuysen's Executrix vs. Vermeulen*................................... 76

LEGITIMATE PORTION—*Mutual Will—Trebellianic Fourth.—Inofficious Sale and Bequest.—Fidei-Commissum.—Lex Hac Edictali.—Ord. No.* 6, 1843, § 48.]—Where the husband of a testator's daughter surrendered his estate in insolvency before the testator's death, the testator can by subsequent will or codicil impose on the daughter's legitim certain *fidei-commissa*, which will prevent the absolute property in the legitim vesting in the daughter or her husband to whom she was married in community, and will, to some extent, preserve it for the children of the marriage. *Blignaut's Trustee vs. Cilliers' Executors and others*... 206

LEX HAC EDICTALI.—See Legitimate Portion.

LIBEL—*Injuria literalis : what constitutes.*]—*Vigors vs. Campbell* 120

LIQUIDATION ACCOUNT—*Trustees' Commission.—Ord.* 6, 1843.]—The Court would not depart from the tariff of trustees' charges fixed by Ord. 6, 1843—(viz., 5 per cent. on movables, 2¼ on immovables)—by allowing to a trustee 5 per cent. on the whole purchase amount of a farm sold before the insolvency, when, in fact, the insolvent had himself, before insolvency, received a portion of such purchase money, and the trustee had only recovered the balance, although after the expenditure of considerable labour in securing the adoption of the sale by the trustee of the purchaser who had likewise become insolvent. *Re Insolvent Estate of H. Denison*... 5

—— Amendment *of*.—See Falcidian Fourth.—Trustees.

MAIN ROADS ACT (10 *of* 1864).—*Divisional Council—Action to recover subsidy. Error of law—Action to recover money paid under. Port Elizabeth Divisional Council vs. Uitenhage Divisional Council*..... 221

MARINE INSURANCE.—*Argument on plaintiffs' exceptions to defendants' pleas.*]—A policy of marine insurance against bar-risk contained the words " warranted free of average, unless general, or the vessel be stranded," and in a subsequent portion, "and warranted free from particular average." .The vessel having stranded on the bar in crossing, the assured claimed particular average. The insurers resisted the claim on the strength of the words secondly quoted. HELD, for the purposes of the pleadings, that as, in the opinion of the Court, the ordinary legal effect should be given to the words, " or the vessel be stranded,"—to wit, that the insurers thereupon became liable to pay particular average, the defendants' plea of no particular average under the policy was no answer to the declaration on the policy ; and the plaintiffs' exceptions were sustained accordingly. *De Pass & Co. vs. Trustees Frontier Fire and Marine Insurance Company*.. 28

MARRIAGE—Proof of, in an action for Divorce : what held sufficient.—
Children, custody of, with father, after mother's adultery proved in
action for Divorce.] *Prickett vs. Prickett*........................... 25
—— Proof of in an action for restitution of conjugal rights. *Rykie vs.
Rykie*... 114
MASTER.—*Insolvent Estates.*—*Costs.*—*Taxation*]—It is the duty of the
Master to tax attorneys' bills of costs filed in insolvent estates,
and to charge 4 per cent. for the taxation. *Re Insolvent Estate
Jahre*... 17
MASTER AND SERVANT..141, 2
MEDICAL CHARGES—*Recovery of.*]—A medical man in this Colony has
a common-law right to sue for and recover fees due to him ; which
right prescribes, by statute, in three years, under the provisions of
Act 6, 1861. *Fleck vs. Moller*...................................... 118
NUISANCE—Interdict granted to prevent. *Dickson vs. Town Council,
Cape Town*... 13
OATH.—See Seduction.
ONUS PROBANDI.—See Public Roads Act.
Ordinance 6, 1843.—See Liquidation Account.—Trustee.
—— „ „ §§ 2, 5.—See Sequestration.
—— „ „ § 52.—See Trustee, removal of, for insolvency.
—— No. 104, § 21.—See Executor.
—— 6, 1843, § 42.—See Trustee, removal of, under.
—— „ „ §§ 26, 39, 40.—See Trustee, election of, confirmed.
—— „ „ §§ 84, 86, 88.—See Undue Preference.
—— „ „ § 48.—See Legitimate Portion.
—— „ do.——See Trustee.
—— 6, 1853, §§ 32, 50.—See Customs Regulations.
—— 15, 1845, § 3.— See Will.
PARTNERS' PRIVATE ESTATE.—See Sequestration, voluntary.
PLEADING.—Ultra vires must be specially pleaded. *Smith vs. Standard
Bank*... 253
——. See Ferry.
POWER OF ATTORNEY.—One of two trustees cannot sign a valid power
of attorney authorizing the commencement of an action ; the power,
to be good, must be signed by both. *Walker & Co. vs. Becton's
Trustees*.. 225
PRE-EMPTION—Right of. *Joseph vs. Peacock*......................... 247
PRESENTATION.—See Provisional Sentence.
PRISONERS' STATEMENTS — Mutiny Act, § 85......................... 148
PROVISIONAL SENTENCE—*Endorsement.*]—Where a promissory note
bore several endorsements, the last but one of which was "Pay
A. F., Esq., order, D. E. & Co.," and the last "L. Bros.," with no
intermediate endorsement by A. F., and where L. Bros. sued F. D.
R., the drawer of the note ; the Court took objection to the absence
of endorsement by A. F. On averment that the note, though
endorsed by D. E. & Co., with intention to hand it over to A. F.,
had, in reality, never quitted the possession of D. E. & Co., and
that A. F. did not reside within the Colony, the Court required
these facts to be stated in an affidavit, and a copy of the affidavit
to be served upon the defendant. But the defendant making no

appearance thereafter, provisional sentence was granted against him accordingly. *Lamb Brothers vs. Rousseau* 3, 139

PROVISIONAL SENTENCE.--*Presentation.*]--Presentation at the "Colonial Bank, Cape Town," is not a regular presentation where the note is made payable at the " Colonial Bank " only. But where there is no Colonial Bank, nor branch bank, nor, indeed, any bank at all, at the place where the note is drawn, and where there is only one Colonial Bank in the Colony, and that at Cape Town, the presentation will hold good on affidavit made of these facts. *Van der Byl & Co. vs. Wid. Du Plessis*............. 2

——— *Sheriff's Service, when insufficient.*]—*Wykham vs. Kingon*......... 24

——— on summons in principal case refused. *S. A. Loan and Investment Company vs. Jacobs and Another*............................ 6

——— Costs in. *A. vs. B*................ 240

PUBLIC BODIES' DEBTS ACT (No. 11 of 1867)—*Proceedings under. In re Ceres Municipality*... 234

PUBLIC ROADS ACT (9, 1858)—*Notices under §§ 38 and 39.—Onus probandi.*]—Proof of the due issue of by the Divisional Council notices required by the 38th and 39th sections of the Public Roads Act, does not rest upon the Council, in favour of whose proceedings the doctrine of "*omnia rite esse acta*" will prevail; it lies upon defendants maintaining the non-issuing of such notices, to prove that allegation, unless *mala fides* should *prima facie* appear.—See *Reed, Appellant vs. Divisional Council, Port Elizabeth*.............. 110

QUITRENT.—See Magistrates' Courts.

RECEIVING STOLEN GOODS—*Guilty Knowledge*................................ 141

RENT.—See Attachment for.

RESIDENT MAGISTRATE—*Contempt of Court.*]—It is beyond the power of Resident Magistrates, under section 45 of Act 20, 1856, to sentence for contempt of Court prisoners undergoing trial on a substantive charge; that section applying only to bystanders and others not in custody. *Queen vs. Schwartz*................... 13

RESIDENT MAGISTRATE'S COURT.]--Is it ground of objection to an action by a Civil Com., *nomine officii*, for arrear quitrent, that he is himself the Res. Magistrate to try the case. *Basson vs. Cir. Com., Paarl* 235

RETAINER—*Special.—Costs.*]—Special retainer to counsel, allowed in taxation, as between party and party.—*Municipal Commissioners of Ceres vs. Arnholz*... 2

RIVER.]—Where by Government Proclamation the "right bank" of a river was declared to be the boundary between two divisions, the Court held, on appeal (reversing the judgment of the Circuit Court), that the right bank extended to the water's edge at low, and not at high-water mark. *Divisional Council, Port Elizabeth, vs. Divisional Council, Uitenhage*................................... 40

SALE "*according to Diagram.*"—See Land Beacons Consolidation Act.

——— *Conditions of.*—See Warranty.

——— AND BEQUEST.—*Inofficious.*—See Legitimate Portion.

——— AND PURCHASE.—See Custom of Trade.

——— of half of a farm to a third party, contrary to the agreement between former joint-owners of the farm, stipulating for the right of pre-emption set aside. *Joseph vs. Peacock*.................. 47

SCHEDULES.—See Sequestration, Voluntary.
SEDUCTION.—*Action of.*]—The man's oath is entitled to preference over the woman's if there is no *aliunde* evidence to support her statement 244
SEQUESTRATION, VOLUNTARY.—*Partner's Private Estate--Schedules— Ord.* 6, 1843, § 2.]—Order for voluntary sequestration of a partner's private estate made by the Court without the production of the usual schedules, upon affidavit that such schedules could not be framed. *Re G. H. Merring* 12
—— *Compulsory, decreed after assignment.*]—Where it was specially provided in the deed that in the case of fraud, or non-acceptance by particular creditors of *pro rata* dividends, the assignees, the present plaintiffs, " might take any proceedings they may think fit for the recovery of their said claims," non-acceptance of the dividend having been proved, the Court held that, under the circumstances of the case, the defendant could not set up the deed of assignment in bar of the plaintiffs' present application for compulsory sequestration. *Doare & Dietz vs. Korsten*... 17
—— *Assignment.—Ord.* 6, 1843, §5.]—Order for compulsory sequestration refused, on return of *nulla bona*, where an assignment was working more beneficially to the creditors. *Trustee De Vos vs. Bourhill & Co.* 1
SHEEP LEASE.—See Undue Preference.
SHERIFF'S SERVICE—*When insufficient.*—See Provisional Sentence.— Default.
SHIP ARREST.—See Arrest.
SUMMONS—*Misdescription of Defendant in. Nicholson's Trustee vs. Coetzee*.. 239
SURVIVOR.—See Will, Mutual.
TAXATION.—See Master.
TELEGRAPH ACT (20, 1861)—*First proceedings under. Wollaston vs. Wehmeyer*.. 243
TENANT.—See Attachment.
TRANSFER.—See Will, Mutual.
—— Unconditional Transfer to a third Party, contrary to agreement of former joint-owners for pre-emption, set aside. *Joseph vs. Peacock* 247
TREBELLIANIC FOURTH.—See Legitimate Portion.
TRUSTEE.—*Removal of, for Insolvency, must be upon due notice to such Trustee.—Ord.* 6, 1843, § 52.]—SEMBLE. It is no good objection to the competency of a plaintiff trustee that he is insolvent, if the creditors have not removed him from the trust. *Re Insolvent Estate A. A. Jonker*... 21
· —— *Removal of, under Ord.* 6, 1843, § 42.]—Where it was proved to the satisfaction of the Court that the trustee had offered a creditor, an auctioneer, the sale in the estate in return for his vote, although such offer was refused by the creditor, who, in point of fact, voted for another creditor. *Preuss & Seligmann vs Bosman*................. 113
—— *Removal of.—Master's Practice. In re Estate A. B.*............... 250
—— *Election of, confirmed.—Ord.* 6, 1843, §§ 26, 39, 40.]—Where at a meeting of creditors for the election of a trustee. A is proposed, and receives the votes of eight creditors, representing over £10,000, while the vote of one creditor, representing over £12,000, is recorded against the election. HELD: That A is, notwithstanding, duly

elected trustee by majority in number and value, inasmuch as the single creditor (who was desirous of electing B) should have duly proposed B, in order that there might be a contest. Having omitted to do so, his vote was of no effect. *Gowie & Co. vs. Smith*.......... 10

TRUSTEE.—*Election of, set aside.*]—Where the chief creditor in an insolvent estate compulsorily sequestrated, on his application, being resident at a considerable distance from the town at which the second meeting of creditors was to be held for the election of trustee, mistook the proper post by which to dispatch the power to prove debt and vote for himself, as sole trustee, in consequence of which mistake the power arrived too late for the meeting; at which meeting the representative of the only other creditor entitled to vote had voted for himself as sole trustee, and was elected accordingly, the Court, on the application of the chief creditor, relieved him from the consequence of his mistake by setting aside the election had, and ordering a fresh one to take its place, giving, however, to the respondent to this application, the elected trustee, his costs of appearing to oppose the application. *Deare & Dietz vs. Honeyborne*............. 107

—— *Appointment of confirmed* (Ord. 6, 1843, §§, 26, 39, 40). *Re Insolvent Estate Archer*,.. 105

—— *Insolvent's titles and muniments vested in.*]—The 48th section of Ordinance 6, 1843, vests in an insolvent's trustees not only the landed property itself, but also all title deeds and muniments of title connected therewith, which must, therefore, be surrendered to him by the possessors thereof at the time of insolvency. *Matthew's Trustees vs. Stewart*.. 251

—— *Charges of.*]—The Court refused to allow a Cape Town trustee his travelling expenses to Worcester, the present, and Malmesbury, the former, seat of the insolvent's business. *In re De Kock's Estate*... 252

—— *Commission of.*—See Liquidation Account.

—— are liable to be sued for road and other rates, inasmuch as by the 48th Section of Ordinance 6 of 1843, the estate has become vested in them, and by Section 41 of Act 9, 1858, Divisional Councils are entitled to recover from the owners of property on which assessments have been levied. *Re Dreyer's Estate*............................ 246

—— See Power of Attorney.

UNDUE PREFERENCE (*Insolvent Ordinance*, 6, 1843, §§ 84, 86, 88).—
Sheep Lease.]—T. let to A. 1,050 sheep for a year, for £64; A. binding himself to pay T. "a fair and reasonable sum for the difference in value (should there be any) between the said sheep when hired and returned." A considerable number of sheep died while in A.'s possession. Notwithstanding this, shortly before his insolvency, A. simply, and without further inquiry or accounting, returned to T. 1,050 sheep, some bearing T.'s marks, some marks of other persons. HELD (on appeal, confirming the judgment of the Eastern Districts Court, CONNOR, J., *diss.*), that this delivery, *per aversionem*, of the whole number, was not protected by the 86th section of the Insolvent Ordinance, not being in the ordinary course of business.—FURTHER, that although T. had by letter requested A. to send the sheep to a particular farm, where T. might regularly lease them to A.'s son, "so as to be beyond the casualty of hungry

creditors," HELD (reversing to this extent the judgment of the Eastern Districts Court, CONNOR, J., *quoad hoc*, concurring), that this expression was not proof of collusion, to support a forfeiture under the 88th section, inasmuch as A. had certain bond creditors pressing him at the time, and it might have been the intention of T., therefore, to protect sheep which were still legally his own property from seizure in execution by such creditors. The 86th section, being highly penal, must be liberally construed in favour of the creditor, and collusion only found where other means of fairly accounting for the conduct of the parties have failed. *Tucker vs. Austen's Trustee* 145

ULTRA VIRES.—See Pleading.

WARRANTY.—Where conditions of sale stipulated that the article sold shall be taken by the purchaser at his risk, and there is no clear evidence of a warranty by the auctioneer, such auctioneer is not thereafter liable to the purchaser. *Von Ludwig vs. Van Reenen*... 244

WILL set aside for non-conformity with the provisions of Ordinance 15, 1845; which requires that wills shall be signed or acknowledged by the testator in the presence of two competent witnesses, present and subscribing thereto at the same time. *Laubscher vs. Basson's Executor* 251

—— *Mutual.—Transfer by survivor contrary to terms of, set aside.*]—Husband and wife by mutual will appointed the survivor sole heir; by codicil they thereafter prælegated to the children of the marriage certain two farms, subject to a life usufruct in favour of the survivor. The wife died, the children were put in possession, and annually delivered to the survivor, at his request, a certain quantity of grain in lieu of his life usufruct. The husband remarried, and thereafter transferred to the children of the second marriage one half of the farms already prælegated to the children of the first marriage. HELD (confirming *Brits vs. Brits* and *Hofmeyr vs. De Wet*), that the surviving husband having accepted benefit under the mutual codicil, was precluded from changing, after his first wife's death, the dispositions in such codicil contained. Wherefore the transfers in prejudice thereof were set aside, and the children of the first marriage declared entitled to the whole of the prælegated farms accordingly. *Oosthuysen vs. Oosthuysen*............................... 51

—— See Legitimate Portion.

—— Construction of.—See Falcidian fourth.

—— *Mutual.— Will by Survivor contrary to terms of, set side, and Transfer of a Farm ordered under the Mutual Will.*]—Husband and wife executed a joint will, whereby they made the survivor sole and universal heir or heiress of all the property of the first dying, movable or immovable, to be enjoyed as sole and own property, with the qualification that the survivor should educate and support the children of the marriage until majority, marriage, or other approved state, and then pay to them such amount of money as legitim as the survivor should conscientiously and according to the state of affairs, find to be due. The will also contained a reciprocal appointment of the survivor as executor or executrix of the predecessor, and administrator of the estate, and the usual reservatory clause. Further, a clause which directed that in the event of the survivor remarrying, such survivor should, before such remarriage, have the whole estate valued. In respect of one-half of the whole estate, the predecessor nominated the children of the marriage his or her heirs in such half or equal portions; and special provision was also made that in case of remarriage the survivor should, nevertheless, enjoy possession of the property until the time fixed for paying the legitim in case of no remarriage. The estate was meanwhile to be converted into money, but from the sale was to be exempted the farm Doorn Kraal, which the survivor might take possession of for the sum of 11,000 guilders, under an obligation to make it devolve on the son of the marriage, Hans Jacob Brits, or his children, if he should predecease the surviving spouse. The wife died first; and the husband, after a term, remarried, and made a will whereby he revoked the first will of himself and his first wife so far as Doorn Kraal was concerned, and directed the farm to be sold, and the proceeds applied to the purposes of his sole will. The son of his first marriage had died, leaving a son, who, after the death of his grandfather, brought this action against the executors appointed by the grandfather's sole will, praying that they might be decreed to give him possession of the farm Doorn Kraal on his paying the 11,000 guilders; and that the will of his grandfather, so far as it revoked the bequest of the farm aforesaid, might be set aside as null. The Court gave judgment in terms of the prayer of the declaration, thereby affirming that a joint will dealing *re singulari* was not revocable by the survivor, as subsequently in Neethling's case (*post*) it affirmed that a joint will was not revocable by the survivor where it dealt *universitate*. *Brits vs. Brits. Appendix*.. 312

WILL.—*Close.*— *What is included under.*]—All papers found in a close will by the notary, at his opening thereof must, where such close will has been executed and superscribed with the required solemnities, be taken to form part of such will, leaving any contrariety or repugnance between the separate papers so enclosed for the consideration and construction of the Court. *Hofmeyr vs. De Wet. Appendix*.. 317

—— *Mutual.—Action to set aside a separate Will and Codicil by a Surviving Spouse in opposition to the terms of.*]—Where spouses made a joint will, directing, as to the whole common estate, that the survivor should enjoy the usufruct thereof during life, and that after her death the common estate should, after the deduction of certain legacies, form a poor fund for the support of indigent relations, and where for twelve years the surviving widow enjoyed the usufruct accordingly.—HELD: that by her adration and acceptance of such benefits under the joint will, she could not after her husband's death make a separate testamentary disposition in opposition to the terms of the joint will aforesaid; wherefore her separate testamentary disposition so made was set aside accordingly ....*Ibid.*

WITNESSES' EXPENSES.—*Act* 4, 1861, § 8.]—Parties to a case are allowed witnesses' expenses where the Court is of opinion they were "necessary witnesses." *Van Wyk vs. Van Wyk*.................... 252

SUPREME COURT REPORTS.

1868.

PART I.

TRUSTEE DE VOS, APPLICANT.—BOURHILL & CO., RESPONDENTS.

(In Camerâ.)

Compulsory Sequestration.—Assignment.—Order for Compulsory Sequestration refused where an Assignment was working more beneficially to the Creditors.

Cole, for applicant, moved for the compulsory sequestration of respondents' estate, upon a return of *nulla bona* to a writ issued on an award duly made a rule of Court. The award had reference to a pending action of account between the parties. Between the time of the commencement of the action and the order of reference to the arbitrator, respondents had assigned their estate; but the applicant was no party to the deed of assignment. The deed, applicant alleged, was a side-wind to deprive De Vos's estate of its rights under the award.

Porter, for respondents, read affidavits to show that an assignment would work more beneficially for the creditors than a sequestration. The assignees had already paid eight shillings in the pound to the concurrent creditors, and a second dividend of four shillings would shortly be ready for distribution. The assignees, moreover, were working the estate gratuitously, and had thus saved considerable expense. The applicant's claim amounted to but £160, including costs, while the great bulk of the creditors were for the assignment.

The applicant had been offered and had declined his dividend under the deed of assignment.

The Court (BELL and CONNOR, JJ.) refused the order. The assignment was clearly for the benefit of the creditors. It was, of course, open to the applicant to dispute the validity of the deed on cause shown; but assuming the deed to be good, then, as the order for sequestration would

1868.
January 7.

Trustee De Vos, Applicant.
Bourhill & Co. Respondents.

B

1868.
January 7.
———
Trustee De Vos, Applicant.
Bourhill & Co., Respondents.

bring no benefit to the creditors, but would rather deprive them of such benefit, the Court was not disposed to decree sequestration.

Order refused, with costs.

[Applicant's Attorneys, *Berrange & De Villiers*.]
[Respondents' Attorney, *E. Hull*.]

MUNICIPAL COMMISSIONERS OF CERES *vs.* ARNHOLZ.

(In Camerâ.)

Special Retainer to Counsel.

January 23.
Municipal Commissioners of Ceres
.vs.
Arnholz.

Porter, for defendant, took the opinion of the Court upon a question of taxation of counsel's fees. The case of the Ceres Municipal Commissioners *versus* Arnholz, involving water-rights, was heard at the Tulbagh Circuit Court in October, 1867. There being only one advocate on the Tulbagh Circuit, and he retained for the plaintiffs, the defendant came specially to town to secure the services of an advocate by a special retainer of twenty-five guineas, besides the ordinary fee at the trial. The question now arose whether such retainer should be a charge between party and party, or between attorney and client. There was no appearance on the other side.

The Court took time to consider; and, *postea* 28th January, *in camerâ*, allowed the charge as between party and party, in this case.

[Applicants' Attorneys, *Fairbridge & Arderne*.]

VAN DER BYL & CO., *vs.* WID. W. P. DU PLESSIS.

Provisional Sentence.—Presentation.

February 1.
Van der Byl & Co.
vs.
Wid. W. P. du Plessis.

Reitz prayed provision on the following promissory note:

"Tulbagh, 15th August, 1867.
"£23 7s. 6d.

" Four months after date I promise to pay to Mr. C. P. du Plessis, or order, the sum of twenty-three pounds seven shillings and sixpence, value received. Payable at the Colonial Bank.

"WID. W. P. DU PLESSIS."
(Endorsed)—"C. P. DU PLESSIS.
"J. WIENER.
"VAN DER BYL & CO."

The notarial certificate of Mr. Notary Tredgold was of presentation on the 16th December, at the request of Van der Byl & Co., "at the Colonial Bank, Cape Town."

1868.
February 1.

Van der Byl & Co.
vs.
Wid. W. P. du Plessis.

The Court did not think that the presentation "at the Colonial Bank, Cape Town," was presentation at the Colonial Bank of the note; but being informed from the Bar that there was no Colonial Bank, nor branch Bank, nor any other Bank, at Tulbagh, required an affidavit to that effect; and that there was no other Bank in the Colony called "the Colonial Bank" except at "Cape Town."

Postea: (the case was not mentioned again during term).
[Plaintiffs' Attorneys, *Hofmeyr, Tredgold & Watermeyer.*]

LAMB BROTHERS *vs.* ROUSSEAU.

Provisional Sentence.—Endorsement.

On the 12th January, *Cole* prayed provision on the following promissory note:

January 12.
February 1.

Lamb Brothers
vs.
Rousseau.

"Wagenaar's Kraal, 29th March, 1862.
"£100 12s.
"On the 1st of August, 1862, I promise to pay Messrs. Lamb Bros., or order, the sum of £100 12s. sterling, for value received.
F. D. ROUSSEAU."

(Endorsed)—" Pay J. B. Auret, Esq., or order.
"LAMB BROS."

"Pay to the order of Messrs. Lamb Bros., without recurrence to me.
"J. B. AURET."

"Pay to the order of Messrs. Dunell, Ebden & Co.
"LAMB BROS."

"Pay A. Forsman, Esq., or order.
"DUNELL, EBDEN & CO."
"LAMB BROTHERS."

As the last endorsement was by the holders of the note, the plaintiffs, *Cole* scored it out, as usual, before praying provisional sentence.

But the Court inquired how the note had got into the hands of Lamb Bros. & Co. without a special endorsement by Forsman. And the case stood over accordingly.

1868.
January 12.
February 1.
Lamb Brothers
vs.
Rousseau.

On the 1st of February, *Cole* again prayed provision on the note, which then had the endorsement, "Pay A. Forsman, Esq., or order.—Dunell, Ebden & Co.," scored out; and opposite it was written, " Cancelled,—Dunell, Ebden & Co., 21/1/68." And after the " Lamb Brothers " endorsement, which Cole had scored out, appeared " Dunell, Ebden & Co."

Cole stated that the note had never been in the possession of Forsman, who was out of the Colony; and Dunell, Ebden & Co. having cancelled their special endorsement to him, the difficulty was removed.

But the Court thought Forsman had the title *ex facie* the note; coupled with which was the antiquity of the note. Moreover, the only note served on the defendant was the note with the incomplete endorsement, before the cancellation by Dunell, Ebden & Co. The summons being, therefore, a bad history of the bill, subsequent identification would be difficult if the Court granted provisional sentence, and Forsman wished, hereafter, to take action on the note.

The case, therefore, stood over for the production of an affidavit (a copy to be served on the defendant), setting forth that Forsman never had possession of the note and was not now in the Colony. The Court would then consider whether provisional sentence should be granted, or the principal case gone into. The Court intimated that it required the affidavit, not because of the striking out of the endorsement, but of the consequent irregularity of the summons, which did not set out the note as altered.

Postea: (the case was not mentioned again during term).
[Plaintiffs' Attorneys, *Fairbridge & Arderne*.]

TRUSTEES NATAL LAND COMPANY. *Ex parte.*

Dissolved Joint-stock Company.—Receivers, Liquidators and Managers of.

February 1.
Trustees Natal
Land Company.
Ex parte.

Porter moved on behalf of Dr. Fleck and Mr. F. G. Watermeyer, trustees of the Natal Land Company, for an order appointing " receivers, liquidators and managers " of a dissolved joint-stock company. On the 1st November, 1854, the company was formed, in Cape Town, for the purchase and re-sale of Natal lands. It was arranged by the deed that the partnership should last till the 1st November, 1864, when it expired by efflux of time, being still the holder of lands at Natal, registered there in its name. The deed made no provision as to the mode of winding up; and acccordingly nothing had since been done in liquidation; but he now applied as above. All the shareholders except one, Mr. Zeederberg, residing at Natal, and whose estate had been sequestrated, had consented; and, to avoid difficulties, whether on the part of Zeederberg, or otherwise, the authority of this Court was now sought to enable transfer to be given at Natal. The proposed "receivers, liquidators and managers" were domiciled in this Colony.

1868.
February 1.
Trustees Natal Land Company.
Ex parte.

[CONNOR, J.—Zeederberg's estate being sequestrated, he has no real or personal right left him in respect of the company. And, again, what jurisdiction has this Court to appoint liquidators in a foreign jurisdiction?]

If the lands are sold, who is to give title? That is the difficulty. We want an order appointing three men entitled to go into the Registry of Deeds in Natal and make transfer. A federal head is wanted for the transfer. The deed is dead. In *Lindley on Partnership*, vol. 2, p. 856, the Court made an order appointing a receiver to a Brazilian Mining Company.

BELL, J.—Does not the power of the directors continue for the winding up, just as the power of the partners in a dissolved partnership would so continue? The common law of the country requires an ordinary partnership to wind up its affairs after dissolution, and so it is here.

CONNOR, J.—The Natal Court, if applied to, would make an order on the Registrar of Deeds to pass transfer. If it refuse to make such an order, then this Court might act.

The Court, on these grounds, declined to accede to the application, leaving it to applicants to go to the Natal Court, as suggested by CONNOR, J.

[Applicants' Attorneys, *Fairbridge & Arderne*.]

RE INSOLVENT ESTATE OF H. DENISON.

Liquidation Account.—Trustees' Commission.

Porter moved for the confirmation of the liquidation account in this estate. The Master had objected to the commission charged by the trustee, viz., 5 per cent. on £1,953 17s. 2d.,=£97 13s. 10d., being of opinion that there should be a charge of 2½ per cent. on £1,561 2s. 8d., and 5 per cent. on £392 14s. 6d. The insolvent had a half share in the farm Clifton, and, before the sequestration of his estate, sold it to one Henry Roberts for £4,950, receiving £1,694 before sequestration, and leaving a balance due at that time of £1,561 2s. 8d. Then Roberts surrendered, and it became a question between the two estates whether Roberts's trustees should adopt the sale, Ultimately, they elected to do so, but not until there had been a great deal of correspondence on the matter.

February 1.
Re Insolvent Estate of H. Denison.

1868.
February 1.
Re Insolvent Estate of H. Denison.

Porter submitted that the money, being paid into Denison's estate, was a movable, on which the trustee was entitled to charge the usual 5 per cent. The principle to be laid down was that wherever fixed property was found in an estate unsold, so that the trustee had the selling, the customary 2½ per cent. would be sufficient; but where the property was sold before sequestration and part paid, and a balance remaining (or even the whole unpaid), the trustees could claim on the money recovered as a movable. If a bond had been passed for the money, the trustee, merely recovering on the bond, would have received 5 per cent., while here the trustee of Denison's estate had been put to unusual labour in arranging with Roberts's trustees.

The Court, however, would not allow more than 2½ per cent., intimating that some strict legal line must be kept to in dealing with such charges.

[Applicants' Attorneys, *Fairbridge & Arderne.*]

S. A. LOAN AND INVESTMENT COMPANY *vs.* WIDOW JACOBS AND ANOTHER.

Provisional Sentence, on Summons in principal Case, refused.

February 1.
S. A. Loan and Investment Company *vs.* Widow Jacobs and Another.

Griffith, Att.-Gen., applied for provisional sentence on a mortgage bond for £850 (with interest), passed by defendants in favour of plaintiffs. The summons was in the principal case, the plaintiffs having been advised there was a bad case on provision. The defendants were in default. Only provisional sentence was now asked, with the costs of pleadings, &c. If granted, it would be unnecessary to call further witnesses now, and expenses would be saved to defendants.

At the request of the Court, *Griffith* stated the facts on which plaintiffs had believed provisional sentence would have been refused by the Court if applied for. Rutherfoord was an agent employed by defendants to negotiate the loan, and, without authority from plaintiffs, had received and appropriated the amount of capital and interest.

[CONNOR, J.—By your summons you have not asked provision; nor have you called upon defendants to acknowledge or deny their handwriting. How, then, can you claim provisional sentence?]

But we have sought final judgment; and, instead of putting defendants, who are in default, to further expense, by calling witnesses to prove the execution of the bond, &c., we now ask for provisional sentence only.

HODGES, C. J.—I doubt our power to grant provision on pleadings in a principal case. It is hard for the parties, but you will have to go on in the usual way,

BELL, J.—If the defendants are as anxious to save expense as you are, a motion to consent to judgment absolute will effect that purpose.

Griffith thereupon asked for adjournment of the case accordingly.

[Applicants' Attorneys, *Reid & Nephews.*]

1868. February 1.

S. A. Loan and Investment Company vs. Widow Jacobs and Another.

LUBBE AND OTHERS *vs.* BURTON.

Costs of abandoned Motion under Divisional Councils Consolidation Act.—It is the duty of the Civil Commissioner of a Division to produce to registered Voters the Nomination List for Candidates when application is made within the limits of time fixed by the Act.

By a notice of motion dated the 20th December, 1867, Willem J. B. Lubbe and eight other registered voters for the Divisional Council of Clanwilliam called upon the respondent, H. F. Burton, Civil Commissioner of that division, to show cause, upon the 13th of January, 1868, or as soon after as counsel could be heard, "why you shall not be ordered to deliver up to the applicants for inspection a certain requisition purporting to have been sent by certain voters of Ward No. 6 in the Division of Clanwilliam to one John R. Cousert, requesting him to be put in nomination as a candidate for the said ward in the Divisional Council of Clanwilliam; and, further, why you shall not pay the costs of this application."

February 4.

Lubbe & Others vs. Burton.

No further action having been taken in the matter, *Griffith, A.-G.,* this day moved for the respondent's costs, as of an abandoned motion.

De Villiers, for the applicants, opposed the motion for costs.

The circumstances of the case, as disclosed by applicants' affidavits, were the following: The Ward No. 6 being vacant, it became necessary under section 16 of Act No. 4 of 1865, to send in to the Civil Commissioner a written nomination of candidates. A nomination was got up for John R. Cousert, and there being no other candidate, he was, without a poll, declared duly elected—the 15th, 16th and 17th sections of the Act, as to notice in the *Gazette,* having been properly complied with by the respondent. Some of the present applicants (being unaware, as they alleged, of some " material changes in the law," which they did not define) had not seen the notice under Act 4 of 1865, and, therefore, they averred, were unable to nominate a candidate. Thereafter, the election of Cousert was gazetted, on the 4th October.

1868.
February 4.

Lubbe & Others
vs. Burton.

Two of the applicants afterwards proceeded, upon the 28th October, to the office of the respondent, for the purpose of "seeking an inspection of the requisition of Cousert, with a view of ascertaining by whom the said requisition was signed," they having been informed by one G. J.v an Taak that he had signed a requisition offered to him for signature as a requisition to one John Foster, whereas it subsequently appeared to have been a requisition to Cousert. A verbal interview was held with the Magistrate; and the applicants, in their affidavits, alleged "that the respondent then refused to entertain their request, without giving any valid or substantial excuse for such conduct." Thereafter, one of the applicants, " acting upon the principle that the document in question was a public one, and entitled to be inspected by any registered voter," addressed, upon the 25th of November, the following letter to the respondent:

"Clanwilliam, 25, 11, 67.

" The Civil Commissioner, Clanwilliam.

" SIR,—On the 28th of October last I, together with Mr. Barend Lubbe, requested you to show us certain requisition sent to Mr. John Cousert, requesting him to stand as candidate for the Divisional Council for the Ward No. 6. You then refused to hand it over to us. As I consider it a public document, I now again address myself to you with the request to be allowed to see said requisition. Should I be refused, I hereby give notice that I will make a motion before the Supreme Court of this Colony to order you to hand such requisition over to us.

" I am, &c.,

" W. P. B. LUBBE."

Receiving no immediate reply, he sent this further letter, upon the 26th November:

"Clanwilliam, 26, 11, 67.

" The Civil Commissioner of Clanwilliam.

" Sir,—I most respectfully beg to bring to your notice that you have as yet not yet complied with my request expressed in my letter of yesterday's date, nor yet sent me a reply, as you promised to do. I now beg to state that unless I receive such reply on or before Monday, the 2nd of December next, I will deem it as a refusal on your part to comply with my wishes as stated in said letter.

" I have, &c.,

" W. P. B. LUBBE."

To this he received, upon the 30th November, an answer declining to accede to the request. Thereupon, the notice of motion of the 20th December was served. Subsequently Cousert, resigned his seat in the Council, upon the 26th December. The applicants having, as they alleged, gained their object, were content to allow the matter to drop, each party paying his own costs.

1868.
February 4.

Lubbe & Others vs. Burton.

In the affidavits for the respondent it was submitted that under the 41st section of the Act, Cousert, and not the respondent, should have been served with this notice, as there was no allegation by the applicants that the respondent's proceedings had been " wilfully wrong." Secondly, that Cousert having resigned, the necessity for a motion had ceased. Thirdly, that, if still required to answer to this notice, section 37 of the Act required, in substance, that complaints with regard to taking polls for the election of Divisional Councils should be made to the Civil Commissioner in writing, and if not made within seven days after the poll "no notice shall be taken of them, nor shall the poll so taken be capable of being afterwards impeached by such complainant in any action or proceeding at law." And section 49 provides, in substance, that complaints against the eligibility of candidates under the 19th section shall always be lodged within seven days after the day of poll. Cousert having been nominated on the 30th September, and there being no opposition, he was elected upon that day, which must be taken, for the purposes of this application, to have been the day of polling alluded to by the Act. The applicants, however, had not moved in the matter until the 28th October. Section 41 of the Act, moreover, fixed a period of " forty-two days next after the pronouncing of any decision by the Civil Commissioner" as the term " within which complainants who have complained within the seven days may apply to a competent court." This time also the applicants had allowed to elapse. The notice for the election had been given in the manner required by section 16 of the Act; but under section 18 it was expressly laid down that no failure to comply with the provisions of section 16, even had they in this case not been so complied with, by respondent, should vitiate or affect any election under the Act; which respondent urged as another ground for rejecting the present motion. The respondent further said "that he considered himself fully warranted and justified in declining to exhibit or hand over to the brothers Lubbe" the requisition referred to ; and submitted to the Court " that the Act 4, 1865, in no wise requires the Civil Commissioner to exhibit such nominations, the said Civil Commissioner being by section 19 entrusted with the duty of ascertaining

1868.
February 4.

Lubbe & Others
vs. Burton.

the legality of such nomination, and being answerable to his official superiors, and not to the applicants, as voters." The requisition to Cousert purported to be signed by six registered voters of the Ward No. 6, attested by three witnesses. This being the sole nomination, respondent, under section 25 of the Act, had declared by advertisement in the *Gazette* that no poll would be taken, the said Cousert having been duly elected. From further affidavits for the respondent it appeared that Cousert's reason for his resignation, as stated by himself in writing to the Divisional Council, was " in consequence of having ascertained that his election has caused dissatisfaction in the district." There were also further affidavits denying the statements of Van Taak; alleging that special notice of the day of nomination had been given by private persons to the applicants; and verifying as genuine the five signatures to Cousert's requisition, altogether independent of Van Taak's, five being the number required by the Act.

CONNOR, J.— The question of costs, then, seems to rest upon the question whether registered electors are entitled to see the nomination of candidates for the Divisional Council.

De Villiers.—It was a public document, which it was the respondent's duty, both upon general principles, and especially from the nature of his office in a country division, to have at once shown.

Griffith, A.-G. (*contra*).—What is the object of seeing the requisition, even before the poll? The Civil Commissioner had, under the Act, no power of testing the validity of any objections the applicants might have raised upon so seeing the nomination. It was, therefore, as far as the election was concerned, a useless request, unattended with any possible advantage.

[HODGES, C. J.—The advantage may have been that seeing the nomination list would, perhaps, have enabled the applicants to give voters notice not to vote for the nominated candidate, lest their votes should from informality be thrown away.]

Under any circumstances, the applicants allowed the seven days and the forty-two days to pass before they proceeded. Therefore, they are not now entitled to relief. This is not a case, on their own admission, in which they asked to see the nomination list in sufficient time to raise objection. The first request was too late. And even if the Civil Commissioner were, in courtesy, though not in strict law (for the Act is silent on the point), required to show the nomination list to voters applying within the seven days, he is not, under any circumstances, bound after that time ; otherwise he may be continually applied to for old nominations, the exhibition of which can serve no real purpose to applicants. The application was long after any step could have been taken.

CONNOR, J.—It certainly is doubtful whether, if it is too late to serve any purpose, a Civil Commissioner is bound to exhibit.

De Villiers in reply.

HODGES, C. J.—The parties applying were voters. They were refused more than once. According to the construction I put upon the Act, the nomination, after it is sent in to the Civil Commissioner, is a public document, greatly affecting the voters of the division, and therefore open at any time to their inspection, to ascertain, for instance, whether there may not be an infringement of the requisites of the 16th section, and also of the proviso of the 19th section. If, as the result of inspection, it appears that the nomination is not signed by five competent persons, as required by the Act, although it is quite true the Civil Commissioner cannot interfere, it may be important the voters should know. According to the spirit of the Act, if not the letter, the voters have an interest in the inspection, and therefore are entitled to inspect, either before or after the election. It is said this application not having been made until the forty-two days had expired justified the Civil Commissioner in his refusal, but I cannot agree to that. The respondent is not entitled to his costs. Each party, therefore, will pay his own.

BELL, J., concurred generally. The applicants were wrong in their application to the Civil Commissioner, because the seven days and the forty-two days had expired; and if the Civil Commissioner had at the first verbal interview, upon the 28th October, based his refusal upon that ground, that no good could be gained now, I might have given him his costs against the applicants. But he did not. These country farmers are not cognizant with the law, as it is in English; and the Civil Commissioner should know that, and give them every information in his power, when applied to. The applicants must pay their own costs, and the Civil Commissioner his also.

CONNOR, J.—I am of opinion that before the election, the Civil Commissioner's office (I draw a distinction between the Civil Commissioner and his office) is bound to let registered electors see the nomination list. But I am certainly not prepared to say that after the days fixed by the Act have passed the Civil Commissioner may not refuse to show the nominations.

BELL, J., added: I do not mean to say that it is the duty of the Civil Commissioner to show the nomination list after the

1868.
February 4.

Lubbe & Others vs. Burton.

expiration of the days fixed by the Act. But in this case the Civil Commissioner, when first applied to, did not put it upon that ground. He claimed a general right of refusal, which I cannot say he possesses.

The Court made no order, beyond ordering each party to pay his own costs.

[Applicants' Attorney, *Tiran*.
Respondents' Attorney, *Van Zyl*.]

RE G. H. MEIRING.

Order for voluntary Sequestration of a Partner's Private Estate made by the Court without the production of the usual Schedules, upon affidavit that such Schedules could not be framed.

February 4.
Re G. H. Meiring.

The partnership estate of Meiring and Co. was placed under voluntary sequestration upon the 23rd October, 1867; and *Porter* to-day moved, upon the petition of G. H. Meiring, one of the partners, that the order then made for such partnership sequestration should now be extended, by modification, to the sequestration of the private estate of G. H. Meiring. It was an application of the first impression, but the circumstances were peculiar.

The petitioner stated in his petition that one of the callings of the partnership was that of auctioneer. That as, by law, auctioneering licences cannot be taken out in the name of a firm, he had taken out such licence individually, but that all his transactions had really been for account of the firm.

CONNOR, J.—Would not the proper course be to surrender the petitiorner's private estate?

Porter.—His affidavit states that his private estate and the partnership estate are so mixed that it is impossible for him to make up schedules for the separate surrender of his private estate.

CONNOR, J.—There is nothing in the insolvent Ordinance requiring schedules before the acceptance of a surrender. If the Court is satisfied of the petitioner's inability to prepare schedules, and is of opinion that sequestration should be decreed, it has it in its power to accept the surrender of Mr. Meiring's private estate immediately.

BELL, J.—The practice has been to prepare schedules, but the law does not require it.

The Court hereupon accepted the surrender without schedules.

[Applicants' Attorney, *Van Zyl*.]

THE QUEEN vs SWARTZ.

It is beyond the power of Resident Magistrates, under section 45, Act 20, 1856, to sentence, for contempt of Court, prisoners undergoing trial on a substantive charge: that section applies only to bystanders and others not in custody.

This was the review of a sentence for "contempt of court," passed by the Resident Magistrate of George upon a prisoner who was undergoing trial on a charge of assault. During the proceedings he behaved insolently to the Magistrate, and said to him, amongst other things, "You lie." Whereupon the Magistrate, under the 45th section of the Magistrates' Courts Act, sentenced him to a week's imprisonment, for contempt of court. The records, having been sent down to Cape Town, as required by the same section of the Act, came before CONNOR, J., the Judge of the week, who, doubting the power of the Magistrate, under the Act, to commit for contempt a prisoner already in the dock on a substantive charge, transmitted the papers to the Attorney-General, who to-day mentioned the case to the Court, and argued, in substance, that the words of the section are general, "any person," and would include a prisoner in the dock.

CONNOR, J.—But how can such "offender be taken into custody and detained until the rising of the Court," when he is already in custody and undergoing trial?

The Court held that the conviction for contempt should be quashed; the words of the section not applying to a prisoner undergoing trial.

1868.
February 4.

The Queen vs. Swartz.

DICKSON, APPLICANT, vs. TOWN COUNCIL OF CAPE TOWN AND ANDREW McKENZIE, MUNICIPAL CONTRACTOR, RESPONDENTS.

Nuisance.—Interdict granted to prevent the further deposit of town filth in the Capel Ditch.

Gritffih, A.-G., for applicant, moved on notice of motion calling upon respondents to show cause why they should not "be interdicted from depositing, or causing to be deposited, the filth of Cape Town in the Capel Ditch.

Porter, for the respondents, opposed.

From voluminous affidavits read on both sides the following seemed to be the short history of the application :

A ravine, called the Capel Ditch, runs down from Table Mountain, from the direction of Platteklip, crosses Upper Roeland-street in the vicinity of the Cape Town prison,

February 6.

Dickson, Applicant, vs. Town Council of Cape Town & Andrew McKenzie, Municipal Contractor, Respondents.

1868.
February 6.

Dickson, Applicant, vs. Town Council of Cape Town & Andrew McKenzie, Municipal Contractor, Respondents.

continues its course across Sir Lowry-street, under the Castle bridge, along the Castle moat, and empties itself into the sea on the eastern face of the Imhoff Battery. Some years ago a barrel-drain was constructed by the Municipality in the lower half, from Upper Roeland-street downwards as far as Sir Lowry-street, and covered in by the deposit of town filth, exclusive of ordure and offal. In the early part of January last the Town Council received a letter signed by forty inhabitants, requesting that the upper portion, from Roeland-street towards the mountain, might be filled in in like manner. It was then resolved to lay a barrel-drain, and allow the contractor for cleaning the streets to deposit the dirt over it. There was nothing in writing between the Town Council and the contractor as to the kind of deposit to be made; but it was averred that the instructions were not to deposit anything offensive, and that these instructions had been carried out. The affidavits for the respondents stated that the work would be a public improvement, and, amongst others, included the affidavits of seven medical practitioners and two chemists, in favour of the work, provided the reclaimed land was not hereafter built upon. For the applicant were read, amongst others, the affidavits of five medical men, besides two chemists, stating that, under any circumstances, the work would be prejudicial to health. The present applicant had, before the work was commenced, addressed a letter to the Municipality, desiring them to desist; and a memorial to the same effect, signed by seventy-two inhabitants, was also presented. But the work was proceeded with notwithstanding. The affidavits, as a whole, appeared *primâ facie* of a contradictory character as to the probable effect on the health of the town, and as to the exact nature of the deposit made. It was further alleged that the ditch, in its present state, was a considerable nuisance, and that the covering in would take four years to complete.

Griffith, A.-G., submitted that the weight of the affidavits was in applicant's favour. Even if the existing open ditch were a nuisance, it was the duty of the Town Council to abate it, under the 72nd section of the Municipal Act, 1 of 1861, but not by creating an additional and greater nuisance. In many cases the Court might not grant an interdict for nuisances, but this was an extraordinary case; for here the nuisance, when once committed, would be irremediable and irreparable. The applicant's affidavits clearly showed that the nature of the deposit included town sweepings, dead fowls, fish, pig entrails, and offal generally.

Porter, for respondents.—There is such a conflict of evidence that the Court cannot grant an interdict, either interlocutory or permanent. The essential requisite for such an interdict as is now sought is, that it must be clearly made out that the nuisance committed is one detrimental to public health. (*Story's Equity Jurisprudence*, sect. 922, 923, 924.) This is rather a case for civil action or criminal indictment. Even if an occasional dead fowl, or the like, is deposited with the other dirt of the town, that is not in itself ground for an interdict, if shown to be accidental and not intended. (*Swain vs. Great Northern Railway Company*, 10th *Jurist*, 1864, N. S. p. 191, citing and confirming *Attorney-General vs. Sheffield Gas Company*, 16th *Jurist*, p. 677.)

Griffith in reply.

The Court granted the interdict unanimously, on the ground that the contract between McKenzie and the Town Council, which the Court had required to be produced and had examined, was for removing all the dirt of the Town, fish-market, shambles, &c, including, therefore, matter of offensive description; there being nothing to show that it was not contemplated to deposit all this in the locality in question, or that that had really not been done. The Court considered all the medical evidence in the case, although *primâ facie* contradictory, to be, in reality, against the respondents, as their own medical evidence was to the effect that the land reclaimed should not be built upon at any time, inasmuch as the ground would in that case require to be opened; and it must be taken that in such case the effect would be dangerous to the health of the town, unless deodorising agents were well and thoroughly mixed with the whole bulk of the deposit, which the affidavits showed had not been done. Costs to be costs in the cause, if proceeded with.

[Applicant's Attorneys, *Hofmeyr, Tredgold & Watermeyer.*]
[Respondents' Attorneys, *Fairbridge & Arderne.*]

RE ESTATE OF GEORGE SOUTHEY, OF GRAAFF-REINET, DECEASED.

Where the Surviver and Executor under a Joint Will becomes insane, the Court, if satisfied upon affidavit as to such incapacity, will under Section 21 of Ordinance No. 105, direct a Meeting for the election of a fresh Executor.

Mr. and Mrs. G. Southey, married in community of property, made their mutual will in the usual way, appointing each other their executors *reciproce*. Mrs. Southey subsequently became insane. Mr. Southey then executed a

1868.
February 6.
Re Estate of George Southey, of Graaff-Reinet, deceased.

codicil (without date), alleging therein his wife's insanity, and appointing his two sons of the marriage, executors of his estate. He died on the 8th November, 1867. This codicil, being underhand, and not containing a reservatory clause, was bad. Its appointment of executors was also bad. There were seven children of the marriage, all taking rights under the will.

Porter now moved for an order upon the Master to convene a meeting of the next of kin of the said George Southey, for the purpose of electing an executor, or executors, to administer the estate. Such an application had been made to the Master, but he had declined, on the ground that by the will an executrix having been nominated, she was the only person entitled to be appointed until she shall either decline so to act, or be declared incapacitated by the Court.

Affidavits of Dr. Maasdorp and the Rev. Mr. Steabler were read, to show the widow's insanity.

Bell, J.—Will not the proper course be an action *de lunatico inquirendo*? How can we pass over the executrix of the will without a declaration of insanity, had after the usual formal proceedings?

Connor, J.—By Section 21 of Ordinance 104, it is provided "that where any person or persons duly appointed to be executor or executors of the deceased, shall have become incapacitated to act as such, then, and in every such case, the Master shall call a meeting of the next of kin, for the appointment of executor dative." Now if the Court should be satisfied from the affidavits here, that the widow is "incapacitated," then we may grant the order.

The majority of the Court (Hodges, C. J., and Connor, J.) took this view of the matter, and, alleging its satisfaction with the case of "incapacity" made out in the affidavits, granted the order.

Bell, J., dissented, on the ground that it was a dangerous principle to declare the widow "incapacitated" under the section referred to, which would, in fact, amount to a declaration of legal insanity, upon affidavits only. He would never make such an order without having the parties whom it was sought to declare insane personally before him, in open Court, on proceedings in the ordinary way in such cases.

[Applicants' Attorneys, *Reid & Nephew.*]

Re Insolvent Estate Jahre.

It is the duty of the Master to tax Attorneys' Bills of costs filed in insolvent Estates; and charge to Four per Cent. for the Taxation.

Porter moved for the confirmation of the liquidation account in the above estate. The Master had withheld his usual certificate of non-objection on the ground that the bill of costs of Mr. Attorney J. Ayliff had not been taxed ; and had claimed 4 per cent. for the taxation. The opinion of the Court was desired upon the point whether it is to be laid down as a rule of practice that every bill of costs filed by an attorney in an insolvent estate must be taxed by the Master, and upon payment of 4 per cent.

1868. February 11. ― Re Insolvent Estate Jahre.

The Master informed the Court that the charge of 4 per cent. for taxation of attorneys' bills dated from 1828, but that this charge was first extended to attorneys' bills in insolvent estates about a year ago.

Porter, for applicants.—There can be no objection to the reasonableness of the amount claimed. No objection has been made by the creditors, although the account has lain the usual time for inspection here and in Graham's Town. But the chief object of this application is to have a definite rule laid down for the guidance of the side-bar.

Griffith, A.-G.—I do not appear formally for the Crown ; but, as the matter is raised, I submit that the only legal voucher for the attorney's bill of costs is the Master's *allocatur* on taxation, and that that applies in insolvent as well as solvent estates.

The Court held that the practice recently introduced by the Master should be adhered to for the future ; and that all such bills of costs should be taxed *item per item,* subject to a payment of 4 per cent. for taxation.

[Applicants' Attorney, *Van Zyl*]

Deare & Dietz *vs.* Korsten.

Compulsory Sequestration decreed after Assignment.

Porter prayed final adjudication of sequestration (provisional order granted by the Chief Justice *in camerâ* on the 7th December, 1867), and produced the Deputy Sheriff's return of *nulla bona* made on a writ executed 9th December, 1867, on judgment absolute for £3,847 9s. 8d., obtained in the Circuit Court for Beaufort, 8th October, 1866 ; the defendant Korsten having then filed a confession.

February 13. ― Deare & Dietz *vs.* Korsten.

1868.
February 13.
Deare & Dietz
vs. Korsten.

Cole opposed the adjudication, on the ground that a deed of assignment had been entered into between the plantiffs and defendant.

He produced the deed, dated Port Elizabeth, 30th May, 1867, alleging the debt of £3,847 9s. 8d. due to plantiffs by defendant, besides a balance due on consignment account, and debts to other parties amounting to £406. Alleging, further, the defendant's inability to meet these claims, the deed proceeded, in regular form, to assign to Deare & Dietz, for the benefit of the creditors, the immovable property, movable property, debts, &c., with authority to sell and dispose thereof, appointing the partners of the firm attorneys for that purpose, and concluded thus :

" The said Deare & Dietz further engage, as long as the said Korsten shall fulfil the promises hereinbefore on his part entered into, not to sue the said Korsten for the amount aforesaid owing by him until the said assigned estate shall be liquidated and an account thereof rendered by them. And it is further agreed that if it shall appear that the said Korsten has wilfully withheld or concealed any property or money belonging to him, or debts due and owing by him, or if he shall at any time refuse to assist the said firm in collecting and getting in the said assigned estate ; or if any of his creditors shall refuse to accept a *pro rata* dividend on the amount of their claims, or such other terms as may be offered by the said Deare & Dietz, and shall in any way interfere with the property hereby assigned, then the said firm shall forthwith be at liberty to take whatever proceedings they may think fit for the recovery of their said claim," &c. " And the said Korsten shall be precluded from pleading anything hereinbefore contained in bar of such legal proceedings."

For the defendant was produced his affidavit, setting forth " that he had, as stipulated by the said deed, rendered, and is still rendering, every assistance to his assignees, and doing all that is in his power to do for the benefit of the estate."

For the plantiffs were produced affidavits setting forth that the defendant had wilfully concealed the existence of a debt due, or pretended to be due, by him to his brother, Jacobus Korsten, who afterwards claimed a sum of £300 with interest, sued for the said sum on the 26th August, and recovered judgment in the Supreme Court ; in execution of which judgment the Deputy Sheriff attached all the available goods under the assignment, having made forcible entry into the defendant's former place of business, then in charge of a clerk of Deare & Dietz. Further, that Messrs. Fasche and Fittig, creditors of the defendants for £30, refused to accept a *pro rata* dividend, or any other terms of composition under the assignment, but had obtained judgment in the

Magistrate's Court for Prince Albert, and issued execution in August, 1867 (before J. Korsten), when certain goods included in the deed of assignment were sold in satisfaction. Further, that a claim had been made by defendant's attorneys, on the 14th January, in the name of the High Sheriff, to a certain sheep lease assigned in the deed, but subsequently sold in execution. That, finding all the valuable assets of the estate were thus being taken out of their hands, and applied in payment of the debts of other creditors, the plaintiffs recovered judgment for their claim in the Beaufort Circuit Court, when the defendant confessed judgment. That since the assignment the plaintiffs had paid £150 to a clerk of defendant for salary due before assignment, £25 to defendant himself for expenses, and had expended considerable sums in endeavouring to work out the assignment; while the entire amount received by them under it was £168 13s. 10d.

1868.
February 13.

Deare & Dietz
vs. Korsten.

There was also produced the affidavit of a clerk in plaintiffs' employ, who took charge of the assigned goods at Willowmore, on the 14th June, 1867, setting forth that, whilst he was in possession, the messenger of the Magistrate's Court for Prince Albert entered the stores with a writ of execution at the instance of F. and F., and "notwithstanding a verbal protest by deponent against such measure," removed and sold the goods. That F. and F. had bought in, for 25s., and for Korsten, a cart and horse included in the assignment. That F. and F. were paid in full under the writ. That deponent then returned to Port Elizabeth, to consult his employers, and in his absence the second seizure was made, on the writ of J. Korsten, of the remainder of the goods, which goods were sold on the 9th September, after the deponent had again returned to Willowmore; the Deputy Sheriff on that occasion breaking open the stores, notwithstanding another "verbal protest."

No answering affidavits on the part of defendant were put in, in consequence, it was alleged, of shortness of time.

Porter, for applicants, submitted that defendant having thus violated the provisions of the deed of assignment, could not now set up that deed. If set up at all, it should have been set up in the Circuit Court at Beaufort, instead of which a simple confession was filed. Korsten was in league with his creditors, F. and F., to defeat the assignment. F. and F.'s refusal to accept the *pro rata* dividend also entitled the plaintiffs to proceed, notwithstanding the deed.

[BELL, J.—I cannot understand the plaintiffs' proceedings. Why did they not protect themselves under the deed of assignment? And if they have failed to do so, why should they now come for compulsory sequestration?]

We may perhaps get more under the sequestration than under the deed, as matters now stand. The sequestration

1868.
February 13.

Deare & Dietz
vs. Korsten.

will carry the fixed property. Besides, it will open the door for a full inquiry, in insolvency, into the suspicious circumstances of the case.

[CONNOR, J.—Can you get the benefit of a return of *nulla bona* which you yourself occasioned, by the action at Beaufort?—All the property had been assigned to you. You were in possession of the movable property.]

But no movable property capable of being seized by the writ was *in rerum naturâ*. It had been taken by previous creditors, under a collusive legal process.

[CONNOR, J.—Will subsequent sequestration defeat the deed of assignment?]

When the parties waive the deed it will be defeated. Deare & Dietz have waived it. And Korsten, by his own fraudulent proceedings, in violation, has legally waived it.

Cole, for defendant, said he had not had time to put in answering affidavits, but he did not ask now for time, because defendant was without means. The plaintiffs had had full assignment in their hands. It was the stupidity of their own clerk which had interfered with their interests under the deed.

The Court appeared to feel considerable difficulty in acceeding to the adjudication at first, but ultimately granted it.

HODGES, C. J., thought the deed, if set up at all, should have been set up at the Beaufort Circuit, when the Judge on Circuit would have refused provision, and ordered the principal case to be proceeded with, giving scope for full inquiry. But the defendant had confessed judgment, instead of setting up a plea in bar. The case came under the 17th section of the Insolvent Ordinance, and he could only add the defendant had shown no cause why final adjudication should not be adjudged.

BELL, J.—Deare & Dietz had everything under the deed, and could have got all under it that they can get by the sequestration, but they have not protected their own interests under the deed. The only good that can result from the sequestration, perhaps, is the inquiry that will be made, and possibly fraud established. However, Deare & Dietz are by far the largest creditors under the deed. The other amounts are trifling; and as the deed is just capable of the construction that Deare & Dietz had other remedies besides the deed, therefore the sequestration may be adjudged.

CONNOR, J.—The sequestration is sought on two grounds: one, the non-acceptance by F. and F. of the *pro rata* dividend; the other, fraud on the part of Korsten. The former seems to me at present to be the clearer objection of the two. And inasmuch as the deed provides that in case of such non-acceptance of the *pro rata* dividend the plantiffs might "take any proceeding they may think fit for the recovery of their said claims." I take it that that includes this application for a compulsory sequestration.

[Plaintiffs' Attorney, *Van Zyl*.
Defendants, Attorneys, *Berrangé & De Villiers*.]

1868.
February 13.
―――
Deare & Dieta
vs. Korsten.

RE INSOLVENT ESTATE A. A. JONKER.

Trustees.—Removal of, for Insolvency, must be upon due notice to such Trustees.

Porter moved for the discharge of an order made *in camerâ* upon the 23rd January last," authorizing the Master to call a special meeting of creditors in this estate for the purpose of electing trustees," they having, as alleged, both surrendered their estates as insolvent; on the ground that the order had been made without notice to the trustees then sought to be removed.

It appeared that Messrs. E. Dobson and D. J. Aspeling, as joint trustees of the insolvent estate of Jonker, brought an action, in that capacity, against the executor dative of Adolph Jonker, and obtained judgment. Before the judgment, which involved the realization of certain landed property, and certain further proceedings in law, could be carried into execution, the trustees surrendered their estates,—Aspeling on the 6th May, 1865, and Dobson on the 13th September, 1865. Matters then remained in abeyance until the 23rd January, 1868, when Messrs. Fairbridge and Arderne—who had been the attorneys in the action, and were still creditors for costs, and acting in the original suit, being requested by the trustees to proceed, and apprehending that the prosecution of the further proceedings necessary would, if made in the name of the insolvent trustees as plantiffs, be open to exception—moved for an *ex-parte* order of removal, under the 52nd section of the Insolvent Ordinance, when the Court made the order above stated.

Porter, for the trustees.—There are two questions to determine. First, whether or not a motion for removal under the 52nd section must not be upon notice to the trustees, or upon a rule *nisi*; secondly, whether Fairbridge and Arderne, although they were the attorneys in the litigation about to be resumed, are sufficiently within the meaning of "parties interested in the suit" referred to in the 52nd section of Ordiance 6, 1843, as to be competent to make the motion. As to the first point, the necessity of notice is shown by the fact that Aspeling had, in fact, been rehabilitated on the 20th June, 1867, although Dobson's estate is still, it is true, under sequestration. Some difficulty

February 13.
―――
Re Insolvent
Estate A. A.
Jonker.

1868.
February 13.

Re Insolvent Estate A.A. Jonker.

was apparently apprehended on the point that the trustees having surrendered, would be incompetent plaintiffs in the further proceedings contemplated. But I take it to be clear that when a defendant is sued by a trustee who is insolvent, such defendant has nothing to do with the fact that the creditors have not removed the trustee ; and, not having been removed, such trustee is a competent plaintiff. The 52nd section does not provide that insolvency shall, *ipso facto*, be a cause of removal, and if creditors choose to take no steps, defendants have nothing to do with the non-action of creditors. Then, on the second point the application must be made by creditors of the insolvent, and not creditors of the trustees, which is what Fairbridge and Arderne really are. They were therefore incompetent, under the 52nd section, to move.

De Villiers (for Fairbridge and Arderne).—The Master was in Chambers, and duly reported the insolvency of both the trustees. Besides, the insolvency of the trustees might be a good exception to an action brought by them.

[CONNOR. J.—Why?

[BELL, J.—Under what section is there any objection to an insolvent trustee proceeding, if creditors have not removed him ?]

The Court, by a majority (BELL, J. and CONNOR, J.), held that the order should be set aside ; that all subsequent proceedings should drop, and matters remain as they were.

HODGES, C. J—We were satisfied in Chambers, upon the Master's report, as to the insolvency ; and I doubt whether, under the 52nd section, it has not been the practice to order a new election, as was done in this intance. However, the majority of the Court being of a different opinion, the order must be set aside ; and the notice to appoint new trustees falls with it.

BELL, J., was for discharging the order on the ground of want of notice to Messrs. Dobson and Aspeling.

CONNOR, J.—When an order is made *ex parte*, the other party may move to set it aside, on cause shown. Here the cause as to both trustees is, that the application was made, in reality, on the part of nobody. It was not made on the part of Fairbridge and Arderne as creditors, nor is it now supported by them as creditors. That in itself is enough to discharge the order. As to the question of a trustee's subsequent rehabilitation, that is an important one ; and I think it is too late to come and remove a trustee because he has once been insolvent, if he has already got his rehabilitation. But there is no necessity to decide that point now. The order was granted under a mistake on the other point alone.

Order set aside accordingly.

[Applicants' Attorney, *Fairbridge & Arderne.*
  Respondents' Attorney, *E. Hull.*]

RE HENRY HAWKINS.

Appointment of Curator Bonis.

Porter moved for the appointment of a *curator bonis*, with power to transfer certain landed property. In 1853 Hawkins left this colony for Australia, leaving behind him, in the colony his wife, Sarah Hawkins, and an only child of the marriage. Before leaving, he had, by last will, bequeathed to his wife, for life, with remainder over to the daughter, a certain piece of ground, situated upon the Camp Ground, near Cape Town. From Australia he had written several times to his wife; the last letter dated in 1857, and stated an intention of returning to the Cape. Money had been forwarded through an agent at the Cape, to an agent in Australia; but nothing more was heard of Hawkins. Special inquiry was made through the Colonial Office of Victoria, in October, 1864; but no tidings could be procured. After Hawkins's depature from the Colony, his daughter had married one Hunt, and subsequently to the marriage, Mrs. Hawkins died. An offer had lately been made by a neighbour for the piece of ground above referred to; and the object of the present application was to appoint a *curator bonis*, with authority to make transfer. In the will, Hawkins had stated that the ground was bought with funds brought by his wife. It was therefore suggested that the Board of Executors, who would be executors under the will if he were dead, should be appointed curators. The application was made, not upon any section of Ordinance 105, but rather on the general law; and it would be necessary to give the person appointed a special authority to transfer.

1868. February 13

Re Henry Hawkins.

But the Court were inclined to treat Hawkins as dead; he not having been heard of for more than seven years. And the matter stood over for a reference to authorities on this point.

Postea, 5th March, the Master was instructed to report whether the sale was for the benefit of the minor.

[Applicants' Attorney, *Buissinne.*]

EXECUTORS WATERMAN, APPLICANTS.— WOLFREY, RESPONDENT.

Curator Bonis.

Porter moved for the sequestration of respondent's estate. In 1862, Wolfrey passed a mortgage bond for £100 in favour of one Henry Adams, by whom it had been ceded to applicants. Wolfrey had left the Colony in 1855 without

February 18.

Executors Waterman, Applicants; Wolfrey, Respondent.

1868.
February 18.

Executors Water-
man, Applicants;
Wolfrey, Respon-
dent.

satisfying the debt, and had thereby committed an act of insolvency, under the 4th section of Ord. 6, 1843. The only other creditor was a bond creditor for £45.
It appeared that Wolfrey had left Cape Town, soon after passing the bond, for Port Elizebeth, where he was for some time resident. Inquiry had been made at Port Elizabeth, but without success.

CONNOR, J.— If a mortgagor goes away, leaving property secured and rents accruing, is it not rather hard to say that he has, under the 4th section of the Ordinance so absented himself " with intent to defeat his creditors" as would make him commit an act of insolvency ? Will not the better course be to appoint a *curator bonis*, and proceed against him ? (*Sande Decis. Fris.*, 4, 9, 8.)

Porter ultimately undertook that a special notice should be inserted in the *Gazette*, intimating that upon the 12th April, the Court would be moved to appoint a *curator bonis*.

[Applicant's Attorney, *Buissinne.*]

WYKHAM *vs.* KINGON.

Provisional Sentence—Sheriff's Service.

February 20.
Wykham *vs.*
Kingon.

Provision was prayed upon a promissory note drawn by defendant in favour of plaintiff. The service of the summons on defendant was personal, " by delivering to him a copy thereof, *as also a certain promissory note*. Defendant replied, ' I will attend to it.' "

The Court sent the return back to the Sheriff for amendment.

[On the same day, the Court granted provisional sentence in *Van der Byl vs. Hoffman* on a promissory note where the Deputy Sheriff's return of service was the delivery of a copy of the summons, " as also of the promissory note. " And in *Collisons & Co. vs. Wiese,* where plaintiffs sued as the cessionaries of a mortgage bond, the service being personal, " as also copy of the mortgage bond and act of cession."]

[Applicant's Attorneys, *Fairbridge & Arderne.*]

BOARD OF EXECUTORS, APPLICANTS.—HELENA JACOBA STIGLING, RESPONDENT.

Where an Order was granted attaching a tenant's Goods for arrear Rent, but before it could be executed the Tenant had removed the goods into another House, where she was not, however, a Tenant for hire,—the Court ordered the removal of the Goods into the House from which they had been so taken away.

On the 19th February, an order was granted by CONNOR, J., in *camerâ*, at the instance of the present applicant, attaching the movables of the respondent for rent of a certain house. During the time the order was being granted, the respondent removed the movables into another house belonging to a Mrs Breda. *Porter* now applied for an order to continue the attachment of the goods in the house to which they had been so removed; and produced an affidavit by Mrs. Breda that her house was not let to respondent, nor to anybody in her behalf.

The Court authorized the removal of the goods, by the Master's messenger, from Mrs. Breda's house into the house from which they had been taken away, an inventory being taken; and without prejudice to the rights of the respondent (who did not appear) to have this order set aside.

[Applicants' Attorneys, *Reid & Nephew.*]

1868.
February 20
Board of Executors, Applicants;
Helena Jacoba Stigling, Respondent.

PRICKETT *vs.* PRICKETT.

Proof of Marriage in an action for Divorce.

In this case, which was an undefended action at the instance of the husband against the wife, for divorce, on the ground of adultery, it was proved that the parties had married at Simon's Town, in 1860, and had removed to Graham's Town in 1864; that in November, 1865, the wife returned to Simon's Bay and was delivered of a legitimate child; that she remained in Simon's Town, without being visited by her husband, and was delivered of a second child in May, 1867. The adultery was clearly proved; but *quoad* the proof of marriage,—

Cole produced from the Colonial Office a certified copy of the marriage register of St. Frances' Church, Simon's Town, proving the marriage of parties of the same name upon the day on which the plaintiff (who had been examined *de bene esse* at Graham's Town) had sworn to his marriage. But no proof of the handwriting of the officiating minister or attesting witnesses was given. The other evidence of the

February 25.
Prickett *vs.* Prickett

1868.
February 25.

Prickett vs. Prickett.

marriage was that of the midwife, who, having been present at both the last deliveries, proved the adultery. She swore that she was acquainted with the parties before marriage; that she was in the house of the defendant's mother upon the day of the marriage; that she saw the parties go to church and return home from the church; and that she knew them to live as man and wife until their departure for Graham's Town.

The Court held this sufficient *primâ facie* evidence of the marriage to support the action. And as to the custody of the three legitimate children, all with the mother, ordered them to be handed over to the care of the father on his sending for them.

[*Et vide, as to proof of marriage, Croeser vs. Croeser, Menz. Rep.* 267. *Hoffman vs. Hoffman, do.* 281. *Kemball vs. Kemball, do.* 281.]

[Plaintiff's Attorneys, *Fairbridge & Arderne*.]

A. DE PASS, APPLICANT.—OWNERS BARKS "TIGRIS" AND "EUNOMIA," RESPONDENTS.

Arrest of part interest in a Vessel at the suit of a co-part Owner in another Vessel refused.

February 25.

A. de Pass, Applicant; Owners Barks *Tigris* and *Eunomia*, Respondents.

Porter moved for the arrest of respondents' interest in the bark *Tigris*, now in Table Bay, under the following circumstances. The applicant is the owner of the bark *Southern Cross*, which was lying at anchor in Simon's Bay, when, on the 11th instant, she was run into by the bark *Eunomia* which was leaving the bay, and, without stopping, the *Eunomia* proceeded on her voyage. The damage done to the *Southern Cross* was calculated, including demurrage, at £142; and for this amount it was now sought to arrest the *Tigris*, which was in part owned by Mr. H. Smith, of Scarborough, owner of the *Eunomia*. It had been intended to arrest the *Eunomia* in Algoa Bay, where she was expected to call, but she had not done so. Mr. Smith was unrepresented here. Messrs. Rutherfoord Brothers had acted as agents until the clearance of the vessel, which was now ready to sail for the West Indies. The captain had not received formal notice of this application, but had been corresponded with, and knew it would be made, but did not appear.

[BELL, J.—Is there any instance of an arrest of this kind, —by which the part owners of the *Eunomia* who are not part owners of the *Tigris* may be damnified by the arrest of the vessel?]

The application has only just been handed to me, and presses, so that I have not consulted authorities. The only difficulty is that the owners of the *Eunomia* are not precisely the same as the owners of the *Tigris*. But I apprehend it is clear that if there were a judgment of this Court against the owners of the *Eunomia*, under that judgment the interest of those owners in both that ship and the *Tigris* would be attachable. It is the common case of a partnership, where the partnership property must be attached as a whole, in order to get at the interest of the part owners. The damnification of the respondents could be avoided by security rendered. The Court would attach the part interest of the owner of one farm in another. It is true a farm is not, as a ship is, movable; but there is no distinction in the principle of part interest to be applied.

1868.
February 25.

A. de Pass, Applicant; Owners Barks *Tigris* and *Eunomia*, Respondents.

[BELL, J.—Then to take the case of a 1,200-ton ship, do you maintain that such a ship could be arrested here for a debt due by the owner of one sixty-fourth part in her, who was the owner of another vessel through which the debt arose?]

I do. If a writ of execution were issued against a farm held by different owners, in undivided shares, however small, the Sheriff would seize the whole to eliminate the share of the debtor. It is a responsibility inseparable from the partnership.

CONNOR, J.—But would ship-owners be identical with farm-owners? Is there not a great distinction between the case of a movable ship and immovable land? We have had no case like this. By attaching the ship we would injure absent owners.

HODGES, C. J.—It is, *primâ facie*, a strong proceeding to make such an arrest without clear authority. It would be better to postpone the application till later in the day, and search for authorities.

The case accordingly stood till later in the day, when

Porter stated he had not found any specific authority in regard to ship arrests; but he again submitted that upon general principles of partnership the matter was plain. The property of the partnership is liable to execution for the debts of a partner, and the Sheriff would sell the undivided share of that partner. It required no authority to prove that anything which can be seized in execution of a judgment is arrestable to found jurisdiction for a judgment. And then we are brought round to consider what is the position of a creditor of a part owner who has judgment and has no means of obtaining the fruits of that judgment except through the interest of his debtor in a ship. This is a point of some importance. It is not an uncommon thing to find the master of a vessel the part owner; and supposing he

1868.
February 25.

A. de Pass, Applicant ; Owners Barks *Tigris* and *Eunomia*, Respondent.

incurred a debt in Cape Town—which debt I will assume was not contracted for ship purposes, both himself personally and the vessel would be arrestable, or the creditor would be defeated. In *Lindley on Partnership*, Vol. 1, p. 584, it is laid down that it is much better for partners to give security for defaulting partners, than that honest creditors should be disappointed. And further, that undivided shares in partnerships cannot be seized without seizing the whole partnership property. Bodily seizure is the principle on which the Sheriff proceeds, and then he holds with a dead hand as regards the other partners. This is shown by Lindley to be the new rule, in contradistinction to the old rule, which was the opposite.

The Court declined making the order.

HODGES, C. J., said the argument for the applicant was rested mainly upon a judgment already recovered. But this is not that case; and, in the interest of ships visiting Table Bay, the Court would be slow to grant such an order without direct authority upon the subject.

BELL, J., considered such an order would be unjust and oppressive. There was no analogy between arresting goods on shore in a debtor's country and arresting a ship sailing on the high seas. Otherwise, one ship might be arrested to satisfy the liabilities of part owners in nineteen other vessels. There was no comparison between the inconvenience the *Tigris* would be put to and the slighter inconvenience of the applicant going to Scarborough to the owners.

CONNOR, J., thought the authorities on the question of partnership were analogous; but yet it was a serious step for the Court to take without a more direct authority on the subject of ship arrests.

[Applicant's Attorneys, *Fairbridge & Arderne*.]

DE PASS & CO. *vs.* TRUSTEES FRONTIER FIRE AND MARINE INSURANCE COMPANY.

Argument on Plaintiff's exceptions to Defendant's pleas.—A policy of Marine Insurance against Bar-risk contained the words " warranted free of average, unless general or the Vessel be stranded," and in a subsequent portion, " and warranted free from particular average." The Vessel having stranded on the Bar in crossing, the Assured claimed particular average. The Insurers resisted the claim on the strength of the words secondly quoted. Held, for the purposes of the pleadings, that, as in the opinion of the Court the ordinary legal effect should be given to the words "*or the vessel be stranded,*"—*to wit, that the Insurers thereupon became liable to pay particular average, —the Defendants' plea of no particular average under the Policy was no answer to the declaration on the Policy; and the plaintiffs' exceptions were sustained accordingly.*

The defendants were summoned to answer the plaintiffs in an action of debt. Upon the 26th February, 1867, and at Graham's Town the plaintiffs, by their agent, Bertram, applied to the defendants to grant a policy of insurance upon the schooner *Lightning*, their property, against certain risk of damage or loss in entering or quitting Port Alfred, which is what is commonly called a bar harbour, at which there was kept a steam-tug for towing vessels entering or quitting the harbour across the bar of the harbour. The Company agreed to grant the policy for £800, "which insurance is hereby declared to be" [here the further printed words of the form of the policy—" goods warranted free of average, unless general, or the vessel be stranded, namely"— were erased, and the following substituted in writing:] "hull and tackle of *Lightning* against bar risk only, to go in and out, tug to be employed; warranted free of average, unless general, or the vessel be stranded." The policy then went on to say, " And we covenant and agree that the insurance aforesaid shall commence upon the said ship at Port Alfred on the hull and tackle of the ship *Lightning* from the time of her being taken in tow by the steam-tug *Alfred*, against bar risk only, both in and out of the river, and warranted free from particular average," &c., &c. The whole of this clause, except the introductory words, " And we covenant and agree that the insurance aforesaid," was in writing.

The plaintiffs' declaration averred that after the making of the said policy, to wit, upon the 4th of March, 1867, the *Lightning* arrived with a cargo of merchandise at or off the harbour, for the purpose of crossing the bar, this being the voyage in reference to which the plaintiffs had effected the policy. The steam-tug was employed to tow the *Lightning*, and took her in tow from the roadstead outside of the harbour, the *Lightning* having previously been furnished by the said tug with a skilled pilot to navigate her. That in crossing the bar, and whilst still in tow by the steam-tug, the vessel struck repeatedly and heavily upon the bar, ceased to obey her rudder, and immediately after drifted to and became stranded upon a spot at or close beside the bar, thus sustaining still further damage. That thirty minutes afterwards she was got off. Having been thus stranded, the plaintiffs averred that the Company became liable to pay to the plaintiffs the particular average, amounting to £281 17s. 5d., as ascertained by an average adjustor; which claim was,

1868.
February 27.

De Pass & Co. *vs* Trustees Frontier Fire and Marine Insurance Company.

1868.
February 27.

De Pass & Co. vs Trustees Frontier Fire and Marine Insurance Company.

without objection to the amount, repudiated by the Company. Wherefore the plaintiffs prayed judgment.
To this declaration the defendants pleaded the general issue, and two special pleas. Firstly, that the plaintiffs did not offer the defendants an opportunity of inspecting the vessel and estimating the damage, but sent her on a further voyage to Simon's Bay, in the course of which voyage she was damaged. That the plaintiffs caused the repairs to be made at Simon's Bay without licence or consent of defendants; and that the expense so incurred exceeded the expense which would have been incurred at Port Alfred. Secondly, "that the damage or loss in the declaration alleged to have been sustained is altogether in the nature of particular, and not general average."

The plaintiffs, in their replication, excepted to the first special plea, on the grounds that the matters in the plea alleged do not, nor any of them, admit or confess and avoid the material facts alleged in the declaration, nor constitute or comprise a bar or answer to the action; and that the said plea is double or multifarious, and is so framed as to embarrass the plaintiffs in replying, seeing that it makes two or more averments distinct and separate in their nature, and such as should not be included in one and the same plea, inasmuch as they do not tend or conduce to, or constitute, one single point or proposition set up as a defence to the said action of the said plaintiffs; and that the said plea does not, in reference to the alleged failure by the said plaintiffs to offer or afford inspection of the said schooner, state at what place such offer should have been made, or at what place such inspection should have been afforded, nor that the said plaintiffs had time and opportunity to have made such offer, or afforded such inspection, if minded so to do; and that the said plea does not in reference to the certain damage alleged to have been received by the said schooner on her voyage to Simon's Bay, aver that such damage, so received formed the whole or any part of the damage claimed for in this action; and that the said plea does not, in reference to the repairs which the said plaintiffs are alleged to have caused to be made without the licence or consent of the defendants, aver that such licence and consent were not applied for by the plaintiffs to the said defendants; and that the said plea is in other respects informal and insufficient."
And as to the special plea secondly pleaded, the plaintiffs likewise excepted to the same as bad in substance on this ground: "That admitting, as the said plaintiffs do admit, and as they have, in fact, by their declaration already alleged, that the damage or loss claimed for by them in this action is altogether in the nature of particular, and not general average, the said plaintiffs say that the said defendants are liable for

such particular average, under and by virtue of the policy of assurance in the said declaration set forth."

1868.
February 27.

De Pass & Co. vs. Trustees Frontier Fire and Marine Insurance Company.

To this replication the defendants rejoined that the exceptions were bad in law, and prayed judgment accordingly.

Porter for plaintiffs.—The exception to the second special plea is the most important, because if the Court is against the plaintiffs, there is an end of the case.

[*Griffith, A. G.*, for defendants.—I submit to the exception on the first special plea, and only desire to argue that in the second.]

The policy is carelessly drawn; but the general words in the subsequent part of it, " free from particular average," cannot relieve the defendants from the responsibility of the words in the preceding part, " or the vessel be stranded." As to the exact force of the words " unless general, or the vessel be stranded," *vide Arnold on Insurance*, vol. 2, p. 851. It means that the Company will pay for any damage in the nature of particular average if the ship be stranded. If doubtful, the policy must be construed most strongly against the defendants, they being the stipulators, who, by the civil law, framed the question to be answered, and against whom therefore, the construction is to be taken most rigidly. Here the Company has said it will pay particular average if the ship be stranded; and it cannot be said that the words "if the ship be stranded" are to go for nothing, for they were first erased from the printed form to be re-inserted in writing.

Griffith, contra.—The stipulator here is the assured, and not the insurer. Therefore the ambiguity, if any, is in our favour. This is a particular insurance against bar risk, but there are, as is natural, a great many unnecessary provisions left in the policy, such as are, for instance, contained in these words: " And touching the adventures and perils which the capital stock and funds of the said Company are made liable unto, or are intended to be made liable unto, by this insurance, they are those of the seas, men-of-war, fire, enemies, pirates, rovers, thieves, jettisons, letters of marque and countermarque, surprisals and taking at sea, arrests, restraints, and detainments of all kings, princes, and people of what nation or quality soever, barratry of the masters and mariners, and all other perils, losses, and misfortunes," &c., &c. These words, although inserted, would not apply to the particular bar risk. And in the same manner, the words " unless the vessel be stranded" did not apply either. The clauses cannot both stand; and the question is, which is to stand? I contend that the particular words " warranted free from general average " will, in the case of a particular risk, govern the general words of the policy; as deeds of release in

1868.
February 27.

De Pass & Co. *vs.*
Trustees Frontier
Fire and Marine
Insurance Company.

England, although general in terms, are confined to the particular intended release.

The Court upheld the exceptions, with costs, on the ground that, in its opinion, effect should be given to the words " unless the ship be stranded ;" and that the fair and honest construction of the policy was to construe the subsequent words " warranted free from particular average " as if the words " except as aforesaid " had been inserted ; the ambiguity having evidently arisen from a clerical mistake in the Company's office.

[Plaintiffs' Attorneys, *Reid & Nephew*.
Defendants' Attorneys, *Fairbridge & Arderne*.]

SAGET, APPLICANT.—BATAILLOU, RESPONDENT.

Discharge of Arrest—Cancellation of Bail Bond.

February 29.

Saget, Applicant;
Bataillou, Respondent.

Cole moved, under the 135th Rule of Court, for the discharge of an arrest granted by BELL, J., yesterday, on a demand for £100 made by respondent, a resident in Cape Town, upon the applicant, the master of the French ship *Ploermel*, on the point of leaving Table Bay.

It appeared that the respondent had called applicant a liar, upon the 31st January, whereupon the applicant struck him in the face. A claim of £100 damages followed upon 4th February, but was taken no notice of by applicant. It was repeated upon the 18th February, when applicant's attorney repudiated the claim, and requested that the action might be tried during the February term, so as not to detain the applicant or his vessel. Nothing further was done by respondent until the 27th February, when the vessel was ready for sea. The arrest was then procured, returnable upon the 4th March. A bail bond was given by the applicant according to the form prescribed by Rules of Court.

Cole maintained the proceedings were in abuse of the power of arrest; the claim, in the first instance, being a ridiculous one under any circumstances. And secondly, it could have been proceeded with before and settled by the Magistrate, or in this Court.

[CONNOR, J.—Ought not your motion to be to cancel the bail bond ? The condition of that bond being to appear and stand the judgment of the Court, the arrest is at an end.]

If the arrest is not now set aside, it will continue until the return day on the writ.

[CONNOR, J.—When you arrest a man on a writ returnable on a certain day, and the party arrested gives bail, the arrest is done with. The Court would never be applied to on the return day to confirm the writ. The bail bond holds during the action.]

1868.
February 29
———
Saget, Applicant;
Bataillou, Respondent.

Upon the return day of the writ the case should, in strictness, be placed upon the roll, as if it were a provisional case, and a motion made, either that it should continue, or be discharged. And, if so, the 135th Rule lays down that it is not compulsory to wait for the return day, seeing that the return day may, under that Rule, be "anticipated." To avoid any technical difficulty, however, the applicant is willing to surrender himself to the Sheriff, if necessary.

Bond contra.

The Court set aside the arrest, and cancelled the bail bond, with costs.

HODGES, C. J.—The process of the Court has been most improperly used, for an oppressive purpose. The claim was unfounded; for the striking in the face was a natural consequence of the imputation made. The case might, under any circumstances, have been heard before the Magistrate, or this Court, before now; intead of which, the proceedings are put off until the last moment of the vessel sailing. I have no doubt the arrest ought to be set aside, and, if necessary, the bail bond also. The applicant must have his costs of coming here to set aside the arrest. This Court is bound to protect foreigners from such improper arrests.

BELL, J., concurred.

CONNOR, J.—I should have a doubt, on a matter of form, whether the motion should not have been to set aside the bail bond; but it is not for me to settle the practice of the Court. As to the claim, it is a monstrous one. If a man calls another a liar, he must be prepared to receive the consequences. The applicant ought never to have been arrested; and it would be very hard, in that case, if the bail bond could not be set aside.

[Applicant's Attorney, *E. Hull.*]
[Respondent's Attorney, *T. Dickson.*]

COLLISONS & CO. *vs.* SCHMIDT.

Defective Service.

De Villiers, for plaintiffs, prayed judgment absolute, defendant being in default of appearance, upon a claim for £16 14s. for goods sold and delivered.

February 29.

Collisons & Co. *vs.* Schmidt,

On reference to the service of the summons, the return of the Deputy Sheriff was found to be as follows:

" On the 11th day of January, 1868, I have repaired to the residence of W llem Gerrit Schmidt, and have then and

D

1868.
February 29.
———
Collisons & Co.
vs. Schmidt.

there, in his absence, duly served upon W. G. van Enter, with whom the defendant resides when he is at home, and delivered to him a copy thereof; and his answer was, 'Schmidt is on togt. I will give it to him when he returns.'"

But the service of the notice of trial (forwarding the declaration at the same time, as filed upon default of appearance) was as follows:

"Upon the 11th February, 1868, I served upon Willem Gerrit Schmidt a certain original notice," &c., "by leaving the same nailed to the door of the residence of the said Schmidt."

The Court would not proceed with the case, but adjourned its hearing *sine die* in consequence of insufficient service. The case to be re-set down for trial.

[Plaintiffs' Attorneys, *Read & Nephew*.]

HONNEYBORNE, APPELLANT.—TINLEY, RESPONDENT.

Where an Enrolled Agent in the Prince Albert Magistrate's Court appealed to the Supreme Court against an Order that he should be struck off the Roll, the Court set aside the Order on account of the non-hearing of Apellant's evidence.

February 29.
Honeyborne, Appellant; Tinley, Respondent.

Porter, for appellant, moved the Court to set aside, under section 37 of Act 20, 1856, a judgment delivered by the repondent in his capacity as Acting Resident Magistrate for the division of Prince Albert, by which judgment the appellant, an enrolled agent in the Magistrate's Court for that division, was struck off the roll.

The facts of the case were briefly these. Upon the 16th of January, 1868, Mr. Borcherds, Resident Magistrate for Prince Albert, was trying the case of the Queen *vs.* Lys Sauel, for assault. The appellant appeared for the defence, and took exception to the competency of the Magistrate on the ground of having had improper intercourse with the prisoner. An altercation ensued, and the Magistrate said "surely, the prisoner has been put up to it." The appellant replied that, if anyone said he had put the woman up, such person lied. The Magistrate subsequently wrote to Government upon the subject, reporting the appellant, and charging him with having used words calculated to provoke a breach of the peace. The appellant also reported the Magistrate, and preferred a similar charge against him. The Government appointed the respondent, who is the Resident Magistrate for the adjoining division of Beaufort, Acting Magistrate for the division of Prince Albert, and commissioned him to inquire into the charge and counter-charge. The respondent thereupon proceeded to Prince Albert, and summoned Honeyborne to appear and answer to having openly insulted the presiding Magistrate by making the statement above referred to, and raising the same as an objection to his proceeding in the case, " although it appears, from the statement of the said Lys Sauel that she did not authorize the said Honeyborne to raise the said objection." Upon the appointed day the respondent sat, and heard sundry witnesses in support of the summons. The appellant then proposed " to lead evidence to prove that he had been informed of the cohabitation by the party in whose favour the exception was taken, and also had cautioned her at the time she signed the power of attorney with respect to the statements she made. Further, that the statement as to cohabitation was made voluntarily, and without any attempt on his part to induce her to say what she did; and that the objection to the competency of the presiding magistrate was considered by him a good and valid one." From the record of proceedings it appeared that the " Court refused to admit the evidence, and that it overruled the objection on the ground of cohabitation, or any complaint from the woman in question, as the same is not before the Court, or in question." And the respondent then proceeded to deliver the following judgment: " To be struck off the list as an enrolled agent of the Court of the Resident Magistrate, Prince Albert, subject to review if called, on the ground of his (Honeyborne) charging the Magistrate while on the bench with cohabiting with a woman, then and there charged before the Court with assault, and on that occasion and others being disrespectful to the Magistrate ; and that my own observations and inquiries have satisfied me that it is for the interest and respectful order of this Court that he be removed from the roll." Adding certain " Memos. to their Honours the Judges," to the same effect.

Porter, for appellant.—The respondent's proceedings have been wholly irregular. He was a Government commissioner to inquire into both the charges, whereas he has only taken notice of that brought by the Magistrate. Here, again, his proceedings were irregular, for he issued a summons under the criminal branch of the department, and instead of fineing or imprisoning under the Act, which is all he could even then do, he turns it into an investigation of the conduct of an enrolled agent, and that, moreover, when the defendant had not been summoned as an enrolled agent to show cause. On that ground alone the respondent was wrong ; but even had his proceedings been regular, the rejection of the evidence tendered by the appellant was wrong. The appellant

1868.
February 29.
___

Honeyborne, Appellant; Tinley, Respondent.

1868.
February 29.
Honeyborne, Appellant; Tinley, Respondent.

was justified in raising the exception, if duly authorized. Indeed, he would have been guilty of misconduct if he had refused to make the objection when his client, after caution, desired it. No practitioner in any court can be struck off the rolls of that Court because, acting by the instructions of his client he takes such an exception. The question then resolves itself into this: Was this a *bonâ fide* objection, made on instruction? On this material point the respondent refused to hear the evidence tendered. The imputation of lying, alleged to have been used to the Magistrate by appellant, was hypothetical, and not, under that hypothesis, unjustifiable. On the grounds stated, I submit, these proceedings should be set aside for irregularity; without prejudice to any further proceedings to be hereafter taken.

There was no appearance for respondent.

The Court ordered the proceedings to be set aside.

HODGES, C. J.—The judgment pronounced was a most serious one to the appellant; and we must therefore see that the proceedings were regular. I must say it appears to me the respondent has mistaken his course altogether. As far as I can see, the wish of the Government was, that he should hear the cross charges. The Government desired to ascertain the truth in a matter seriously affecting the administration of justice. Instead of holding such inquiry, the respondent issued a very peculiar summons, not even calling upon or giving the appellant any notice to show cause why he should not be struck off the roll of agents. The proceedings were informal in these respects; but even had they been regular, the respondent should have heard the evidence in behalf of the appellant. It was an important point to inquire whether the appellant had been instructed by the woman, or whether he acted from malice towards the Magistrate. The respondent had nothing to do with striking the appellant off, under any circumstance. His duty was limited to reporting to Government the result of the proceedings. Without, however, saying anything about the merits, all the Court does now is, to say that the respondent arrived at his decision without jurisdiction, and irregularly.

BELL, J., concurred generally as to the irregularity of the proceedings, and as to the limitation on the respondent to inquire into the cross actions, and nothing beyond. The summons assumed the truth of the Magistrate's account. The respondent was only a commissioner to make certain inquiries on behalf of Government. The appellant's mouth had been shut on the great point of the case, as to the *bonâ fides* of the agent's instructions. Even if the Magistrate may not have had such connection as was alleged, yet if the woman told the agent that he had, and authorized him, as agent, to take such objection, the appellant was fully justified in so doing. There may have been, for all we can tell, sufficient cause for the removal of the agent on the ground of insulting and overbearing manners; but as far as they have yet gone, the whole proceedings must be set aside, and proceeded with *ab ovo.*

CONNOR, J.—I am not quite prepared to say that the respondent had not jurisdiction. I presume that Magistrates hold during pleasure; and in the case of an officer who holds during pleasure, appointing another displaces him. The respondent, I am inclined to think, was the acting Magistrate to adjudicate; and, supposing he were the legal Magistrate, then, under the 17th section, he had jurisdiction. Possibly, therefore, he had a legal right to arrive at the decision as to the striking off the roll. But the case, as now presented to us, cannot stand; for the respondent has refused evidence upon a most material point. It was argued for the plaintiff that an agent is bound to follow implicitly the instructions of his client. I doubt that, and apprehend that it is for the agent to excise his own discretion. We are bound, in the absence of evidence to the contrary, to assume that the agent made the objection *bonâ fide*; and however painful the objection, I am not prepared to say that the respondent may not have shown he was warranted in taking such an exception. The great irregularity in the proceeding was the rejection of the justifying evidence; and, confining myself to that for the present, I am of opinion that the proceedings, as they stand, do not show a case for striking the appellant off the roll.

Proceedings reversed, with costs.

[Applicants' Attorneys, *Fairbridge & Arderne.*]

1868.
February 29.

Honeyborne, Appellant; Tinler, Respondent.

ARNHOLZ, APPLICANT AND ORIGINAL PLAINTIFF.—
DIVISIONAL COUNCIL OF TULBAGH, RESPONDENTS
AND ORIGINAL DEFENDANTS.

Divisional Councils Consolidation Act. What is a Divisional Councillor's "direct or indirect interest" in a Council Contract under Section 75?

This was an appeal from a judgment of the Resident Magistrate for Tulbagh, on a claim for work done by one Warwick, the account for which had been passed by the Tulbagh Divisional Council, with the words written thereon, " Please pay to Mr. A. Arnholz, for value received.—W. Warwick."

1868.
March 8.

Arnholz, Applicant and Original Plaintiff; Divisional Council of Tulbagh, Respondents and Original Defendants.

1868.
March 3.

Arnholz, Appli-
cant and Original
Plaintiff ; Divi-
sional Council of
Tulbagh, Re-
spondents and
Original Defen-
dants.

It appeared that Arnholz, who was a member of the Divisional Council for the Ceres ward, had, in conjunction with the Civil Commissioner of Tulbagh, the chairman of the Divisional Council, but without an express resolution of the Council, authorized Warwick to perform certain urgent repairs to the Ceres bridge for the sum of £7. Afterwards, Mr. Arnholtz, who is a storekeeper at Ceres, influenced, as he alleged, by feelings of kindness towards Warwick, advanced him £7 in cash and food during the progress of the repairs, and then took from him the order upon the account, as above stated. Arnholz presented this account, with the abovementioned order written thereupon, at the following meeting of the Divisional Council of Tulbagh, when the account was passed. A Mr. Wiener, who was a storekeeper at Tulbagh, with a branch at Ceres, was acting secretary to the Council at the time. Upon being applied to he alleged that the original account had been lost, that the words forming the order to pay had not been endorsed thereon at the time the Council passed the account, and that he had subsequently paid the amount to one Henry Kilgour (who, it appeared, was the manager of Wiener's Ceres business), for which payment he held the receipt of Warwick, attested by two witnesses. The original account, and order endorsed thereon, on which the plaintiff founded his claim, not being forthcoming in the Court below, the Magistrate, although there was secondary evidence of its existence, nonsuited the plaintiff on that ground.

Porter for appellant.—There has been unfair proceeding on the part of Wiener to get his own account paid rather than Arnholz's account.

[CONNOR, J.—Section 75 of the Divisional Councils Act, 6 of 1865, provides that no Divisional Councillor shall be "directly or indirectly interested in any contract." Was not Arnholz virtually interested in the contract made with Warwick?]

There were two separate stages,—The contract to do the work, and the agreement to receive payment. Arnholz was not interested, in terms of the Act, in either ; but if, for arguments sake, he was interested in anything, it was in the agreement to pay, and that was after the contract for the work had been finished. If the Civil Commissioner had advanced the money, would he have come under the Act?

[CONNOR, J.—Arnholz advanced a certain sum on the credit of the contract. Was that not being interested in the contract?]

All his interest, if any, lay in the passing of the account But the Chairman of the Council had as much interest, because he, as one of the contracting parties, was liable. As to the cession of the claim, by *Voet* 18, 14, 15, it is good without intimation to the debtor. The only liberation is by a *bonâ fide* payment by the debtor to the cedent. Here it is questionable whether money ever passed on the receipt given by Warwick to Kilgour, for the attesting witnesses have not been produced. And under any circumstances, it was a *malâ fide* payment by Wiener to himself, to defeat Arnholz's claim.

1868.
March 3.

Arnholz, Applicant and Original Plaintiff; Divisional Council of Tulbagh, Respondents and Original Defendants.

Griffith, A.-G., for respondent.—Wiener has paid the amount to Kilgour on Warwick's receipt. If there has been fraud on the part of Warwick, Arnholz can go against him, or he can go against Wiener ; but not against the Divisional Council, which has already paid the debt. Moreover, under the Act, the contract was bad ; Arnholz being a Divisional Councillor.

The majority of the Court (HODGES, C. J., and CONNOR, J.; BELL, J., dissenting) held that Arnholz was interested in the contract under the Act, and therefore could not sue upon it.

CONNOR, J.—The writing by Warwick on the account produced by Arnholz is said to have been a cession of the debt, but it looks more like a bill of exchange ; and if so, there has been no acceptance by the Divisional Council. But assuming even that it is a cession of the worth of the contract, that will come under section 75 of the Act 6 of 1865. Either Arnholz was the agent of Warwick—and then payment to the principal discharges the debtor—or he is himself the owner of the worth of the contract. That is, under the Act, an illegal engagement, and the plaintiff cannot bring an action on it. Although; I do not believe this was the ground of the decision in the Court below, still, as the law of the land, as contained in the Act, need not be pleaded, we can notwithstanding hold that the plaintiff, on the ground now stated, was incapacitated from suing.

BELL, J., conceded that if the section applied the result just stated would follow, but on no view of the case could he regard the section as of any application. Arnholz was not interested in the contract under the Act ; besides, the Council had had presented to them the account with the cession at the foot of it, and had passed it, and thus approved what had been done and bound itself to pay. As to the terms of cession many a mortgage bond had been declared provisionally executable upon a similar cession. Even if not a cession, it was a bill of exchange, and then it was clear the Council had by passing the account with the endorsation thereupon accepted the bill. The plaintiff would be unjustly treated if he did not receive the amount and costs.

1868.
March 3.

Arnholz, Applicant and Original Plaintiff; Tolbagh, Respondents and Original Defendants.

HODGES, C. J., did not see how the plaintiff had made out a contract, express or implied, upon the part of the Council to pay him this amount; but even had there been such an undertaking, he concurred that the matter fell within the 75th section of the Act, and that, on this ground, the judgment of the Court below should be sustained and the appeal be dismissed with costs.

[Applicant's Attorneys, *Fairbridge & Arderne*.
Respondent's Attorneys, *Hofmeyr, Tredgold, & Watermeyer*.]

DIVISIONAL COUNCIL, PORT ELIZABETH, APPELLANTS AND ORIGINAL DEFENDANTS.—DIVISIONAL COUNCIL, UITENHAGE, RESPONDENTS AND ORIGINAL PLAINTIFFS.

Where by Government Proclamation the "right bank" of a River was declared to be the boundary between two Divisions, the Court held on appeal (reversing the judgment of the Circuit Court) that the right bank extended to the water's edge at low, and not at high-water mark.

March 4.
March 12.

Divisional Council, Port Elizabeth, Appellants and Original Defendants; Divisional Council, Uitenhage, Respondents and Original Plaintiffs.

This was an appeal from a judgment of the Circuit Court for the division of Port Elizabeth, given upon the 28th October, 1867, in an action to recover the amount of certain tolls.

The circumstances in which the action originated in the Court below were as follows: Prior to 1848, the divisions of Uitenhage and Port Elizabeth, which now are distinct and independent divisions, were both included in the division of Uitenhage. In that year, Port Elizabeth was, by proclamation of the 8th March, created a separate division, and the boundary line between the two divisions declared to be "down the right bank of the Great Zwartkops River to its confluence with the sea." In 1850, a pontoon was placed upon the Zwartkops River, the proceeds falling into the general revenue. In 1859, the pontoon was superseded by a bridge called "Rawson Bridge," and a toll established by the Government. The toll-bar was placed upon the bridge itself, and was regulated under the provisions of Ord. 9, 1858. The proceeds continued to go to Government until the passing of the Road Act, No. 10 of 1864, when the maintenance of the main roads of the Colony was handed over to the Divisional Councils. Rawson Bridge being situated upon the main line of road between Port Elizabeth and Graham's Town, the toll-bar upon it came under the Act from 1st January, 1865. Until the 27th February, 1867, the tolls were divided equally between the two Divisional Councils of Uitenhage and Port Elizabeth; but since that period they have been wholly claimed by the Divisional Council of Port Elizabeth. The Divisional Council of Uitenhage accordingly brought an action in the Port Elizabeth Circuit Court, claiming the whole amount of the tolls collected from 1st March, 1867, on the ground that the toll-bar on Rawson Bridge was in the Division of Uitenhage; or otherwise, the half of the tolls, under contract between the two Divisional Councils and custom prior to 1st March, 1867.

1868.
March 4.
March 12.

Divisional Council. Port Elizabeth, Appellants and Original Defendants; Divisional Council, Uitenhage, Respondents and Original Plaintiffs.

The case in the Court below mainly turned upon the construction of the Proclamation, and the definition of what was the "right bank" of the Great Zwartkops River. The presiding Judge (FITZPATRICK, J.) held that the Division of Uitenhage extended to the high-water mark of the river on the right or Port Elizabeth bank; and that the toll-bar, being forty-four feet below high-water mark, was within the Division of Uitenhage, which was therefore entitled, under section 4 of Act 10 of 1864, to the whole of the tolls taken.

The evidence taken below having been read,

Griffith, A.-G. (with him *De Villiers*), for appellants.—The sole question in the case is,—is the toll-bar within the boundary of Port Elizabeth, or not? This depends upon the construction of the words in the Proclamation, "the right bank of the river." I am willing to concede that a grant to the sea, *quoad* proprietary rights, is a grant to the sea at high-water mark; but no authority can be produced on the other side to apply that principal to a question of jurisdiction. So, also, if lands are conveyed to a private person, the boundary being a river, that is also up to high-water mark. But not where a river is made the boundary of counties, or divisions, as is the case here; for then the right of jurisdiction is raised, and the proprietary principal fails. If a crime were committed when the river was at low-water mark, between that mark and high-water mark, I submit the criminal would be liable to apprehension on a writ issued in Port Elizabeth without any necessity for delay by first procuring the indorsation of the writ at Uitenhage. The right bank of the river extends to that part where the river runs at its lowest. That is the bank on which, in the days of the pontoon, the one end of it rested at low water. Then, again, it is clear on the evidence that by certain embankments raised at the construction of the bridge, the high-water mark was thrown more to the Port Elizabeth side than it was at the time of the Proclamation of 1848. But I maintain it is the bank as it stood at the time of that Proclamation which must guide, and not the bank as subsequently altered. We have had possession, and it lies upon the other side, who now claim

1868.
March 4.
March 12.

Divisional Council, Port Elizabeth, Appellants and Original Defendants; Divisional Council, Respondents and Original Plaintiffs.

what we had possession of, to show that the high-water mark at the date of the Proclamation would not include the toll-bar in the Division of Port Elizabeth. In common language, the " bank of the river" is the bank which the river makes; and that must be taken at low water, because this is a tidal river, and the tidal water is sea water, and not river water.

Porter (with him *Cole*), in support of the judgment below.—We agree that the case turns upon what is the meaning of the words "right bank." The bank is that kind of thing which if it were the case of a canal, in Holland, it would be the duty of the parties in the neighbourhood to keep in good repair. Our law, following the civil law, makes a clear distinction in private grants between *agri limitati and illimitati*. (*Voet*, 41, 1, 15.) Defining the bank of a river, it means that boundary which remains stationary,—on which grass grows; and any other view would lead into great difficulties. As to the question of jurisdiction, by Ordinance No. 73, where a crime is committed within two miles of the boundary line of the division, both divisions have jurisdiction specially conferred upon them. The banks of a river are the natural wall confining the rising and falling water, whether from its source or by tidal accessions. It is a limit created by nature. I adopt the opinion of *Paulus* (*Dig.*, 43, 12, 3), that the banks of the river are those which contain the "*flumen plenissimum*." The mud bank left by the receding of the water at low tide is not the bank of the river. Next, as to the alteration of the embankment. The alteration was made by Government, and a bank might change by lawful permanent works; but in reality no substantial change was made.

Cole, on the same side, quoted *Kent's Commentaries*, vol. 3, p. 427, original paging, and the note.

Griffith, in reply.—The quotation from *Kent* refers entirely to proprietary rights, and has no bearing on this case. *Voet*, 43, 12, and 43, 13, clearly defines what *ripa fluminis* is.

Cur. adv. vult.

Postea, March 12, the court held (reversing the judgment below) that the right bank of the river extended to low-water mark.

CONNOR, J., delivered the following judgment: The appeal in this case from the decision of the Circuit Court of Port Elizabeth involves the question whether the boundary of a division of the Colony, which it is provided shall be " down the right bank of the said river " (the Great Zwart-kops) to its confluence with the sea, extends, where the river is tidal, over ground not covered by water when the tide has receded, *i.e.*, at low water. The Court below decided that the banks of the river did not extend below those elevations which are, according to the evidence, as well marked as the walls of a house, and which contain the *plenissimum flumen*, to use the expression of *Paulus* (*Dig.*, 43, 12, 3), supposing—which we shall see is at least doubtful—that the *flumen* in this expression includes the influx of the tide. My doubts (for I have had them) whether the decision in the Court below was not correct arose not only from its appearing more in accordance with the term "bank," as understood in ordinary parlance, but also because no other right bank of the river was shown in the evidence to exist; and because what the tide daily covers, not all the day, but two hours in the twenty-four, would seem to be the bed of the river, and therefore distinct from the bank. *Gothofredus*, for instance, in his *Notes to Dig.*, 43, 12, 1, says that "Rivers consist of three things,—the bed, the banks, and the water."

The Roman lawyers do not give us much direct assistance on the point involved here, because the Mediterranean is, we may say, a tideless sea. *Ulpian* says expressly (*Dig.*, 43, 12, 5): "The bank will be rightly defined thus: That which contains the river, holding in the natural force of its course. But if at times (*quando*) it has increased temporarily by showers, *or by the sea*, or by any other means, it does not change its banks. No one says that the Nile, which covers Egypt by its increment, changes or enlarges its banks; but, when it has returned to its perpetual measure, the banks of its bed are to be guarded." We see that here he expressly speaks of an increase to a river by the sea; but it is, as I have said, very likely that the influx of tides was not present to his mind. But then we have the *Digest* annotated by distinguished jurists, to whose minds tides would be present; and they do not, as far as I am aware, correct the generality of *Ulpian's* statement. *Gothofredus* has this note to *Ulpian's* definition, as above, of the bank (*x*): "Say, more plainly, the bank is defined by the natural course of the river, not from its increase by showers, *or by the sea*, or by any other means. *Pothier* also—as to what *Ulpian* says, that when "the river has returned to its perpetual measure, the banks of its bed are to be guarded"—says that "perpetual" there means natural; and that the banks referred to by *Ulpian* are the banks of this bed which it then (*iam*) occupies. These are therefore, finally, properly said to be the banks." Now, of course, the increase by showers, and the sea, is "natural," in the sense of being brought about according to the laws of nature, and not by artificial means: therefore "natural," when used by these jurists as exclusive of these means, must, I apprehend, be understood to mean what is usual in the river, as a river proper.

1868.
March 4.
March 12.

Divisional Council, Port Elizabeth, Appellants and Original Defendants; Divisional Council, Uitenhage, Respondents and Original Plaintiffs.

1868.
March 4.
March 12.
———
Divisional Council, Port Elizabeth, Appellants and Original Defendants ; Divisional Council, Uitenhage, Respondents and Original Plaintiffs.

What is a river? The word is derived, apparently, through the French, from the Latin *Rivus*, which comes, I apprehend, from the Greek *Rheo*, to flow. But our term "river" corresponds, I should say, not with the Latin *Rivus*, but with *Flumen*, which, of course, also comes from a word signifying to flow (*fluo*); and *Flumen* is said by *Ulpian* "to be distinguished from *Rivus* by magnitude, or by the estimation of those living around it" (*Dig.*, 43, 12, 1.) *Rivus*, then, apparently corresponds with our *stream* or *brook*, or, when smaller still, *rivulet* ; but the flowing from which both names are derived is a flowing by reason of the earth's gravitation, downwards to the sea, as the lowest. And a bank's being right or left is decided by what would be so on the supposition of the river being a person walking in the direction in which it flows. Now all this is reversed in reference to the tide. It advances against the earth's gravitation, up, instead of down. And, according to the rule which I have mentioned, the right bank of the river would be the left bank of the tide. In truth, then, the course of the tide is not the natural course of a river. It is the reverse of that. And it is not to be said that it is so when the tide is receding, because this must derive its character from that of which it is the reaction, viz. : the flow of the tide. Nay, so diverse are the river and the tide, that while the former is, as I have said, so called from flowing downwards, the tide is alone said to "flow" when it is flowing upwards. Well, then, if the tide is not the river, is but a disturbing element, an invasion of the river, we must look for the banks to those elevations which contain the river proper, and that is, the river at low water,—in cases, at least, in which the sea is then wholly absent and the river is free and separate from the tide. The term "bank" implies, I think, *elevation*. We do not confine the term to rivers. Then we have the term "embankment;" and the Latin *Ripa* is probably derived from *repo*, to creep : all these expressions appearing to imply a slope, or other elevation. *Voet* (43, 12), referring to a paragraph in the *Digest* which is not, I think, easy to translate (43, 12, 3), describes the banks of a river as "beginning from where the earth begins to slope (*vergere*) from the flat (*plano*) down to the water." In the argument in *Brown vs. Gufy* (2 *Moore*, P. C., N. S., 341), this passage is quoted from *Hilliard on Torts*, p. 106 : "One of the accompaniments of a river, technically so called, is the bank. It is said the banks of the river are those elevations of land which confine the waters when they rise out of the bed; and the bed is that soil so usually covered with water as to be distinguished from the banks by the character of the soil, or vegetables, or both, produced by the common presence and action of flowing water." This, as I have already intimated, must, I apprehend, be confided to the river's water, not extended to the tide's water. There may, I apprehend, be a tidal bed and a river bed. And the fact of the ground under the tide being left bare at low water, implies that such ground is higher than the river. There is no doubt, however, but that in *Sæbriskto vs. the East India Company* (10 *Moore, P. C.*, 140), the soil under the water at high water in the river Hooghly, at Calcutta, is dealt with as the bed of the river; then there was no occasion there to distinguish between the tidal bed and the bed of the river proper. Nor does it appear, I think, that the bed was left uncovered at low water.

In *Brown vs. Gufy* (10 *Moore, P. C.*, 341), the defendant was sued by a mill-owner in Canada for erecting a wharf on a tidal river which bounded his property. The defendant admitted that the ground on which he had built the wharf was covered with water at high tides; and in the judgment of the Privy Council this passage occurs (362): " It was then said that, however the law might be, if the bank on the face of which the wharf is built, were the private property of the defendant, a distinction is to be made, because the bank is in truth, part of the bed of the river and a portion of the public domain, and that a work erected upon it is a public nuisance of which any person interested has a right to complain. That the bank in question is part of the bed of the river, and a portion of the public domain, is not in terms expressed by the pleadings. The averment was said, at the bar, to be contained inferentially in the statement that the wharf erected by the defendant would traverse the whole of the river, which it would not do unless the bank formed part of the river. If fact were essential to our decision, in this case, we should feel great difficulty in holding that the plaintiff had either sufficiently put it in issue by his declaration, or established it by evidence." Now from an earlier part of the report (346) we find that the plaintiff gave evidence to establish, *inter alia*, three points: 1. That the river Beaufort was a tidal and public river, and navigable at spring tides as high as his mill; 2. That the land on which the respondent had built the wharf was covered at high tide during a large part of every month; 3. That the wharf projected, in some places, even into the bed occupied by the river at low water. And, as I have said, it was not denied by the defendant that the ground on which the wharf was built was covered with water at high tides. Yet the Judicial Committee would, as we have seen, have found great difficulty in holding that this bank, the site of the wharf, was shown to be part of the bed of the river.

Brissonius, "De Significatione Verborum," ad verbum Ripa says: it is known to grammarians that *Ripa* is said of rivers as *Littus* is said of the sea." that is apparently, that what is shore *quoad* the sea, is bank *quoad* a river. And he adds that Pliny calls the bank "the margin of the river." Shakspere, we know, speaks of "the beached margent of the sea," and Wordsworth of "the margin of a bay." Now, then, if what is "shore" *quoad* the sea is "bank" *quoad* a river, and we can ascertain that what is under the flux and reflux of the tide, in the sea, is *shore*,—this may help us in deciding whether what is covered at high water and uncovered at low water, in a tidal river, may not be the *bank* of the river. *Littus* is, in the *Digest* (50, 16, 96), defined to be " as far as to where the greatest wave of the sea reaches." This, of course, means from that point back to the sea. The question of the extent of the shore, with reference to the tide, was very fully discussed in *The Attorney-General vs. Chambers* (23 *Law Jl.*, *ch*. 3, 662). The case was heard before Lord Chancellor Cranworth, assisted by Mr. Baron Alderson and the present Lord Wensleydale, then Mr. Baron Parke. There being no doubt but that *primâ facie* the Crown is entitled to the shore, the question in the case was, what *was* the shore to which the Crown was so entitled? The Judges gave their opinions; and the Lord Chancellor concludes his judgment by saying: "The learned Judges whose assistance I had in this very obscure question point out the limit in leasing such land" (*i.e.*, land not cultivable referred to by Lord Hale) "as the line of the river in a high tide between the springs and the neaps; all lands below that line are more often than not covered at high water, and so may justly be said, in the language of Lord Hale, to be covered by the ordinary flux of the sea. This cannot be said of any land above that line; and I therefore concur with the able opinion of the Judges whose valuable assistance I had, in thinking that the true river line must be taken as the boundary of the right of the Crown." Earlier in his judgment the Chancellor says: The right of the Crown to the *littus maris* (whatever that means) is not disputed. The question is, what is the *littus maris*?" and this question he answers as we have seen. Further on he cites Mr. Justice Holroyd, as saying in *Blundel vs. Catteral* (5 B. and Ald., 268): "By the common law it (that is, the sea shore) is confined to the flux and reflux of the sea at ordinary tides, meaning the land covered by such flux and reflux." In the note to the *Report* (663) an extract is given from Lord Hale's treatise *De Jure Maris*, in which, among other things he says: "The shoar is that ground that is between the ordinary high-water and low-water mark. This doth *primâ facie*, and of common right, belong to the King, both the shoar of the sea and the shoar of the arms of the sea." We see, then, that not only does the *littus maris* extend under the flux and reflux of the tide, but that nothing else is, properly speaking, shore. If, therefore, *ripa* is *quoad* a river what *littus* is *quoad* the sea, it seems clear that in a tidal river the *bank* includes that which extends under the flux and reflux of the sea.

1868.
March 4.
March 12.

Divisionrl Council, Port Elizabeth, Appellants and Original Defendants; Divisional Council, Uitenhage, Respondents and Original Plaintiffs.

In *Lord vs. the Commissioners for the City of Sydney* (12 Ald. P. C., 473), overruling the decision of the Court below it was decided, *inter alia*, that by a grant by the Crown to an individual of land described in the grant as bounded on two sides thus, " and on the east side by a south line to a small creek, and on the north side by that creek and the waters of Botany Bay, at the mouth of Cook's River," the grantee was entitled to the soil *ad medium filum* of the creek: though it was contended that the strict construction of the grant, which the Crown was entitled to, would prevent that construction, as that by which a thing is bounded is outside the thing. The creek is described in the *Report* (477), as " an unnavigable stream of fresh water which flowed into Botany Bay," and therefore did not resemble, probably, the river here; but in the argument for the respondents the following passage is cited (483) from *Angell on Tide Waters*, p. 7 : " The well-settled rule of the law of nations is, that where an arm of the sea or a river is the boundary between two nations or states, if the original right of jurisdiction is in either, in the absence of any convention respecting it, each holds to the middle of the stream. But where one state is the original proprietor and grants the territory on one side only, it retains the river within its own domain, and the newly established state extends to the river only, *and the low-water mark is its boundary.*" But counsel adds, " This was held by the Supreme Court of the United States in reference to the river Ohio, of which the State of Virginia was the original proprietor, and had granted the territory on one side only to Kentucky." We can hardly conceive anything in terms more applicable to this case than the passage in *Angell* ; we are not, however, told the exact terms in which the boundaries of Kentucky were described.

On the whole, I have come to the conclusion, though I can easily understand a different decision being arrived at on Circuit, that the right bank of this tidal river extends at least to low-water mark, and therefore, beyond the place where a plumb-line from the toll-bar would meet the ground. I have arrived at this conclusion upon the principles which

1868.
March 4.
March 12.
Divisional Council, Port Elizabeth, Appellants and Original Defendants; Divisional Council, Uitenhage, Respondents and Original Plaintiffs.

I have endeavoured to explain; and one must feel glad if a result, evidently the more convenient of the two, and that which we can hardly doubt would, if the circumstances had been present to the minds of those who directed the boundaries, have been adopted by them, is that which is required by the principles of law applicable to such questions. Whether this decision is calculated to create any difficulty as to the proprietorship of the bank, between high and low-water mark, need not now be discussed. The case of *Brown vs. Gufy,* which I have already referred to as before the Privy Council, seems to have approached the question, without, however, there being occasion for its being decided. It will probably be found that even for the purposes of questions of property, the ground between high and low-water mark in a tidal river may, without inconvenience, be deemed the bank of the river proper. I concur in thinking that the decree of the Court below should be reversed, and that there should be judgment for the defendants (the appellants here) in the action.

[Applicant's Attorneys, *Reid & Nephew.*]
[Respondents' Attorney, *D. Tennant.*]

J. O. SMITH & CO. *vs.* STEWART.

Where it appeared from the record that a case had been sent up to the Supreme Court by the Eastern Districts Court, under section 24 of Act 16 of 1864 (there being a difference of opinion), but for the adjudication of one exception only, and not for the hearing of the whole case, the Supreme Court declined to hear argument on the exception, and remitted the record to the Eastern Districts Court for amendment.

March 5.

J. O. Smith & Co

This was an action for the delivery of certain promissory notes.

On the 6th May, 1867 the plaintiffs were creditors of Kirkwood, Holland & Co., a mercantile firm, carrying on business at Port Elizabeth, for £473 4s. 6d. On that day, at a meeting of creditors of Kirkwood, Holland & Co., the Standard Bank of British South Africa, through its duly authorized agent, James Tudhope, then the local Manager of the Port Elizabeth Branch, agreed, on receiving cession of the plaintiff's claim, and the release of Kirkwood, Holland, & Co., to guarantee the plaintiffs fifteen shillings in the pound, in four equal instalments, by bills at six, twelve, and eighteen months. Some difficulty had, however, since arisen on the part of the Bank; and the plaintiffs, still willing to carry out the guarantee, and tendering the stipulated cession of their claim, now brought this action for the delivery of the four notes.

1868.
March 5
———
J. O. Smith & Co. *vs.* Stewart.

The defendant took three principal exceptions to the declaration; to wit, firstly, that the defendant had been sued in his capacity as general manager of the Bank, whereas the Bank was a corporation, enrolled in England under the Joint-stock Banking Acts of 1857 and 1858, and therefore should have been sued in its corporate capacity and name; secondly, that there was a variance between the summons and the declaration, inasmuch as Tudhope had made the agreement, and not the defendant Stewart; thirdly, that the case should have been against Tudhope.

The case came on for hearing before the Eastern Districts Court. The Judges of that Court (DENYSSEN and FITZPATRICK, J. J.) differed on the first exception, and removed the case to the Supreme Court, under the 24th section of the Eastern Districts Court Act, 16 of 1864, with a record stating that the cause had been so removed "for the adjudication of the exception." The plaintiffs had put down the case on the cause list "for argument on the exception." It did not distinctly appear from the proceedings whether the other exceptions had been considered and disposed of by the Eastern Districts Court.

Cole, for defendant, stated that the first exception was the matter really before the Court; and was proceeding to argue, in support thereof, that the Standard Bank of British South Africa, being a corporation created in England, must therefore be sued in its corporate capacity; and, secondly, that a corporation which is duly created in the country where it is so created, is recognized by the courts all over the world, by comity of nations,—when he was stopped by

The Court drawing attention to the passage in the record of the Eastern Districts Court "for the adjudication of the exception," and inquiring whether by this it was not to be understood that the case had been only partially removed; whereas, under section 24, read in the light of section 29, only the "whole case or proceedings" could be so removed. As no positive information could be furnished by the Bar upon the point, whether the other exceptions had been considered and already disposed of, or whether the exception first taken had been taken first in order, and the Judges had differed thereupon, leaving the other exceptions open for consideration,—the Court declined to hear the case, and ordered it to be sent back to the Eastern Districts Court to amend the record by a remittal of the whole case to this Court, instead of the removal of an exception only. The

E

1868.
March 5.

J O. Smith & Co.
vs. Stewart.

Court intimated its strong opinion that when such difference of opinion arose on the Eastern Districts Bench, the 24th and 29th sections of the Act required the removal of the whole case, instead of only a part thereof, to this Court, notwithstanding the circumstance that the difference of opinion may have arisen on only one part of the case.

[Plaintiff's Attorneys, *Reid & Nephew*.
Defendant's Attorneys, *Fairbridge & Arderne*.]

SUPREME COURT REPORTS.

1868.

PART II.

OOSTHUYSEN *vs.* OOSTHUYSEN.

Mutual Will: Transfer by Survivor contrary to Terms of, set aside.

Husband and wife by mutual will appointed the survivor sole heir; by codicil they thereafter prælegated to the children of the marriage certain two farms, subject to a life usufruct in favour of the survivor. The wife died, the children were put in possession, and annually delivered to the survivor, at his request, a certain quantity of grain in lieu of his life usufruct. The husband re-married, and thereafter transferred to the children of the second marriage one half the farms already prælegated to the children of the first marriage. HELD *(confirming* BRITS *vs.* BRITS, *and* HOFMEYR *vs.* DE WET) *that the surviving husband, having accepted benefit under the mutual codicil, was precluded from changing, after his first wife's death, the dispositions in such codicil contained. Wherefore the transfers in prejudice thereof were set aside, and the children of the first marriage declared entitled to the whole of the prælegated farms accordingly.*

This was an action to have the plaintiffs' right under a mutual will and codicils declared, and a transfer by defendant in contravention of those rights set aside.

Mr. and Mrs. Oosthuysen, sen., married in community, executed their mutual will on the 8th October, 1817, instituting the survivor sole and universal heir, on condition of " educating and supporting the children until majority, marriage, or other approved estate, when to each shall be paid, for father or mother's portion, such amount as the

1868.
March 5.
May 19.

Oosthuysen *vs.* Oosthuysen.

E 2

1868.
March 5.
May 19.

Oosthuysen vs.
Oosthuysen.

survivor shall find in conscience, and according to the position of the estate, to be due," &c.; and further, appointing each other guardians and executors *reciproce*. By a codicil, in October, 1831, they altered their will under the reservatory clause, and prælegated to the plaintiffs, Ockert Jacobus and Daniel Johannes Oosthuysen, the only children of the marriage, and then still minors, two farms in the division of Beaufort, upon condition that the survivor of the marriage should have a life usufruct in the farms. In 1836, Mr. and Mrs. Oosthuysen removed into the Colesberg division. In September, 1837, they executed a second codicil, appointing the plaintiffs executors, without, however, revoking the former appointment of the survivor; and subsequently sold the prælegated farms in the Beaufort division, with the consent of the plaintiffs, on the understanding that they would purchase two other farms in the Colesberg division and bequeath them in lieu of the Beaufort farms, and upon the same conditions; which was done by a second codicil in 1840. Thereafter, the plaintiffs came of age, and were put in possession of the farms, and effected improvements to the value of £1,800 or £1,900. In 1846, Mrs. Oosthuysen died. The survivor, as the active executor, proved the will, as plaintiffs alleged, and paid to the plaintiffs their filial portions under it, awarding the same to himself. And in lieu of his life usufruct elected to take a certain annually delivered quantity of grain. Six months afterwards, Mr. Oosthuysen was married again to the present defendant. By the second marriage he had two children, still minors, also made defendants to this suit, through the defendant as their natural guardian. In 1866, notwithstanding that he was an heir of the first wife, and had, as plaintiffs alleged, adiated the inheritance as such heir, he proceeded to make transfer of half the prælegated farms to his second wife, in trust for the two children of the second marriage. The plaintiffs accordingly brought the present action against their father, in his individual capacity, and in his capacity as father and natural guardian of the two minors of the second marriage; and against the second wife, in her capacity as trustee for the minors.

Evidence taken *de bene esse* at Colesberg having been read,

Porter, for plaintiffs (with him *Reitz*), produced the liquidation account of the first marriage, signed by D. Arnot, q.q., and awarding to the plaintiffs and the survivor their filial portions in respect of the movable property of the estate, the farms not being included in the account. He also produced receipts said to have been given by plaintiffs for such portions, and argued that this account, taken in connection with the receipts, the proving of the will, and taking out letters of administration by the survivor, and the annual rental taken in consideration of foregoing the right of life usufruct and allowing the plaintiffs to remain in possession of the farms, amounted to an adiation of inheritance under the mutual will and codicils. He then relied upon the adiation to show that old Oosthuysen had lost testamentary power of disposition over any part of these farms. The only case in England on the subject of mutual wills was that of *Dufour vs. Pereira*, 1 *Dick.* 419, cited in 1 *Williams on Executors*, ed. 1867, p. 120, in which it was decided that where a wife had been bequeathed an interest under her husband's will, plainly pointing to an intention that the property after death should go in a certain way,—she was precluded, having accepted the interest, from making any alteration in the devolution, on the ground that, by the force of an express or implied contract, the survivor was prohibited from making such alteration. In *Hofmeyr, Neethling's Curator, vs. De Wet, Neethling's Executor*, decided in the Supreme Court, 9th August, 1853, after elaborate argument, citing every authority that could be produced, it was held that a will made by a survivor in opposition to the mutual will of herself and husband should be set aside. In that case, as also in the prior case then cited, *Brits vs. Brits*, 20th February, 1842, there was clear adiation. But it is a question which may arise in the present case, and is well worthy of consideration, whether adiation is essential, although it may be usual ; or whether the contract contained in the mutual will is not completed by the death of the first-dying, and by the fact that the survivor has allowed the deceased to die without notice of an intention to change that contract. The only case that looks the other way is *Scorey vs. Scorey.* (*Menzies*, p. 231.) But that went on the ground of the legal presumptive coercion on the part of the husband over the wife by virtue of the marital authority, and will not therefore bear upon the case where the husband is the survivor. There never has been a decision, it is believed, that the husband, being the survivor, must adiate in order to be bound ; and, the point being open, it is submitted that reason and authority are in favour of holding that where the husband is bound by a mutual will, made in such a way that if there were adiation he would be bound, he is bound by the contract contained in the mutual will even without that adiation. He admitted that adiation runs through the cases decided; but still submitted that in this case of a husband being the survivor, adiation is not in strictness necessary. But even were it so, there has in this case been adiation of a two-fold character, though one would be sufficient. The husband took his share of the movables, and also his life interest, or its equivalent in

1868.
March 5.
May 19.
Oosthuysen *vs.*
Oosthuysen.

1866.
March 5.
May 19.
Oosthuysen *vs.*
Oosthuysen.

grain, in the immovables prælegated. Now, if he took only sixpence of the property of the deceased, he must not dispute the will of the deceased, but must hand over the thing prælegated. The liquidation account, although signed by Arnot, q.q., is identified and fixed upon the survivor by the fact that letters of administration were issued to him as executor under the will. As executor, it became his duty to lodge an account; and this is the only account lodged, which shows that the survivor awarded, and the receipts show that he paid, to the plaintiffs their filial portions under the will.

De Villiers for defendants.—When a survivor acts as executor, it does not follow that he adiates his inheritance under the will. His duty as executor is one thing; his adiation as heir is a totally distinct thing. There is no proof here of adiation on the part of the surviving husband, which, he submitted, was essential. The liquidation account produced is not signed by the survivor, but by an agent, whose authority is not proved; because he has never been examined before the commissioner. As to the receipts produced, they come from the custody of the plaintiffs themselves. There is no proof of receipt or payment on the face of the account itself. Then, by the will of the survivor, Oosthuysen, on the 6th April, 1867, he revokes the prælegacy in the will of 1817, *quoad* his own half share; and, supposing no adiation to be established, that was open to him. But, moreover, under any circumstances, the adiation must not be a mere general adiation, but an express adiation of the particular benefit; and here there has been no adiation of the life usufruct of the farms, the benefit in this case, for the plaintiffs have always been in possession. (*Boel ad Loen. Decis.* 137, p. 792). And the same authority further lays down that after the dissolution of the marriage the survivor may keep the benefits under the will, and at the same time revoke the other bequests in the joint will *quoad* his half. *Vide* especially *Art. 50 and Art. 51 of the Statutes of Antwerp*, cited by *Boel*, and stated to be followed by nearly all the other States of Holland. Lastly, under the joint will, it was open to the survivor to have, at all events, cut off the plaintiffs with the legitimate, if so minded.

Porter, in reply to the quotation from *Boel*, cited *Van der Keessel, Thesis* 283. He further maintained that it is out of the power of the survivor under the mutual will, in which he himself takes a child's portion, to cut off the children with the legitimate. The two forms of will most generally in use—namely, that in which the survivor and children of the marriage are made joint heirs, and that in which the survivor is made sole and universal heir, with the burthen of educating the children until they become of age, or until they obtain some other approved state, and of then paying out to them such portion as the survivor shall conscientiously find to be due to them according to the position of the estate at the time,—in point of fact amount to the same thing: that the survivor cannot cut of the children of the marriage with the legitimate only. (*Oosthuysen and Du Toit vs. Mocke*, decided in the Supreme Court on the 19th December, 1865.)

Cur. adv. vult.

Postea (May 19) the Court gave judgment for plaintiffs.

HODGES, C. J., having re-stated the facts of the case, observed upon the evidence as follows: The evidence taken under commission established most of the material allegations contained in the declaration. It appeared that the two farms Groot Fontein and Drie Fontein were purchased by the father of the plaintiffs in the lifetime of their mother, and that one of the plaintiffs occupied Groot Fontein, and the other Drie Fontein, since 1838. A short time after the death of the defendant's wife, he said to the plaintiffs: " There are your farms ; build and plant on them as much as you like ;" and it was proved that the value of the farms had been materially increased by the labour and expenditure of the plaintiffs. A certain portion of the produce of the farms was from time to time given by the plaintiffs to the defendant, and the plaintiffs still remained in occupation. The following extract from the evidence given by one of the plaintiffs describes the position of the parties:

" My mother afterwards died. After her death, my father told me that I should go and call my brother ; that we should go and divide the lands. We divided the lands,—the sowing lands, I mean. When we returned, my father said to us: ' My children, I am old ; you must sow, and give me the half of the corn, the half of the barley, and the half of the oatsheaves.' We did so ; we gave the half to our father every year. Subsequently, my father sent for us again, and said : ' My children, I will make another agreement with you. You must give me each 25 muids of corn ; and of the barley and oatsheaves one half the produce.' When we gave half the produce, we always first deducted the seed. After the death of my mother, my father said to us: ' Build and plant on the farms, and make them to your liking. I now give the farms up to you altogether.' We then built houses and kraals, and planted vineyards and trees. My father said : ' After my death, it is all yours.' We built houses and made gardens on both Groot Fontein and Drie Fontein. On the latter the gardens are not so extensive."

The plaintiffs also proved that upon the death of their

1868.
March 5.
May 19.

Oosthuysen *vs.*
Oosthuysen.

mother a liquidation account of the estate of their late mother was prepared, and that the same was filed with the Master on the 11th March, 1847. In the distribution account, one half of the amount was awarded to the father, as surviving spouse, and also one third of the residue as a child's portion; and receipts given to the father by the plaintiffs, acknowledging the receipt from him of the amount of the remaining two thirds of their mother's estate, are also in evidence. There was no proof offered that the defendant had at any time expressed any intention of repudiating the joint will until he made the transfers already referred to in favour of his children by the second marriage. The question the Court, upon these facts, has to decide is, whether the plaintiffs are entitled to the relief which they claim in this action? I am of opinion that they are. No doubt can be entertained that the general rule of law is that a joint will made by husband and wife, although made on one sheet of paper, is to be considered as two separate wills, which each is at liberty to revoke with respect to his or her share of the joint estate. But this general rule is subject to limitations. For instance, if the joint spouses have benefited each other, and have jointly and by common consent directed how the joint estate shall go after the death of the survivor, such survivor cannot, after the adiation of the estate and the enjoyment of the benefit, make another testament of his or her share of the joint estate, contrary to the will of the first-dying. *Van Leeuwen* (*Censura Forensis*, 3, 11, 7) says:
"If two spouses in a joint will reciprocally institute each other heir, under the condition that all the goods remaining at the death of the survivor shall be left to A and B, the survivor, if he have adiated the estate of the first-dying, cannot afterwards dispose even of his own share in a different manner contrary to the mutual will, their estate having, as it were, become consolidated, in which case, only, the free revocation of testaments is prevented; because the one has with the consent of the other made a will of the goods of both and part of them, and that disposition, which otherwise would be revocable on the part of the testator, passes into a contract on the part of the one consenting to it, and becomes irrevocable. This limitation against revocation must be confined to the case where the one, in disposing of the goods of the other by his consent, or both disposing reciprocally of the joint estate by consolidation, substitution, fideicommissum, or any other mode, institutes the other heir, or leaves him the usufruct or any other benefit, in which case it is the common opinion of the doctors that the other having adiated the inheritance or enjoyed the benefit of what was left, cannot, even for his share, alter the disposition, because

it is considered as only one disposition made of the single joint patrimony consolidated by mutual mixture." I may add that all the authorities bearing on this point, here treated on by *Van Leeuwen*, were cited in the elaborate judgment delivered on this point on the 9th August, 1853, in *Hofmeyr vs. De Wet, Executor of Neethling*; and as this case appears to fall within the principle there established, I am of opinion that our judgment ought to be for the plaintiffs, with costs.

1868.
March 5.
May 19.

Oosthuysen *vs.*
Oosthuysen.

BELL, J.—The question which has arisen in this case was very fully considered by the Court in the year 1853, in the case of *Neethling vs. Neethling*. In that case, the rules of law in regard to cases of the present nature were fully gone into by the Court, and the arguments for the defendants in favour of the revocability of the mutual will by the survivor having been urged at great length, and with so much subtlety and ingenuity, by Mr. Porter, then Attorney-General, and by my ever-to-be-lamented brother, Judge Watermeyer, I was induced to examine all the commentators very carefully before delivering my judgment; and after hearing the argument for the parties in the present case, I have not seen occasion to alter the opinion which I then delivered. The will in the case of *Neethling vs. Neethling* disposed of the *universitas* of the estate of the two spouses—and the chief argument of the defendants was rested upon that fact; they conceded that if the bequest had been confined *ad rem singularem*, it would have been irrevocable by the survivor, and that it was with reference to that case only that the passage in *Grotius*, 2, 15, 9, was applicable; but that when the will dealt with the *universitas* of the estate of the spouses, the will was revocable by the survivor, and for this *Leonius* was referred to as authority. The argument did not prevail, and the Court by its judgment in Neethling's case affirmed that a mutual will of the nature of the will in that case was not revocable by the survivor, even where it dealt with the *universitas* of the two spouses. As the will in Neethling's case was not confined *ad rem singularem*, it may be said that although it suited the case of the defendants to admit that a will so confined would be irrevocable, that admission ought not to bind the defendants in the present case, where the bequest in question is confined *ad rem singularem*. That is just. But, unfortunately, the defendants in Neethling's case showed that their admission was neither voluntary nor gratuitous, for they accounted for it by referring to the case of *Brits vs. Brits*, which was decided by this Court in February, 1842, and has been referred to by the plaintiffs in support of their argument for the irrevocability of the testament. I have sent for the record in the case of *Brits vs. Brits*, and I

1868.
March 5.
May 19.

Oosthuysen *vs.*
Oosthuysen.

find that the will in that case is almost identical with the will in the present case, so much so as almost to suggest either that the wills in both cases were made after a common form, or that they had both been prepared by one and the same notary. In the case of Brits, as in this case, the spouses executed a joint will, whereby they made the survivor sole and universal heir or heiress of all the property of the first-dying, movable or immovable, to be enjoyed as sole and own property, with the qualification, in either case, that the survivor should educate and support the children of the marriage until majority, marriage, or other approved state, and then pay to them such amount of money as *legitim* as the survivor should conscientiously, and according to the state of the affairs, find to be due. The testator also in both cases appointed reciprocally the survivor to be executor or executrix of the predecessor and administrator of their estate, and in both cases the will contains the usual reservatory clause. So far, the will in either case dealt alone with the *universitas* of the estate of both spouses, and was, as I before mentioned, nearly identical in terms. But in Brits's case the will provided for the case of the survivor re-marrying, by a clause which directed that in such event the survivor, before consummation of his second marriage, should have the whole estate valued, and in regard to one half of the whole estate, the predecessor nominated the children of the marriage his or her heir in such half or equal portions. But special provision was made that in such a case the survivor should nevertheless enjoy possession of the property until the time fixed for paying the *legitim* in case of no re-marriage. The estate was meanwhile, however, to be converted into money; but from the sale was to be excepted the farm Doorn Kraal, which the survivor might take possession of for a sum of 11,000 rixdollars, under an obligation to make it devolve on the son of the marriage, Hans Jacob Brits, or on his children, if he should predecease the surviving spouse. The wife died first, and the husband after a term re-married, and made a will, whereby he revoked the joint will of himself and his first wife so far as Doorn Kraal, and directed the farm to be sold and the proceeds applied to the purposes of his sole will. The son of his first marriage had died, leaving a son, who after the death of his grandfather, brought an action against the executors appointed by the grandfather's sole will, praying that they might be decreed to give him possession of the farm Doorn Kraal on his paying the 11,000 rixdollars, and that the will of his grandfather, so far as it revoked the bequest of the farm, might be set aside as null. The Court gave judgment in terms of the prayer of the declaration, thereby affirming that a joint will dealing *re singulari* was not revocable by the survivor, as subsequently in Neethling's case it affirmed that a joint will was not revocable by the survivor where it dealt *universitate*. In the present case, the will having dealt *universitate*, only a codicil was executed by the spouses, in these terms :

1868.
March 5.
May 19.

Oosthuysen *vs.*
Oosthuysen.

" We, J. J. Oosthuysen and A. M. Strydom, do hereby declare, by virtue of the power given to us in the aforesaid will, and the reservatory clause of the same, to bequeath and prælegate to our sons, O. J. and D J. Oosthuysen, together with all such children as may be procreated in our present marriage, the quitrent farms, &c., with this provision, that the said quitrent farms shall not, until after our death, be taken by our said children, then, by them, or their lawful descendants, for ever to be possessed as their own and lawful property, without the interference of any person."

Subsequently the two farms mentioned in this codicil were sold by the testators, and two farms, called Groot Fontein and Drie Fontein, were purchased in their stead—and, as the plaintiffs swear, this sale and purchase were not made without their previous consent first asked and obtained. A codicil executed 14th December, 1840, was in these terms :

" We, the undersigned testator and testatrix, do hereby declare that these two quitrent farms, named Groot Fontein and Drie Fontein, we bequeath to our sons, O. J. and D. J. Oosthuysen,"—instead of those I have mentioned as having been sold.

The testatrix died in July, 1846. Unfortunately for the sons, the father married a second wife in the year 1864, and either through the influence of this wife, or for her sake, made a sale of one half of the two farms, and passed transfer of them to her, in trust for the children of the second marriage.

The object of this action is to have it declared that these transfer deeds were illegal, and to have them set aside as void, the father having no more than a life usufruct of the farm. The facts of the present case differ in some trifling respects from those in *Brits vs. Brits*. But substantially the two cases, so far as principles of law are concerned, are the same ; and Brits's case is so directly in point, as to show that the question raised between the parties in the present case has long since been *res judicata* in favour of the plaintiff. The language of the will precludes the possibility of saying that the instrument can be read as two wills, one by each of the spouses, dealing separately with their respective shares of the estate. They dispose reciprocally of the joint estate, and make one disposition of the single joint patrimony consolidated by mutual mixture, in the words of *Van Leeuwen*; they dispose by mutual consent of the joint estate, in the words of *Van der Keessel;* and they acted together,

1868.
March 5.
May 19.
———
Oosthuysen vs.
Oosthuysen.

testating the one spouse upon the goods of the other, each giving to the other the power of so doing, in the words of *Voet*; and according to these authorities, the will in such circumstances was irrevocable by the survivor. So long as the two spouses continued in life, it was in the power of both to have revoked this will entirely, or it was in the power of either to have revoked it so far as it affected his or her share of the joint estate. But so soon as death had closed the door against the possibility of revocation by one of the testators, it closed the door against the power of revocation by the surviving testator. And for an obvious reason. But for this mutual will, the predeceasing testatrix might have disposed of her half of the farms very differently from giving her half of them to the surviving testator for his life enjoyment, and her half of the rest of the estate to him in fee ; and the inducement for her to give in this way may have been the fact that the surviving testator had given his share in the same way that she had disposed of her half. The present case seems to me to come exactly within the category stated in *Boel on Loenius, Dec.* 137, *p.* 784, where he says : " Si ita duo simul testentur, ut quisque non de suis sed alter de alterius bonis vice quasi mutuâ aut uterque de suis simul et conjugis bonis, ex mutuo consensu supremæ faciat voluntatis testationem."—In which case the commentator says, revocation by the survivor is not permitted, neither is it permissible in the case " cum conjuges de utriusque bonis indistincte in unis tabulis testantes inter liberos aut etiam inter extraneos declarant dispositionem fore prioris decendentis in solidum." (*Loen., p.* 780.) I am, therefore,—without going so fully into the law of the subject as was done by me almost too elaborately in the case of Neethling, to which I have already referred,—of opinion that the judgment of the Court ought to be for the plaintiffs, and with costs. I have not gone into the question of adiation, because the evidence upon this subject is not altogether satisfactory. There is enough, however, to confirm, and it was not necessary to support the conclusion at which I have arrived.

CONNOR, J.—It was contended in this case, on behalf of the defendants, that adiation of the inheritance by the surviving spouse was necessary to his being bound by the provisions of a mutual will which he had concurred with his deceased wife in making, so far as those provisions affected his half of the common estate ; and it was further contended that here there was no such adiation. Upon this latter point, it was urged that the defendants' main witness to disprove adiation,—viz., the surviving spouse, and the father at once of the plaintiffs and the minor defendants,—was shut out from being a witness through an irregularity committed by the commissioner for taking the evidence; as he postponed, at the instance of the plaintiffs, the examination, for the arrival, which never happened, of an absent witness for the plaintiffs, and because this main witness for the defendants died in the following month, and has consequently never been examined; and that, therefore, all the evidence in the case should be disregarded. This result, however, the defendants cannot be entitled to, as they had a remedy in their hands by applying to this Court; and not having availed themselves of it, it would be out of the question to exclude now, absolutely and for ever, all evidence on the part of the plaintiffs.

1868.
March 5.
May 19.

Oosthuysen vs.
Oosthuysen

As, however, there was no doubt, to some extent, a failure in the object of the commission, as far as that was to take the evidence in the case generally, I proceed to consider the first of the above propositions, viz., whether there was here any occasion for adiation of the inheritance, to render the first-dying spouse's part of the mutual will binding on the survivor, the plaintiff's father, in reference to the interest thereby devised in the two farms in question to the plaintiffs. To consider this question, first, upon principle—What is or was adiation? The word purports to be a translation of the Latin *aditio*, composed from the two words *ad ire*. The person or persons instituted by a will as heir or heirs of the testator adiated the inheritance to which he was so instituted by "going to" it by expressly or impliedly accepting this institution. That some person or persons should be instituted as heir was, in the old law, deemed requisite to the validity of a will, as distinct from a codicil, and there were matters which a will proper could alone effect, and which, therefore, a will which did not institute an heir failed to accomplish, unless it contained a clause providing that if it could not operate as a will, it should operate as a codicil. Now, when it is remembered that will-making is to be favoured, we cannot but feel certain that so technical a rule, with so technical an exception as that which I have just described, would be open to be assailed and undermined, and, as the occasion for wills increased with the advance of society, to be finally swept away. Why should the rule ever have existed? Simply, I apprehend, because it was thought requisite for the security of the creditors of the deceased that there should be a person designated by the will to whom they should look for the payment of their debts, who should be a representative of the testator. If the instituted heir "took to," or "went to," or *adiated* the inheritance, he was liable personally for the testator's debts. He had, as a general rule, the administration of the testator's property, and if by his administration he could not or did not raise enough out of it to pay the testator's

1868.
March 5.
May 19.

Oosthuysen *vs.*
Oosthuysen.

debts, he was liable personally for the balance ; if he made more out of the estate than was sufficient to pay debts, and legacies, and the like, he was entitled to keep the balance. The office resembled in many respects that of executor of a will under English Law, until a comparatively recent period, as far as relates to personal property, except that if the executor were careful as to his acts, and also as to his pleading, if sued by a creditor, he might escape having to pay any of the debts of the deceased personally. So much has this resemblance struck others, that in the English folio translation of *Domat*, the word *executor* is, as far as my memory serves me, generally used to represent the *hæres* of the Roman Law. The instituted heir had a certain period given him for deliberation as to whether he would " take to " the inheritance or not, for him to be able to ascertain whether the liabilities he would incur would equal or fall short of the benefits he would derive. If an only heir, or all of them, if more than one, would not adiate, the will became void. (*Grotius*, 2, 24, 19.) We can hardly, I think, conceive any more vexatious snare for an ignorant testator than a technical system of that kind is,—a system which I think Courts of Justice ought to be glad to avail themselves of authority for declaring it to be obsolete or superseded. And it appears to me that the law of this Colony has, in fact, interposed. Under it the administration of the estate of a deceased person is (Ordinance No. 104) given to an executor, testamentary or dative, instead of to the heir. The heir, *qua* heir, cannot now adopt his own mode of administering the estate. The executor by law administers, and lessens the estate by his commission ; and he can, under the Insolvent Ordinance, subject the estate to the provisions of the Insolvent Law. There seems to be, therefore, hardly any opportunity for the heir to adiate. If he be not executor, the adiation is the province of the executor ; if the heir be executor, his acts are to be referred to that capacity, and not to that of heir. There seems then, to me to be much ground for contending that this Court is warranted in holding that a testamentary heir is now in this Colony to be regarded rather as a residuary legatee than as an heir in the Roman Law sense ; and that adiation, if it remain to any extent, remains only in name ; that it has, to all substantial effects and purposes, been merged in executorship, and become a nullity, on the principle of the maxim, *cessante ratione legis cessat et ipsa lex* ; and the case is the stronger here, as the reason of the law has ceased through the express provision of another and later law ; and because the old law was one which it was desirable should cease.

I have said that it appears contrary to principle to

hold that the heir, as such, incurs now any personal liability, or is more than a residuary legatee ; and this leads to the further consideration that, if so, the inheritance can now never be *damnosa* ; if there be no balance above debts and legacies and costs of administration, the heir gains nothing, but in no case could he lose anything ; and, therefore, his adopting the inheritance would always be presumed where the presumption were possible, and the more so if such adoption were essential to the rights of third parties.

1868.
March 5.
May 19.

Oosthuysen *vs.*
Oosthuysen.

But though I cannot but regard these considerations as of weight, I should be unwilling, at least if they were not essential to the determination of this case, to rest my judgment upon them ; and I therefore proceed to consider whether, according to Roman-Dutch Law, unaffected by the law of this Colony, adiation of the inheritance was essential to the binding force of a mutual will of spouses, such as that before the Court in this case. It is, I think, to be seen from *Van der Linden's* (our latest Dutch jurist) mode of expressing himself, that something like that which has been done in this Colony, the substitution of the office of executor for that of heir, was then gaining ground in Holland. He goes into what, from the concise nature of his work, may be called a detail in reference to executorship (*pp.* 147, 8). Then, with reference to the remedies of legatees, in which term he evidently includes *fidei-commissaries* he expressly (*p.* 146) says that the personal action lies not only against the heir, but against the executor. Now we know as a general rule, that of the three actions for legatees and *fidei-commissaries*, under the Code (6, 43, 1), the personal action only lay against the heir if he adiated (*Huber, Prælect* 2, 20, 34); so that there seems to be much ground for supposing that *Van der Linden* regards an acting executor in the position, for this purpose, of an heir who had adiated, at least with reference to the nature of the action which the legatee, &c., might institute against him.

Grotius (2, 4, 6) having stated that a will was invalid if no heir were instituted, in the note (by, I apprehend, *Groenewegen*) there is a reference thus : " But see *Groenewegen De Legibus Abrogatis ad Inst.* 2, 20, 34 " and upon looking at this, we find that *Groenewegen* says that several authors whom he names, including *Vinnius* and *Christinœus* (*Decis.* 247, 7), deny that the institution of an heir was then necessary to a testament, both the name and law of testaments and codicils being confounded by their practice ; and he refers to his own observations (*Inst* 17, 7) in favour of the opinion that a will without an instituted heir may revoke another will—an opinion which, he says, " without doubt obtains, if credit is to be given to those who, the name and law of testaments and codicils being confounded in practice (*per mores*), deny that

1868.
{ March 5.
May 19.

Oosthuysen *vs.*
Oosthuysen.

the institution of an heir is now necessary to the essence of a testament." He refers, also, to his observations on *Inst.* 2, 25, s. ult., to the same effect, stating it there to be the opinions of the authors on practice; and adds, "hence, also, there is no impediment by our customs to an inheritance being given and adeemed directly by codicils, and also a disinheriting provided for."

The most recent Roman Law, too, itself, in the *Novels*, interposed against the severity of the old Roman Law in reference to non-adiation destroying the will, by giving legatees and *fidei-commissaries* an action against the heir to compel his adiating for their benefit, without injury to himself (*Voet*, 28, 3, 14; *Van Leeuwen*, *Cens. For.* 1, 3, 10, 15); and the older Roman-Dutch jurists say that the like benefit existed among them, by means of the codicillary clause usually inserted in wills; but *Van der Linden*, as a later writer, goes further, and expresses himself on the point in this way (*p.* 156), that when a will becomes void by the heirs being unable or unwilling to adiate, the legacies must be paid, "especially when the will contains the codicillary clause;" clearly not confining the preservation of the legacies in the will on non-adiation to cases in which there is the codicillary clause, as would rather seem to have been intended by *Voet* and *Van Leeuwen* (*ubi supra*), and *Sande Decis.* 4, 4, 10.

There is therefore, I think, considerable ground for coming to the conclusion, both on the principles of Roman-Dutch Law in its latest day, and still more on the existing law here in reference to executors, that unless we are bound by some decision in the Court that I am not aware of, we ought to include among the *leges abrogatæ*, the whole system of institution or non-institution of heirs, or of adiation or non-adiation of inheritance, as affecting the validity of wills in the whole or in part. 1 may add that it is not to me at all clear that there is not a sufficient codicillary clause in the mutual will in this case to confer upon it any security to be obtained from that clause. There is also the circumstance that the devise of the farms in question is itself by a codicil.

It is not contended here that the will of the wife, the first-dying spouse, or rather, her part of the mutual will, is not, and has not always been since her death, perfectly valid and effectual; but the non-adiation must have been in respect of *her* inheritance; and if the old law on that subject applied, the wife's will must by the non-adiation have been detroyed except perhaps as to the legacy of the farms in question. Destroyed, *inter alia*, as to the appointment of the survivor as executor, would it lie then in the survivor's mouth, supposing he was confirmed as executor, to say that by his non-adiation the will of which he had had himself confirmed as executor was destroyed? I assume here that the survivor did obtain letters of administration, though, as I shall hereafter observe, that fact does not seem to be in issue in the case.

But though the argument was directed mainly to strict adiation of the inheritance, it was no doubt intended to include the case of the surviving spouse's accepting or not benefits under the will of the first-dying. Putting aside, then, the question of adiation of the inheritance, I proceed to consider this: Was the surviving spouse bound by the mutual will in reference to its bequest of the two farms in question to the plaintiffs, so that the survivor, their father, could not by deed or further will alter that disposition, as he, in fact, endeavoured to do? In considering this question as to mutual wills generally,—viz., the power of the survivor to make different dispositions from those contained in the mutual will,—there are, I think, two main points to be settled: Has the first-dying spouse purported to dispose of property of the other; and (2) if so, is the other bound thereby? On the first question it appears to have been decided in this Court in a case of *Brits vs. Brits*, in 1842, cited in *Hofmeyr vs. De Wet*, decided in 1853, that when the spouses by a mutual will had bequeathed a particular piece of property of the joint estate to a particular person, the surviving spouse could not change this disposition after the death of the other. In other words, as I understand it, in a case like that (and this case is so), each spouse is construed to have disposed of the other's interest in the particular piece of property. And this is, I think, the right conclusion, viz., that in such a case each spouse has directed by his or her part of the will, that the legatee should have the whole of the particular piece of property bequeathed. Well, then, when this is so, what is it that takes place upon the death of the first-dying spouse, with such a mutual will remaining unaltered? His or her part of the mutual will then becomes an effectual testamentary instrument disposing of the whole of the particular piece of property—disposing of one-half of it as the testator's own, disposing of the other half of it, viz., that of the survivor, by the survivor's assent. We are bound to assume the assent from the nature of the common act. All the jurists tell you upon the authority of the Roman Law, that one person may dispose of another's property.(*Christinæus, Decis.* 6, 58; *Van Leeuwen, Cens. For.* 1, 3, 11, 7.) How, then, does the other testator, the survivor, become bound by that disposition? *Christinæus* (*Decis.* 6, 58) says the survivor is bound if, after the death of the other, he or she expressly or tacitly approve of the will. *Grotius* says (2, 15, 9) that if the survivor accepts benefits under the will of the first-dying,

F

he or she cannot alter the dispositions of the will of the first-dying. *Van der Keessel* (*Th.* 283) would appear to make the will of the first-dying prevail, generally upon the common consent appearing, save, perhaps, so far as it allowed the property to go to the survivor's heirs.

I cannot but think, myself, that some confusion has arisen on the subject of mutual wills from its not being sufficiently borne in mind that each part of the mutual will is a distinct will (*Van Leeuwen, Cens. For.* 1, 3, 2, 15, 16), and that therefore, *prima facie*, the like rules must apply to each part of a mutual will, in like manner as if it were a single separate will. And I apprehend that the whole idea of the mutual will operating as a contract on the part of the spouses, and thus affecting the survivor's power of revoking his part of a mutual will, only leads to confusion and contradictions. *Huber* (*Prælect.* 28, 3, 4) says that to hold that a solemn agreement by way of contract would enter into a will, and an action *ex contractu* arise therefrom, and the law of last wills and of acts *inter vivos* be confounded in that way, seems unheard of and intolerable; that the force of such a contract is only that of an asseveration, which, though sworn to, would give no right of action; that there is no inheritance or testament of one living. (*Dig.* 18, 4, 1.) He says also (*Prælect.* 2, 17, 3) that the rule of law that a man's will is ambulatory to the very end of his life (*Dig.* 34, 4, 4) must prevail; and that two testators are in no wise mutually bound by the mere fact of making a will by mutual consent, because that a contract cannot consist with the act of devising, *i.e.*, a person making his or her will is not to be understood to be undertaking a contract.

The true way of viewing the question is, I apprehend, without regarding questions of contract or irrevocability of the survivor's will, to inquire what the part of the mutual will which has come into operation by the death of the first-dying spouse purports to devise, and how far it is effectual for that purpose. If the first-dying has disposed of part of the property of the survivor, and the survivor, after the other's death, has accepted a benefit under the other's part of the mutual will come into operation on that other's death, then, by the ordinary testamentary principle of election, he or she is estopped from saying that his or her share of the property did not pass as the other's will directs; and, so far, that property has ceased to be the survivor's property; and though he can revoke his part of the mutual will, yet he cannot alter the disposition by the other's will of the property so affected by it, because, as I have said, it has ceased to be the survivor's property.

This mode of regarding the question, viz., that, except for

the purpose of ascertaining what property purports to be affected by it, each part of the mutual will is to be considered as if it were a single and separate will, appears to me to be not only the most simple and satisfactory, and that which is most in accordance with the law of wills, but that it also reconciles the essential parts of all the authorities of weight, avoids their inconsistencies, and shows that points which appear to be in conflict among them are, in truth, not essential in the question. I say *inconsistencies*, for surely it is one to hold that the mutual will is a contract which has become sealed and enforceable by the death of the spouse first dying, and yet also to hold that it depends on a voluntary act of the survivor, after the other's death, whether or not he or she will be bound by this contract, which according to the hypothesis, was on the first death a complete contract; that the survivor can escape from the contract if he do not adiate the inheritance or accept the benefits under the will of the first-dying. Surely then, again, it would be an anomaly in the law of wills, that the survivor should live, it may be for many years, bound by a last will and testament of his own, but one which is irrevocable by him. But there is no such anomaly in a person's having by an act *inter vivos* left himself without any devisable interest in a property which previously was his, and which he could then have disposed of as he pleased.

It is clear from the authorities in *Boel's Loenius' Decisions* (*cas.* 137) that other jurists of great name, as well as *Huber*, have maintained that the survivor's part of a mutual will cannot be irrevocable during his life. It will be observed that there *Decker* is shown to have thought that when the eminent jurists whom he refers to—*Antonius Faber, Peckius, Everard, Sande,* &c.—say that the survivor's part of the will is not irrevocable, they say so without reference to two instances of mutual wills which he states; but the first of these comes within the principle of the property of the survivor passing under the will of the first-dying; and the second is a case in which by the mutual will the testators expressly purport to bind the survivor from revoking; and this evidently introduces quite a distinct question, viz., whether a testator can by his will bind himself against revocation, whether precautions for his own security against being entrapped into a revocation the will may specify and render necessary.

Van Leeuwen, in the *Censura Forensis* (1, 3, 11, 7), approves highly of *Decker's* mode of stating the obligation that the surviving spouse is under of not departing from the mutual will, as if that obligation of itself made the survivor's part of the mutual will irrevocable; and *Van Leeuwen* says that that principle was followed in their practice, and refers for this, *inter alia*, to *Grotius* (9, 15, 2), who, as we have seen, introduces the elements of the survivor's accepting the benefits of the will of the first-dying in order to his being first bound; and bound against what? Why, against disposing differently from the provisions of the will of the deceased. *Van Leeuwen* also alludes, almost angrily, to those who, though eminent jurists, deny that the will of the survivor ever becomes irrevocable by him; and insists that this may be so, but only in one case, viz., that in which the survivor is instituted as heir of the other, and then adiates or accepts the benefits, thus introducing the inconsistency which I have already referred to, of a contract being adopted or rejected at the choice of one contractor after becoming complete; but he proceeds to say that it must be clear that the spouses or the first-dying bequeathed of the other's property, and gave the benefits on that condition. Thus again reconciling the case to the principle which he had before in the same section stated, viz., that it was clear from the *Digest* (20, 6, 11) and the jurists, that one person can devise of another's property, and bequeath by his consent, and to his prejudice. And this principle, as I have said, satisfies all the requirements of the case, without resorting to the anomaly of the will of a living person being irrevocable by him during his life. When by the mutual will the survivor is instituted heir of the first-dying, and this one's part of the mutual will is so expressed as to pass effectually part of the property of the survivor, a charge in the nature of a *fidei commissum* is imposed on the survivor in reference to his own property; and the case must be regulated according to the usual rules relating to such testamentary dispositions.

These principles appear to me to be quite consistent with what one of our latest Roman-Dutch Law authorities says— I allude to *Van der Keessel* (*Th.* 283),—I cite from the Latin edition, 1800: " The surviving spouse, who, with the first-dying, devised of the common goods, and was made heir to him [or her], cannot otherwise dispose of that part of the common property which ought to return to the substitutes of the first-dying, but of that part which is to come to his or her own heir, he may rightly make his will" (referring, *inter alia*, to *Boel ad Loen. Decis* 137) " unless it have happened (*forte*) that both spouses have disposed, by common consent, of the common patrimony, or a part of it;" and he refers for this last proposition to *Voet* (28. 3, 11), who says there: "Nor finally, does it prevent a change of testament by another later one, that one has made his testament not alone, but together with another in the same paper (*tabula*), whether each has disposed separately of his own substance, or both

together dispose of the common mass of the patrimony
dealt with in common (*communicati*). Otherwise, if two so
devise together that they devise by way of last will, not of
their own, but one of the goods of the other, as if by mutual
interchange (*vice quasi mutua*), or each of his own and his
spouse's goods together by mutual consent, according to
what is explained (23, 4, 63). And to this, also is to be
reduced the case of two spouses, who devising by one paper
together, leave legacies to certain persons to be paid from the
common mass of the patrimony, without distinction, whether
they be of the kindred of the husband or wife, or neither,
and then each separately disposes of their own part which
each has in the common mass; when in these things so
disposed of in common, in opposition to those separately left,
each cannot but appear to have devised the goods of the
other by his or her consent; that hence these very legacies
(*hæc ipsa legata*) seem to be so confirmed by the death of one
spouse that they cannot be recalled by the will of the survivor
in whole or in part (*Respons. Juris. Holl.*, 2, 275). It is
plainly beyond doubt that the survivor cannot revoke the
testament of the deceased spouse made in the same paper."

I have cited this passage from *Voet*, not only as explanatory
of *Van der Keessel's Thesis* (283), but as also bearing upon
the construction of the codicil of the mutual will in question
in this case. *Van der Keessel's Thesis* seems to me to lay
this down, that when the surviving spouse is effectually
burdened with a *fidei-commissum*, either as to the other's
half of the common property, or the survivor's own, or any
part of either, he cannot alter this disposition, but he can
make a new will as to anything not the subject of such a *fidei-
commissum* or the like. It will be observed that *Van der
Keessel* makes use of the expression " otherwise dispose of
the property in question ;" not that the survivor's part of the
mutual will is irrevocable ; nor, I may add, does he refer to
adiation, nor indeed to acceptance of benefits ; but this latter
may probably be implied as having been expressly mentioned
by *Grotius* in the passage to which the *Thesis* applies.
Though there are, as it appears to me, as I have already
stated, some passages in *Van Leeuwen's Cens. For.* (1, 3, 11,
7), which tend to introduce confusion in the discussion of
questions relating to mutual wills, yet his language in his
Roman-Dutch Law (3, 3, 8) is, as far as it goes, quite consistent with what appears to me to be the correct expression
of the legal proposition involved in the question of irrevocability of the survivor's will. He says there: " When two
married persons have reciprocally benefited each other, and
thereby directed how the goods of the common estate should
devolve after the death of the survivor of them, which sur-

<small>1868.
March 5,
May 19.

Oosthuysen *vs.*
Oosthuysen.</small>

1868.
March 5.
May 19.

Oosthuysen vs.
Oosthuysen.

vivor having enjoyed the benefit, *cannot dispose of his or her share by last will;*" and this, he says, was decided in two cases, one in the High Court at Mechlin, and the other by the Court of Holland. This was, in effect, also the decision, on much deliberation, of this Court in 1853, in the case of *Hofmeyr v. De Wet.* How far this latter decision was intended to overrule certain propositions to be found in *Van Leeuwen's Cens. For.* (1, 3, 11, 7), and *Voet* (23, 4, 63), as to the construction to be put upon the mere fact of two spouses dealing in common with the common property, and the position to be found in other jurists, that the mere direction that property shall go to the survivor's heirs, is not binding on him or her (*Boel's Leonius' Decis.* 137), may perhaps be doubtful, but it is not here material.

It appears to me, therefore, that the questions to be decided in reference to a mutual will, under the like circumstances as exist in the case before the Court, are these: Did the first-dying spouse's part of the mutual will purport to dispose of the property in question? If so, did the surviving spouse become bound on or after the death of the first-dying by that disposition, as far as it related to his (the survivor's) share in the property in question? The material parts of the mutual will in this case are as follows:

"Now proceeding to the election of heirs, the testators declared to nominate and appoint each other reciprocally; that is, the first dying, the survivor to be sole and universal heir or heiress, and such of all the property of the first-dying, movable and immovable, actions and credits, inheritances and successions, nothing excepted, to be had and enjoyed by the survivor of them for ever, as sole and own property, without gainsay of any one, in such manner, however, that the survivor shall be obliged to educate and support the child or children already and to be procreated in their marriage, until their majority, marriage, or other approved states; when to each of them shall be paid, for father's or mother's portion, such amount of money as the survivor shall find, in conscience and according to the state of affairs, to be due; but, in case the survivor shall enter into a second marriage, such survivor shall be bound, before the solemnization thereof, to nominate and appoint two good and impartial men as superintending guardians in respect of the minors' portions (*Kinderbewys*), without, however, being bound to pay the portions of such minors earlier than before stated, but the same shall remain in the custody of the survivor—it being the express will and desire that the survivor should remain in the full and undisturbed possession of the estate in order the better to educate and support the minors for the usufruct of their inheritances until the period aforesaid."

The testators then appoint each other reciprocally to be the executor or executrix of "this their will," as also administrators of their estate, and also guardians of their minor heirs. They also " reserve to themselves power to alter at all times, this their last will (except the appointment of heirs), and to add thereto, or revoke, such matter as they may in time be minded, either by separate act or at the foot hereof, desiring that all such alterations in or additions to this will, signed by them, shall be considered as herein word for word inserted." They also declare their desire that the will "may have effect either as last will or donation *causa mortis*, or as may be found best to consist in law, notwithstanding the omission of any forms which they (the testators) consider as inserted therein, with a request that the benefits of the law may be extended thereto."

1864, March 5; May 19.

Oosthuysen. *vs.* Oosthuysen

This last clause is that which I have referred to as possibly a sufficient codicillary clause to prevent any injury from non-institution of an heir, or, I may add, from non-adiation by the heir. (*Voet* 28, 3, 14; *Van Leeuwen, Cens. For.* 1, 3, 10, 15; and 1, 3, 3, 10; *Sande Decis. Fris.* 4, 4, 10.) It was not argued here that the revocation clause applied to any but a joint revocation. It appears to me to be clear that in this will, which related only to the inheritance generally, each spouse must be considered to have been devising only his or her own half. Mr. Porter, the plaintiffs' counsel, stated it to have been decided in this Court that in such a will the surviving spouse is entitled absolutely to a child's portion. And from instances which have come before me, I think it not unlikely that that is the construction commonly adopted in practice; but it is not, I think, easy to understand the principle upon which that decision proceeded if the words corresponded with those used here. It would, I apprehend, be more easy to come to that conclusion if the will were framed as that in *Hofmeyr v. De Wet*, in the Supreme Court, in 1853, in which the surviving spouse and the children were instituted as heirs together. Then there is the case of *De Smidt v. Burton* (*Menzies' Reports*, 222), in which the mutual will was, I think I may say, allowing for difference in translation, in the very words of this will; and there the Court held (227) that under those words the widow, the surviving spouse, was entitled beneficially to the interest of the property during the only child's minority, but there is not the slightest intimation that she was entitled absolutely to a child's share, which in that case would have amounted to half, there being but one child. The Court is stated (227) to have held that by the will "the testator had, as he lawfully might do, given the usufruct of the interest, and other profits aforesaid, to his surviving widow during his son's minority; and that he had done this by virtue of the clause in his will by which he had appointed his surviving widow sole and universal heiress of all his movable and immovable property, actions, credits, inheritances, and bequests, nothing in this world excepted to be possessed by the survivor as his or her free and unencumbered property, without any gainsay of anyone; upon condition, however, that the survivor should be bound to bring up, maintain, and support such child or children as might be procreated within the marriage, in an honest, Christian manner, until their majority, &c.; when to each of them, for and in lieu of their paternal (or maternal) inheritance or share, should be paid out such amount of ready money as the survivor would deem in conscience to be sufficient in respect of the amount of the estate," with a provision similar to that in this case, with reference to the survivor's marrying again. The point is only of importance here with reference to the liquidation account, if that were properly in evidence in this case.

The testators, in this case now before the Court, subsequently made the first codicil to their will: it is dated October 12, 1831, and is thus translated:

"We, Jacobus Johannes Oosthuysen and Anna Magdalena Strydom, do hereby declare, by the power and authority given to us in the reservatory clause in the said will, bequeath, and prelegate to our sons, Ockert Jacobus Oosthuysen and Daniel Johannes Oosthuysen, together with all such children as may be procreated in our present marraige, the quitrent farm called Vrolykheid, and half of the quitrent farm called Fondeling, near Lever Water, both situated in the field-cornetcy Traka, in the division of Beaufort, without paying anything of the same into our estate; with this provision, that the said quitrent farms shall not, until after our death, be taken by our said children, then by them or by their lawful descendants, for ever to be possessed of as their own lawful property, without the interference of any person."

The testators then, by a further joint codicil of 15th September, 1827, appointed " as executors and guardians of our property, movable and immovable, both our sons and inheritors—viz., O. J. Oosthuysen and D. J. Oosthuysen, with power of assumption and surrogation." Then, by another joint codicil of 7th October, 1838, they exclude the Master of the Court from the management of their property. And afterwards they made another joint codicil, dated 14th December, 1840, in these terms:

" We the undersigned, testator and testatrix, do hereby declare that these two quitrent farms, named Groot Fontein and Drie Fontein, situated in the division of Colesberg, we bequeath to our sons, O. J. Oosthuysen and Daniel J. Oosthuysen, instead of those situated in Zwartberg, with the same right and condition as stated in the will."

The wife, the plaintiffs' mother, died on the 30th July, 1846, and the husband, the plaintiffs' father, married again on 8th February, 1847. On the mother's death, the only two children of the first marriage, the two plaintiffs, had attained age, and consequently, unless the first part of the will entitled the survivor to a child's share in the inheritance, the father would have been entitled to nothing under the institution as heir.

The first question to be decided appears to me, as I have already intimated, to be, did the codicils relating to the farms purport to be a devise by each spouse of the other's as well as his or her own share in the farms of the two sons, the plaintiffs? And it is, in my judgment, clear that we are bound to answer that in the affirmative, upon the authority of the decision of this Court in *Brits v. Brits*, and *Hofmeyr v. De Wet*; and the case here is perhaps the stronger, as we have the circumstances of change in the form of expression referred to by *Voet* (28, 3, 11) in the passage which I have already cited. I think, too, that, independently of authority, that conclusion ought to be arrived at. I grant that where the survivor is to be held barred from contesting that what was his property has passed under the will of his predeceased spouse, such ought to be the clear construction of the mutual will,—the construction which any one of ordinary capacity would put upon the words,—or else that the construction in that way of the words used should have been irrevocably settled in law. The question on that point is, as it appears to me, this: Would any person reading those words conclude from them that each spouse intended that the sons should, after the death of the surviving spouse, have the whole of the farms between them? Because, if so, the consequence seems to me to be that each testator consents to the other bequeathing to that effect; and that each part of the mutual will gives the whole; then that the bequest becomes binding, upon either part of the mutual will becoming, by the death of that part's testator, a speaking, effectual, binding will. The first part of the mutual will, in respect of which this coming into force by death happens, conveys the property to the legatees, the survivor's part of the mutual will becomes *quoad* that property, or that interest therein, *functus officio*, the title has vested in the legatee, just as it would under a single, separate, valid will. The survivor has the benefits of survivorship, but he has also its inconveniences; and among the latter is this, that (at least if he accepts the benefits) he has allowed the will of his wife, a will then becomes irreversible, to pass away this property which was once his. I think that this conclusion is the clearer in the present case from the words used after the devise, viz., that it is to be "without paying anything of (? for) the same into our estate, with this provision, that the said quitrent farms shall not until after our death be taken by our said children, then by them or by their lawful descendants for ever to be possesed of as their own lawful property." It appears to me that, I may say, every person would understand these words as giving the whole of both testator's interest in the two farms to the plaintiffs after the surviving spouse's death, in like manner as they give the usufruct of the whole to the survivor for his life.

The second question, then, according to what I have already intimated, to be considered is : Did the wife's devise of the husband's share of the farms in question bind him? It does not appear from the statement of the case of *Brits v. Brits*, which I have referred to, that the surviving spouse was there held bound by reason of his having accepted any benefits; nor is that condition mentioned in the passage of the *Digest* cited by *Van Leeuwen* (*Cens. For*. 1, 3, 11, 7), as to one person's devising another's property with his consent. *Christinæus*, too (*Decis*. 6, 68), seems to recognize approval of the will after the death of the first-dying as sufficient to bind the survivor in such a case. It was urged here, on behalf of the plaintiffs, that the liquidation account filed with the Master as to the wife's estate, and which it was said must be taken to have been filed by the authority of the husband, as her executor, and which shows that he takes to himself a child's share, shows that by that he accepted a benefit under the wife's will. But independently of the question which I have already alluded to, as to whether the wife's will purported to give him any such benefit, I am unable to see how the liquidation account is in evidence as against the defendants here ; it does not purport to be signed by the father, nor is there any direct evidence that it had his authority. And though receipts by the plaintiffs to the father are put in for amounts which, assuming the liquidation accounts to be correct, would be for proper amounts solely on the supposition that the father took a child's share, yet it is, as I have said, difficult to find any legal evidence to connect the father with the liquidation account, however little we may doubt it in point of fact. It was stated that letters of administration were granted of the wife's will to the plaintiffs' father as executor ; but this is not averred in the declaration, and is therefore hardly admissible as a ground of decision. It is difficult, too, to understand how, without any renunciation by the plaintiffs, the father could have been alone confirmed as executor, if the codicil appointing the plaintiffs executors has been produced to the Master. And as these letters of administration were apparently not granted to the father until after his second marriage, the circumstances connected with this grant might have been material ; for I need hardly say that if the father had so soon after his wife's death suppressed all the codicils of the mutual will, this would go so far to show that subsequent acts of his were not intended by him to have been in pursuance of codicils which he had so treated. On the other hand, if these codicils were produced with the will, that might tend to an opposite conclusion. I mention this as showing that the fact of the letters of administration not being relied on in the declaration, makes it dangerous to draw any conclusion from them in the plaintiffs' favour. There is, however, evidence in the case to show that the father, after the wife's death, approved of her will; that he told the sons the farms would be theirs, and encouraged them to build and to plant; and there is strong evidence to show that when, upon the plaintiffs hearing that their father had transferred half of the farms to his children by his second marriage, they, in the presence of witnesses who have been examined, expostulated with him, and urged upon him his previous statements to the effect which I have mentioned, he admitted his having made them. There is evidence to show that he received from his sons crops and payments which, it is contended on the part of the plaintiffs, represented his life usufruct ; and though it is urged for the defendants that these receipts are to be referred to his half share of the farms under the community of property with his first wife, I think it right to refer these receipts by him to a character consistent, and not to one inconsistent, with the wife's will, which he so approved. If I were to decide in favour of the defendants here, I should have not only to come to a different conclusion from that which I have just expressed in reference to the character in which the plaintiffs' father required and received from them these payments out of the farms, but I should also have to decide that a bequest with consent by one person of another's property is not binding without some further act by that other after the death of the testator, and that mere approval of the will then is not a sufficient act for that purpose. I can have little doubt, too, in point of fact, but that the surviving spouse here also received a child's portion out of his wife's estate, and as bequeathed to him by her will, though I do not think the fact so proved as to be a ground for my judgment. On the

1868.
March 5.
May 19.
———
Oosthuysen *vs.*
Oosthuysen.

whole, therefore, I feel bound to come to the conclusion that there ought to be judgment for the plaintiffs. I may mention here that the transfers to the children of the second marriage purport to be for value; no defence is, however, raised on that ground, nor is there any evidence of any payment of money, or the like, in respect of them.

[Plaintiffs' Attorneys, *Hofmeyr, Tredgold, & Watermeyer.*
Defendants' Attorney, *De Korte.*]

ESTERHUIZEN'S EXECUTRIX, APPELLANT; VERMEULEN, RESPONDENT.

Land Beacons Consolidation Act, construction of.—Decision of Commissioners appointed under, reversed on appeal.

" *Sale according to diagram," effect of. Original beacons, and occupation according to, prevail over diagram and grant where the dispute as to such diagram and grant is raised within the* 30 *years after the passing of the Act. And where upwards of* 17 *years before the passing of the Act Esterhuizen had commenced an action against respondent as to boundaries, but upon advice by Counsel that according to the then state of the law, having purchased* " *according to diagram," he would be unsuccessful in the action; and where, accordingly, he withdrew the action and abandoned homestead and spring of water to respondent, but, after the passing of the Act of* 1865, *revived his former dispute, which was thereupon inquired into by the Commission, and decision given against him;* HELD: *That notwithstanding the abandonment aforesaid, no vested right had accrued thereupon to respondent; but that it was open to Esterhuizen, availing himself of the provisions of the Act, to have a fresh inquiry into the merits of the dispute.*

1867.
Dec. 9.
1868.
Feb. 18.
„ 27.
May 19.
———
Esterhuizen's
Executrix,
Appellant;
Vermeulen,
Respondent.

This was the first appeal heard since the passing of the Land Beacons Consolidation Act, from a decision of Commissioners appointed under that Act. The facts of the case and the chief arguments of counsel (*Porter* for applicant, *De Villiers* for respondent) will be found fully stated in the judgments given below. Esterhuizen having died since action commenced, his widow and executrix testamentary was made plaintiff on the record.

On the 9th December, 1867, Porter had argued appellant's case *ex parte*, and the Court then reversed the decision of the Commissioners.

On the 18th February following, *De Villiers*, for respondent, prayed for a re-hearing, on the ground that, by insufficient service, there had been no appearance for respondent on the previous occasion. *Porter* not objecting, the Court fixed the re-argument of the case for the 27th February, and, after the re-hearing upon that day, took time to consider.

Postea (19th May), the Court (by majority, HODGES, C.J., *dissentiente*) gave judgment in favour of appellant. There being a difference of opinion on the Bench, judgment was first delivered by

1867.
Dec. 9.
1868.
Feb. 18.
„ 27.
May 19.

Esterhuizen's Executrix, Appellant; Vermeulen, Respondent.

CONNOR, J., who said: This case comes before the Court by way of appeal, under sections 55—59 of the Land Beacons Consolidation Act (No. 7, 1865), from a decision come to by a majority of the three Commissioners selected under the Act to settle disputed beacons, as between two farms of the names of Draai River and Sillery Fontein. The question in dispute may be shortly stated to be, whether beacons F and C, or E and D, shall be held to be the common beacons of the two farms; this involving the further question, whether the stronger spring of the two Kook Fonteins, and the homestead, are to belong to the appellant or to the respondent. Two of the three Commissioners decided that E and D were to be such beacons. In other words, they decided the dispute in favour of the respondent; and hence this appeal.

The case was argued before the Court on the part of the appellant, the respondent not appearing, on the 9th December, 1867, and we concurred in reversing the decision of the majority of the Commissioners. A motion was made in the following term to have that decision of ours opened, on the ground that the Conditional Order, granted under section 57 of the Act, on the respondent to show cause had not been duly served on him. Notice of this motion was given to the appellant; and Mr. Porter, as her counsel, not objecting to it, the Court allowed the case to be reopened, and it accordingly came on again for argument on 27th February last.

I wish to observe that the service of the Conditional Order upon the respondent appears to me to have been irregular on this account, that the person who served it (the son of the appellant) could not read the order; and, this being so, I cannot understand how he could rightly swear that the copy served by him was a true copy. It appears that the respondent could not read the order either, neither he nor the person serving it being able to read English. The return day of the Conditional Order was in last August, but the case was not brought on then, but stood over *sine die*, and was not argued until the 9th December; and as the respondent had never appeared, and had no further notice after the irregular one to which I have referred, it was certainly

1867.
Dec. 9.
1868.
Feb. 18.
" 27.
May 15.

Esterhuizen's Executrix, Appellant; Vermeulen, Respondent.

desirable, as he wished it, that he should have a fresh opportunity of being heard. Every care had been taken by the Court at the first hearing that he should not be prejudiced by his absence, as not only were all the facts and evidence accurately stated in detail, and the grounds of the decision of the Commissioners known, but the written argument of the respondent's agent sent in to the Commissioners was read aloud in Court here by myself.

As nothing to the contrary has been stated, I conclude that all the preliminary steps required by the Act to be taken for the submission of the question for decision by, and selection of, Commissioners, were duly performed; and I shall briefly state what these are. By section 3 of the Act, the Divisional Council of each division may divide it into sections or areas, giving (section 7) notice of the boundaries of such sections or areas, and the owners of half the immovable property in any such area may obtain from the Governor an order for a resurvey thereof, for the purposes of the Act. (Section 8, &c.). When the Proclamation for this purpose has been issued, and notice published, all the owners of immovable property in the area are to put up provisional beacons, where they think they ought to be, and if they differ among themselves as to the position of any beacons, each is to put up provisional beacons in the places where he thinks they ought to be ; but in this case such beacons " shall not be evidence, to any extent, of the rights of parties, but only of the fact that such rights are or may be in dispute." (Sections 13, 14.). The appointed surveyor is to begin the survey (section 15) within a certain period after the notice ; and the Divisional Council hereby (section 31) require all the landowners within the area to deliver to them all their (the owners') title-deeds and diagrams, and they are to point out to the surveyor, on his application, their respective beacons, and " to admit or deny, by some writing witnessed by not less than two witnesses, the correctness of any of the beacons of any adjoining farm, which beacons abut upon their own farms." (Section 32.). If the surveyor find that any dispute exists regarding boundaries which cannot be settled among the parties, he is to give notice of the dispute, and of the parties, to the Divisional Council (section 36), which is to frame a list of six men ; and if the dispute is between the owners of two farms only, each owner may attend and strike off two names, the person who strikes off first being ascertained by lot (sections 37—39), and the remaining two, with the Civil Commissioner, are to form the Commission. (Section 43.) Notice of the day of hearing is then to be given ; and the Commissioners being on that day assembled and sworn, and being assisted by the surveyor who reported the existence of the disputes, or another surveyor, to be approved of by the Surveyor-General, they are to try the case, " so as to ascertain where, according to real and substantial justice between the parties, the disputed beacons ought of right to stand." (Sections 44—46.)

Section 47 then provides that, to determine this real and substantial justice, " the Commissioners will take into their consideration the particular circumstances of each particular case, but they will, as general principles, be expected to recognize and act upon the rules following, that is to say :" Six rules are then given which are thus to guide the Commissioners, some of which I shall have to refer to more particularly hereafter.

The persons whom both the appellant and respondent here represent purchased the two farms in question about the year 1837, on the same day, at a sale by the executors of a person of the name of Joosté, who had been in his lifetime the owner of both farms ; and as they, we must take it to be admitted, purchased " according to diagrams," and, as it was also admitted that any land included in both diagrams of the original Government grants, that is to say, any " overlap" in the diagrams, would not give the applicant the beacons F or C claimed by her, it was argued for the respondent that the Court ought not, on principle, to put such a construction on the Act as to hold that under it those beacons should be awarded to her ; for that each of the buyers having purchased " according to diagram," and there being no question but that the appellant's diagram did not give her what she claimed, and that the respondent's diagram did give him all that he claimed, to take this from him and give it to the appellant, as the previous decision in this Court would do, would be to make the Act work an injustice by depriving the respondent of a vested right, and giving to the appellant property which the person whom she represents had not purchased, and which the person whom the respondent represents had purchased.

It appears that six or seven years after the purchase from the executors of Joosté, some question having arisen between the owners of the two farms as to their extent, a surveyor, Mr. Bird, was called in, by both the owners apparently, to state what each was entitled to under their diagrams. It was not contended on behalf of the respondent that Mr. Bird was called in to do more than to represent, by beacons and diagrams, what ground was included in the diagrams annexed to the original grants of the farms, and according to which, as I have said, the executors of Joosté had sold ; in fact, to explain visibly what the diagrams meant. He surveyed, and, as he thought, found,—and the

1867.
Dec. 9.
1868.
Feb. 18.
„ 27.
May 19.

Esterhuizen's Executrix, Appellant ; Vermeulen, Respondent.

1867.
Dec. 9.
1868.
Feb. 18.
" 27.
May 19.

Esterhuizen's
Executrix,
Appellant ;
Vermeulen,
Respondent.

correctness of his survey is not disputed,—that F and C were not, according to the diagrams, proper boundary beacons, and that E should be substituted for F, and D for C, in order that the beacons should correspond with the diagrams. The effect of this change was to deprive Esterhuizen, the owner of the farm Draai Rivier, of the spring of water, one of the two Kook Fonteins known as Klein Kook Fontein, though the stronger of the two, and of the ground upon which his house stood. This was in the year 1843 or 1844. Esterhuizen accordingly left his house, built another for himself in another part of the farm, and commenced an action against the executors of Joosté for compensation for his loss ; but it being ascertained by his counsel that he had bought " according to diagram," the action was not proceeded with. He subsequently died, and his widow is, it has been assumed in and for this proceeding, the person now representing him.

With reference, then, to the Land Beacons Act, we have, as I have said, to take it that a resurvey has been had, under that Act, of the area in which these farms are situate ; that the surveyor, in the progress of his survey, ascertained that there was a dispute between the owners of these farms in reference to beacons ; that he reported this fact ; that the subsequent proceedings which I have referred to, as directed by the Act, followed ; and that they terminated in the decision of the Commissioners which I have mentioned.

The main point relied on, as I have said, on the part of the respondent,—indeed, I think I may say the only point urged,—and it is certainly one well deserving attention, is : Are we to construe this Act so as to take away property from one person whose it is in law, to give it to another whose it is not in law ? The proposition that legislative enactments are not to be construed so as to deprive parties of vested rights, unless it is clear from the words and context of the enactment that the Legislature so intended,—unless, in truth, an opposite construction would be incompatible with a fair and reasonable construction of the Act,—is, I apprehend, at once an undoubted rule of construction, and one of great importance for courts of justice to maintain. Any departure from it must tend to shake the confidence of all men in the security of their rights ; and it is unfair for the Legislature itself, which has a right to expect that so self-evident a principle of justice ought to be borne in mind by courts of justice in construing the words which it may have used, and which, in human fallibility, may not be perfectly the very words which in strictness ought to have been used to convey the meaning of the Legislature, subject to the qualifications which justice requires.

In the first place, then, can it, upon any fair and reasonable construction of the language and scope of the Act No. 7, 1865, be held that the Legislature did not by it intend to take from any person any land which his diagram purports to give him? So far from that, we find that the first rule which, under section 47, the Commissioners are, in a dispute such as this, to act upon, provides that "the original beacons of farms pointed out at the original measurement thereof shall be deemed" to define the farms, "notwithstanding that such beacons may not correspond with the original diagrams, or with the extent of land which the original title-deeds purport to grant." Here is an express provision that, in a dispute between two owners of two adjoining farms, the original beacons are to decide what extent of land they are thereafter to have, without regard to the amount which the diagrams or the grants express, in their different modes, to give them. Can this rule be fairly construed so as to except the cases of purchasers purchasing according to diagram: or to except cases in which, if you put it in operation, it will take something from one of the parties which his grant and diagram in law gave him? This rule expresses to be subject to only one qualification, that of the second rule (*b*), which, as I understand it, provides, in substance, that if for thirty years beacons other than the original beacons have been taken by the parties disputing, or those under whom they claim, to have been the true beacons, the Commissioners shall regard them as such. The third rule (*c*) then provides that when any land included within the "original beacons" (not the diagram or grant) of an older grant has afterwards been included within the diagram or beacons of a later grant, thus occasioning an "overlap," the older grant shall prevail, unless (by rule *d*) the old beacons had fallen down and the parties interested in the older grant had not attended at the inspection for the later grant, or (by rule *e*) if for thirty years beacons other than the old beacons had, as provided by rule 2 (*b*), been taken to be the true beacons. Now the effect of the first exception (rule *d*) from the third rule (*c*), would be apparently to take away a vested right in the owners under the older grant, by reason of the negligence. Again, the third rule shows itself wholly indifferent as to what the older grant or diagram may have purported to do. The beacons at its original measurement are to decide the right, be the grant or diagram what they may. Now, if the older grant did not purport to convey all the land within its beacons, and the later grant did purport to convey the surplus, those claiming under the later grant had a vested right in law to the "overlap;" and yet this rule takes it from them. And the two exceptions to the operation of the

1867.
Dec. 9.
1868.
Feb. 18.
" 27.
May 19.

Esterhuizen's Executrix, Appellant; Vermeulen, Respondent.

G

*1867.
Dec. 9.
1868.
Feb. 18.
" 27.
May 19.

Esterhuizen's
Executrix
Appellant;
Vermeulen,
Respondent.*

rule are regulated, not in the least by the nature of the grant or of the diagram, but solely by the beacons, and by the conduct of the parties in reference to the beacons. And in the exceptions to the rule, the claimants under the later grant who are to succeed, are to do so solely with reference to their beacons, and not with reference to their grants or diagrams,—namely, their original beacons, under the first exception, and the thirty years' beacons under the second. Then the last rule (6), under section 47, takes the case of one party relying on his diagram, and insisting that the beacons have been shifted, and the other party insisting that the diagram is erroneous; and the question which the Commissioners are directed to decide is, whether or not the beacons are original and authentic.

It may, moreover, be asked, if property vested in law in one person is to be taken from him, under the Act, and given to another, what provision is there for the transfer of the property from the one to the other? This, however, is not left unprovided for by the Act. By sections 60 and 61 it is provided that after the decision of the Commissioners, or, if there be an appeal, of the Court, "the same proceedings and consequences shall take place in regard to new diagrams and fresh grants as are hereinbefore provided with respect to the farms which are in the 16th section of this Act mentioned, precisely as if the beacons established by such decision had been beacons originally admitted to be true and correct." Then we find that the 16th section provides that when the surveyor finds that the beacons of any farm or number of farms are admittedly correct, he shall frame an accurate diagram of every such farm, taking the same to be the area represented by such admitted beacons, whether the said beacons shall or shall not coincide with the existing diagram of such farm, or with the extent of land which shall by the title-deed of such farm purport to have been granted. Sections 17 and 18 then provide for transmission of the diagram through the Divisional Council to the Surveyor-General, "in order that a fresh grant founded upon the resurvey and new diagram" may be issued; and (section 19) upon the issue of the fresh grant all existing title-deeds or transfer deeds of the farm are to become void.

But, it may be said, if rule (*a*) of section 47 is to prevail,—though its effect be to take one man's property, belonging to him in law, and give it to another in all cases within the terms of the rule, and not within the exception in rule (*b*), is that effect to be given to it in a case in which this Court, suppose, had already decided that beacons other than the original beacons were the rightful beacons in law; or if the parties had by contract between themselves agreed that

that should be so ? If, notwithstanding such a judgment or contract rule (a) were held to apply, and the party against whom the judgment had gone, or who had bound himself otherwise by contract, were under that rule to be reinstated indefeasibly in the position he had been driven from in law, or by his own contract, there can be no doubt but that such an effect of the Act would properly shock men's sense of right and justice, and yet the case is not expressly excepted out of rule (a). We must, however, remember that under the Act there is no place for a Commission to be appointed unless there be a dispute about beacons. Well, then, after such a judgment, or contract, no matter what the party touched by the judgment or contract might say to the contrary, there would not and could not be any dispute about the beacons,—all questions as to which had been disposed of in the modes suggested,—and upon the judgment or contract being brought to the surveyor's notice, he ought not to report the existence of any dispute; or, if he did, the Divisional Council ought not to act on his report; and their acting would, of itself, be good cause for applying for relief to this Court.

1867.
Dec. 9.
1868.
Feb. 18.
" 27.
May 19.
Esterhuizen's Executrix, Appellant; Vermeulen, Respondent.

Does it, then, make any difference, as contended for by Mr. De Villiers, on behalf of the respondent, that the sale to the persons whom the parties here represent— the sale of the two farms on the same day by the executors of Joosté—was " according to diagram?" What is a diagram? It is a figure bounded by lines drawn between points, which are supposed to represent the positions of beacons. The most ordinary understanding, therefore, perhaps, among parties knowing the farms, of the expression is, selling by beacons. That the seller is supposed to say to the buyer : " There are my beacons; I don't bind myself to the amount of land, but whatever it is, you are to get it, and no more." A diagram is, however, part of the grant, or transfer. And when a sale is represented to be " according to diagram," especially by executors, or others not personally interested, the meaning would probably be held to be, that the vendor intended to sell, and the purchaser to buy, all that the grant and diagram would have enabled the seller to establish his right to in law, if he had continued owner; all that, and no more. Then the Land Beacons Act interferes, and provides, in the cases to which it applies, that persons shall be able, and only able, to establish their right, under their grants and diagrams, to that amount of land which the original beacons admit of. So far as this differs from diagrams and grants, the latter are to " become cancelled, void, and of no effect" (Section 19.) The new diagram is to represent the area included within the original

G 2

1867.
Dec. 9.
1868.
Feb. 18.
„ 27.
May 19.

Esterhuizen's Executrix, Appellant; Vermeulen, Respondent.

(or 30 years) beacons, whether the said beacons shall or shall not coincide with the existing diagram of the farm, or with the extent of land which shall by the title-deeds of such farm purport to have been granted. (Sections 16 and 60.)

In truth, the idea upon which the Land Beacons Act was founded was probably this: " The old diagrams are imperfect; but the great majority of the owners of farms, and especially of those who ought to be most regarded in a Colony, those who occupy and cultivate their farms, depend much more upon their visible beacons, as to the extent of their farms, than upon deeds and diagrams. The differences between the beacons and the diagrams are, after all, in respect to the size of the farms, but small, and it is better, and, on the average of cases, the fairer and wiser plan, in a conflict between beacons and diagrams, to let the beacons prevail. It is possible, though unlikely, that cases of much hardship may arise; but the great balance of convenience and substantial justice will be on the side of a plan, the object of which is certainty of title and the preventing future disputes and wrongs, by correcting the surveys, and diagrams, and deeds, while there is time, according to the visible muniments of title, viz., the beacons." I am not advocating the principle of the Act, which has, I believe, been criticized; but it seems to me to be idle to say that these considerations are not of weight. Whether thirty years was too long a period before substituted beacons should prevail may, I think, be questioned. This, too, may I think be said, that if the advocates of the Act wanted a case to justify the conclusion at which I have supposed them to have arrived,—that much more injustice would be avoided by following beacons rather than diagrams,—they could not well expect a stronger one than that before us, in which, upwards of twenty years ago, the husband of the applicant was turned out of his house and home because, on a scientific examination of diagrams, it was discovered that the existing beacons,—according to which, in substance, I am satisfied the two farms were sold and bought, to and by him and his neighbour respectively,—ought to have been some yards in a different direction, the difference, unluckily, including his house and homestead, and their supply of water, the existence of which together where they were was the strongest evidence as to what men's beliefs had been as to the real boundaries.

Being therefore clearly of opinion that this case is not prevented from being within the Act by the form of the sale of the two farms to the persons whom the parties here represent, I can very shortly dispose of that part of it which depends upon the facts given as in evidence. It was, indeed, hardly contested by the learned counsel for the respondent that if the case were within the Act, the beacons F and C ought to be held to have been the original beacons. It is to my mind clear, upon the evidence, that these were the beacons set up on the original measurement of the farm Draai Rivier; that they continued to exist as such beacons till the year 1843 or 1844; that (whether or not at the official inspection the Civil Commissioner gave any directions, as the witness Visser states, to the surveyor to make an alteration, yet) no alteration of those beacons was, in fact, made; that Kock and Joosté, the successive owners of both farms, regarded F and C as the beacons; that these were so regarded by all sellers and buyers and others, at the sale by Joosté's executors to the persons whom the parties to this case represent; and that they continued to be the beacons until, in 1843 or 1844, the Surveyor Bird being called in to ascertain what, according to the diagrams, ought to be the beacons, the beacons E and D were substituted for F and C. Whether if that substitution had lasted for 30 years the case would have come within the exception to rule (*a*) of section 47, contained in rule (*b*), it is needless here to inquire, as the period of 30 years has not, of course, yet run. But this exception in rule (*b*) is in the appellant's favour, to this extent, that it shows that the Legislature, contemplating a long disregard of the original beacons, refused to allow that to prevent their prevailing in a dispute, unless the disregard had lasted for 30 years.

I know that the evidence that the beacon F was not set up before the inspection, and the witness Visser's evidence that the Civil Commissioner acceded to his (Visser's) expostulation against giving Kook Fontein to the farm Draai Rivier, as the farm Sillery Fontein had been earlier applied for, and accordingly directed the surveyor to make an alteration,—has been supposed to create a difficulty as to F and C being within the terms of rule (*a*) of section 47, " the original beacons " of the farm " as pointed out at the original measurement thereof." I cannot say I feel that difficulty. F and C were, in fact, the beacons so pointed out, and any supposed directions to the contrary were not, in my opinion, visibly acted on by their being removed and others being set up. They were, as far as I can judge, the common beacons of the two farms till Bird's survey. The direction to make an alteration, if given, was given in the absence of Mr. Kock, the person then interested in Draai Rivier, and for whom it had been surveyed; and Mr. Porter suggested that as he became after this, and before the issue of the grants, owner of both the farms, the alteration having become im-

1867.
Dec. 9,
1868.
Feb. 18,
" 27.
May 19.

Esterhuizen's
Executrix,
Appellant;
Vermeulen,
Respondent.

material, was probably for that reason not carried out. For, as was also suggested, as Visser states that he only knew of one Kook Fontein, and called it Groot Kook Fontein, while that one connected with beacon F was more generally known as Klein Kook Fontein, and there was another Groot Kook Fontein, which was and is included in the farm Sillery Fontein, it may have been thought that Visser had made a mistake as to the source of water he spoke of not being included in the farm, and that therefore the alteration which he suggested was necessary.

This old gentleman speaks, too, in reference to old transactions occurring upwards of thirty years ago, and the contemporary written records, so far from bearing him out, go to show that the alteration which he thinks he suggested was not only not acted on by a change of visible beacons, but that this was done intentionally. His recollection is that he urged the change as a measure strongly required in justice to the farm Sillery Fontein for its supply of water. Assuming this, and that his suggestion had been adopted, can we believe that in the Civil Commissioner's official inspection report as to the water supply of this farm, this source, which had been the subject of discussion, and of a change of beacons, after the survey of the farm Draai Rivier,—this source, I say, of water-supply should have been omitted to be mentioned? And yet so it is. The farm Sillery Fontein is, in the inspection report, stated to be supplied with water by the fountain called Sillery Fontein, and no other source of supply is mentioned. The same report, no doubt, states that there should be a condition that the cattle of Draai Rivier should have a "drinking" at the Groot Kook Fontein. And it may be said this shows that there may be a source of water-supply on the farm Sillery Fontein, which is not mentioned in the inspection report; but, then, this in no way corresponds with the evidence, which is to the effect that this Kook Fontein, though called "Groot," was weak of water. The fountain in dispute is, as I have said, called " Klein Kook Fontein."

In the Civil Commissioner's inspection report as to Draai Rivier, that farm is stated to be supplied with water " by the Draai Rivier and Kook Fontein." The supply had been originally, in the report, apparently, stated to be by two fountains and periodical floods; but this is struck out, and what I have already mentioned (as to the Draai Rivier and Kook Fontein) is substituted. Now, the diagrams, as far as I understand them, show that the spring called Sillery Fontein is far from all the boundaries of the farm Sillery Fontein, that is, in the centre of the farm, but that the Groot Kook Fontein, though within the farm Sillery Fontein, is very near to the boundary between it and Draai Rivier. And all this goes, in my mind, to indicate that what old Mr. Visser was impressed by when he gave his evidence was probably this: that it was originally intended to include in Draai Rivier both the Kook Fonteins; that he objected to this; that consequently the Groot Kook Fontein was included within the farm Sillery Fontein, and a "drinking" at it given to the cattle of Draai Rivier, but that Klein Kook Fontein was intentionally left with Draai Rivier as formerly,—in fact, that it was never proposed to take it from it.

1867.
Dec. 9.
1868.
Feb. 18,
" 27.
May 19.

Esterhuizen's Executrix, Appellant; Vermeulen, Respondent.

The only objection, as far as I am aware, to this construction is, that the inspection report as to Draai Rivier does not mention, as the contemporary one as to Sillery Fontein does, that there should be a "drinking" for the cattle of Draai Rivier at the Groot Kook Fontein, and that, therefore, the statement in the report that the farm Draai Rivier is supplied by Kookfontein is to be supposed to refer to this proposed servitude of a "drinking." This, however, seems to me an insufficient objection. The question as to water, to be answered in the report, is, "How is the land supplied with water during the different seasons?" Now, this form of expression certainly seems to refer rather to water on the land, than to a proposed right of sending cattle into another farm to drink. There is no doubt but that there are two Kook Fonteins. Only one of them is referred to in the two inspection reports of the farms if that now mentioned in the answer before us, as to the farm Draai Rivier, is not the Fontein in dispute. It is called in this answer simply Kook Fontein, while in the contemporary document, as to Sillery Fontein, the water at which it is proposed to give the "drinking" is called the *Groot Kook Fontein*. The presumption is that they were different. And as the fountain in dispute is the stronger of the two, it is not unlikely that it should be called simply Kook Fontein. I think it probable that the other was called *Groot*, because of its marshy nature, and its site, consequently, being spread out.

On the whole, I am satisfied that F and C were the original beacons within the meaning of the Act, and that our former decision declaring this to be so, and that they should now prevail, and that the decision of the majority of the Commissioners the other way should be reversed, was correct.

There remains the question of costs. When this case was last before the Court, the costs of the proceedings and appeal were given to the appellant, on account of the irregular service of the notice to show cause. I do not think that the respondent ought to have to bear the costs of that argument. Then when I remember that this whole

1867.
Dec. 9.
1868.
Feb. 18.
     27.
May 19.

Esterhuizeu's
Executrix,
Appellant;
Vermeulen,
Respondent.

dispute has been in a great measure occasioned by an act to which both the late owners, represented by the appellant and respondent, were parties, viz., the calling in of the surveyor, Mr. Bird, I should be strongly disposed to say that each party's costs of these proceedings should be borne by themselves; but then I should expect, in that case, that there should be no claim on either side in respect of improvements on, or the occupation of, the premises in dispute.

BELL, J.—The contest in this case is between the owners of the respective farms of Draai Rivier and Sillery Fontein as to which of them is entitled to a fountain called Klein Kook Fontein.

In 1830 Draai Rivier was surveyed for Kock, for the purpose of a Government grant, Erasmus having previously applied for a grant of Sillery Fontein. Before the grants were issued Kock purchased from Erasmus his chance of the grant of Sillery Fontein. Kock being thus in right of both grants, should they be issued, had the two farms surveyed by Meiring, a Government surveyor, under directions which De Kock gave him to put a beacon at a point F between the two farms. This would throw the fountain in question into Draai River. After this survey had been completed, and not till then, the Civil Commissioner of the division held an inspection of the two farms. This he did so late as the year 1837.

In November, 1838, the Government issued a grant of Sillery Fontein, with a condition in it that "the cattle of the farm Draai Rivier should be permitted to drink at the Groot Kook Rivier," and thereafter, in December of the same year, a grant was issued of Draai Rivier. In the same year, 1838, Kock sold both farms to Joosté, who died also in the same year.

After Joosté's death, his executors put up the two farms for sale, and Esterhuizen bought Draai Rivier, while Vermeulen bought Sillery Fontein. Each of these purchases was "according to diagram."

Kock, during his possession from 1830 to 1838, had erected and possessed a homestead near to the beacon F and the Fountain Klein Kook Fontein, that fountain and the homestead being assumed to be within Draai Rivier.

In 1844, Vermeulen, who had become the proprietor of Sillery Fontein, as before mentioned, raised a question as to boundary, insisting that by the diagram attached to his transfer deed, the boundary between the two farms brought his farm much within what had been occupied by Esterhuizen as Draai Rivier, and embraced Klein Kook Fontein; the truth being that Kook Fontein, the true subject of dispute, was made to appear by both diagrams to be on both farms.

To settle this dispute Bird, a surveyor, was employed, and he, after survey, declared Vermeulen to be in the right, and, of his own authority, Bird had a beacon erected at a point, E, which, according to him, ought to form the beacon between the two farms.

1867.
Dec. 9.
1868.
Feb. 18.
„ 27.
May 19.

Esterhuizen's Executrix, Appellant; Vermeulen, Respondent.

Esterhuizen, the proprietor of Draai River, being advised that according to the then state of the law, diagrams must prevail over beacons, abandoned any idea of disputing the right to this fountain with Vermeulen, dropped an action which he had brought for that purpose, and removed his homestead from the letter F, betaking himself to another homestead more within the farm. This course he took undoubtedly with much reluctance and against his self-conviction as to his own rights, and under the compulsion of what he was given to understand was the then state of the law.

Subsequently, the Act No. 7 of 1865 was passed, and Esterhuizen then bethought him that he would take advantage of that Act, and try if he could not establish F as the boundary beacon. Accordingly, he presented an application to the Divisional Council, by whom a Commission was issued in terms of the Act, and the result of the proceedings before that Commission was the affirmance of what Bird had done in 1844, when fixing E as the true beacon between the farms, instead of the beacon F. Against that decision of the Council Esterhuizen took an appeal to this Court, as allowed by the 55th section of the Act, and gave due notice thereof. When the day for hearing the appeal arrived, no appearance was made for Vermeulen, and this Court, after hearing counsel for Esterhuizen, who in the course of his address read what may be called two able pleadings, which had been submitted to the Divisional Council, on behalf of Esterhuizen and Vermeulen, respectively, this Court reversed the decision of the Divisional Council, and affirmed F to be the proper beacon between the two farms.

On a subsequent day, Vermeulen appeared by counsel and stated that he thought that something more than the notice which had been served upon him was necessary before he should appear in Court. In this way he accounted for his absence at the hearing of the appeal, and unfortunately his excuse was admitted, and the case was again heard, and it now stands for judgment; but I have not heard anything to induce me to alter the opinion I formed when the case was heard *ex parte*.

The evidence satisfies me that a beacon was placed at the point F before any other beacon whatever was in existence, and while as yet the two farms were owned by one and the same proprietor, by Kock, and that it continued to stand and be recognized as a beacon during the tenure by Joosté of

1867.
Dec. 1.
1868.
Feb. 18.
" 27.
May 19.
Esterhuizen's Executrix, Appellant;
Vermeulen, Respondent.

both the farms under the two Government grants, and that matters remained in this state from 1838, when Joosté died, until 1844, although Vermeulen had, in 1838, or some time between that year and 1844, got a transfer from Joosté's executors according to diagram, the diagram showing the beacon F to be within Sillery Fontein.

It is not therefore until 1844 that the beacon at the point E had any existence in fact. That beacon, therefore, can in no sense of the word "original," used in the Act, be the original beacon. In truth, there was no original beacon "as pointed out at the original measurement,"—the words of sub-division (a) of section 47,—unless the beacon F is to be taken to be such beacon.

The objection to holding it to be such original beacon is, as I understand it, that at the time the farms were surveyed and this beacon fixed, no inspection by the Civil Commissioner of the district previous to a survey, as required by the Government regulations at the time, had yet taken p'ace.

The first and second articles of the Regulations of 30th September, 1814, direct that all applications for farms should be referred to the Landdrost and Heemraden for examination, and that a Commission, consisting of the Landdrost and one Heemraad, assisted by a sworn surveyor, should repair to the ground in question, and, after having heard the parties, and had pointed out to them the lands desired, the surveyor should measure the lands in presence of the field-cornet, who should point out the springs, and take care that sufficient landmarks were forthwith erected at the several angles. By the third article the surveyor was to furnish a diagram to the Landdrost, who, by the fourth article, was to forward this to the Governor. "The object of His Excellency," says the 5th article, "being to save all unnecessary expense to the parties applying, and to preserve uniformity in the survey and impartiality to the parties, relies upon the zeal and local knowledge of the Landdrost, Deputy Landdrost, and Heemraden, that they should arrange the several applications in the mode best calculated to effect economy, expedition and general accuracy, by pointing out the surveyors, successively in their order, the different lands applied for, so that surveyors may proceed with dispatch, and without interruption, by which much expense will be saved."

It is, no doubt, true that inspection by the Landdrost and Heemraden should have preceded the survey which took place when the beacon F was erected, whereas it would appear from the evidence that the inspection was not held until seven years after the survey and erection of the beacon.

This was, no doubt, highly irregular and reprehensible on the part of the Civil Commissioner, or whomsoever the delay was imputable to, as tending to defeat,—as, in fact, it has defeated,—the object specified in article 5 of the Regulations; but having said this, all is said that can be said. It is a totally different thing to say that the survey held seven years before inspection, according to which possession was held during that time, and for six years after inspection had taken place, is to go for nothing,—there is no authority in the Regulations for drawing any such consequence. In my opinion, the inspection must be held to draw back by relation to the year 1830, and prior in that year to the survey; that it is to be held as having been made *nunc pro tunc.* It might have been otherwise if, on the actual inspection taking place, the Civil Commissioner, who came in place of the Landdrost and Heemraden, had, upon good grounds, stated to and allowed by the Governor, dissented from or disallowed any part of the survey; but that even is doubtful. At any rate, I see no evidence of such dissent or disallowance. The only thing of the kind is a statement by some of the witnesses that some one, on behalf of Erasmus, who had applied for the Grant of Sillery Fontein, but afterwards sold his chance of his grant to Kock, objected, in the absence of Kock, who had applied for the grant of Draai Fontein, that Draai Fontein ought not, in fairness, to include Klein Kook Fontein, and that the Civil Commissioner assented to the objection, and said he would direct the surveyor (who had seven years before made the survey) to make an alteration of the beacons in accordance with the objection. That evidence, such as it is, is open to three observations. In the first place, the evidence does not satisfy me that, there being two Kook Fonteins, Groot and Klein, the Civil Commissioner really understood which of them the objection regarded, Groot Kook Fontein, or Klein Kook Fontein; but, in the second place, assuredly, however the Civil Commissioner may have understood the objection, and whether he did or did not give directions to the surveyor,—as to which there is not a particle of evidence,—no alteration of the beacons was actually made in accordance with the objection which is supposed to have been taken, but beacon F was allowed to remain exactly as it had been originally fixed until the year 1844, when Bird made his survey for the parties; and, in the third place, it was not competent for Bird, without any directions from the Civil Commissioner, or any other public authority whatever, to disturb the beacons. Nay, I apprehend it was not competent to the Civil Commissioner to give the directions to the original surveyor as to the alteration of the beacon, which he is stated by the witnesses to have

1867.
Dec. 9.
1868.
Feb. 18.
„ 27.
May 19.

Esterhuizen's Executrix, Appellant;
Vermeulen, Respondent.

1867.
Dec. 9.
1868.
Feb 18.
" 27.
May 19.

Esterhuizen's
Executrix,
Appellant;
Vermeulen,
Respondent.

promised to give. He might have altered his report of inspection to the Governor, leaving His Excellency to deal with the matter, but it was no part of his duty to give or to withhold fountain, or anything else. His duty was merely to inspect and report. In my opinion, therefore, beacon F must be considered to be the original beacon, in the language of subdivision (*a*) of section 47 of the Act, which the Divisional Council was bound to adopt when ascertaining the rights of the parties, and that this must be held even " notwithstanding," in the language of the subdivision, " it may not correspond with the original diagrams, or with the extent of land which the original titledeeds purport to grant ;" because if there were no other reason, in the language of subdivision (*b*) of the same section, there was no other " certain, well-ascertained beacon which had been for an uninterrupted period of 30 years or upwards, next before the day on which the Commission," *i.e.*, of the Divisional Council, " in the particular case was in manner aforesaid selected or obtained, recognized by the parties who dispute the same before the Commissioners, or those under whom such parties claim, as the true and proper beacon which can be taken to be, and to have been, the original beacon."

Subdivision (*c*) of the same section, 47, directs that where land included within the original beacons of an " older grant" has afterwards been included within the diagram and beacons, or diagram or beacons, of a " later grant," the right of the older grant to the overlap shall prevail, unless in the cases stated in subdivisions (*d*) and (*e*). But subdivision (*c*) cannot apply to the present case. No doubt the grant of Sillery Fontein, instead of being made contemporaneously with the grant of Draai Rivier, like the applications for the grants, happened, apparently through the accidental arrangements of the Surveyor-General's office, to be issued in November, while the grant of Draai Rivier was not issued till the following month of December ; but according to an equitable and just construction of the Act, that accidental circumstance could not, in my apprehension, constitute the grant of Sillery Fontein the " older grant"— it is rather to be treated as contemporaneous with the grant of Draai Rivier ; especially when it is remembered that before either grant had been issued, De Kock had, by purchase from Erasmus, acquired right to the land in both of the grants.

Nay, more, even if the grant of Sillery Fontein were to be treated as the " older grant," there was not " any land included within the original beacons " of Sillery Fontein, treating the grant of it as of the " older grant," which had "afterwards been included within the diagram and beacons, or diagram or beacons, of a later grant," treating the grant of Draai Rivier as the "later grant." The fact is just the other way, for holding beacon F to be the original beacon, as, for the reasons I have given, I think it must be held to be, the overlap between the points F and E was included within the original beacons, not of Sillery Fontein, treating the grant of it as the "older grant," but of Draai Rivier, treating the grant of it as the "later grant."

1867
Dec. 9.
1868.
Feb. 18.
" 27.
May 19.
———
Esterhuizen's Executrix, Appellant;
Vermeulen, Respondent.

Subdivision (c) therefore, not having application to the case, it is not necessary to consider the qualifications upon that subdivision created by subdivision (d).

If the case is to be decided upon the terms of subdivision (f), which probably is the one most applicable to this particular case, then I am of opinion, for the reasons I have before given, that beacon F was an "original authentic beacon," which was shifted by Bird the surveyor, without any authority, and that the diagrams' in so far as they do not give effect to this beacon, are erroneous.

In every view, I am of opinion, that the judgment of this Court reversing the order of the Divisional Council, pronounced at the first hearing of the appeal, was correct, and ought now to be adhered to.

I have looked through the Act to see if it gives the Court any power to consider the question of meliorations and dilapidations, with a view to adjusting the rights of the parties in this respect, because we were informed by the evidence that the appellant, Esterhuizen, had sustained injury by the removal of his homestead from the disputed ground in the year 1844, and, on the other hand, that the respondent had since that year made meliorations on the same ground. But I have not found any authority in the Act for considering this question. If it exist, an enquiry into this matter no doubt should be made. If it do not exist, I am afraid that in a proceeding entirely authorized by the Act, the Court cannot take such power to itself, and that the parties must take some course independent of the Act, if they desire to have the rights in this respect ascertained.

With regard to costs, I am disposed to think that, as Vermeulen, at the time he purchased from the executors of Joosté, must have been aware of the long existence of the beacon F and of his predecessor's possession according to that beacon, he must have raised the dispute which has caused all the inquiry before the Divisional Council upon the hope that he might be borne out in his unjust claim by the mere terms of his transfer "according to diagram," and the circumstance of the diagram, erroneously, as he must have known, giving him the land in dispute,—he ought

1867.
Dec. 9.
1868.
Feb. 18.
" 77.
May 19.

Esterbuizen's
Executrix,
Appellant;
Vermeulen,
Respondent.

therefore to bear all the costs of the survey and proceedings before the Commission and Divisional Council, and of this appeal—but, in any view, that he ought to pay the costs of the second hearing of the appeal, which was occasioned entirely by his default in not appearing at the first hearing.

HODGES, C.J.—On the 1st November, 1838, a Government grant, with diagram, attached, was issued of the farm Sillery Fontein, and on the 31st December, in the same year, a similar grant, with diagram, was issued of the farm Draai Rivier. The appellant is the owner of Draai Rivier, and the respondent of Sillery Fontein. It was an undisputed fact in the case that, according to these diagrams, a homestead with a fountain of water adjoining fell within the boundaries of Sillery Fontein, and for several years before the proceedings hereinafter referred to (under the Act No. 7, 1865) were taken, the owner of that farm had remained in undisturbed possession of the homestead and fountain. The interest in both these farms had originally belonged to one Kock, and he sold them both to one Joosté, whose executors sold the same by public auction, according to diagram, to the respective purchasers of the two farms now belonging to the appellant and respondent. After the sale, the purchasers entered into the occupation of their respective farms, and the purchaser of Draai Rivier held the homestead and fountain before mentioned, but some misunderstanding having arisen on the subject of the boundaries of the farms, Bird, a surveyor, was called in at the joint expense of the two proprietors, and he, investigating the titles and referring to the original diagrams, placed beacons which threw back the homestead and fountain to the farm Sillery Fontein, and the then owner of Draai Rivier, apparently acquiescing in the decision, quitted the possession of that part of the farm, but brought an action against the executors of Joosté for selling to him, as a part of the farm Draai Rivier, the homestead and fountain already referred to. When the case was ready for trial at the Circuit Court, the plaintiff was advised that, as he purchased the land according to diagram, and as the diagram excluded the homestead and fountain, he would be probably unsuccessful in his action, and he therefore withdrew, and no further proceedings were at that time taken. Had no subsequent legislation on the subject of disputed boundaries taken place, no doubt can, I think, be entertained that the title of the owner of Sillery Fontein would have remained undisturbed. But these two farms having been included in an area or section under Act No. 7, 1865, the surveyor employed by the Divisional Council reported the dispute, as he is directed to do by the 36th section, and a Commission was duly issued to inquire into the circumstances of the case;

and, after a long and expensive inquiry, the majority of the three Commissioners decided in favour of the respondent, the owner of Sillery Fontein; but one of the Commissioners dissented from their decision, whereupon the defeated party appealed to this Court in pursuance of the 55th section of the Act; and there has been transmitted to us the report of the Commissioners and the evidence, documentary and otherwise, of a very voluminous character. A rule to show cause, directed to the respondent, was then granted under section 57, but on the return of the rule no person was instructed to appear on behalf of the respondent, and the Court, after hearing counsel for the appellant, decided in his favour; but the respondent having subsequently asked for leave to reopen the question, and that application not being opposed by the learned counsel who appeared for the appellant, we had the advantage of hearing counsel on both sides, and my learned brothers have, as we have heard, continued of the same opinion as they entertained in the first instance; but I confess that further reflection on this somewhat intricate case has induced me to come to the opinion that the majority of the Commissioners came to a correct judgment. I should have satisfied myself with stating this without further comment, but as this is the first appeal which has been heard under the provisions of the new Act, and as it involves a point as to the construction of the 47th section, I shall explain the grounds of my decision. That section directs that, "in determining what real and substantial justice between the parties truly is, the Commissioners will take into their consideration the particular circumstances of each particular case, but they will, as general principles, be expected to recognize and act upon the rules following," one of which is that, "the original beacons of farms, as pointed out at the original measurement thereof, shall be deemed to denote and include the true and proper farms as granted and intended so to be, notwithstanding that such beacons may not correspond with the original diagrams, or with the extents of land which the original title-deeds purport to grant."

1867.
Dec. 9.
1868.
Feb. 18.
,, 27.
May 19.

Esterhuizen's Executrix, Appellant; Vermeulen, Respondent.

It is quite clear that the dispute in this case arises from a variance or difference between the diagrams and a certain beacon called beacon F in the various plans which were produced before the Commissioners and transmitted to us with the other evidence. The history of that supposed original beacon is detailed by Kock, who was one of the most important witnesses examined. He deposed that he, probably with a view of sending in a request for purchase, had both these farms surveyed (by what authority does not appear), and that Draai Rivier was surveyed by Stretch, a

1867.
Dec. 9.
1868.
Feb. 18.
" 27.
May 19.
Esterhulzen's
Executrix,
Appellant;
Vermeulen,
Respondent.

Government surveyor, about a year before Sillery Fontein. That was in 1829 or 1830. Sillery Fontein was surveyed by Meiring, also a Government surveyor, and Kock directed him to survey up to the said beacon F, which was no doubt set up by Stretch, and which threw the fountain and the site of the homestead into Draai Rivier. It was upon this site that Kock, before any title was issued, built a portion of the homestead. In 1836 or 1837, Kock sold his interest in both these farms to Frans Joosté. Kock further deposes that a few months after Draai Rivier had been surveyed by Stretch, the inspection of the farms took place by Mr. Truter, the Civil Commissioner of the district, and that Mr. Stretch and the field-cornet were present. Kock gives no particulars of what transpired at this inspection, and it is even possible that he was not aware that the Commissioner disapproved of the beacon F, which had been placed by Stretch as the boundary of Draai Rivier. As it has been already stated, Kock afterwards sold his interest in both these farms to Joosté, and the executors of Joosté sold both of them at an auction, according to diagrams, to the different purchasers, who subsequently called in Bird to survey, and Bird, disregarding altogether the beacon F, put up beacons according to the diagrams, and the beacon F was destroyed or taken down and not set up again until after the passing of the Act No. 7, 1865. The evidence adduced on the part of the respondent, the owner of Sillery Fontein, leads me to the conclusion that the beacon F cannot and ought not to be, under the circumstances which were proved, considered to be "an original beacon pointed out at the original measurement," within the meaning of that word, as used in paragraph (a) section 47 of the Act of 1865. That beacon was erected by Stretch, at the instigation of Kock, several months before the inspection took place. Had the Civil Commissioner, who fulfilled the duties formally performed by the Landdrost, approved of that beacon when he held his inspection, no doubt the beacon would have been an original beacon, although it was irregularly put up by Stretch before the inspection. But, so far from that beacon being approved of, there is evidence to show that directions were given by the Civil Commissioner to Stretch to remove it. This he probably neglected to do, but the diagrams were, nevertheless, issued as if he had performed his duty, and the diagram on the grant of Draai Rivier is stated to be "from the original framed by Surveyor Stretch." If, therefore, the evidence I am now about to read can be relied upon, it is abundantly manifest that it was through Stretch's neglect that all this protracted and most expensive litigation has unhappily arisen.

An aged witness, Gerrit Visser, speaking of the transactions at the inspection, says (I cite his own words) : "I have resided here ever since 1812, and am in my 80th year. The commission of inspection of the farm Sillery Fontein, to the best of my recollection, arrived here in October, 1832, and consisted of Mr. Truter, Civil Commissioner of Worcester, and his clerk, Mr. Scholtz. Surveyors C. L. Stretch and P. Meiring accompanied them. The field-cornet was Albert Smit. I was appointed by the Civil Commissioner to act in his stead, and did so. The Civil Commissioner stated that they had met for the purpose of inspecting the farms Draai Rivier and Sillery Fontein, and said that he had given the fountain called Groot Fontein to Draai Rivier, whereupon I objected, saying ' It is not right, sir, as Sillery Fontein is the older request of the two.' The Civil Commissioner replied, ' We have already given it to Kock' (the owner of Draai Rivier); whereupon I again said, ' It is not right, because Draai Rivier has been surveyed before an inspection, which is illegal, as the Government instructions were that an inspection before a survey should take place.' Mr. Truter then said that he should be obliged to alter it, to which I replied, ' It is my desire.'

"The surveyor, Stretch, was then ordered to return to Draai Rivier, and alter his survey of that farm which he had surveyed eight or ten months before ; and Mr. Meiring was at the same time ordered to include the Groot Fontein in the survey of Sillery Fontein.

"The Groot Fontein at the homestead was the one spoken of at the inspection,—at least I presume so, as I knew of no other.

"I do not remember that Kock was present at the inspection. Mr. C. Erasmus, the applicant for Sillery Fontein, was not there; but his son, Jan Erasmus, came here the next day while the commission of inspection was still here. I remember seeing the beacon on the ' Nek,' and marked F on the tracing. I was surprised to see it, since Mr. Stretch had been ordered back to alter the beacons of Draai Rivier."

This witness having deposed that young Erasmus represented his father at the inspection his evidence on this point is confirmed by young Erasmus, who was also examined. He says : " I believe that Mr. Kock owned Draai Rivier at that time. I was present at the inspection of Sillery Fontein, which took place at Elandsberg—the farm of Mr. Gerrit Visser, sen. I was appointed by my father to attend that inspection in his stead. The inspection was appointed to take place at Sillery Fontein; but my father not being there, I overtook the Commission at Gerrit Visser's. When I got to Mr. Visser's, it was the day after the inspection took

1867.
Dec 9.
1868.
Feb. 18.
  „ 27.
May 19.

Esterhuizen's Executrix, Appellant ; Vermeulen, Respondent.

1867.
Dec. 9.
1868.
Feb. 18.
" 27.
May 19.

Esterhuizen's Executrix, Appellants;
Vermeulen, Respondent.

place there. I cannot remember whether Mr. Kock was there. Mr. Visser told me that he acted for my father the day before, in his absence. Mr. Truter told me that he had included the Groot Fontein at the homestead in Sillery Fontein. At that time, and long before, the lower fountain was called Groot Fontein."

It now becomes important to ascertain what regulations were in force relating to surveys and inspections at the period when these two farms were thus inspected by Truter. I find them in a document bearing date the 30th September, 1814. The regulations are as follows:

"Art. 1. All applications which may be referred to the Landdrost and Heemraden for examination shall be distinguished and arranged in lists.

"Art. 2. These lists being made out, a Commission, consisting of the Landdrost and one Heemraad, assisted by one of the sworn surveyors, shall repair to the field-cornetcy, and there (after having first heard the field-cornet and the interested parties specially to be summoned for that purpose, and being informed of all the circumstances from the different parties, which Government should be acquainted with), on the applicants pointing out the several lands to the surveyor, he shall proceed from place to place and measure the same, in presence of the field-cornet, who is to point out to the surveyor all springs, &c., and take care that sufficient landmarks be erected at the several angles forthwith.

"Art. 3. The Commission having thus inspected those lands, and pointed the same out to the surveyor as aforesaid, shall be considered as having terminated its proceedings; and the land-surveyor, in the presence of the field-cornet, is to continue his operations in the same order, and in the manner prescribed; after which he is to furnish the Landdrost with a diagram of each place, drawn out according to the form directed in the surveyor's instructions.

"Art. 4. Immediately on the receipt of this diagram, the Commission shall send in their report to the Governor, stating therein all the circumstances, as well regarding the nature of the ground as with respect to the applicant, according to such orders as already exist or may be given hereafter."

Here we see that the inspection ought to precede the survey which the surveyor is bound to make according to the directions he might receive from the Civil Commissioner, and the diagrams of both the farms are consistent with the directions which Visser swears he heard Truter give to Stretch.

There are one or two additional circumstances which confirm me in the view I take of this case. In the grant of Sillery Fontein there is an express reservation that the cattle of the farm Draai Rivier shall be permitted to drink at the Groot Kook Fontein. If this had been distinctly shown to be the fountain at the homestead, the respondent's right to the fountain (which, as I have before said, was excluded by Stretch's beacon F) would have been most clearly established by the express words used in the grant. But there was shown to be another fountain on Sillery Fontein, higher up than the homestead ; and it was contended that this was the fountain referred to. But there was not wanting evidence on the other side to show that this fountain was an insignificant one, incapable of supplying cattle with water to any useful extent ; also, that the fountain at the homestead bore the name of Groot Kook Fontein. I may also remark, incidentally, that as the grant of Sillery Fontein was older than that of Draai Rivier, any overlap would belong to the former by the express provision of the 47th section, letter (c), of the Act No. 7, 1865. For all these reasons, I think that the beacon F was not such an original beacon as was contemplated by the Legislature in the 47th section of the Act. It never was an original beacon, because it was neither planted by the surveyor by the order of the Civil Commissioner, whose duty it was to inspect the farm, nor was it ever adopted or approved of by him. The memorandum, in the handwriting of Mr. Charles Bell, on the diagram of Draai Rivier, to this effect, i.e., that it was prepared from the " original " (meaning original diagram) prepared by the surveyor, Stretch, shows that Stretch, in all probability, acted on the instructions he received, but at the same time neglected to have the beacon taken down ; and thus he brought about this most expensive litigation, which will, I fear, prove all but ruinous to some of the parties interested in the decision. I may, with truth, say that although this Court is not responsible for the costly machinery now provided, we may well caution landowners to pause before they set it in motion when beacons or boundaries are disputed. Surveyors are necessarily called in, agents and interpreters employed, and the Commission sit as often and at as many places as they think necessary. In this case, adjourned meetings were held, and the costs are necessarily very great ; and as a right of appeal is given to this Court, no man can predict the pecuniary losses he may sustain before the litigation attending a disputed beacon is terminated. As I have already intimated, my opinion is that the finding of the majority of the Commissioners in favour of the respondent ought to be confirmed.

1867.
Dec. 9,
1868.
Feb. 18,
,, 27.
May 19,

Esterhuizen's Executrix, Appellant;
Vermeulen, Respondent.

The Court allowed the appeal, and confirmed its order made on the 28th February, except as to costs : now ordering each party to pay her and his own costs ; the respondent undertaking not to make any claim or sue for ameliorations.

[Appellant's Attorneys, *Hofmeyr, Tredgold & Watermeyer*.]
[Respondent's Attorneys, *Fairbridge & Arderne*.]

SILBERBAUER vs. RUTHVEN.

(In Camerâ.)

Arrest, discharge of, where at the time of the arrest the arresting Deputy Sheriff had not a Copy of the Writ in his possession, but acted solely on Telegraphic Message from the Sheriff in Cape Town.

1868.
March 17.
" 19.
Silberbauer vs.
Ruthven.

Porter moved upon notice to plaintiff to show cause " why the arrest, or pretended arrest, of defendant effected by the Deputy Sheriff of Port Elizabeth, on the 6th day of February last, shall not be declared legally null and void, upon the ground that the said arrest was effected without the said Deputy Sheriff producing any lawful writ of arrest, or having or being able to produce such writ to defendant, and being consequently unarmed with any sufficient power or authority to capture the defendant and convey him to gaol; and why said arrest, or pretended arrest, and all other subsequent proceedings of the plaintiff thereunder, shall not be set aside, with costs."

It appeared from the plaintiff's affidavits (which were unanswered by the defendant, as it was alleged, from want of time) that the defendant, being indebted to plaintiff in the sum of £24 13s. 6d., assigned his estate in Cape Town, with the consent of all his creditors, except the plaintiff, and proceeded to Natal in the steamer *Natalian*. *En route*, the steamer called in at Algoa Bay, where the local Deputy Sheriff went on board, and arrested the defendant for the sum stated to be due to the plaintiff. The writ had been taken out in Cape Town on the 3rd February. On the same day, or next, plaintiff's attorneys telegraphed, on behalf of the Sheriff, to Port Elizabeth, to arrest the defendant. On the 4th February, the writ of arrest itself was posted in Cape Town. On the 5th February, the Deputy Sheriff at Port Elizabeth proceeded on board the *Natalian* to arrest the defendant, but was not able to recognize him. On the 6th, he again went on board, arrested the defendant, and conveyed him to the Port Elizabeth gaol, where he had ever since been detained. On the 7th February, the writ of arrest itself arrived in Port Elizabeth, and was then for the first time in the hands of the Deputy Sheriff, the whole of whose previous proceedings had been carried on on the authority of the telegram.

Porter maintained the arrest was illegal. By the 14th Rule of Court, the writ was directed to the Sheriff or his Deputy, who were required to give the defendant a copy of the writ if demanded. Although the affidavits did not state that the Deputy Sheriff, in this case, had been requested by the defendant to give him a copy of the writ, yet it followed from the terms of the Rule of Court that he must, at all events, have a copy in his possession. No legal arrest could therefore be made by the Deputy Sheriff on a telegraphic or any other message. In England, if a bailiff make an arrest without warrant, it will be set aside, even if the writ is in the hands of the Deputy Sheriff at the time. (*Archbold's Practice, by Chitty, 9th ed., p.* 568.) And a copy of the writ must be delivered to the defendant on making the arrest (*p.* 728). And when a *capias* has been irregularly issued, the person arrested under it cannot be detained in custody; nor even detained upon a *capias* afterwards regularly issued (*p.* 702).

[BELL, J.—Have you any authority for the proposition that arrest by telegraphic message is illegal?]

No. But, certainly, under our own Rule of Court, to act upon anything else than the warrant would land us in inextricable difficulties.

Cole, for plaintiff, showed cause, and referred to the return of the writ, which ran thus: " The defendant has been duly arrested on board the steamer *Natalian*, and placed in custody in the gaol of Port Elizabeth. Percy Vigors, High Sheriff, 7th March, 1868." The rule of the Court always has been not to go behind the Sheriff's return. If there has been an unlawful arrest, the party arrested has his remedy against the Sheriff. By Ordinance No. 37, 1828, the Sheriff is required to give the defendant, at his request and cost, a copy of the writ. The Deputy Sheriff is not recognized by the law at all. If the Sheriff therefore received the writ, and it was possible for him to arrest the party five minutes after at Port Elizabeth, he could do it. Under any circumstances, there was no request here by the defendant to the Deputy Sheriff for a copy of the writ. In the English practice, the writ is issued to the Deputy Sheriff, and not to the High Sheriff. The Deputy Sheriff then gives a copy to the bailiff who arrests, but keeps the original in his own office. The Deputy Sheriff here is analogous to the English bailiff; and, therefore, if the Sheriff had the writ in his possession, it was sufficient, and he could instruct an arrest by telegraph.

Porter in reply.—In *Nesbitt & Dickson vs. Richardson* (*Menz.* 562), the Sheriff returned a due arrest, but the Court heard affidavits to show the illegality of the arrest in respect to the *locus quo*, and then went behind the return. Among the papers here, is the receipt by the gaoler of Port Elizabeth for sustenance money, dated the 6th of February, showing, therefore, the real date of the arrest.

Their Lordships (HODGES, C.J., and BELL, J.) took time to consider. And later in the day it was announced to

1868.
March 17.
„ 19.

Silberbauer *vs.* Ruthven.

the parties, through their attorneys, that the arrest was held invalid; and an order was made for the defendant's discharge and the setting aside of all proceedings, which had got so far as setting down the plaintiff's declaration by default of appearance. It was understood that their Lordships having differed, CONNOR, J., was consulted in the interim, and had agreed with HODGES, C.J. (BELL, J. *dissentiente*), that the arrest should be set aside.

Postea, 19th March (CONNOR, J., on Circuit).
Porter applied for and obtained the costs of the motion to set aside the writ.

HODGES, C.J., then said: After the sitting in Chambers on Tuesday there was merely an intimation to the parties to set aside the arrest, but the case is an important one, and I should like now to state the grounds on which I founded my decision. If I had given a formal judgment I should have done it in these terms: I decide this case upon the single ground, namely, that the Rule of Court No. 14 shows that it was the duty of the Sheriff's deputy to be in a position at the time he made the arrest to give defendant, upon demand, a copy of the writ of attachment, by virtue of which the arrest was made. It is admitted that the Sheriff's deputy had not in his possession either the original writ or a copy of it, but it is not necessary to decide in this case whether it is essential that the original writ should have been in his possession at the time of the arrest. It would, I think, be a most dangerous thing to hold that a person is to take it for granted that another, who says he has a writ to arrest him, but who does not produce even a copy of the document, speaks truth.

BELL, J.—I should not have alluded to this matter had it passed *sub silentio*. As it is, however, I think it right to say that I cannot concur in the opinion just given. The terms of the Rule of Court make it necessary that if a person at the time of his arrest requires the production of a copy of the writ he shall be entitled to it, and if this defendant had made the application at the time, and the Sheriff could not have complied with it, I should have said at once that the arrest was bad. But it is one thing to say the arrest is bad when the debtor is refused what he is entitled to in law, and another thing to say that it is bad when he never applied for it. If there had been any words in the rule to the effect that the Sheriff should not presume to execute a writ without having the writ, or a copy of it, in his possession, that would have been another matter. I have not come to the conclusion that a Sheriff can always execute a writ without having a copy in his possession, but I am hardly disposed not to allow the public to avail themselves of the progress that has been made in science to facilitate the operations of the law. I would rather be inclined in many cases to allow the telegraph to be used for this purpose; observing cautiously, at the same time, that I would not give sanction to the notion that it should be always done, or that the service would be a good service if the party objected to it at the time of the arrest.

1868.
March 17.
„ 19.
Silberbauer vs. Ruthven.

Postea (later on the same day),
Porter again moved for an order restraining the plaintiff from re-arresting the defendant, who was still in custody, and whom it was intended to serve with a new writ of arrest.

Their Lordships granted the order: on the ground that, on inquiring carefully into the alleged cause of debt, they were not of opinion that the debt on which the arrest was sought was satisfactorily established.

[Plaintiff's Attorneys, *Berrangé & De Villiers.*]
[Defendant's Attorneys, *Fairbridge & Arderne.*]

GOWIE & CO., APPLICANTS; SMITH, RESPONDENT.

(In Camerâ.)

Trustee, Election of, confirmed.—Insolvent Ordinance, §§ 26, 39, 40.

Cole moved to set aside the election of the respondent as trustee in the insolvent estate of Thomas Beeton. The motion was opposed on several grounds, but the one on which the application was based was stated in the notice to be " That at the meeting held before Mr. Wolfe, Acting Magistrate of Graham's Town, for the election of a trustee, Smith was not elected by the greater part in number and value of the creditors present, but that his election was opposed by the greater amount in value, and that, in declaring him to be elected, the Acting Magistrate had exceeded his authority, and acted in violation of the 26th, 39th and 40th sections of the Insolvent Ordinance, or the spirit and intention thereof."

1868.
April 14.
Gowie & Co., Applicants; Smith, Respondent.

Porter opposed the motion.
It appeared that Mr. C. R. Gowie and Mr. F. Hall (then Secretary to the Union Fire and Marine Insurance Company of Graham's Town) were originally appointed joint trustees of the estate. Hall left the Colony, and the Eastern Districts Court, on being applied to under the 52nd section of the Insolvent Ordinance, removed him from the trust, and

1868.
April 14.

Gowie & Co., Applicants; Smith, Respondent.

ordered a new joint trustee to be elected in his stead ; Mr. Gowie to act as sole trustee in the interval. The proceedings for the new election took place on the 25th March. Mr. J. J. H. Stone, as attorney for Gowie & Co., proposed "That it is not desirable to appoint another trustee in the estate ; and that it remain under the sole administration of Mr. C. R. Gowie." Whereupon it was moved by Mr. Ayliff, as attorney for Mr. G. D. Hinds, and seconded by Mr. J. E. Wood, on behalf of Wood & Sons, that Mr. R. S. Smith (who had succeeded Hall as secretary in the Union Company) should be appointed trustee. This motion was merely stated in the minutes to have been "opposed" by Mr. Stone, but when put to the vote, eight creditors, representing £10,705 12s. 1d., voted for Smith, and one creditor, the applicants, for £12,432 10s. 3d., voted against it. The Acting Magistrate declared Smith duly elected in the room of Mr. Hall, subject to the decision of the Master of the Supreme Court.

The Court (HODGES, C.J., and BELL, J.) held that the Ordinance contemplated the nomination of a second candidate if the first candidate proposed was objected to ; and if the creditors who objected to Smith had brought forward a candidate of their own, so that there would have been a choice for the creditors between the two candidates, there would probably have been no election, because number and value did not concur. But under the circumstances of this case, the Eastern Districts Court having ordered the election of a new trustee, the parties who objected to Smith had missed their course altogether. Instead of contenting themselves with "opposing" an only candidate nominated, they should have proposed another candidate, and then there would have been no election. And their Lordships were not prepared to say whether in that case the Court would order the election of a new trustee to fill the place of one who had left the Colony, or died, or whether it might not have been considered sufficient to leave the estate in the hands of Mr. Gowie as sole trustee. That point had never been decided, and it need not be decided now. But at present, the majority which voted for a new trustee having voted for Smith, both in number and value, the Court would confirm his appointment.

Application refused accordingly, with costs.

[Applicant's Attorneys, *Reid & Nephew*.]
[Respondent's Attorney, *Van Zyl*.]

SMITH AND ANOTHER vs. PINTO.

(In Camerâ.)

Appeal.—Leave to appeal from a Magistrate's Judgment granted, after time for noting fixed by the Act had expired.

Bond, for defendant, moved for a rule *nisi* calling upon plaintiffs to show cause why the proceedings in the case heard before the Resident Magistrate of the Paarl should not be quashed.

1868. April 23.

Smith & Another, vs. Pinto.

The action was for £7 10s., the value of certain wood, cut by defendant on plaintiffs' land. The defendant had been first summoned to answer a criminal charge, but that was withdrawn, and the plaintiffs proceeded civilly. At the hearing on the 23rd March, the defendant excepted, that, as the Magistrate had given advice to the plaintiffs, and had also, before the trial, made enquiries from the defendant, he was incompetent to try the case. It did not specially appear from the record what became of the exception; but judgment was given for the plaintiffs with costs. The defendant then, it was alleged, mistaking his course, put in a protest, grounded on Ordinance 40, section 5, which is a criminal Ordinance, instead of, under the 33rd section of Act 20, 1856, entering an appeal on the next court day at furthest.

Bond submitted that it was incompetent for a Magistrate to decide on an exception taken to his own competency. (*Van Leeuwen, Cens. For. pt.* 2, *lib.* 1, *c.* 26, *par.* 5; *Brunnemanus ad Cod.* 3, 1, 16.)

But the Court inquired whether the defendant had a defence on the merits independent of the exception; and, being answered affirmatively, gave the defendant leave to appeal.

HODGES, C.J.—The proper way to proceed would be by appeal if there is a defence on the merits. The time has now gone by, according to the strict letter of the law, but we sometimes extend that. We will do so now, and give defendant a power of appeal, under the 33rd Section of Act 20, 1856.

[Applicants' Attorney, E. *Hull.*]

IN RE INSOLVENT ESTATE EDMUND ARCHER.

(In Camerâ.)

Trustee, Appointment of, confirmed.

Porter, on behalf of J. H. Parker and T. H. Jones, creditors in the abovementioned estate, moved for the

1868. April 128.

In Re Insolvent Estate Edmund Archer.

1868.
April 28.

In Re Insolvent Estate Edmund Archer.

appointment of Mr. W. Moir, of Queen's Town, in his capacity as Secretary to the Queen's Town Fire Insurance, Loan and Trust Company, as trustee in the estate.

It appeared that at the second meeting of creditors, on the 2nd March, Messrs. Moir and Croxford (the latter in his capacity as Secretary to the Graham's Town Fire and Marine Insurance Company) were proposed as trustees At the first meeting the following creditors had proved debts: J. H. Parker, £1,180; T. H. Jones, £815; D. Bradfield, £37 9s. 1d. Bradfield had given a power of attorney, dated 24th February, to Moir, to prove debts and vote in the choice of trustees. At the second meeting the following debts were proved: Eastern Province Guardian, Loan and Insurance Company, £582 5s. 10d.; Messrs. Blaine Brothers, £634 5s. 4d.; D. Bradfield, £30 11s. 8d. But Bradfield had then given a power of attorney, dated 2nd March, to Mr. R. Jefferson, to prove this second debt and vote in the choice of trustees. On proceeding to the choice of trustees, Parker, Jones and Moir (on the first power of Bradfield), the aggregate of their respective proofs of debt being £2,032 9s. 1d., voted for Moir. The Eastern Province Guardian, Loan and Insurance Company, Blaine Brothers, and Jefferson as the agent of Bradfield on the second power, the amount of whose proofs were £1,247 2s. 10d., voted for Croxford. The Magistrate did not accept the vote of either agent representing Bradfield, being doubtful which power entitled to the vote; and the votes then admitted being equal in number, no election followed.

Porter admitted that, with respect to the vote of Bradfield, that given for Croxford, being on the power latest in date, must prevail. Even then, however, although Croxford would have the greater number, he would not have the greater value, for the amounts would still stand £1,995 to £1,216 11s. 2d.: leaving a majority in favour of Moir. Mr. Croxford resided in Graham's Town, 140 miles from Queen's Town, where the assets of the estate are; so that, in this respect, Mr. Moir was the more desirable trustee.

Cole opposed the motion.

But the Court ordered the appointment of Mr. Moir, as prayed.

[Applicants' Attorney, *De Korte*.]
[Respondents' Attorney, *E. Hull*.]

DEARE & DIETZ, APPLICANTS ; HONEYBORNE, RESPONDENT.

Trustee, Election of, set aside.

Where the chief creditor in an Insolvent Estate compulsorily sequestrated, on his application, being resident at a considerable distance from the town at which the second meeting of creditors was to be held for the election of trustee, mistook the proper post by which to dispatch the power to prove debt and vote for himself as Sole Trustee, in consequence of which mistake the power arrived too late for the meeting, at which meeting the representative of the only other creditor entitled to vote had voted for himself as Sole Trustee and was elected accordingly, the Court, on the application of the chief creditor, relieved him from the consequence of his mistake by setting aside the election had, and ordering a fresh one to take place, giving, however, to the respondent to this application, the elected trustee, his costs of appearing to oppose the application.

1868.
May 15.

Deare & Dietz, Applicants ; Honeyborne, Respondent.

Porter moved to set aside the election of respondent (not yet confirmed by the Master) as trustee of the insolvent estate of Cornelis Korsten, of Willowmoore, in the division of Prince Albert, under the following circumstances :

Messrs. Deare & Dietz, last term (see Part 1, p. 17), obtained the compulsory sequestration of Korsten's estate. The second meeting of creditors was appointed to be held in the town of Prince Albert upon the 30th March last. Messrs. Deare & Dietz, who are merchants at Port Elizabeth, and were creditors for £3,847 9s. 8d. with costs (the claims of the other creditors being £108), were desirous that one of the firm partners, Mr. Henry B. Deare, should be appointed trustee. The firm had been in the habit of corresponding with the insolvent at the village of Willowmoore, and of forwarding their letters to him by the post which left Port Elizabeth on Fridays, at 4 o'clock, and passes up the Long Kloof, from a certain point of which it was then carried by a branch to Willowmoore. Under the belief that the post to Prince Albert from Port Elizabeth went by the same route, *vià* Long Kloof, Mr. H. B. Deare posted to the address of Mr. Z. J. Muller, an agent residing at Prince Albert, a proof of debt and power to vote for his (Mr. Deare's) appointment as sole trustee. The post from Port Elizabeth by the Long Kloof route closed at Port Elizabeth at 4 o'clock on the 20th March, and it was sworn that the letter was posted in Port Elizabeth before that hour. But the Post between Port Elizabeth and Prince Albert went in reality by a different route, through Beaufort West,

1868.
May 15.
Deare & Dietz, Applicants;
Honeyborne, Respondent.

and that post closed at 3 o'clock on the 20th March. In consequence of this mistake, the letter was delayed a week in the Port Elizabeth post office, and only reached Prince Albert on the 2nd April, and therefore too late for the meeting of the 30th March,

It further appeared that at the second meeting Mr. Z. J. Muller proved an open account debt due to himself for £23 3s. 6d, and the respondent, Mr. B. S. Honeyborne, proved, as the agent of Mr. G. Rex, a sum of £84 11s. 4d., being the balance of the purchase money of an erf, with interest. These were the only claims proved. Proceeding to the election of a trustee, Mr. Honeyborne, as the agent of Rex, being the only creditor over £30, voted for himself, and was declared elected. It was alleged in an affidavit of Mr. H. B. Deare, and not answered on the other side, that the claim of £84 filed by Rex was for the balance of the purchase price of certain landed property which had never been transferred, and that it was possible the trustee in Korsten's estate would find it desirable, for the benefit of the creditors, to abandon the purchase rather than pay the balance in order to obtain transfer, in which case it would be doubtful whether Rex would be a creditor at all. The concluding section of Mr. Deare's affidavit ran thus :—" And this deponent lastly says that he is desirous, on behalf of the said firm, to be himself appointed trustee of the said estate, in order to diminish, as far as possible, the very heavy loss sustained by his own firm, and that it would cause very great inconvenience and injustice to his said firm if, through a mistake in posting a letter, the management of the estate should be taken out of their hands and entrusted to the said B. S. Honeyborne, on the vote of one person who may, in all probability, not be entitled eventually to rank as a creditor at all, or for more than a very small amount."

For the respondent was produced the affidavit of Mr. Honeyborne, in which, *inter alia*, it was alleged that he believed it to be for the general benefit of the estate that the election should not be set aside, as he is a totally disinterested party, having no end to serve but the creditors' welfare. He has an extensive knowledge of the neighbourhood in which insolvent's business was carried on. He is also, comparatively speaking, on the spot, can personally superintend the management of the estate, and inquire into and examine the books and transactions of the insolvent, and can command many sources for obtaining valuable information regarding the said estate ; while Mr. H. B. Deare, should he be elected, will have the interest of the firm of which he is a partner uppermost, and would labour under a great disadvantage in conducting the administration of the estate through a local deputy, and would otherwise be obliged to encumber it with the expense of one or more journeys from Port Elizabeth to Willowmoore. "And this deponent lastly saith that he believes his said election to have been strictly in form, and that he conceives there are no legal grounds upon which the said applicants can come into this Honourable Court to have the same set aside."

1869.
May 15.
—
Deare & Dietz, Applicants;
Honeyborne, Respondent.

Porter, for applicants.—The facts disclosed in the affidavits amount to an accident over which applicants had no control. The equities of the case are altogether with them; and this is, therefore, a fitting instance for the exercise, by the Court, of that discretion which all Courts have over accident, and more especially of that equitable discretion which the Court would exercise in cases of insolvency.

Cole, for respondent.—Everything was done in proper form at the second meeting. The mere fact of applicants having posted a letter wrongly cannot now upset these proceedings. It was their own carelessness, or ignorance of postal arrangements, and not, therefore, an accident over which they had no control. There is nothing in the Insolvent Ordinance which justifies this application. Again, the respondent would have the advantage of being a local trustee, and there is no allegation in the applicants' affidavits that the respondent is an unfit person for the office. Applications of this nature may be made in very many cases if now allowed.

The Court held that the election should be set aside; the respondent being, however, allowed his costs of appearance to oppose this motion.

HODGES, C.J.—There has been a failure in holding such a meeting as the Ordinance contemplated for the election of trustees. The applicants undoubtedly intended to appear and vote in respect of the large debt for which they were creditors; and something very like an accident over which they had no control seems to have prevented them. Upon the whole, I think, if respondent is paid the costs of being brought here to oppose this motion, the Court should make an order setting aside the election, and declaring that another meeting should be held.

BELL, J.—I concur. It is said that applications of the same kind may be made in many cases. When those cases occur we will deal with them. It is true there is nothing in the Insolvent Ordinance which applies to the present case; but that Ordinance has not dealt, either, with other cases which might happen. If with any truth of language it could be said that the second meeting here was a meeting of creditors, probably the Court would refrain from meddling with the election; but it is absurd to say this meeting really was such a meeting. It does sometimes happen that credi-

1868.
May 15.

Deare & Dietz,
Applicants;
Honeyborne,
Respondent.

tors will not come to the meetings, and that then one person happening to be present votes for himself, and secures his election as trustee ; and to that there can, in such a case, be no objection if the creditors choose not to attend. But the meaning of the section was to give creditors an opportunity of voting ; and where there has been such a mistake as took place in this case, where nothing was imputable, as far as I can see, to the applicants, it would be applying rather strong language to say that there has been such a meeting of creditors as the Ordinance contemplated. I think the meeting has failed, and has not taken place ; and that the case is pretty much the same as that which happened the other day (*Re Archer, ante, p.* 105), where, the majority in value being on one side and the majority in number on the other, the Court ordered a new election.

CONNOR, J.—As the rest of the Court has so decided I am sure it must be the best conclusion at which to arrive ; but I doubt whether there is anything in the Ordinance which authorizes this application. The only imputation cast upon the election of Honeyborne is that he elected himself. But that was also the object which the other side wished to secure,—the election of themselves,—and the result of the order the Court will now make will probably be that the other side will elect themselves accordingly. But yet, as there has been, in truth, a mistake, or an oversight, perhaps the equity of the case will be met by a new election, if the respondent is paid his costs,—although I doubt how far the Ordinance authorizes such a decision.

BELL, J.—I do not wish it to be understood that I think the Ordinance expressly authorizes this decision. But I apprehend the Court should, in dealing with such cases, not specially embraced by the Legislature, give them such a construction as it is not unreasonable to suppose would have been given had the case suggested itself.

[Applicants' Attorney, *Van Zyl.*
Respondent's Attorneys, *Fairbridge & Arderne.*]

REED, APPELLANT ; DIVISIONAL COUNCIL OF PORT ELIZABETH, RESPONDENTS.

Public Roads Act.—Notices under Sections 38 *&* 39. *Onus probandi.*

Proof of the due issue of Notices required by the 38*th and* 39*th Sections of the Public Roads Act,* 9 *of* 1858, *does not rest upon the Council, in favour of whose proceedings the doctrine of* " omnia rite esse acta" *will prevail: it lies, therefore,* *upon Defendants maintaining the non-issue of such Notices, to prove the allegation, unless mala fides should primâ facie appear.*

This was an appeal from the judgment of the Resident Magistrate of Port Elizabeth, in a suit between the Divisional Council of Port Elizabeth, plaintiffs, and J. S. Reed, defendant, for the amount of the annual rate, duly assessed in terms of Act No 9, 1858, and Act No. 10, 1864, upon the immovable property of the defendant, for the year 1865.

1867.
Nov. 28.
1868.
May 15.
——
Reed, Appellant;
Divisional
Council of Port
Elizabeth,
Respondents.

By the 38th section of Act 9, 1858, a notice of thirty days to members of the Divisional Council is required to be given before the assessment of the rate, and the publication of a notice in the *Government Gazette* for a similar period, and in, at least, one of any newspapers published in the division. By the 39th section the Divisional Council is required to give thirty-one days' previous notice in the *Gazette*, or by posting notices, of the day upon which such rate is due, and of the amount of the rate.

The chief defence of the defendant in the Court below, and re-urged by him in appeal, was that no such notice had been given. There were other grounds of defence, but they were passed over by the Court. The respondents proved the giving of the notice required by the 39th section, but did not show the notice required by the 38th.

After hearing the arguments of *Cole* for applicant, and *Porter* for respondents, the question before the Court resolved itself into this: On whom rests the *onus probandi* the notice ?

Porter, for respondents, had maintained that in regard to the proceedings of a public body such as the Divisional Council of Port Elizabeth, the doctrine *"omnia rite esse acta præsumuntur"* should apply ; and that it was not the duty of the respondents, therefore, to prove such notice, but, on the contrary, it was the duty of the applicant clearly to establish that no such notice had been given, which he had not done.

Cole had maintained that the applicant was not bound to prove the negative, and that the Court had, in fact, adjourned the hearing of the case from the 28th November, when it was part heard, until to-day, with the special object of enabling the respondents still to prove all the notices. But, on this last point, he could produce no specific order of the Court to that effect.

The Court dismissed the appeal, with costs, on the ground relied upon for respondents, that " *omnia rite esse acta,*" &c.

HODGES, C.J.—This was an action brought to recover rates under sections 38 and 39, Act 9, 1858; and the answer

1867.
Nov. 28.
1868.
May 15.

Reed, Appellant;
Divisional
Council of Port
Elizabeth,
Respondents.

set up by the opposite party is, that it is incumbent upon the Divisional Council to show that the notice to the several members of Council was given, under section 38. Now it appears to me the rule " *omnia rite esse acta*" ought to operate in this case. No attempt had been made by the appellant to show that the members did not get the notice; and that a sufficient quorum really did appear is proved by the fact that the rate is in existence. The *Gazette* has been produced containing the notice, and evidence has been given of the publication of the notice in the local papers. But it, moreover, seems to me at all events open to great doubt whether the proviso at the end of section 39 does not apply to both the notices referred to in the 38th and 39th sections. That proviso declares : " Provided, further, that it shall not be necessary in any suit or proceedings for the recovery of such rate to prove anything further, as to due notice thereof having been given, than the publication of the announcement thereof in the *Government Gazette*." This proviso was no doubt inserted in the Act to prevent frivolous objections. If the appeal had been founded on the fact, either that no notice whatever was given, or that the rate had been levied at a packed meeting, these would be grounds for quashing the proceedings. But this has not been the ground of objection; and I take it that we must now presume that all that passed at the Council meeting in reference to this rate passed after due notice, unless the contrary could be shown by the appellant.

BELL, J.—The appellant suggests the possibility,—for it comes to no more,—that each member of Council may not have got the personal notice. If this objection were good in the mouth of the appellant, it might be so in the mouth of every one liable to pay the rate ; and what position would a Divisional Council be placed in then, if they were obliged to satisfy every ratepayer that they had complied with all the requisites of the Act ? Every year the Council would be involved in a host of difficulties. I take it that it is to be presumed, until the contrary is shown, that the officers of the Council have complied with the 38th section. And this is only subject to the observation that if any person liable to pay the rate can show *mala fides*, by want of personal notice to a certain number of Council members, with the view of prejudicing the public interest, such ratepayer would be entitled to relief. It is true the proviso of the 39th section, if read strictly, may be read as being confined to the 39th section only ; but yet it is perfectly capable of argument, from the reason of the thing, that it may be supposed to apply to both the 38th and 39th sections.

CONNOR, J.—The only difficulty in the way of presuming notice is, that if the notice has been given it must be lodged somewhere. The officers connected with the Divisional Council have been examined in this case in the Court below; but no one of them says the personal notice was really given. But with respect to the proviso to the 39th section I think it is, under all the circumstances of this case, a fair construction to put upon that proviso that it applies to both the 38th and 39th sections, and I accordingly prefer to base my judgment upon that ground than upon any presumption of notice.

1867.
Nov. 28.
1868.
May 15.

Recd, Appellant;
Divisional
Council of Port
Elizabeth,
Respondents.

[Appellant's Attorney, *E. Hull.*
Respondents' Attorney, *Van Zyl.*]

PREUSS & SELIGMANN, APPLICANTS; C. J. BOSMAN, RESPONDENT.

Trustee, Removal of, under Section 42, *Ordinance* 6, 1843.

This was a motion upon notice to the respondent to show cause why his election as trustee in the insolvent estate of Abraham Phillipus Faure, of Tulbagh, should not be set aside, and the respondent declared incapable of being again elected trustee, under the provisions of sections 41 and 42, on the grounds, amongst others: " 1. That the respondent had an interest in the estate opposed to the general interest of the creditors. 2. That from the nature of the respondent's claim as a creditor and the proof of debt, the said claim and proof of debt would have to be carefully investigated. 3. Because the respondent had contrived, or been privy to, a plan or arrangement by which debts or securities really belonging to one or more persons have been divided amongst a great number of persons, for the purpose, merely, of increasing the number of votes at the election of trustee, and thereby influencing the same. 4. Because the respondent promised and offered to certain of said creditors a pecuniary inducement, or other valuable consideration, in return for their votes, and for their influence in other estates in his favour as such trustee. And further to show cause why a fresh election of another trustee or trustees, in respondent's place, should not be directed to take place; with costs of this application against the respondent personally."

1868.
May 15.

Preuss & Seligmann,
Applicants;
C. J. Bosman,
Respondent.

The affidavits on both sides having been read, the first three objections raised fell away on argument. The fourth proved to be the only substantial objection in the case.

In support of this fourth objection, *De Villiers,* for applicants, read a passage from the affidavit of Mr. Edmund C. Durham, partner in the firm of Messrs. McIntyre and

I

1868.
May 15.

Preuss & Selig-
mann,
Applicants;
C. J. Bosman,
Respondent.

Durham, auctioneers and agents, of Ceres, who deposed "that the said Bosman attempted to obtain deponent's vote and the votes of other creditors whom he suppposed deponent could influence, by promising, in return for such votes, to give deponent's firm the sale of the said estate ; threatening, in case of refusal, to select some other person to be his auctioneer, as trustee of the estate."

Amongst the affidavits read by *Porter*, for the respondent, was that of the respondent, Bosman, who, in reference to the allegation contained in Durham's affidavit, so far from denying it, distinctly deposed " That shortly before the second meeting of creditors the deponent casually met the said Durham, in Cape Town, in the office of the Cape Commercial Bank, when the said Durham, in the presence of D. A. de Villiers, offered to join this deponent as co-trustee in said estate. That deponent refused to join him, but stated that if he, Durham, would give him his votes and those he held, deponent would agree to give his firm the sale. But that no other offer or bribe was held out by this deponent ; but the said Durham refused to give this deponent his vote ; nor did he at the second meeting vote for his deponent as such trustee, nor did any of his friends."

The Court, under the 42nd Section of Ordinance 6, 1843, set aside the election on the fourth ground stated in the notice of motion, without giving any opinion on the other parts of the case ; and gave costs against the respondent personally, as prayed; declaring him, further, to be incapable of being re-elected trustee in the said estate.

[Applicants' Attorneys, *Fairbridge & Arderne*,]
[Respondent's Attorney, *De Korte*.]

RYKIE vs. RYKIE.

Proof of Marriage in an Action for Restitution of Conjugal Rights.

1868.
May 17.

Rykie vs Ryke

In this case, which was an undefended action, at the instance of the husband, for restitution of conjugal rights, the plaintiff swore to his marriage with Christina Elizabeth Langenhoven, at Somerset West, before the Rev. Mr. Reitz, on the 17th January, 1860 ; and that they had lived together until the end of 1864, when the defendant deserted him, taking with her three children of the marriage.

De Villiers, quoad the marriage, produced from the Colonial Office a copy, certified by " L. Adamson, Chief

Clerk of the Colonial Office," of the "duplicate original register" of a marriage celebrated at Somerset West, on the 17th January, 1860, between a man named Petrus Andries Jacobus Rykie and a woman named Christina Elizabeth Langenhoven. He referred to section 21 of the Marriage Order in Council of 1839 (*vide Cape Statute Law p.* 453), which provides that every copy of the "duplicate original register," "certified under the hand of the Colonial Secretary to be a true copy, shall be good evidence of the facts therein recorded before all Courts and in all proceedings whatsoever in which it shall be necessary to give evidence of the marriage to which it shall relate."

The question was thrown out by the Court, whether the oath of the husband swearing to the marriage was sufficient to connect himself and wife with the marriage described in the register, so as to show that the parties named in the register were the parties to this suit,—inasmuch as although the register in question was made evidence by the Ordinance, proof *aliunde* was still required to identify the parties to the proceedings before the Court as the persons named in the register, and in this case the only such proof offered was the evidence of the husband. But the Court ultimately granted the decree, and made the order returnable upon the first day of next term, so as to allow the defendant to appear, if she chose, then to make any representations in the matter she might consider necessary.

[Plaintiff's Attorneys, *Berrange & De Villiers*.]

POCOCK, APPLICANT.—STOLL, RESPONDENT.

Arrest : personal, civil.

On the 12th September, 1866, the respondent (who had been the defendant in an action in which judgment had gone in his favour, with costs amounting to £35 1s. 1d.) obtained a decree of civil imprisonment against the applicant (the plaintiff in the action) for that amount. The warrant was issued upon the 14th September, and the arrest effected upon the 11th October.

Subsequently, applicant served upon the respondent notice of a motion calling upon him to show cause upon the 29th November, why the arrest "should not be declared illegal, having been made in a wrongful manner and on the premises of the applicant, and why the applicant shall not be entitled

1866.
Nov. 29.
1867.
Feb. 28.
1868.
June 4.

Pocock,
Applicant;
Stoll,
Respondent.

to be released and discharged from gaol, with costs of this application, or why the applicant shall not have such other relief as may seem meet."

On the 29th November (by consent of *Porter*, of counsel for applicant, and *Griffith*, *A.G.*, for respondent), the application was ordered to stand over *sine die*; it being further ordered, by consent, " that Pocock be liberated from imprisonment until the further hearing of the case, on his giving security to the extent of £50 to the satisfaction of the Resident Magistrate of George, to surrender himself in case the Court should, upon further argument, be of opinion that the arrest was legal." The application stood over accordingly, from time to time, until the 28th February, 1867, when

Porter, for applicant, read the affidavit of respondent, which set forth, that on the day of arrest he was standing in the back-yard of his own house, in York-street, George Town, at about two or three yards' distance, at the utmost, from his house, when he was arrested and conveyed to gaol. That the said back-yard was part and parcel of deponent's residence and premises then occupied by him. That it was surrounded with a strong spar fence, about four and a half feet high, and having a gate, closed with a movable chain, opening into deponent's said premises. That the back-yard is separated from the side-yard of the house by a small cross fence, and from the front or court-yard by another cross fence made of spars, nailed to uprights or posts. That while engaged in chopping wood in this back-yard, he was suddenly and violently sprung upon, without any document or paper being shown him, by one Johannes du Plessis, assisted by one Johannes Brittain, who had both obtained illegal and forcible access to deponent's premises and yard by coming from the street into the court-yard and then climbing over or forcing themselves through the cross fence. That then some paper was exhibited to him, and Du Plessis said, " You must come to Swemmer's."

There were also produced the affidavits of W. Jackson, Mary Ann Stevens, Mary Pocock, H. A. Pocock (this deponent spoke of the paper being held out by Du Plessis before the arrest), Ann E. Pocock, Elizabeth Allpass, Mary C. Partridge, Lucy Heine, and Mary C. Allpass.

For the respondent were produced the affidavits of Mr. J. P. Swemmer, son of the Deputy Sheriff, who swore to being present when the writ was handed to Du Plessis; of Du Plessis, who swore to being entrusted with a writ of arrest, with which he proceeded to applicant's, and, holding it in one hand, tapped him on the shoulder with the other, and arrested him in the usual form, and that he had subsequently shown the writ to one Fox, who came to the rescue of Pocock; of Johannes Brittain, in corroboration of Du Plessis; of Stephen Pressnell and C. J. Holtzkramp, and of Mr. F. A. Swemmer, Deputy Sheriff, who deposed to having entrusted the writ of arrest to Du Plessis, who, after arresting Pocock and returning to deponent's office, returned the writ in Pocock's presence. Certain plans, showing the positions, were also produced.

1866.
Nov. 20.
1867.
Feb. 28.
1868.
June 4.

Pocock,
Applicant;
Stoll,
Respondent.

Porter.—The arrest was illegal, as much so as if the parties arresting had broken open the door of Pocock's dwelling-house and dragged him out. In *Nesbitt & Dickson vs. Richardson* (*Menz.* 562) the arrest was declared illegal; and that was an *a fortiori* case, for a reference to the affidavits in that case (which affidavits and the records of the case itself are now in court) shows that there the arrest was at Richardson's garden-gate and twenty paces from his dwelling house. Secondly (as was maintained in Richardson's case), the arresting parties were legally unauthorized to make the arrest, not having been lawfully appointed deputies of Sheriff, and not having exhibited to the respondent their writ or authority. The writ only authorizes the Sheriff or his deputy; and the handing over of the writ to third parties is not lawful. A warrant must be exhibited by the Deputy Sheriff in serving. (*Blackstone* 1, 344. *Chitty*, 9th ed. 1566.)

Griffith, A.G., for respondent.—The case in *Menzies* only rules this: that, whether the arrest was legal or illegal, in the first place,—as to which the Court gave no judgment, —the Court would not make absolute a rule ordering execution on the person of Richardson within his dwelling-house. But how does that make out that the original arrest was legal? As to the second point *contra*, the warrant was sufficient if parol, and need not necessarily be in writing. It is the custom of the country for third parties, empowered by the Deputy Sheriffs, to arrest on parol warrants to themselves, provided they exhibit the writ at the time of arrest.

Cur. adv. vult.

Postea (June 4, 1868.)

Porter said he had been informed by the Attorney-General, who had been of counsel for Stoll in the argument, that he was not now further instructed; and he had also been informed by Messrs. Hofmeyr & Co., who had been the attorneys, that there would be no further appearance in the proceedings on behalf of Stoll. He would therefore ask for the costs of proceedings. He re-stated the facts of the case, and was about requoting the authorities, when he was asked by

[BELL, J.—Is there any necessity now for going into the merits of the arrest, or of the decision in *Nesbitt & Dickson vs Richardson*, as the respondent now makes no appearance?]

Porter, accordingly, made no reference to authorities beyond handing in a translation of a passage from *Peckius*, p. 199, for information hereafter, should a similar case occur.

The Court then made the following order:—" The respondent having failed to appear in pursuance of the notice duly served upon him, it is ordered that the application for costs incurred by the applicant be granted as prayed. The applicant being restricted from bringing any action against the respondent for false imprisonment, or otherwise."

HODGES, C.J.—It will be understood that this leaves the case in *Menzies* just where it was; and that the order the Court now makes cannot be cited as having approved, or not approved, of that decision, one way or the other.

BELL, J.—The decision in *Menzies* was very much doubted by my late Brother Watermeyer, J.; and the argument in this case stood over from time to time, to allow us an opportunity of again consulting with him. But his death prevented that; and as it was his strong opinion that the decision was not based upon the true principles of Roman-Dutch Law, I am anxious to save the case, so as to keep the point open for future discussion, if necessary.

[Plaintiff's Attorneys, *Hofmeyr, Tredgold & Watermeyer.*]
[Respondent's Attorneys, *Fairbridge & Arderne.*]

FLECK *vs.* MOLLER.

Medical Charges, Recovery of.

This was an undefended action for the recovery of £35, balance of account for medical attendance during the years 1866 and 1867.

De Villiers, for plaintiff, proved the usual notices of service, &c., and called

Dr. Fleck, who deposed to attendance during 1866, and charges during that period, amounting to £45, and to having sent in his account for " Medical Attendance during 1866," without specifying the items. In April, 1867, he received £30 on account from defendant, who promised the balance, but never paid it. During 1867 his charge for attendance was £20, and he sent in a similar account for that year. This latter amount the defendant also promised, but had failed to pay; and with the balance it made up the sum claimed. His charge was at the rate of five shillings a visit. He made that charge on the authority of a tariff drawn up by the Medical Board in 1830, and still unchanged.

1868.
June 2.
Fleck *vs.* Moller

HODGES, C.J., asked under what authority the plaintiff, being a medical man, sued for his fees?

De Villiers referred to the 5th section of Act No. 6, 1861, which recognized the right to do so by establishing a prescription of three years for the action.

The Court gave judgment for the plaintiff, with costs.

HODGES, C.J., observed that the Court would have been better satisfied if the plaintiff had sent a specified account, although it might not be that the plaintiff was bound to furnish such account unless applied for by the defendant. The law of the Colony as to entitling a medical man to recover was clearly different from the law of England.

BELL, J., concurred. Independently of what was the distinctive law here, perhaps the plaintiff would have been even successful in an action in England, seeing that there was a positive promise to pay the two accounts, and he could therefore have recovered on that contract. But he concurred also in the opinion that it was desirable that patients should be furnished with specified accounts, so that they might have fair opportunities of objecting. If such an account had been demanded in this case, and not furnished, he would not have been inclined to give the present judgment.

CONNOR, J., concurred; and judgment went accordingly.

[Plaintiff's Attorneys, *Redelinghuys & Wessels*]

[*Et vide Drew vs. Executors of Wolfe*, decided by the Supreme Court on the 16th February, 1858. In that case the Court (BELL, Acting C.J., CLOETE, J., and WATERMEYER, J.) decided that a medical man's action to recover charges is prescribed in two years, calculating up to the commencement of the suit. This decision was founded upon the Placaat of C.V. of 1540, which the Court decided is not, as to medical men, in disuse. And it was the rule laid down by this decision which was subsequently extended in the enactment of Act 6, 1861.]

VIGORS vs. CAMPBELL.

Injuria literalis: what constitutes.

Evidence.

1868.
June 9.
„ 10.

Vigors vs.
Campbell.

This was an action brought by the plaintiff, the Sheriff of the Colony, against the defendant, Dr. Campbell, of Uitenhage, formerly a Deputy Sheriff for that division, for £1,000 damages for the publication in the *Port Elizabeth Herald* newspaper, of the 28th February, 1868, of the following letter, alleged by plaintiff to be a false, scandalous, malicious and defamatory libel:

" THE HIGH SHERIFF AND HIS DEPUTY AT UITENHAGE.

" Uitenhage, Feb. 26, 1868.
" To the Editor of the *E. P. Herald.*

" SIR,—You may suppose that for some time past the relations between the High Sheriff and myself have not been very cordial. You know all the circumstances attending the appointment of Mr. Knight to Alexandria. That was the first open attempt to force me to resign. As that had only the effect of drawing from me an indignant letter and charges of untruthfulness on his part, he next called on me to answer an asserted extract from a letter which bore no signature, and which contained the grossest falsehoods. This I treated as it deserved, but at last the indignant contempt which I heaped on him made him wince and dismiss me. I shall not trouble you with the extract referred to, or any portion of the correspondence which ensued, as it will all be published; but Mr. Vigors knew at the time that he wrote that inquisitorial letter, and demanded an immediate reply, that that reply, or the documents in support of it, could not reach him in time to prevent the course he has taken, and which, despite all his valueless assertions, he intended from the first to take. He wished to intimidate me, and he failed. I ever talked publicly of my impending dismissal—taking care to make known the causes. He brought charges against me on an anonymous malignant fasehood, or, worse still, on a malignant falsehood, the author of which he knew, but dared not avow. I vindicated my own independence, and challenged him to give up the name of his authority. My demand was met by silence; whilst he aggravated his conduct by further persistent evasions. Mr. Vigors used a falsehood for his own purposes; he endorsed it and made it his own, and became liable for the consequences. He denied most earnestly having any connexions with persons here, yet his last letters prove incontestibly that he has employed a system of espionage, which, to the lasting disgrace of the Government, has come into vogue since the departure of that true gentleman, Sir George Grey; and Mr. Vigors culminated his disgraceful and underhand proceedings by daring to accuse me of want of veracity—an accusation which, so well am I known, merely recoils on himself.

" After such treatment, could you believe, sir, that during my two years' term of office I could only get my money from him by repeated applications, and at last by threatening to sue him ? He borrowed £109 from me, kept it for a year, and on returning it at last, doubted whether I could claim interest. He still owes me a considerable sum of money. Is it any matter of surprise that those of his deputies who have no private means, get into difficulties ?

" Parliament has shown a strong disposition to do away with this absurd official, and, as anything that throws light on the working of a public department is of use, I claim the insertion of this letter.

"Yours, &c.,

"AMB. GEO. CAMPBELL."

The innendoes drawn in plaintiff's declaration were as follows : " Meaning and intending thereby that the said plaintiff, as such High Sheriff, has conducted the business of his said office in a disgraceful and underhand manner, by making use of false charges, knowing them to be false, for the purpose of dismissing the said defendant from his office of Deputy Sheriff, and by carrying on a disgraceful system of espionage over his deputies. And also, that during the two years in which the said defendant held the office of Deputy Sheriff of Uitenhage, he, the said plaintiff, as such High Sheriff, wrongfully, and in violation of his duty and obligations, retained and withheld, for his own uses, certain lawful fees and expenses in his possession, then due and payable to the said defendant as such Deputy Sheriff, and afterwards had only paid the same under threat of legal proceedings to be instituted against him by the said defendant. And also, that he, the said plaintiff, as such High Sheriff, had improperly borrowed for his own uses the sum of one hundred and nine pounds sterling from the said defendant and wrongfully detained it from him for a year. And also, that he, the plaintiff, as such High Sheriff, is still lawfully indebted to the said defendant in considerable sums of money, in fees and disbursements, which he, the said High Sheriff, wrong-

1868.
June 9.
" 10.
Vigors vs.
Campbell.

fully and unlawfully detains from him, the said defendant. And also, that the plaintiff, as such High Sheriff, is in the habit of improperly and wrongfully withholding, for his own uses, from his deputies, fees and disbursements lawfully due to them, and of improperly borrowing from such deputies various sums of moneys, and wrongfully detaining them, whereby it is no matter of surprise that one or more of his deputies who have no private means have got into difficulties. And, generally, that the said plaintiff, as such High Sheriff, has conducted himself in an arbitrary, inquisitorial and disgraceful manner towards the said defendant, and other Deputy Sheriffs. By means of the committing of which said grievances by the said defendant, the said plaintiff hath been and is greatly injured in his good name, credit and reputation, as such High Sheriff and otherwise, and brought into public scandal, infamy and disgrace."

The defendant pleaded the general issue, and then the following special pleas :

" And for a further plea to so much of the said supposed libel as regards the printing and publishing, or causing to be printed and published, of the certain words following, that is to say, ' after such treatment, could you believe, sir, that during my two years' term of office, I could only get my money from him by repeated applications, and at last by threatening to sue him,' the defendant says (in case the plea first pleaded should be adjudged insufficient for the defence of this action, but not otherwise), that he, the defendant, was, as Deputy Sheriff of Uitenhage, entitled to certain fees for his work and labour, which were payable to him through the said plaintiff, as Sheriff of the Colony, and that he, the said defendant, was at all times, during his term of office as such Deputy Sheriff, compelled to make repeated applications to the said plaintiff for the payment of the said fees, by reason that, by or through the want, on the part of the said plaintiff, of due and proper care and attention on the part of the said plaintiff, a time much longer than was reasonable or necessary was by the said plaintiff allowed to elapse before obtaining for and paying over to the said defendant his said fees ; and, in particular, the said defendant says that certain fees due to him in his aforesaid capacity from the Colonial Government, amounting to £98 6s., and which should and might, but for the default and neglect of the plaintiff, have been paid to the defendant in or about the month of October, 1866, were not paid to him until June, 1867, or thereabouts, and that the delay in making such payment was caused by the neglect and default of the said plaintiff in his office of Sheriff; and further certain other fees also due to the said defendant from the said Colonial Government, and amounting to £73 1s. 6d., and which should and might, but for the default and neglect aforesaid, have been paid to the defendant in or about the month of February, 1867, were not paid to him until the middle of the month of April, 1867, and that the delay in payment was caused by the same neglect and default of the said plaintiff as aforesaid.

" And the said defendant further saith, that he did, to wit, on the 17th January, 1868, give the said plaintiff notice that he, the said defendant, would be compelled to sue him for the recovery of his said fees then due and unpaid. Wherefore the said defendant says that he printed and published, and caused to be so printed and published, the certain words in the introductory part of this plea mentioned, as he lawfully might, for the cause aforesaid; and this he is ready to verify; wherefore he prays judgment if the said plaintiff should have or maintain his action against the said defendant for or in regard to the words in the introductory part of this plea mentioned.

" And for a further plea as to so much of the said supposed libel as regards the printing and publishing, or causing to be printed and published, the certain words following, that is to say : ' He borrowed £109 from me, kept it for a year, and on returning it at last, doubted whether I could claim interest,' the said defendant says (in case the plea first pleaded shall be adjudged insufficient for the defence of this action, but not otherwise), that next before the time at which the said defendant was appointed such Deputy Sheriff as aforesaid, one Herbert Longlands filled the office of such Deputy Sheriff, for whom the said defendant was as surety, bound to make good to the said plaintiff all moneys lawfully payable to or claimable by the said plaintiff, as Sheriff, for or on account of any levies made by the said Herbert Longlands as such Deputy Sheriff.

" And the said defendant further saith, that the said plaintiff did on the 18th of January, 1866, represent to the said defendant that he, the said plaintiff, would, as Sheriff, be called upon on the 1st of February, 1866, to pay two certain sums amounting together to £109, to certain persons for whom, or on whose behalf, the said Herbert Longlands had, as Deputy Sheriff, levied and made the said sums respectively, and requesting the said defendant to forward to the said plaintiff the said sum of £109, in order to enable him to pay the two certain sums aforesaid.

" And the said defendant says, that, believing such representations of the plaintiff to be true, he did, in or about the month of January, 1866, send such sum of £109 to the plaintiff; but the defendant says that he has since, and before the publication of the said supposed libel, discovered,

1868.
June 9.
" 10.

Vigors v.
Campbell.

as the fact is, that at the time the plaintiff made the aforesaid representations, and the defendant remitted the said sum, the plaintiff had in his hands, or should and might have had, but for his own default and neglect, fees due to the said Herbert Longlands as such Deputy Sheriff, to an amount more than sufficient to cover the two certain sums aforesaid, and any sum or sums which the plaintiff might or could have been called upon to pay in respect of any levies made by the said Herbert Longlands.

" And the defendant further says that no part of the said sum of £109, so sent by the defendant to the plaintiff upon the representation aforesaid ever was, in fact, paid or applied by the plaintiff in or towards the payment of the said levies, or in or towards payment of any other moneys due from or on account of the said Herbert Longlands in his said capacity of Deputy Sheriff ; but the defendant says that the said plaintiff kept and retained the said sum of £109 in his hands until the month of December, 1866, when he returned the same to. the defendant ; but the plaintiff refused, and still refuses, to pay any interest for the time during which the said sum so remained in his hands.

"And the said defendant submits to this Honourable Court, that the obtaining by the said plaintiff from the said defendant the sum of £109 aforesaid was, under the circumstances aforesaid, a transaction which the said defendant was warranted in treating as a loan ; wherefore the said defendant says that he printed and published, and caused to be printed and published, the certain words in the introductory part of this plea mentioned, as he lawfully might for the cause aforesaid, and this he is ready to verify ; wherefore he prays judgment if the said plaintiff should have or maintain his action against the said defendant for or in regard to the words in the introductory part of this plea mentioned ; and he prays judgment against the plaintiff for his costs of suit."

The plaintiff, by way of replication, excepted to the defendant's pleas, on the ground that they were not an answer to the whole libel as set forth in the declaration, but only to parts thereof, and therefore insufficient ; to which replication the defendant's rejoinder was the general issue.

As to the exception in plaintiff's replication which *Griffith, A.G.* (with him *Bond*), for plaintiff, proposed to withdraw, being desirous the case should go on the merits, *Porter*, for defendant (with him *Cole*), asked that the exception should be formally overruled, inasmuch as although the general issue in defendant's plea embraced the whole alleged libel, it was competent for the defendant, where the libel set forth contained a number of allegations, to select any one or more of them, and plead to them specially as divisible parts. (*Clarkson vs. Lawson*, 6 Bing., p. 66.)

Exceptions overruled accordingly; *Griffith* not supporting them.

Porter having then admitted publication,

Griffith called the Hon. R. Southey, Colonial Secretary, who deposed to having read the letter in the *Herald*. He did not believe it.

Cross-examined. I know the defendant very well indeed. I remember his writing to me, on the 8th April, 1867. I sent a reply, in my own handwriting, dated the 15th April, 1867. (Produced.) My son is a Deputy Sheriff.

Porter proposed to found upon the letter this question: Have you not written to the defendant that your son and other Deputy Sheriffs of the Colony have frequently complained to you, as Colonial Secretary, of the delays they experienced in getting money due to them from the Sheriff's Department? He maintained that as amongst the plaintiff's inuendoes was the following: " And also that the plaintiff is in the habit of improperly and wrongfully withholding for his own use, from his Deputies, fees and disbursements lawfully due to them, and of improperly borrowing from such Deputies various sums of money," &c.,—it was evidence to the issue raised by that inuendo to ask this question, and in mitigation of damages.

Griffith objected, and cited *Underwood vs. Parkes*, Str. 1,200, quoted in 2 *Starkie on Libel*, p. 87, note. And one Deputy Sheriff's statement that the Sheriff had done wrong, not only was no evidence, but, even if it were, was no justification for another Deputy Sheriff making a libellous charge against the Sheriff.

The Court (HODGES, C.J., *dissentiente*) ruled that the question could not be put.

W. H. Sherman was next called by plaintiff. He deposed that he was a merchant in Cape Town, and had lately been to Port Elizabeth, where he had heard the subject of the libel publicly discussed.

Griffith proposed to ask: As far as you can gather, what was the general impression in Port Elizabeth from these discussions?

Objected to; and question disallowed.

The correspondence in the case having been put in and read,

Porter supported his plea of justification by reading extracts from these letters.

1868.
June 9.
„ 10.

Vigors *vs.*
Campbell.

Griffith called the plaintiff to disprove the charges made.

Postea (June 10), after hearing counsel, the Court unanimously held that the defendant's pleas of justification had completely failed on evidence; and gave judgment for plaintiff for £100 and costs. BELL, J., was disposed to have given heavier damages; but HODGES, C.J., thought the defendant had acted under a certain amount of provocation; and CONNOR, J., thought that, in estimating damages, regard should be had to the character of the libel, and that lesser damages were sufficient in the present case, where the libel consisted of mere abuse, and would, with sensible people, convict itself; as it did not state facts in support of its abusive assertions.

[Plaintiff's Attorneys, *Fairbridge & Arderne.*]
[Defendant's Attorneys, *Reid & Nephew.*]

UITENHAGE DIVISIONAL COUNCIL *vs.* J. S. REED.

Ferry : right of.—Pleading : Non-joinder.

1868.
May 28.
„ 29.
June 19.

Uitenhage
Divisional
Council *vs.*
J. S. Reed.

This was an action to recover £750 "for rent or hire, moneys or compensation, for use and occupation and receipt of tolls," at the Sunday's River Ferry, situated upon the main road from Port Elizabeth to Graham's Town, and within the division of Uitenhage, reckoned from the 1st January, 1865, to the 30th June, 1867, at the rate of £300 per annum, or otherwise an order upon defendant to account with plaintiffs.

It appeared from the evidence that in 1850 the Central Board of Commissioners of Public Roads invited tenders for the right to ferry over the Sunday's River at a particular part, and that the tender of Messrs. John Capper & Co. was accepted for five years, at £75 a year, and a pont, constructed by the firm at its own expense, placed upon the river. At the time of the tender the road and the approaches to the pont were in a bad condition, requiring heavy repairs. These were executed by Messrs Capper & Co., who then represented to the Road Board the expense they were thus put to, and succeeded in, from time to time, obtaining a remission of the rental, until the road should be open for public traffic. In 1858 it was reported to the Board that the road was then in such condition that it could be opened for public traffic, and Capper & Co. were called upon to execute a lease. But although a draft lease was sent to the local road superintendent, Mr. White, and a copy of it was now produced, from among Capper's papers, it was never executed. And from that time to his death, in 1861, Capper paid no rent, his plea being the non-performance by the Road Board and its successors of certain stipulated conditions; nor were any steps taken to enforce payment. Subsequently, in 1861, his executors sold at a public sale to the defendant, certain extensive buildings on the land adjoining the Sunday's River, together with the pont over the river, and the right to tolls, for £4,375, on conditions of sale, which were headed "Conditions of sale of the Sunday's River Ferry, with its land and houses, together with right to lease from Government;" the fifth condition being:' "The property is sold according to title and diagram of the land: to the papers appertaining to the right of lease, and the pont as she now lays in the stream, with her appurtenances." Defendant entered into possession accordingly, but from time to time also declined executing a lease. By Act 23, 1858, schedule A, No. 8, the road from Port Elizabeth to Graham's Town, *via* Sunday's River Ferry, was declared a main road; and schedule B, No. 3, fixed the tariff of fees at the ferry. From and after 1st January, 1859, the Central Road Board was abolished (by Act 9, 1858), and the main roads were placed under the management of a Chief Commissioner and assistance, until by Act 10, 1864, the divisional councils were charged with the maintenance of the main roads of the Colony. On the 16th January, 1865, defendant sublet the ferry to his three sons, for five years, at £500 a year. From 1861 to 1865, defendant had paid no rent, nor had either he or his lessees from 1865 down to the present date.

In the course of the evidence it became apparent that the pont or ferry-boat was not entirely in the division of Uitenhage, but plied between it and the division of Alexandria. Whereupon

Cole (with him *De Villiers*), for defendant, drew the attention of the Court to this fact, and maintained that the plaintiffs had no right to bring this action. If there was a right of action at all, it lies in the divisions of Uitenhage and Alexandria together, by virtue of section 4 of Act 10, 1864. There was, therefore, a non-joinder of co-plaintiff, and he prayed a non-suit, or absolution from the instance. As to the right to claim a non-suit on the general issue pleaded by defendant in this case, he cited *Chitty's Precedents in Pleading*, p. 359, ed. 1836; *Saunders on Pleading*, 2nd ed. vol. 1, p. 10.

Griffith, A.G. (with him *Porter*), for plaintiffs,—admitting that, on the evidence, the Alexandria Divisional

1868.
May 28.
,, 29.
June 19.

Uitenhage Divisional Council vs. J. S. Reed.

Council would, under the Act of 1864, be entitled to half the tolls collected,—maintained that the present action was not one *ex contractu*, but an action *ex delicto*, founded on defendant's tortious occupation; and that, therefore, as against him as a a trespasser, it was sufficient for the Uitenhage Council to sue, accounting thereafter with the Alexandria Council for whatever share might be due to that body.

The Court, after consultation, determined upon hearing the whole case before deciding the point of pleading now raised. The evidence taken *de bene esse* at Uitenhage was accordingly read, and the defendant orally examined.

Postea (May 29).

Griffith, A.G. (with him *Porter*) again maintained, as to the alleged non-joinder, that the foundation of the action was a tort; and that therefore either Council could bring the action. (*Chitty's Pleading*, ed. 1847, by *Pearson*, p. 229, citing *Broadbent vs. Ledward*, 11 *Adolphus and Ellis*, p. 209.) Proceeding to the merits of the case, by section 12, Ordinance 8, 1843, the power was given to the Central Board to erect certain "toll-bars and gates" upon main roads, subject to the sanction of Government. And by section 14 it was provided that toll-gates thus established should be announced by proclamation. Upon the 21st June, 1854, a proclamation was issued, reciting these sections and fixing a tariff. Then, under the Act 23 of 1858, schedule B, No. 3, the "ferry" at Sunday's River is expressly recognized. And even if it be contended *contra* that from 1854 to 1858 there was no legal ferry, it is clear by the legislative recognition that after the Act of 1858 there was. Now, upon any part of a river which is a portion of a public road, and at which there is a regular ferry or toll established, no person can establish himself, whether with his own property or not, and take tolls and ferries. The bed of the river is the continuation of the main road, if the river dried up to-morrow, and is therefore public property. As to the rights of the *fiscus* to the *ripatica*, *Voet*, 49, 14, 3. Then it will be argued *contra* that, according to correspondence between Capper and the Road Board, no rent was to be paid until certain things had been done by the Road Board in the way of constructing permanent approaches to the pont and getting a supply of water. But all that Capper meant was, that the road should be sufficiently open for traffic before rent became payable, and it was declared open in 1858. And under any circumstances, these things to be done were not "conditions precedent" to the demand for rent, but matter of cross-action or set-off.

Reed stands in Capper's shoes completely, and, at the very least, is liable for the £75 a year Capper agreed to pay; but, from the evidence in this case, and taking into consideration the large returns defendant has enjoyed, £300 a year is the proper sum to award.

1868.
May 26.
„ 29.
June 19.

Uitenhage Divisional Council vs J. S. Reed.

Cole, in reply, re-cited the authorities he quoted yesterday as to non-joinder. Capper was not in tortious possession; for there was between him and the Road Board a verbal contract for a lease, and non-payment of rent cannot constitute a tort, and Reed stands in Capper's shoes in this respect. Secondly, no ferry toll was ever legally established by competent authority at Sunday's River. In Ordinance 8, 1843, section 12, there is not a word about "ferries," but only about "toll-bars or gates;" and there being no lawfully constituted ferry, it is open to defendant to take passengers across the river in his private pont, just as much as he could, if he chose, drive passengers through the river in his cart. The Proclamation of 1854 was *ultra vires* the Ordinance 8, 1843, on which it was based; and the mere recital in the Act 23, 1858, of an existing ferry does not legalize that ferry. Defendant has not exacted "tolls," but ferries. Thirdly, on the evidence it is shown that neither the Road Board nor those who succeeded it fulfilled their part of the contract with Capper as to making permanent approaches nor supplying water, and therefore could not now claim rent. And under any circumstances £75 a year is the utmost defendant could be called upon to pay.

Cur. adv. vult.

Postea (June 19),

The Court gave judgment for plaintiffs, for £187 1Cs., with costs.

HODGES, C.J., after re-stating the facts of the case, and tracing the various changes in the constitution of the body to whom was confided the charge of the main roads of the Colony, and the obligation of collecting the tolls, next observed, on the question of pleading set up by defendant as a ground of non-suit, as follows: " Defendant says it has been satisfactorily proved that the Sunday's River is the boundary between the divisions of Uitenhage and Alexandria; and that the Divisional Council of Alexandria ought to have been co-plaintiffs in this action. There appear to me to be two answers to this objection; first, the objection should have been taken by a plea in abatement, which would have given the plaintiffs notice of the objection. It ought not in justice, I think, to be allowed under the plea of the general issue.

K

1868.
May 28.
„ 29.
June 19.

Uitenhage
Divisional
Council vs.
J. S. Reed.

Authorities were cited from the English decisions to show that such a defence is ground of non-suit, but these are cases in *assumpsit* where mutual promises are alleged, and an allegation that a promise was made to A, when the proof offered was that it was made to A and B, is obviously a good ground for non-suit; and thus in *Snelgrave vs. Hunt* in *Starkie's Cases*, 2, 424, it was held that a defendant might object that there is another assignee of the bankrupt still living, who ought to have joined; but Mr. *Starkie*, in citing this case in his *Treatise on the Law of Evidence*, appends the following remark: ' Note that the action was in *assumpsit*.' (2 *Starkie on Evidence*, 174, 3*rd edition*.) He thereby implies that if the action had been in case, and not in *assumpsit*, the defendant could not have claimed a non-suit. The form of pleading in this Court does not raise the technical objection which prevails under the English system, and as it is against equity to allow such objections to prevail, they ought not to be encouraged. Irrespective of this point, I should have been inclined to hold that we may well presume in this case that the Divisional Council of Alexandria have (if they indeed have any interest in the tolls, about which I say nothing) allowed the plaintiffs in this case to let or farm these tolls, pursuant to the last proviso in the 4th section, and that impliedly gives the power to recover them from any one who has received them. This presumption, in the absence of any proof to the contrary, is, I think, justified by the evidence adduced, that the Divisional Council of Uitenhage proclaimed the tariff of the tolls in the *Gazette*, and that Mr. Tennant, their attorney, demanded them from the defendant before this action was brought." With respect to the second point urged for defendant, viz., that no tolls were established at the ferry by any competent authority, the wording of the Act 23, 1858, schedule A, section 7, and schedule B, No. 3, where the Sunday's River " ferry " is specially named, sufficiently answers that objection. On the third point, that the terms upon which Capper was to obtain a lease had never been carried out by the intended lessor, and that various things promised to be done had never been performed, there was no evidence to support the statement; the parties entitled to the tolls could at any time have compelled Capper or his assignee to come to a reckoning for the tolls received by them, although this had, from evident carelessness and indifference of the authorities, never been done. And as to the fourth point, that the defendant, if held liable at all, was only liable for £75, his Lordship remarked as follows : " It is contended for the plaintiffs that the Court should award at least the sum of £300 per annum, or the alternative prayer is that an account should be taken of receipts and disbursements, and that, making all just allowances to the defendant, he should be compelled to pay over the balance of the earnings at the ferry. I find no satisfactory evidence that the profits have amounted to £300 per annum. It was incumbent on the plaintiffs to prove the affirmative, and it is to be observed that the taking of an account over so long a period will be attended with very serious expenses, all of which will probably fall on the defendant. I am therefore of opinion, under the peculiar circumstances of this case, that plaintiffs' damages should be assessed at £75 per annum, being the sum which Capper would have paid if he had accepted the offer made to him by the Road Board, by Mr. De Smidt's letter of the 21st February, 1857. In that case, his lease would have expired on the 1st March, 1862; and as the defendant purchased of Capper's executors, in 1861, he would have been entitled to hold the ferry at a rent of £75 for a short period. There is a class of cases well known which is somewhat analogous to this. It has been often decided that if a person holds over a property after a lease is expired, and nothing is said on either side, he will be held to be liable to all the counts, whether usual or special, which are contained in the expired lease. Here all parties have been to blame. The authorities neglected to enforce their rights against Capper and the defendant, and the defendant, who in his own language stood in Capper's shoes, evaded, by every possible excuse and expedient, the payment of rent. But upon the whole case, I think it will be quite sufficient to require the defendant to pay the costs of this action, and the bygone rent at the rate of £75 per annum."

BELL, J., with reference to the objection of non-joinder, remarked: " If I were compelled to give effect to this exception of non-joinder, taken at the eleventh hour, I must have done so with great reluctance, because it was known by the defendant from the very outset of the proceedings. When the exception was first opened, I suggested whether it might not be convenient to stay proceedings until the Council of Alexandria had had an opportunity of intervening; because if our judgment should prove to be in favour of the defendant, it would be *res inter alios acta*, and could not bind the Council of Alexandria; and so also, if the judgment should be against the defendant for payment of a specific sum, that likewise would be *res inter alios*, and could not bind the Alexandria Council. In this I was overruled, and the argument proceeded; but, in the view I take of the case, no inconvenience need arise from the course which was adopted. Indeed, I was much inclined to overrule the exception upon this ground, that inasmuch as the Council of Uitenhage is undoubtedly entitled to protect the right of ferry against all intruders, it may be presumed to be acting with the authority of the Alexandria Council, to whom, from the public advertisements by the Uitenhage Council, the proceedings of that Council must be known. The action has not, in the legal language of this Court, any particular appellation. In form, it is an action for the payment of a sum of money for the use and occupation of the ferry; but, in substance and effect, it is an action to try the right to the ferry, and that right being, in my opinion, established conclusively to be in the plaintiffs, no inconvenience can arise from the absence of the Alexandria Council, if my opinion shall come to be the opinion of the Court; because the right to the ferry, being established to be in the two Divisional Councils, the Alexandria Council may still be allowed to intervene as co-plaintiffs in taking the account of what is to be paid by the defendant in respect of tolls taken by him at a ferry to which he had no right in law. As to the defendant's second ground of defence, the denial of the existence of any public ferry by law established, although in the proclamation of the 21st June, 1854, the word 'ferry' might not have expressly been mentioned, the object of a ferry was then undoubtedly established. A public road is brought to the edge of a deep flowing river, and a pont is provided for the transport of the traffic from one side of the river to the other, and rates of toll are by the authority of Government proclaimed to be payable for the passage of the river—the first item of the schedule of tolls is 'for every vehicle *crossing* either before or after sunset,' and the seventh and last item is thus worded: ' The above charges shall be double *if the ponts* are required *between sunset and sunrise*.' It is impossible, therefore, to doubt that the toll to be levied was in respect of the passage of the river. There was, therefore, the fact of a ferry being created, and of a schedule of ferry tolls demandable. This would seem to be enough to dispose of the defendant's objection that no ferry had ever been legally created, but an Act, No. 23 of the year 1858, puts this further beyond any possible doubt. The eighth section of schedule 8 of that Act specifies ' the road leading along the flat to Sunday River *Ferry* ' as being one of the main roads of the Colony, for the purposes of that Act. The second section of the Act declared ' that the toll-bars mentioned in schedule B are hereby established, and such persons respectively as shall be authorized by the Governor shall be entitled to demand at every such toll-bar the several tolls which, by the said schedules, are set forth ;' and the third section of the schedule is thus expressed : ' Rates payable at *ferries* on the Swartkops, Sunday, and Breede Rivers, viz., the rates now payable at such ferries respectively.' The expression 'ferries,' with reference to the

Sunday's River, is repeated in the Act No. 3 of 1859, which corrected a mistake in the Act 23 of 1858, in respect of rates 'payable at ferries at Zwartkops, Sunday, and Breede Rivers.' What would constitute a ferry having been established by public legal authority, without the designation of ferry having been at first given to it, we now have the designation given by the same authority ; there is an end, therefore, of the pretence set up by the defendant, that no legal ferry was ever established. As to the third ground of defence, that there could be no right to the compensation claimed by plaintiffs until certain things had been by them performed, whatever contract might have been entered into between the former road authorities and Capper the present plaintiffs have nothing to do with that, seeing that Act 10 of 1864 gives the Uitenhage and Alexandria Council an absolute, indefeasible, statutory right to this ferry and its tolls, which had previously, by law, been in the Crown, or the Government which represented the Crown ; and it gives this title in reimbursement, along with other things, of the expense cast upon them by the Act, of maintaining the main roads and of forming and maintaining the divisional roads. The Act says not one word about any liabilities to which the Road Board or the Chief Commissioner might be subject. It leaves these to be dealt with between the Government, as coming in place of the Road Board, and of the Chief Commissioner, and the persons who might be creditors in the liabilities, and says simply that—' From and after the taking effect of this Act, the tolls taken at toll-bars established, or to be established, on any main road lying or being within any division, and at all ferries upon the line of any such main road, and within such division, shall belong to the Divisional Council of such division.' I am at a loss, therefore, to see how any claims, real or imaginary, which the defendant may have against the Government, as coming in the place of its Road Board and its Chief Commissioner of Roads, can be brought in the present inquiry. But if the Court should be against defendant, and hold that a ferry had been created, the defendant argued that, as he had supplied the pont and worked it, he was entitled to the dues levied for the time bygone, if the passage of the river were to be treated as a ferry ; but he put the case alternatively, as if the passage of the river were part of the main road, and asked if he might not ply his pont in the same way as any coach-owner might ply a coach for fares on any public road or street ? Even if the river were to be taken literally as part of the road, I apprehend that no private individual has a right to place on any public road or street a carriage of such a construction as that it will engross the breadth of the way, and then to say that passengers

1868.
May 28.
" 29.
June 19.

Uitenhage
Divisional
Council vs.
J. S. Reed.

entering it must pay him a certain rate. But that, in truth, is what the defendant did. He placed a pont upon the river which engrossed the point of passage of the river. Taking the other view, and treating the passage of the river as a ferry, the defendant relied upon the fact, which is indisputable, that the plaintiffs had not supplied any pont for the conveyance of the traffic across the river, and he asked why, having done so for them, he should not be allowed to have fairly earned the tolls which were payable? The answer to that question is, that no one may intrude himself into a ferry, and levy the tolls under pretence of serving the public better than the owner of the ferry. According to the passage referred to by the plaintiffs in *Voet* 39, 15, 3, the transport from bank to bank of a public river is among the minor *regalia* of the State. By the law of England, the right is in the Crown, and the owner of an ancient right of ferry, unable to produce any positive grant of it, holds only upon the presumption that such a grant had been made at one time or other, but has been lost. In *Blisset and Hart*, *Full. ni. pri.* 76, it was held that if a man have an ancient ferry, and another set up a new ferry, he will have action against him, for he who has an ancient ferry is compellable by law to keep boats—that is to say, having to be at the expense of keeping boats, his remuneration for so doing by collecting the ferry tolls cannot be diminished by the intrusion of a third party into the ferry; and in *Peter vs. Kendal*, 6 *Barn. and Cr.*, 703, it was held that neglect of duty on the part of the owner of the ferry is no answer to an action against a third party for disturbing the ferry. If the Councils to whom this ferry and the right to levy its tolls was given neglected to perform their duty by making the river as part of the main road passable by bridge, pont, or other contrivance, the remedy for such a state of things is given by the 13th section of this Act to the Council of any division through any part of which the road shall run, or to any landowners, not fewer in number than 25, within such division, but not to the defendant or to any person who may choose to take that upon him. It would be a singular state of things if a private individual could be allowed by law to make profit of the neglect of a public body, such as a Divisional Council, to perform its duties to the public. These ferry dues were given to the Council as a means to an end, the end not being the personal profit of the members of the Council, but the maintenance of this ferry and of the public road which leads to it, a burthen which was cast upon the Councils by the very Act which gives them the toll. As to the last ground urged by defendant, that if he should be found liable to pay anything, the amount would not exceed £75 per annum, the sum which was to have been paid under the contract of 1850 with the Central Board, which the defendant never did and never could be induced to subscribe, I am at a loss, for the reasons which I have already given, to see what the present plaintiffs have to do with what passed or did not pass between the defendant and the Government functionaries before the ferry came into the possession of the plaintiffs. If, independently of these matters, £75 be relied upon as the sum which ought reasonably to be demanded of the defendant, I have seen no evidence to justify such a conclusion. The evidence, such as we have, would, in my opinion, justify a much larger demand. The plaintiffs have demanded £300 a year, and if I am to judge by the evidence, I am inclined to say that even that sum is much within the mark. But, as I suggested at the outset, I am of opinion that before taking the account the Council of Alexandria should be allowed to intervene as plaintiffs, so as to be parties to that proceeding."

1868.
May 28.
" 29.
June 19.

Uitenhage Divisional Council vs. J. S. Reed.

CONNOR, J., after going over the correspondence in the case, said : " This action may be described to be by the plaintiffs against the defendant, on the ground that the defendant has received tolls of the Sunday's River Ferry, which belonged to the plaintiffs. It would, I apprehend, be a mistake to suppose that there was here any grant of a ferry in the ordinary sense of the term. In the description of the line of main road, this ferry at the Sunday's River was included, and ferry tolls were recognized as legally demandable in respect of persons and things ferried over. But no such tolls were ever purported to be authorized as tolls for four years after the agreement with Capper in 1850. I apprehend that where ferry tolls are demandable by law, especially when there has not been any grant of a ferry, there is an implied condition that the public body which demands them shall have the means ready of ferrying over persons, &c. If therefore a right to demand these tolls belonged to the plaintiffs, they must either have had, by themselves or by arrangement with some one else, the means of ferrying over the persons, &c., in respect of whom the tolls were to be paid. The terms of the Proclamation establishing the tolls confirm, I think, this view. The Proclamation is dated 21st June, 1854 (*Gazette*, June 22, 1854)." After a reference to the wording of this Proclamation and of the Act 23, 1858, his Lordship observed : " If there were no contract in the case, and the plaintiffs had a right of ferry, the proper form of action would probably have been such as that in *Newton vs. Cubitt*, 31 L. J., C. P., 246, viz., that the plaintiffs were entitled to the tolls, and that the defendant carried passengers for hire at the *locus in quo*, whereby plaintiffs have lost divers profits which otherwise would have arisen

1868.
May 28.
" 29.
June 19.

Uitenhage
Divisional
Council vs.
J. S. Reed.

to them from the employment of their ferry. But the answer would then probably have been : 'We deprived you of nothing, because during all that time you had no means of ferrying people over and becoming entitled to any tolls.' Nor do I think the cases of private rights of ferry are to the contrary. Because there the property is private property, and no one has a right to have a beneficial enjoyment of it but the private owner ; and if he neglects supplying the means of ferry, that will not transfer the right of ferry to another. Though I should be slow to believe that if a private owner had no means of ferrying, he could recover substantial damages for another's ferrying, if the ferry was in the line of a public road. If, however, the private owner kept up merely insufficient means of ferrying, it may be that the proper remedy would be by an indictment or other proceeding in the name of the Crown. But I am not aware that a private owner of a ferry would have any means of compelling the intruder on the ferry paying or accounting to him for his receipts. His remedy would be by an action for damages, and on this I have already observed. The plaintiffs, or the public whose officers they are, do not appear to me to have been injured by the defendant's maintaining his pont for hire on the river. The plaintiffs have never been ready to put a pont there themselves, and the defendant and those under whom he claims have supplied the public service. If he has not done so under arrangement with them, then they have been in great default. If they have had no pont on the river, they have been entitled to no tolls,and the defendant,therefore, can have deprived them of none. It is therefore, to my mind, essential to the plaintiff's case that I should recognize the pont which has earned the money in question, whether to be deemed tolls or not, as being placed and worked on the river by arrangement with them. And I may observe that the plaintiffs by their letter of June 18, 1867, written to the defendant, recognize him as the manager of the ferry. Can, however, I hold as against the defendant, that he has had his pont on the river by arrangement with the plaintiff ? I think so ; for, that there was such an arrangement is, in truth, his case. It is not the case perhaps of either party on the pleadings: but when evidence is given on a particular subjectmatter affecting the substance of the case, at considerable length by both parties, or by one of them with the tacit acquiescence of the other, then, however, objectionable, or however alien to the object of pleadings in actions, the admission of such evidence may have been, it is impossible in practice to exclude it as an element in the judgment of the Court. Again, we were referred to *Voet*, 49, 14, 3, in which among the *jura fiscalia* is included : ' every right which the

Crown has in the banks of public rivers, in respect of tributes, or of embankments, or of the right of ferrying from bank to bank. And in *Newton vs. Cubitt*, a case of *Blissett vs. Hart, Willes*, 508, 512 (*n*), is referred to by counsel *arguendo*, thus, that there 'it is said to have been held *per curiam* that a ferry is *publici juris*, and that it is a franchise that no one can erect without a licence from the Crown; and when one is erected another cannot be erected without an *ad quod damnum*. If a second is erected without a licence, the Crown has a remedy by *quo warranto*, and the former grantee has a remedy by action.' Not only, therefore, is it part of the defendant's case that there was such an arrangement the provisions of which were made one of the four grounds urged by his counsel in his defence, but there seems considerable ground for holding that some such arrangement was requisite for the legality of his position. Not, however, that I mean to express any opinion that when a public road crosses a public river, and at the crossing ferry tolls are authorized to be taken, and the parties entitled to receive these tolls omit to keep up reasonable means of ferry, any person may not ferry himself over, or be ferried over by any third person; and if he have this latter right, it is difficult to understand how he is not entitled to pay, and the other to receive, hire for being so ferried over. Mr. Justice Willes, in delivering the judgment of the Court in *Newton vs. Cubitt*, says : ' A ferry consists in respect of persons using a right of way when the line of the way is across the water. . . . The franchise is established to secure convenient passages, and the exclusive right is given because in an unpopulous place there might not be profit sufficient to maintain the boat, if there was no monopoly. The ferry is unconnected with the right to land, and exists only in respect of persons using the right of way. . . . The cases on the nature of a ferry are few, and we cite only *Pain vs. Patrick Carth.* 192, where the Court decided that case did not lie for an obstruction of a highway, with special damage ; that a passage over the water is of the same nature as a highway for all people ; and that the plaintiff, who claimed as an inhabitant of Littleport, had not the passage as such inhabitant, but as a subject.' Mr. Justice Willes made these observations in a case in which the plaintiff claimed under an express grant of a ferry, and they seem to me, so far as they apply to this case, to apply *a fortiori*, there being, as I have said here, no such grant of a ferry, or of property in a ferry. It appears to me, therefore, that at once as against and in favour of the plaintiffs, and against and in favour of the defendant, I have to regard the arrangement with Capper as that under which the pont has been maintained, and the payments in question earned and received. That

1868.
May 28.
" 29.
June 19.

Uitenhage
Divisional
Council *vs.*
J. S. Reed.

arrangement I hold to have been in effect this, that of the earnings of the pont the Road Board, and those by whom they are represented, should receive £75 a-year, so much and no more. To what share, then, of this amount are the plaintiffs entitled? I am of opinion to only one-half. The Act 10, 1864, sec. 4, enacts that the tolls taken at all ferries upon the line of any main road, and within any division, shall belong to the divisional council of such division; and if in any case it shall so happen that any ferry, at which there is a toll, shall ply between two divisions, and not be wholly in either of them, then the tolls taken at such ferry shall be divided between the divisional councils of both divisions, share and share alike. I can have little doubt but that before the recent decision of this Court in the *Rawson Bridge* case (*The Divisional Council of Port Elizbeth*, appellants, *vs. The Divisional Council of Uitenhage* respondents.—1. *Buch., Rep.* 40), this ferry at Sunday's River was deemed to be wholly within the Uitenhage division. We, however, in the case which I have mentioned, decided that when the boundary of a district which has been taken out of a larger district is described as being one of the banks of a tidal river, that bank is to be deemed to extend at least as far in as low-water mark. As, then, it is clear from the evidence in this case that at high water the pont advances considerably beyond low-water mark, there can, I think, be no doubt but that the ferry is not wholly in the Uitenhage division, and that, therefore, the tolls, or sums payable in respect of tolls, belong to the two divisions, share and share alike. It must, I apprehend, be held that the rights of the Commissioners of Roads under any contract were, by the Act 10, 1864, transferred to the two divisional councils equally. There has been no new letting of these tolls. There has been no mutual agreement between the two divisional councils that that of Uitenhage should have the letting of these tolls, nor is any such letting under any such agreement the subject of this action, so as to bring the case within the proviso of section 4 of the Act. It was urged on the part of the defendant, that the Divisional Council of Alexandria's not being a party to this action entitled him to an absolution from the instance, on his plea of the general denial; I am, however, not of that opinion; I am not satisfied that even if the objection had been specially made, it could have been allowed to defeat the action. The technial rules of English pleading are not rules of this Court. By technical rules, I mean such rules as derive their force from the mere fact of their being rules. Technical rules of pleading may be requisite in every Court, but those binding in any Court must be technical rules adopted by or for itself. It is said that in cases of contract the non-joinder of a party whose interest as a plaintiff is disclosed in the evidence, is fatal on the general issue. Such a rule may in many cases be requisite on principle. But surely one can imagine cases in which the contract is so several in its nature, or has been so far already performed, as that the non-joinder is excusable. No contract is sued on in this case; the circumstances have come out at the instance of both parties, or at least in evidence not objected to by either. The general issue does, I think, enable the defendant to save himself from any injury or injustice which is shown by the evidence admissible or admitted in the case. It would, I think, be an injury of such a kind to compel him to pay the plaintiffs here the whole of the £75 a year, when they are only entitled to half, and when this judgment could not save him from being sued for half again, by the Divisional Council of Alexandria, whom this judgment cannot bind. The general issue is, I think, sufficient to save a defendant from an injustice of the kind which I have mentioned, but it is not sufficient to save him from an inconvenience. It is an inconvenience to be sued twice by parties who ought to have joined in one action, but if each of those parties only recovers his own rights in his action, the severance in the actions, if not specially objected to, is not to be deemed more than an inconvenience." Observing, finally, as to the amount the defendant was liable, his Lordship considered that that liability should be reckoned as £93 15s., being the one half which the plaintiffs were entitled to of the £75 a year, for two and a half years, from 1st January, 1865. The defendant appeared to have now no rights in the ferry, except, of course, to the pont. This action would be a sufficient determination of any permission by the plaintiffs to his continuing to work the ferry.

The judgment of the majority of the Court was then given for £187 10s., with costs.

[Plaintiffs' Attorneys, *Reid & Nephew.*
Defendant's Attorneys, *Fairbridge & Arderne.*]

1868.
May 28.
„   29.
June 19.
—
Uitenhage
Divisional
Council *vs.*
J. S. Reed.

LAMB BROTHERS *vs.* ROUSSEAU.

(See Part I, p. 3.)

Postea (14th April), Provisional Sentence granted accordingly.

1868.
Jan. 12.
Feb. 1.
April 14.
—
Lamb Brothers
vs. Rousseau

EXECUTORS WATERMAN, APPLICANTS; WOLFREY, RESPONDENT.

(See Part 1, p. 23.)

Postea (12th April), *Bond* appointed accordingly. And (15th May) sequestration decreed.

1868.
Feb. 11.
April 12.
May 15.
—
Executors,
Waterman,
Applicants;
Wolfrey,
Respondent.

MAGISTRATES' REVIEWED CASES.

Warrants of Apprehension should alone be issued on sworn informations laid.

1868.
March 24.

BELL, J., said a case had come before him, as Judge of the week, in which a prisoner, accused of theft, had been tried before a Magistrate, and had pleaded guilty. He was sentenced, and as Judge he (BELL, J.) was asked to review the sentence; but he sent it back to the Magistrate, telling him it was impossible to review a sentence where there was no evidence nor any complaint on oath beforehand. The Magistrate said, in reply, that the copy of the complaint of the farmer whose sheep had been stolen was all the record he had. Now the Ordinance No. 40 required that a Magistrate issuing a warrant for the apprehension of any person, should do it on an information sworn before him: and if that sworn statement of the complainant was sent up, together with the plea of guilty, the Judge would be able to know whether the prisoner had been sentenced properly or not. But when no information of the kind was sent, it was a mere form to forward the sentence and ask a Judge to review it. Singularly enough, along with this came another in the same predicament, where a prisoner was charged with confederating and conspiring with others to escape from gaol. He also pleaded guilty; but what could a black man know of the meaning of confederating and conspiring so as to enable him to plead to such a charge? In that case he returned the papers to the Magistrate at once. He mentioned these cases publicly now, in order to let Magistrates generally know that they had no right to issue warrants of apprehension unless on information sworn upon oath. In the first case, owing to the irregularity of the Magistrate, the time consumed in sending the papers for review, in returning them, and getting them corrected, was such that the accused had suffered all the term of imprisonment to which he was sentenced. This prisoner's sentence had expired on the previous day; and in this case, therefore, the interference of the Court would be unavailing. It was to be hoped, however, that such irregularities would not occur in future.

Master and Servants' Act, 15 of 1866, Sec. 26.

BELL, J., said that among the cases which had come before him during the week, was one in which a boy was charged with absconding from his master's service. He had the charge of some cattle and left them. His master complained to the Magistrate, and a prosecution under the Master and Servants' Act followed. It appeared that the boy had gone away formerly, when the master applied to the father, and the father surrendered him. The second time, however, he refused to do so, saying that the boy had been ill-used, and that he had not been educated and clothed according to agreement. The Magistrate heard the complaint, and convicted the boy, who was sentenced to a very reasonable punishment; but the Magistrate, acting, as he said, upon the 26th section of Act 15, 1856, fined the father in the costs, of all the proceedings, and sent him to prison in default. That section was as follows:

1868.
March 31.

" When it shall be made to appear to the Magistrate that any servant or apprentice, desirous to bring a civil action against his master, or late master, for the recovery of wages alleged to be due, or for the fulfilment of any part of the contract of service, or apprenticeship, or for damages for any breach thereof, or for assault, is from poverty unable to pay the costs of civil process, then the Magistrate shall cause such process, as regards parties and witnesses, to be issued and executed at the public charge, as in criminal cases presented at the public instance, and in case judgment shall be given for such servant or apprentice with costs, then the costs first aforesaid shall be recovered from the defendant and refunded to the public; provided, always, that if at the trial the action shall appear to have been instituted without reasonable or probable cause, and the plaintiff shall fail to pay, or give sufficient security for the payment of the said costs, as also for the costs (if any) awarded to the defendant, then the Magistrate may forthwith commit the said plaintiff to prison, with or without hard labour, for any period not exceeding one month."

Now there was nothing in this section to show that the costs could be recovered from the father in such a case as the present. The complaint was only against the son. It was perfectly clear that the whole of this part of the proceeding was unwarrantable, and, to this extent, the sentence must be set aside, and the costs returned.

Act 17, '67, Sections 7 and 8.

HODGES, C.J., said, a case had been before him this week, where a Resident Magistrate recently tried three

1868.
April 2.

1868.
April 2.

prisoners under Act 17, 1867. The charge against them was the theft of two sheep, or receiving stolen property knowing it to have been stolen. One of the prisoners pleaded guilty to the theft, and the depositions supported the confession. To this person the Magistrate awarded the punishment of one year's imprisonment with hard labour. That sentence was good, and would stand. The other two prisoners pleaded not guilty to the two charges; but the depositions went to show that they were guilty of receiving a portion of the carcases of the stolen sheep. They were therefore guilty of receiving stolen goods, knowing them to have been stolen, and to them as well as to the man who had committed the theft, the Magistrate awarded the punishment of one year's hard labour. Now this Court has always held that the 7th and 8th sections of the Act did not apply to cases where a portion of the carcase of a sheep has been received with a guilty knowledge; therefore the Magistrate had no authority to pass this sentence. Under his ordinary jurisdiction he might have sentenced these two persons to three months' imprisonment, with hard labour, irrespective of the Act of 1867; and under all the circumstances, the Court thought the better course would be to allow the judgment to stand with respect to the man who pleaded guilty; and as there was evidence only to support a conviction of feloniously receiving on the part of the other two, their sentence would be reduced to three months' imprisonment, with hard labour, that being the greatest punishment the Magistrate had power to inflict under his ordinary jurisdiction. He (HODGES, C.J.) might mention that the record did not show that these parties were brought up under the Act of 1867, and therefore it was thought right to deal with the case in the way he had stated.

MASTER AND SERVANT—ACT 15, 1856, § 5.

1868.
April 14.

HODGES, C.J., said, that among the cases which had come before him, as Judge of the week, there was one in which a certain Piet Jackson, a man of colour, was charged with leaving his master's service, with intent not to return. The charge was laid under the 5th section of Act 15, 1856. The defendant pleaded not guilty, and the Acting Magistrate before whom he was brought satisfied himself with taking the evidence of the prosecutor, who deposed that the prisoner was in his service; that he had hired him on the 16th of January, as a shepherd, for twelve months; and that on the 25th of March he left service without leave, and declared that he would not return. This was all the evidence, and the Magistrate, adjudging the defendant to be guilty, sentenced him to two months' imprisonment, with hard labour. Now it was plain that the Magistrate ought to have investigated the case much more particularly. It was perfectly true that by the law of the Colony there might be a hiring by word of mouth for twelve months. But still, when a farmer said that he had made such a hiring, and charged his servant with desertion within the period, the inquiries of the Magistrate should be very close, and he should be careful how he sent a man to prison for deserting service, unless he had thoroughly satisfied himself that a proper bargain had been made between the master and servant; and if, upon due investigation, the Magistrate had been satisfied of the correct nature of the bargain, two months would have been a very proper sentence. In this case, however, there had been no proper inquiry; defendant had been in prison for some days, and the Court thought the best way would be to quash the conviction altogether, and leave the parties to do what they pleased hereafter. Accordingly the conviction would be quashed, and it was to be hoped Magistrates, in cases of this kind, would be more careful in future.

1868.
April 14.

Conviction quashed accordingly.

MUTINY ACT, § 85.—PRISONERS' STATEMENTS.

CONNOR, J., said that under the 85th section of the Mutiny Act a prisoner was charged with having in his possession a military coat, value 15s., the property of Her Majesty the Queen, and sentenced to three months' imprisonment. But under that section of the Act, in the case of a first offence (which this was), there was only power to fine, not exceeding £20, or a forfeiture of treble the value of the property. In the case of second convictions alone could imprisonment be inflicted. At first he thought it would be sufficient to alter the sentence into one of forfeiture of treble value; but he now considered that the proper course would be to quash the conviction altogether. He also wished to draw attention to an irregularity into which Resident Magistrates frequently fell, namely, after trying a prisoner, calling upon him, as in case of a preliminary examination, for a statement of what he had to say, and then placing it on the record. This practice was quite incorrect. When Magistrates tried and sentenced a prisoner (without its being necessary or intended, therefore, that his case should go before a superior court for trial), the prisoner should not be called upon to make such statements.

1868.
June 11.
„ 12.

SUPREME COURT REPORTS.

1868.

PART III.

TUCKER, APPELLANT, AND DEFENDANT BELOW;
AUSTEN'S TRUSTEE, RESPONDENT, AND PLAINTIFF
BELOW.

*Undue Preference.—Insolvent Ordinance, §§ 84, 86, 88
Sheep Lease.*

This was an appeal from a judgment of the Eastern Districts Court, in an action of undue preference.

1868.
May 19.
" 22.
June 19.

Tucker, Appellant;
Austen's Trustee Respondent.

The plaintiff's declaration in the Court below set forth that Richard Austen surrendered his estate as insolvent upon the 12th June, 1867, and that John Croxford, the plaintiff, was thereafter duly appointed trustee. That before the surrender, to wit, on or about the 5th day of April, 1867, Austen had delivered to the defendant, Tucker, 1,050 sheep, of the value of £600, the property of the said Austen. That at the date of this delivery Austen contemplated the sequestration of his estate, and intended to prefer the defendant, who was one of his creditors, above his other creditors. Wherefore an undue preference was claimed under the 84th section of Ordinance 6, 1843, and the re-delivery of the sheep; and further, a forfeiture, under the 88th section, of the defendant's claim as creditor, on the ground of collusion. The defendant pleaded the general issue.

From the evidence taken in the Court below, it appeared that the insolvent and the defendant were connected by marriage. The insolvent was a farmer, and had fallen into difficulties, when, on the 1st April, 1865, the defendant, to assist him, delivered to him 1,050 ewes, on the following document:

"Agreement of hire of sheep, entered into between Henry Tucker, of
Cradock, of the one part, and Richard Austen, of Diamond Dale,

L

1868.
May 19.
" 22.
June 19.

Tucker,
Appellant ;
Austen's Trustee
Respondent.

in the division of Fort Beaufort, of the other part. The said Henry Tucker hereby agrees to let, and the said Richard Austen to hire, for one year, from the date hereof, one thousand and fifty good merino sheep, at a yearly rental of sixty-four pounds three shillings sterling.

" The said Richard Austen hereby acknowledges the receipt of the said one thousand and fifty sheep, and agrees to pay to the said Henry Tucker, at the Eastern Province Bank, Cradock, the said sum of sixty-four pounds three shillings sterling, in half-yearly instalments of thirty-two pounds one shilling and six pence each, the first of which will be due and payable on the first day of October, 1865.

" The said Richard Austen hereby binds himself to pay to the said Henry Tucker a fair and reasonable sum for the difference in value (should there be any) between the said sheep when hired and when returned ; it being mutually agreed that in case of any difference of opinion on the subject the same shall be referred to Mr. Kidger Tucker, whose decision shall be final.

" Thus done at Cradock, on the 1st April, 1865.

"(Signed) R. AUSTEN."

When the lease expired, on the 1st April, 1866, it was, at the insolvent's solicitation, renewed for another year. Four days after the expiration of this second year, at a time when insolvent was admittedly in difficulties, and saw no hope of surmounting them, he sent 1,050 sheep from his farm, Diamond Dale, to Way Plaats, the farm of Mr. K. Tucker, the defendant's brother. On the road, however, a number died from *klaauwziekte* (foot-rot), and the number actually delivered was 830. On the 10th February, 1859, before Tucker leased his sheep, Stone had leased to the insolvent 1,100 sheep, and again 524 more on the 10th February, 1866, under another contract for three years,—which had not expired at the time of the insolvency, but would have run on until the 10th February, 1869,—and had taken a registered bond in security. Stone proved his bond in the estate, with another bond and concurrent claim, amounting to £1,684 3s. 4d.

From the evidence of the trustee it appeared that the scheduled debts were £2,399 16s. 11d., and the scheduled assets £1,492. The assets consisted of a farm, Goshen, in British Kaffraria ; movables, £214 9s. ; and debts due to the estate, £28. The debts proved were £2,139 8s. 2d., of which £1,224 4s. 6d. were preferent, and £915 concurrent On the 1st April, 1867, Austen was insolvent ; his liabilities on that day being £2,983, and assets, £2,156 : deficiency, £826 17s. 6d.

From the insolvent's evidence, it appeared that in the early part of 1867 he knew he could not meet his liabilities, and that in March, 1867, the defendant was aware of his position. Insolvent told him he was in difficulties. Both Stone's sheep and Tucker's he had marked with his own mark, and they ran mixed. All the sheep he possessed on the 1st April, 1867, were 1,553. At that time he owed 1,050 to Tucker, and 1,624 to Stone. He delivered sheep out of the mixed flock.

1869.
May 19.
„ 22.
June 19.

Tucker,
Appellant ;
Austen's Trustee
Respondent.

Among the correspondence between the insolvent and defendant, put in, was a letter from defendant to insolvent dated 12th February, 1867, in which the following passage occurred : " I want you to carry out the arrangement made when you were here, namely, for your son to *trek* up to Way Plaats with the sheep at once. I can then regularly lease them to him, and they will be beyond the casualty of hungry creditors."

Judgment in the Court below was given for £120, as the value of 240 sheep, by which the Court held the defendant had received an undue preference.

In the argument at the bar, on appeal, the insolvency of Austen in April was virtually admitted by

Porter, for appellant. The objections to the judgment of the Court below are three. First, that that judgment was bad generally. Secondly, that the value of the sheep mentioned in the judgment was over-estimated. And, thirdly, that the judgment declaring a forfeiture, under the 88th section, is unsupported by the evidence, and should be set aside. Firstly, the lease is, contrary to the form of most sheep leases, a pure lease, and passed no property to Austen, —as little as the lease of a house would pass the property in that house. The ordinary colonial "sheep lease, " as it is improperly called, does pass property ; but here defendant took the special precaution of framing this lease, by the insertion of clause 3, so as to avoid that result. What is called a " sheep lease," improperly, is, *e.g.*, if A leases to B, for five years, a certain number of sheep of certain specified description and ages, and B stipulates, at the end of the period, to return sheep of the same description and ages as those which A had given him five years before. In that case, it is easy to see, from the conditions affixed, that the identical sheep cannot be returned, and this Court has held, by a series of decisions, that such a contract is not *locatio*, but is a *mutuum*, and that therefore the property in the sheep passes from the lessor into the lessee. Just as if A deposited sovereigns in a bank. Although called a deposit, it also is, in reality, a *mutuum* ; because the bank, even if it kept in its coffers the identical sovereigns, and then failed, would retain the sovereigns in its estate. The deposited sovereigns having been banked for use, and not, as a chest of plate, for instance, in security merely, the property in these sovereigns has passed completely into the bank.

[CONNOR, J.—And that seems to have been the ground of

the decision in the Court below in holding that Tucker was entitled to keep all but 240, which the Court must have considered were not portion of the sheep he had originally leased, but were leased from other parties.] The Court below must clearly have so construed, and rightly, the peculiar words of the 3rd clause of the lease, which speaks of the " difference in value between the sheep when hired and their value when returned," estimated in a certain way, these words contemplating, evidently, the return of the same sheep. And this is also the construction which both parties to the lease put upon it. The insolvent swears, in his evidence, that there was no idea of property passing. And Tucker, in his correspondence, shows that was the very thing he was altogether anxious to avoid. The insolvent was, therefore, not bound to return any of the 1,050 which died; nor to pay for those which so died, in the ordinary course of nature, and without any default on his part, it being a first principle connected with *locatio* that, as long as the hirer takes good care of the thing leased, casualties are at the owner's risk. The value was put into the contract only to determine the rent. This contract, therefore, may be designated as almost the only one of pure hiring which has come before this Court in connection with sheep. Now, it will be said, *contra*, that as it may be shown that 240 sheep of the sheep delivered by Austen could not have been portion of the sheep originally leased, that Austen thereby intended, *quoad* these 240, to prefer Tucker by giving to him what was not his property, but, perhaps, that of other lessors. But if it be conceded that (according to the whole colour of the contract, gathered from that contract itself, and from the way in which it was read by both the parties, according to the evidence in the case) there was an obligation on the insolvent to return to Tucker his 1,050 sheep, and, if Tucker would have been justified in receiving them, and if, therefore, all notion of undue preference falls away, as the Court below has virtually decided it must fall away, in reference to defendant's own sheep,—then arises, in reference to the overplus of 240, the question: did insolvent intend to give Tucker an undue preference in regard to any of the sheep delivered? It is clear that the insolvent drew no distinction between the 240 and the rest. There was a merger of the sheep all into one flock; and thus, although it be true in point of law that Tucker could not have claimed a right of property in more than that portion of his 1,050 sheep which remained at the delivery, namely, 830,—or, it may be, that number with its progeny, because they were all ewes, and *partus sequitur ventrem*,—the offspring follows the dam, still, there cannot be said to have been on the side of the insolvent any intention to give an undue preference, it being impossible to draw any line between the sheep ; and then the transaction resolves itself into one in the ordinary course of business.

[CONNOR, J.—That is to say, under section 86, which proceeds to throw the burden of collusion on the trustee. But, then, did not the Court below find such collusion?]

It may be said, *contra*, that there is proof of such collusion in Tucker's letter of the 12th February, 1867, where reference is made to "hungry creditors." But all that Tucker meant by that expression was that, not having parted with his property in the sheep, he was entitled—as, indeed, he was entitled—to get back his sheep rather than that they should go to such "hungry creditors" as Stone and others, who really were not in the same position as himself, and who might claim what was his, not theirs.

[BELL. J.—But even viewing the matter in that light, what right has Tucker to the 240 sheep?]

In law, Tucker had no right to these sheep, and must have lost them had they been left in the insolvent estate. But the more important question is, in reference to the insolvent with regard to these 240 sheep, was there not in his mind a real and *bonâ fide* belief, although a mistaken one, that there rested upon him the legal obligation to return Tucker all the sheep he did deliver? If so, section 84 will not apply.

[CONNOR, J.—Would it not merely, at farthest, necessitate a different form of action ? Because if Tucker had no claim to the overplus of 240 delivered, the trustee certainly could recover them in some other form of action, although perhaps not, technically, in an action of undue preference. And, again, although it may be said to have been, looking at the intent of the insolvent, a mistaken idea of an ordinary course of business transaction, and therefore protected under section 86, in so far that in such case there is thrown upon the trustee the *onus* of proving collusion,—yet there, then, comes round, on this point of collusion, the letter of February, 1867. Is there not there suggested such a collusion as the 86th section refers to?]

As to the form of action, the trustee might possibly recover by way of *rei vindicatio*, but certainly not in this form of action under the 84th section. And as to the "hungry creditors" remark, the interpretation of this has already been given. If there was upon the part of the insolvent a *bonâ fide* belief that for every sheep which died Tucker was a creditor, and if the delivery of the overplus may be justified on that mistaken supposition, then there could, at all events, be no action under the 84th section, where intention to prefer is the foundation of the action, while here there was no such intention. I will now proceed to argue that the undue pre-

1868.
May 19.
" 22.
June 19.

Tucker,
Appellant ;
Austen's Trustee
Respondent.

1868.
May 19.
" 22.
June 19.

Tucker,
Appellant;
Austen's Trustee
Respondent.

ference must be gathered from the intent of what the insolvent does, and not merely from its effect. This point was discussed at the bar at considerable length in the case of the *Trustees of C. P. Brink vs. the Cape Commercial Bank*, an action of undue preference heard before this Court on February 15, 1867, before Hodges, C.J., and Bell, J., who differed in opinion, and it was arranged it should be argued before a full Bench ; but since that time it has collapsed from want of funds to fight for, and no decision was given. In that case I argued that an insolvent's intention to prefer must be real and not presumptive, and traced the history of the law of the Colony on the subject of undue preferences.

[BELL, J.—I thought the law of the Colony in regard to undue preferences was settled long ago, by a series of decisions, in this court, confirmed by the Privy Council in appeal, in the case of *Smith, Trustee of Taylor, vs. Carpenter.* 12 *Moore, P. C. Rep. p.* 101.]

It is intended, respectfully, to discuss that Privy Council decision, to show, by a subsequent Privy Council decision, that the decision in Smith and Carpenter was founded on a mistaken notion of our colonial law. The Old Insolvent Law, before Ordinance 6, 1843, was contained in Ordinance No. 64, the 7th section of which corresponds, to some degree, with our present 84th section, and was a most destructive one. To establish an undue preference it required merely a knowledge of insolvency, with the effect to prefer,—not the intention, but the effect. The decisions of the Court on this 7th section were most unsatisfactory, and the resu't of long discussions in commercial circles was, that a Committee of the old Legislative Council recommended, in 1842, the assimilation of the law of the Colony to the fraudulent preference of the English law, by substituting, in the 84th section, of what was afterwards Ordinance 6, 1843, the intention to prefer instead of the effect to prefer, hitherto contained in section 7 of Ordinance 64. [Counsel read a passage from the report of the Committee.] Hence it is not carrying out the object of Ordinance 6, 1843, if, for the intention to prefer, of section 84, we in reality substitute the effect to prefer of the former section 7. The intention of the present Ordinance being to introduce the law of England, the 84th section does embrace the law of England, or at least the law of England as it stood in 1843 ; and, consequently, will open the door for the citation in this court of the more recent English decisions, also, for we should not fossilize the law as it was administered in 1843. In England the two elements or conditions of destruction would be : Did the bankrupt contemplate a bankruptcy ? and, Did he intend to prefer ?—Nor would the effect of the preference make out an intention to prefer. Until the decision of the Privy Council in *Smith vs. Carpenter*, it was always thought that English decisions were admissible in argument here. The foundation of the English law is contained in two decisions of Lord Mansfield. First, *Harman and others, Assignees of Fordyce, vs. Fishar, Cowper's Reports, p.* 118. Lord Mansfield gave for the plaintiffs, "because the letter showed that the debtor meant to give a preference (*p.* 125), and this the law does not allow. It is much stronger where the trader mentions that to be his *sole motive*," &c. Now, this is a very strong case, and shows that the motive of the debtor was what was inquired into and weighed with the Court. *Rust, Assignee of Papps, vs. Cooper* ; *Cowper's Reports, p.* 629, is the second of Lord Mansfield's decisions, and that goes to the same effect. Of the intention on the part of the debtor, Lord Mansfield there said "that a fraudulent preference, with a view to defeat the bankrupt laws, is void, and annuls the act. There is a fundamental distinction between an act like that in this case and one done in the common course of business. If, in the course of business, a man pays a creditor who comes to be paid, notwithstanding the debtor's knowledge of his affairs, or his intention to break, yet being a fair transaction in the course of business, the payment is good, for the preference is there got consequentially, and not by any design. It is not the *object*, but the preference is obtained in consequence of the payment being made at that time." These two cases support the proposition that the two criteria of destruction, according to English law, are a contemplation of bankruptcy and an intention to prefer. These decisions of Lord Mansfield's have not, it is admitted, ruled the whole of the English decisions afterwards, for Lord Denman, in a decision in *Adolphus and Ellis*, has laid down that English decisions on this subject are "irreconcilable." For some time they had a destructive tendency, but the Courts, it will be shown, have now come back to the ancient ways of Lord Mansfield's decisions. This is seen by the observations of the Judges in *Edwards and others, Assignees of Oak and Snow, vs. Glyn and others* (5th Jurist, 1859, p. 1397), where Erle, J., said " that the tendency of the Courts at one time was to enable the assignees of a bankrupt to set at defiance the principles of right, and to sweep in and take all the property of the bankrupt over the general body of creditors ; and the object of Parke, B., was to stem the tide in that direction." And instances are then quoted from decisions named, and particularly the case of *Brown vs. Kempton, in error,* 19 *L.J.C.P.,* 169, is quoted by Crompton, J., to show that the payment must be a voluntary one, according to the recent decisions ;

1868.
May 19.
" 22.
June 19

Tucker, Appellant ;
Austen's Trustee
Respondent.

*1868.
May 19.
„ 22.
June 19.
Tucker,
Appellant;
Austen's Trustee
Respondent.*

and if pressure is applied it is not a voluntary payment, and not a fraudulent preference. It is clear, therefore, that the tide has turned, and that the Judges in England are now adhering to the Mansfield principles, which are in the ascendant. The next case is from the 11th *Jurist* (1865), *p.* 155, *Bills and another, Assignees, vs. Smith,* where Cockburn, C.J., also clearly laid down "that it must be borne in mind that the true question in all these cases is, whether the intention with which payment was made was to defeat the operation of the bankrupt law." And the case shows generally that the motive of the debtor was the question left to the jury to determine. Then, again, in the 8th *Jurist* (1862), p. 181, of *The Bank of Australia, Appellant, vs. Harris and another, Respondents,*—a case which was before the Privy Council. Our colonial case of *Smith vs. Carpenter* was tried in appeal before the Privy Council in 1858, whereas this case now quoted is one of 1862. It is an appeal from Australia, and it is important to notice this. Mr. Justice Menzies was the author of our late Ordinance 64, but Mr. Justice Burton assisted greatly in its preparation, Mr. Justice Burton was promoted to the Bench in Australia, and he introduced our late Ordinance 64 there, with some alterations. It was upon section 7 of that Ordinance, slightly modified, that this appeal came before the Privy Council in 1862 ; and it was there held that the words of the section " have the effect of preferring one then existing creditor to another" apply to a fraudulent preference, and were not intended to apply to any case of preference not fraudulent. *Fisher's Digest,* 1864, *p.* 21, *Ex-parte Seals, in re Baker,* 10th *L. J.,* 315, *N. S.,* shows what is not a fraudulent preference. From all these cases it is clear that it is the intention of the insolvent, and his sole motive, that the Court must look at. The introduction of the law of England into the Colony was intended by the present Ordinance ; but with surprise it was found, in 1858, that a distinction was drawn, in the Privy Council, in the case of *Smith, Appellant, and Carpenter, Respondent* (12 *Moore P. C Rep., p.* 101), between our law and the English law as to what constitutes a fraudulent preference. It is stated that the 84th section does not require, as the English Insolvent Law does, that in order to constitute a fraudulent preference the transaction should be voluntary. And at p. 114, Lord Justice Knight Bruce says, " The present dispute, however, must be determined, not by English law, not upon English decisions, but by a just interpretation of the 84th section of Ordinance 6, 1843, * * * which does not require that in order to constitute a fraudulent preference the transaction should be voluntary." Now, if a man intends to prefer, and makes a voluntary payment, is that not a preference? Can there be a voluntary payment which is not an intention to prefer, or an intention to prefer which is not a voluntary payment? The 71st section of the Ordinance 6, 1843, as to culpable insolvency, classes under that head " the giving an undue preference, as hereinafter defined,"—that is, in the 84th section. There cannot be two definitions of undue preference—the one criminal and the other civil. The same rule must apply to both; and in a criminal case the court would look at the circumstances, and would regard it as essential to ascertain what was passing in the man's mind. It is entirely a jury question what was passing in Austen's mind. There is no difference, in respect of intention, between trying a case of murder and a case of undue preference. It is not the act of homicide makes the guilt, but the intention. And more especially in these sheep cases, the more correct view is to lay down, in respect to the insolvent's intention, that such a transaction is not to be judged of by asking whose sheep are these, and whose are those, but by asking what did the insolvent really mean by their return.

1868.
May 19.
„ 22.
June 19.

Tucker,
Appellant;
Austen's Trustee
Respondent.

Secondly, as to value, *Porter* proceeded to argue that the sheep were of lower value than that put upon them in the judgment. And, lastly, that there was no collusion proved so as to support forfeiture under the 88th section; the " hungry creditor " allusion in Tucker's letter of 27th February having been already explained away.

Postea (May 23).

Cole was heard for respondents. As to the first point, *contra*, that the lease in this case was a pure lease and had not the effect of passing the property from Tucker, as lessor, to Austen, as lessee, it might under other circumstances have been argued that it was not a pure lease, but did pass the property; but the respondent having got judgment below that it was a lease, he must maintain the judgment as it stands and hold that it is good *quoad* the 240. As to the intention of the parties, whatever may have been Tucker's intention, Austen swears, " I marked the sheep with my mark, and mixed them with Stone's, which I got after." It is said Austen was not answerable for loss on the sheep if he took due care. Why, then, should he return the 240 sheep, instead of those lost, as argued *contra*?

[*Porter* (*passim*).—It is necessary to qualify the position taken up for appellant, and to maintain that when Tucker hired his sheep to Austen, the sheep remained Tucker's property. If they lived over the year, but were returned in an inferior condition, the lessee had to repay the difference.

1868.
May 19,
" 22.
June 19.

Tucker,
Appellant;
Austen's Trustee
Respondent.

And if it should happen that they were less in number as well as value, the lessee would have to make up the difference also, under the words quoted in section 3 of the lease, either in money or sheep.] What did Austen think his obligation was? He swears, "Stone's sheep were in the same position as Tucker's." It is not contended, however, that he thought he was bound to give Stone's sheep back. He never did return any sheep to Stone, but he did to Tucker; and this is a clear intention to prefer? Then it is said that the 86th section protects the delivery of the 240. But that delivery did not take place in the way stipulated to be done by the lease, in many respects. Tucker suggested the return of the sheep that "hungry creditors" might be disappointed. Further, by the lease the sheep were to be returned, and carefully examined as to whether they were of the same quality as those delivered, but, on the evidence, nothing of the kind was done. The only desire manifested was to get them from one farm to the other, to disappoint "hungry creditors." It is said that as to the delivery of the 240, a mistaken impression on the part of Austen that he had to return sheep instead of those lost will negative the intention of undue preference. But look at his impression as stated in the evidence: "Stone's sheep were hired in the same way as Tucker's. The identical sheep (Tucker's) were not to be returned, but the same number and value." *Carpenter vs. Smith* is still the law, and is in conformity with the current of decisions of this Court; and although it is argued that the law should not be "fossilized" as it stood in 1843, the current of decisions would require to be overturned for this case, if the doctrine on the other side is to prevail. As to the value, that was rightly fixed in the Court below. And as to the forfeiture, the whole history of the case shows collusion, and a determination to save sheep "from hungry creditors," as expresssd in Tucker's letter of February, 1867. Even were that not collusion, it is a "mutual understanding," which is one of the causes for forfeiture under section 88.

Porter, in reply. The only object Austen had in marking the sheep with his mark was to secure recognition by neighbours. Stone's contract did not expire till February, 1869; so there was no necessity to return his sheep. As to Austen's intention, the moral test is the true test. There is no real distinction between what is called sometimes a fraudulent preference, sometimes a voluntary preference, and sometimes an undue preference. The decisions on all will be found under either head (*Griffith on Bankruptcy*, 1, 428). And a judge, charging a jury in England, would lay down two propositions,—first, did the insolvent contemplate bankruptcy? and secondly, did he intend to prefer?—just the same questions as should be raised in an action of undue preference in this Colony.

Cur. adv. vult.

Postea (June 19) the Court gave judgment.

1868.
May 19.
" 22.
June 19.

Tucker, Appellant;
Austen's Trustee Respondent.

HODGES, C.J., thought it could not be doubted that the facts in the case showed that the original contract was a contract of lease, and not of sale. No property in the sheep, therefore, passsed from Tucker to the insolvent. Had the sheep returned by the insolvent on the 5th April consisted entirely of sheep of the original flock, no doubt could be entertained that the transaction was free from all objection under the Insolvent Ordinance. The insolvent had never acquired any property in the sheep. The lease had expired by effluxion of time, and Tucker had every right to insist upon the sheep being returned to him without reference to the state of the insolvent's circumstances when the lease expired. How, then, was the case altered by the fact that the insolvent returned sheep other than those he had received from Tucker to make up the number? Many of those returned bore Tucker's mark, but a considerable number of them did not, for the rest of the flock were dead; and it was in respect of the sheep without Tucker's mark only that the Court below held the transaction to be subject to the provisions of the 84th and 88th sections of the Ordinance. The lease of the 5th April was not clearly expressed as to the terms agreed upon on the return of the sheep at the expiration of the lease. The insolvent bound himself to pay to Tucker " a fair and reasonable sum for the difference in value, should there be any, between the sheep when hired and when returned." This language might be said to apply to a fall in the price of sheep at the expiration of the lease, or to a deterioration in point of condition at that time, or to a diminution of their number by death or other casualty; or it might be construed with reference to all these circumstances taken together. The insolvent seemed, however, to have considered that if the same number of sheep (1,050) should be returned by him to Tucker the contract would be fulfilled; and if no insolvency had followed, all difficulty would have been avoided. The insolvent, in his evidence, said: " In April, 1867, I had 1,573 sheep in Diamond Dale. At that time I owed 1,050 sheep to defendant, and 1,628 to Stone. All were running together there undistinguishable." The result, therefore, was, that the insolvent, to fulfil his contract with Tucker, made use of sheep which he had obtained on lease from

1868.
May 19.
" 22.
June 19.

Tucker,
Appellant;
Austen's Trustee
Respondent.

Stone or other creditors; and one of the questions to be decided was, whether this transaction was brought within the 86th section of the Act. Was this a delivery of the sheep made by the insolvent to Tucker in the usual and ordinary course of trade or business? His Lordship thought it was not. If the lease had provided that on its expiration the same number of sheep as those leased should be returned to the lessee, much might be urged to show that it was a *bonâ fide* transaction, and that it was therefore protected by the 86th section. But whatever might be the proper construction which ought to be put upon the words inserted in the lease, it was quite clear that it was a recompense in money which was to be paid in respect of any difference in value. " The said Richard Austen binds himself to pay to the said Henry Tucker a fair and reasonable sum for the difference in value." This was the language used; and as the insolvent, who was on the very verge of insolvency, chose to send away sheep to represent the difference in value without coming to any reckoning whatever with the lessor of the original flock, it must be concluded that he did this with the intention to prefer the lessor before his other creditors. Had he come to a reckoning before the delivery, or paid the difference in cash, the transaction would probably have been held to be one in the ordinary course of business; but as it was, his Lordship could not come to that conclusion. But then another question arose. Was this a case where a forfeiture was incurred under the 88th section? To support that conclusion the Court must be satisfied that the evidence proved a collusive arrangement, mutual understanding, or common consent between Tucker and the insolvent, the one to give and the other to get an undue preference. The letter of the 12th February must not be carried beyond its fair import. Tucker might have been speaking of his own sheep, of sheep of the original flock, in respect of which he had never parted with any property, and which creditors, whether " hungry " or not, could not interfere with. Had he suggested that the number should be made up by sending sheep other than his own, there might be some colour for maintaining that there was collusion. But he does nothing of the kind. He probably did not remember the exact terms of the lease when he wrote that letter, and it would be straining the language which he used too far to hold that it contains proof of collusion. His Lordship had always thought that the serious imputation of collusion with an insolvent ought to be as clearly and distinctly proved as if the party were undergoing a trial on the criminal side of that Court. He could not, therefore concur in the judgment below that there was sufficient proof of collusion under the 88th section.

The result was, that the appeal would be allowed so far as the forfeiture was involved, and disallowed in respect of the finding on the 88th section of the Insolvent Ordinance ; each party bearing his own costs of the appeal.

1868.
May 19.
" 22.
June 19.
——
Tucker, Appellant ;
Austen's Trustee Respondent.

BELL, J., after remarking on the difficulties occasioned by the incomplete and irregular state of the correspondence between Tucker and Austen, as put in in the Court below, and also of the oral evidence there taken, and, further, on the embarrassment created by the absence of any notes of the Judges' opinions in giving judgment, proceeded first to consider, independently of that judgment, whether the transaction between the parties was in fact a hiring or a loan ; inclining to the view that it was a loan of £642 by Tucker to Austen, to be repaid on the 5th April, 1866, in money. His Lordship then went on to say :

If the transaction were to be thus treated as a loan to be repaid in money, there would be an end of any question under the 84th section of the Insolvent Ordinance, for, in that view, Tucker would be a creditor of Austen for £642 10s., to be paid on the 1st April, 1866.

It is, no doubt, true that sheep were not altogether put out of the question ; even viewing the arrangement as a loan, there still remained the stipulation in the agreement of the 1st April, 1865, by Austen to pay Tucker " a fair and reasonable sum for the difference in value (should there be any) between the said sheep when hired and when returned." Tucker, though agreeing to change the hiring into a loan, as between him and Austen, retained the security of the sheep for repayment of the loan, through the operation of this clause, which entitled him to the return of " the said sheep," and a fair and reasonable sum for the difference in value " between the said sheep when hired and when returned ;" but in my opinion, according to the plain reading of these terms, his security could not go beyond that.

It was, perhaps, unnecessary to go into this inquiry as to whether the transaction was in fact a loan or a hiring, because the Eastern Districts Court has treated the case as one of hiring, and there is no appeal against their decision on the part of Croxford, the trustee of Austen's estate ; but that view of the matter throws some light on the case, viewing it as one of hiring ; and as such I shall now consider the question raised by the appeal.

Viewed as a case of hiring, Tucker by the agreement No. 8 let, and Austen hired, 1,053 ewes at a yearly rental of £64 3s. sterling, for the whole number ; that is to say, for 1,050 animals, subject to deterioration in value by disease or accident and increase in age and to diminution in number by

1868
May 19.
 " 22.
June 19.

Tucker,
Appellant;
Austen's Trustee
Respondent.

death. Austen was to pay a fixed sum by way of rent, whether he had a return in the shape of wool, or in increase of numbers by birth of lambs, or whether he had no return, or a very small return. This might or might not be a favourable or unfavourable bargain for either of the parties; but there was nothing in it inconsistent with the principles of law; and according to these principles, if there had been no more in the agreement, Austen, on the one hand, would have had to pay the fixed sum, taking his chance of reimbursement or no reimbursement by the fleece of the flock and the increase of numbers by the birth of lambs, and under the obligation to return the very sheep he had hired, so far as death should not have diminished their number. On the other hand, Tucker would have been entitled to receive the fixed rent, whether Austen gained reimbursement by the hiring or not, and to have the very sheep he had hired returned, except in so far as their number might have been reduced by death, without default on the part of Austen in taking due care of them,—the risk of death being with Tucker, as the hirer.

Diminution of numbers by death seems to have escaped the attention of Tucker. His astuteness was directed to guarding against the idea that he was selling instead of hiring the sheep; but loss by death he seems to have overlooked. This is shown by the N.B. to his letter of the 30th May, 1865, in which he says: "You will understand that the drift of clause 3 is to make it clear that hiring is intended, and not selling." It is by the light of this N.B., therefore, that clause 3 is to be read. I have already quoted so much of that clause, but now I will give its full terms. "The said Richard Austen hereby binds himself to pay to the said Henry Tucker a fair and reasonable sum for the difference in value, should there be any, between the said sheep when hired and when returned, it being mutually agreed that, in case of any difference of opinion on the subject, the same shall be referred to Mr. Kidger Tucker, whose decision shall be final."

If the transaction had been one of sale, there obviously could have been no necessity to make any provision for the event of diminution in numbers by death, or decrease in value by deterioration; but if it were one of loan, both of these events were to be provided for, because, from the very nature of the contract, the hirer would, by law, have had to bear the loss arising in either event. Such being the case, this third section binds the lessee, which the law would not have bound him, to pay to the said Henry Tucker a fair and reasonable sum for the difference in value, should there be any between the said sheep when hired and when returned, but it is altogether silent as to diminution of numbers by death. Taking the language of this clause to mean that if there should be any difference in the value of each of the said sheep when returned from what was the value when hired, that would be consistent with the compact of location—consistent, though perhaps unusual; but if the language of the clause is to be taken to mean by the words "the said sheep," the flock of 1,050 sheep, without reference to the identity of each individual sheep in that flock, and by the words "a fair and reasonable sum for the difference in value between the said flock when hired and when returned," that the difference in value might be occasioned either by diminution in numbers through death or by deterioration in the quality of the sheep, then the clause is opposed, in my apprehension, to the contract of location, and takes the transaction out of that category, for the ruling principle in the contract of location is that the thing hired perishes to the owner, if, in its perishing, there be no blame imputable to the hirer.

1868.
May 19.
„ 22.
June 19.

Tucker,
Appellant;
Austen's Trustee
Respondent.

Viewing, therefore, the transaction as one of hiring, I cannot read the agreement in any other way than as an agreement by Austen that he should return the 1,050 sheep so far as diminution by death should not prevent him, and that as to every sheep he did return, if there should be any difference in its value between the time when it was hired and when it was returned, he should be bound to pay that difference in money to Tucker.

The facts are, according to Austen's letter of the 28th May, 1866, that, up to that time, he had lost 711 sheep, little and big, and that perhaps 40 or 50 more would go; and yet the entire number of 1,050 was returned to Tucker, without reference to their identity with those hired or the diminution of numbers by death.

It was strongly urged for Tucker that the return of 1,050 sheep in this way was protected by the 86th section of the Ordinance as a transaction in the ordinary course of trade. That section says "that every delivery made by any insolvent to any creditor in the usual and ordinary course of trade or business, shall *prima facie* be held or taken to have been made or given *bonâ fide*, and without an intention to give to such creditor any preference," although the insolvent may at the time have contemplated the sequestration of his estate.

The agreement of 1st April, 1865, by which Tucker leased the sheep to Austen, did not bind Austen to return the sheep. That obligation arose by law from the agreement being one of hiring—Austen being so bound by law to return the sheep hired. The agreement further bound him

1868.
May 19.
" 22.
June 19.

Tucker, Appellant;
Austen's Trustee Respondent.

"to pay a fair and reasonable sum for the difference in value, should there be any, between the said sheep when hired and when returned."

I apprehend that if this obligation had been worked out, in the ordinary course of business, the first thing that would have been done would have been to ascertain the exact number of the identical sheep that had been returned; then to have ascertained fairly and reasonably the difference between the value of the sheep so returned and the value "of the said sheep" when hired; and this difference having been ascertained, then Tucker would have been in a position to call upon Austen to pay him "such fair and reasonable sum" as had been ascertained to be the aggregate amount of such difference. Not one of these steps was followed. All that was done was to drive out a miscellaneous flock of 1,050 sheep (the number that had been hired), some having the mark of Tucker and some having the marks of other people, and to send these *per aversionem* to Tucker, without the slightest attempt to ascertain their value, or how far it corresponded with the value of the 1,050 sheep leased.

On the assumption, which I take to be the correct one, that Tucker by the agreement of leasing was entitled to the return of the identical sheep, so far only as death had not diminished their number, it may be that those of the 1,050 sheep returned which were not sheep hired were of less value than the difference in value of those returned which had been hired between the time at which they were hired and the time at which they were returned, or it may be that they were of greater value. The truth of this was wholly unascertained at the time at which this action was brought.

The consequence of this state of things, when attempting to apply the 86th section of the Ordinance, will be best seen by supposing that no insolvency or sequestration had occurred. It is obvious that if no sequestration had occurred, the transaction would not have ended by the mere delivery of these sheep. The parties must have come together to ascertain whether Austen had given and Tucker had received too much, or whether Austen had given and Tucker had received too little.

Even if it be assumed, which I take to be erroneous, that Tucker was entitled —for it is the agreement, not the correspondence which must regulate his rights, Austen having been in a state of insolvency during the correspondence,—I say even on the assumption that Tucker was entitled to have 1,050 sheep returned, whether consisting of the sheep hired or of these along with other sheep, so far as death might have diminished the number of those hired, still the 1,050 must be of a value corresponding with the value of those hired ; and if not, Austen was " to pay him a fair and reasonable sum for the difference in value between the sheep " (omitting the word " said " before sheep) " when hired and when returned." But no attempt was made to ascertain this, which would have been the ordinary course of business ; all that was done, as I said before, was to drive out a flock of miscellaneous sheep, and to hand them over *per aversionem* to Tucker, to put them " beyond the casualty of the grasp of hungry creditors," leaving the difference in value still to be ascertained, it might be in favour of Tucker, or it might be in favour of Austen. That Kidger Tucker was to be the person to ascertain the difference in value, to my mind weighs but little. The letter asking the sheep to be sent asks them to be sent to Waai Plaats, to be safe from hungry creditors, not to K. Tucker that he might ascertain the difference of value. That K. Tucker happened to be at the farm at the time the sheep were sent was a mere accident.

I cannot think this is the ordinary course with men of business, or that it would have been followed by Austen and Tucker, if Austen had continued solvent, or that the 86th section was intended to cover it.

The Eastern Province Court has by its judgment declared that an illegal preference over the other creditors of Austen had been received by Tucker, and the amount of that preference they have estimated at £120, as the value of such of the 1,050 sheep returned as were not sheep that had been hired. It is not obvious how the Court arrived at this sum, but the principle of their judgment being, according to the views I take, sound, I think their judgment ought to be affirmed in that respect.

The Eastern Province Court has further declared that this preference was the result of a collusive agreement, mutual understanding, or common consent between Tucker and Austen, and have enforced against Tucker the penalty of the 88th section of the Insolvent Ordinance. I cannot take upon me to say absolutely that in doing this that Court acted erroneously, for there is much to justify it in the evidence. But, on the whole, as the clause is highly penal, it ought to be construed liberally ; and I am disposed to view what passed on Tucker's part as dictated by anxiety that the general bond to Stone should not sweep away his sheep. He was aware of this bond from the beginning, and the correspondence shows that, in assisting Austen, he wished to avoid his sheep being taken to pay the debt for which the bond was given, and that this, rather than an intention to gain a preference over the general creditors of Austen, was what actuated Tucker in obtaining delivery of the sheep. And the difference

1868.
May 19.
" 22.
June 19.

Tucker,
Appellant ;
Austen's Trustee
Respondent.

1868.
May 19.
" 22.
June 19.

Tucker,
Appellant ;
Austen's Trustee
Respondent.

to be observed in construing the 88th, as compared with the 84th, is, that while the operation of the 84th is dependent upon the motives of the insolvent alone, irrespective of those of the preferred creditor, the operation of the 88th section depends upon a combination of the motives both of the insolvent and of the preferred creditor.

I am, therefore, disposed to think that the judgment appealed from should be reversed, so far as it gives effect to the 88th section against Tucker.

CONNOR, J., in the course of his judgment, observed:—
In considering cases of alleged undue preference, it is, I think, right to bear in mind that, as the provisions of the Insolvent Law in question have for their object the defeating of an interest vested in a creditor, we ought, upon the ordinary and well-known principles of construction in such cases, to be satisfied that the circumstances bring the case within the words and meaning of the enactments which, if applicable, defeat the creditor's interest, and work a forfeiture of his demands. It is, I think, well to bear in mind the words of Erle, J., in the case cited in the argument *Edwards vs. Glyn*, 28 *L.J. Q.B.* 351 (358) : " The tendency of the Courts, at one time, was to enable the assignees of a bankrupt to set at defiance all principles of right, and to step in and take all property for the general body of the creditors. An endeavour was made on the part of Parke, B., to stem the tide of this principle of law, by which, at least, great hardship had often been incurred." And he refers to cases in which the law had been corrected, and among them to *Brown vs. Kempton*, a case before the Exchequer Chamber, and on which the Court in *Edwards vs. Glyn* acted. I may add that I think it hardly admits of doubt that, if the case now before the Court had occurred in England, there should have been judgment for the defendant, the creditor, in the action below. I say so because it seems beyond doubt from the correspondence which is in evidence that the creditor here urged, pressed on the insolvent to give him up the sheep. The several letters of 28th May, 1866, 12th June, 1866, 6th July, 1866, and 12th February, 1867, show this. And it is stated in *Edwards vs. Glyn*, by Crompton, J., that in *Brown vs. Kempton* the Judge's direction to the Jury,—that if the payment was made under the influence of the pressure and importunity of the defendant, though, also, with a desire to give him a preference in the Court of Bankruptcy, still the payment was good,—was held by the Exchequer Chamber to be correct.

The case, however, of *Smith vs. Carpenter* (12 *Moore*,

P. C. C. 101) decides that the English authorities do not govern the construction of section 84 of the Insolvent Ordinance of this Colony,—that, in truth, that section must be construed according to the words used in it; and though I have no doubt that Mr. Porter was quite correct in stating in the argument that the intention in framing section 84 was to put the law of this Colony on the same footing on that point as the law in England, yet as the course taken for that purpose was to express in words what the unwritten law of England on the subject was supposed to amount to, and as we have seen the view of that unwritten law was about that time varying in England, the failure, if it be such, to express in a line or two what the law of England was, or ultimately became, was not unlikely, and is only another instance of the truth of the maxim, *Omnis definitio in jure civili periculosa est: parum est enim, ut non subverti possit.* (*Dig.* 50, 17, 202.)

1868.
May 15.
,, 22.
June 19.

Tucker, Appellant; Austen's Trustee Respondent.

The question in such cases for the English Courts is: Was there a fraudulent preference? The question under our Insolvent Ordinance of 1843, is: Was there such a transaction as is described in section 84? We can, I think, imagine cases which would be within that description, and yet not be properly termed, even in law, *fraudulent*. Sections 86 and 88, however, appear to deal with what must be considered acts of *dolus malus*; and it seems to be fair to argue that the English decisions with reference to fraudulent preference are not to be deemed inapplicable to the construction of sections 86 and 88 by reason of any distinction between a fraudulent and an undue preference.

The result of the English decisions would seem, from *Edwards vs. Glyn* and *Brown vs. Kempton*, to be, that if the act may be attributed in part to any motive influencing the debtor's will extraneous to his own choice or preference, though such his preference may have coexisted, the case is not one of fraudulent preference; that, in fact, if there be a sufficient actual cause, which, if existing alone, would not occasion the penalty, you are to attribute the act to that cause and not to hold the penalty to have been incurred.

There is nothing, I think, in the decision of the Privy Council in *Smith vs. Carpenter* (12 *Moore, P. C. C.* 101) to show that, to bring a case within section 84 of the Insolvent Ordinance, the Court must not be satisfied that the debtor not only contemplated the sequestration of his estate, but also intended, by the payment or other act, to prefer, directly or indirectly, the particular creditor above his other creditors. On the contrary, it is said expressly in the judgment that pressure by the creditor may "be so extreme as to negative the intention to prefer." In other words, the pressure may

M 2

1808.
May 19.
" 22.
June 19.

Tucker,
Appellant ;
Austen's Trustee
Respondent.

be so great as that the act by the debtor is to be attributed to pressure, and not to an intention to prefer, though, from his knowledge of his insolvency, he must know that such would be the effect of his yielding to the pressure. But (p. 114) if the pressure by the creditor is neither severe nor terrifying, nor occasioning any alarm to the debtor, and the latter knowing himself to be in a state of insolvency,—that his early stoppage and failure are morally certain,—and being friendly disposed towards the creditor, and desiring to favour and prefer him, does the act which gives the preference, such preference is undue within section 84. And I may add that both these positions are quite in accordance with the rule of the Roman Law, which *Merula* (*De Controvers. Juris.* 17, 43, 3), referring to *Jason* and *Parpuratus* on *Dig.* (12,1,4), says it is evident, from the authorities cited by them, has place in every subject, viz.: that that is to be considered which is principally intended, that being omitted which comes by way of consequence.

The first question in all these cases is, putting out of consideration any section of the Insolvent Ordinance but the 84th: Was what was done an undue preference within that section? I think it is clear that the insolvent in this case must be taken to have contemplated on 1st April, 1867, the sequestration of his estate as likely to take place at an early period. The trustee, in his evidence, states that the insolvent's books showed a deficiency against him on 1st April, 1867, of £826; but then this proceeds on the assumption that the sum of £913 for Mr. Stone's sheep lease was due then, whereas it was not to be due till 1st February, 1869, and therefore the statement of there being such a deficiency is, in strictness, not correct. But still the insolvent was not only subject to this future liability to Stone, but in his evidence he describes himself as, in January, 1867, on his "last legs;" and he was proposing to leave this Colony for the Free State, and was apparently endeavouring to induce Tucker to help him towards that. There is not, therefore, I think, much doubt but that he must be taken to have then contemplated his sequestration as very likely. But it is not to my mind at all clear that, to use the words of the definition (so to speak) in *Smith vs. Carpenter*, being friendly disposed towards the creditor, he was desirous to favour and prefer him. It is not to my mind by any means clear that that was his object in giving up the sheep; that he did not rather do it because he thought he had to do it when the second year of the lease expired. The mode in which the English authorities may, I apprehend, be brought to bear on, for instance, the provisions of section 86 is this: If the transaction was in the usual and ordinary course of business, and the Court thinks that the creditor was acting in reference to it, as a rule, then we ought not to hold him to have incurred the penalty merely because he knew that the affairs of the debtor were embarrassed, and that the act in question would very probably secure him, while afterwards other creditors might lose part of their demands,— that if we see another real motive which may reasonably be deemed to have actually and mainly existed in, and worked on, the creditor's mind, we ought not to reject it, and adopt the hypothesis that there was collusion between the debtor and creditor, " the one to give, and the other to get, a preference over the other creditors of the insolvent, *under colour* of a transaction in the ordinary course of business." These last are remarkable words, and the Court ought, I think, to construe them on the assumption that the Legislature made use of them with all the significance which they purport. Sections 84 and 86 are, I apprehend, to be construed together. This appears from, among other things, the fact that section 88, occasioning the forfeiture of the creditor's claim, does not expressly refer to section 86, it being, I presume, deemed included in the sections which are there named. Section 86, therefore, so far as its provisions are against the creditor's interest,—that is, so far as relates to what I call the exception,—is to be construed strictly ; and I am of opinion that the transaction in question ought not to be deemed within the exception if it appears to have been actually regarded by the parties as in the ordinary course of business ; that the exception applies only when the transaction is colourably, and not really, in the ordinary course of business. We have seen that that principle is recognized in *Smith vs. Carpenter*, with reference even to section 84,— viz., that when you find a real and mainly actuating cause of a nature different from collusion, you are to set down the act to the former cause, and not to the latter. You are not to impute an intention at collusion which will occasion a forfeiture, when there is another ground to which the transaction may, on the evidence, be reasonably referred. And we may, I think, be satisfied that much of the variety of decision which has been mentioned arose from there being a tendency at one time to construe the law loosely, so as to include cases within the penalty, and at another time to adopt a stricter construction.

I have said that it is not by any means clear to me that an intention to prefer Tucker was the occasion of the insolvent's part of the transaction in question ; that he rather gave over the sheep because he thought that he had to do so, *i e.*, had to do so in the ordinary course of business. His letter to Tucker of 6th July, 1866, goes far to show this.

1868.
May 19.
" 22.
June 19.

Tucker,
Appellant ;
Austen's Trustee
Respondent.

1868.
May 19,
„ 22.
June 19.

Tucker,
Appellant ;
Austen's Trustee
Respondent.

He says there: "If you will not accept less than £600, I fear that my efforts to find a friend will be in vain, and little as I like the idea of returning the sheep, it will have to be done. I would, however, stipulate that I be allowed to retain them for the whole of the current year." Here he asks that if the sale cannot be arranged, he may be allowed to keep the sheep till the end or the current year; that is, I apprehend, the current year of the lease, viz., to April, 1867. He would therefore think, and rightly, that when that day arrived, he would have to give over the sheep. In the view which I take of the case, it is unnecessary for me to form a judgment as to how the case would stand if the effect of section 84 were alone before us; but the foregoing considerations are not immaterial upon the question of the transactions being in the ordinary course of business. The correspondence which is in evidence in the case between the appellant and the insolvent satisfies me that the lease was tacitly construed by them both to mean that at its expiration the insolvent should give back sheep,—the sheep which had been originally hired, so far as forthcoming, but so far as not forthcoming, then others. We find the insolvent telling Tucker, in a letter of 28th May, 1866, of deaths by hundreds among the sheep; but this does not prevent Tucker, in his reply, writing of recalling the sheep, or the insolvent treating about the time of their being returned, or a sale to him of them by Tucker. (Letter of 6th July, 1866.) If it be said that under the lease (of 1st April, 1865), a diminution in the sheep was to be paid for,—not to be made up by other sheep,—the answer seems to me to be that it was quite competent for the lessor to consent to take sheep instead of money (which word is, indeed, not used in the lease), and that it is clear to me, as I have said, that that was their tacit, if indeed not express, understanding of their contract. It would, I think, be a strange result, if the insolvent's selling sheep to a third person, and paying over the price to Tucker, would have made the transaction safe as being in the ordinary course of business under the lease, but that his giving the sheep in payment directly to Tucker, instead of their price, prevented this; prevented the transaction being in the ordinary course of business. It has been suggested that if the transaction were of that kind, there would first have been a valuation on behalf of Tucker, in order that he should be paid the difference, if any, in value between the sheep returned and those hired. But we have to remember that under the lease Mr. Kidger Tucker was to be the arbitrator on this point, and the sheep were sent to where he was, viz.: at a farm held jointly by him and the appellant, his brother.

It has been urged also that Tucker intimated to the insolvent that, on the sheep being sent by the insolvent's son to Tucker's farm, Tucker might let them to the son, and it is said that this was not in the ordinary course of business ; but there is not any evidence to show that the insolvent's son was to be in fact only a nominal lessee, and should in fact hold the sheep for the benefit of the insolvent ; so that I do not see how a fresh letting after the expiration of the other lease prevents the giving up of the sheep to Tucker being in the ordinary course of business. I have no doubt but that Tucker was anxious to get his sheep out of the insolvent's hands, and this is, I think, the utmost that Tucker's letter of February, 1867,—in which he alludes to " casualty by means of hungry creditors,"—necessarily means, or requires us to hold it means ; that it may fairly bear this construction : " The time for getting my sheep has come. I have, as you know, long wished to conclude the matter, and I am afraid that while they are with you they may be taken in execution by hungry creditors." And this fear of itself helps to show the understanding on Tucker's part, as there clearly was on the insolvent's, that the latter's liability under the lease might be discharged by sheep other *in specie* than those leased.

1868.
May 19.
" 22.
June 19.
___
Tucker,
Appellant ;
Austen's Trustee
Respondent.

What is " the usual and ordinary course of trade or business " within the meaning of section 86 ? It is, I apprehend, that which is suitable to the nature of the particular business, and might reasonably and probably, and in ordinary course, have taken place without reference to a contemplated sequestration ; and such was, as it appears to me, Tucker's closing his transaction as to the sheep with the insolvent in April, 1867. He had been long reiterating that he should have to close it, and any communications he had with the insolvent were not calculated to lessen his anxiety. The first year of the lease was not made the conclusion of the term, at the insolvent's request ; and it was allowed to continue to the end of the second year, partly, apparently, because the insolvent held out hopes of his being able to find a purchaser for the sheep, which was a mode of concluding the transaction which Tucker would have preferred. In March, 1867, the insolvent went to Cradock, the appellant's residence, to try, apparently, to procure assistance from him towards going to the Free State, and he says that Tucker was then aware how he stood with Mr. Stone. But what would the insolvent tell him on that subject, but that, to the extent of £500 principal, Stone was secured by a second mortgage on a farm valued apparently at £1,250, and that of the remainder making the whole, upwards of £900 would not be due till 1st February, 1869 ? Was the appellant to con-

1868.
May 19.
„ 22.
June 19.

Tucker,
Appellant;
Austen's Trustee
Respondent.

sider himself bound to wait till that date before he concluded his transactions, though he had been so long anxious to conclude them as soon as possible?

The most reasonable construction, I apprehend, of the lease of 1st April, 1865, is this: " I let you a certain troop of sheep, to be returned by you at the end of the lease, and any difference in value, on any ground, between what you return as a whole and what you now get, is to be made up to me." This lease did not, I apprehend, transfer property in the sheep originally let from the lessor to the lessee. When a person lets any property to another for a year, unless it be property which can only be used by being consumed, or unless the term is too long for the things let out to last it in the usual course of things, the presumption is, I apprehend, that the things let are to be returned *in specie*, and there ought to be something in the terms of the lease to show that this is not to be so. In this lease of 1st April, 1865, not only is there no clause inconsistent with its being understood that the same sheep which were let were to be returned to the lessor, but such return seems expressly referred to.

The conclusion which I have arrived at on the whole case is, that the appellant is protected by section 86 of the Insolvent Ordinance, and that there ought to have been judgment in his favour in the Court below.

The Court disallowed the appeal, except as to the forfeiture with costs.

[Appellant's Attorney, *E. Hull*.
Respondent's Attorneys, *Reid & Nephew*.]

DANTU *vs.* WIDOW HART'S EXECUTORS.

Will, construction of.—Liquidation Account, Amendment of. Falcidian Fourth.

1868.
June 26.
July 13.

Dantu *vs.*
Widow Hart's
Executors.

This was an action to set aside the award of the Falcidian fourth made in an executor's liquidation account.

The Board of Executors of Cape Town and Dr. Roux, also of Cape Town, executors testamentary of the will of the late Magdelena Hart, widow of the late William Hart, of Cape Town, were summoned to answer J. W. Dantu, a minor, assisted by C. H. van Zyl, as his curator *ad litem*. By will, dated 4th October, 1865, Widow Hart, having first bequeathed £950 as legacies among twelve different parties —of whom plaintiff was one for £250 (the interest whereof was to be paid him during his minority and the capital on attaining majority)— declared "further to nominate and appoint as the sole and universal heirs of all the residue and remainder of her estate and effects, Solon van Haght and Magdalena Johanna Dantu, born Hendriks, in equal shares and proportions, burthening, however, the inheritance of the last-named with the entail of *fidei commissum*," &c. The executors, on realizing the assets, found the proceeds £850, and then made a *pro rata* distribution among the legatees, giving the plaintiff £134 1s. 6d., instead of £189 6s. 5d., which would have been his legacy had not the executors first deducted the *pro rata* share of the Falcidian portion, which they awarded to Solon van Haght and M. J. Dantu, regarding them as heirs entitled to such portion. And the present action was brought to declare this award a wrong one; the plaintiff, in his declaration, denying that Van Haght and Dantu were heirs under the will.

1868.
June 26.
July 13.

Dantu *vs.*
Widow Hart's
Executors.

The defendants, having first pleaded the general issue, pleaded specially that the true construction of the will was to appoint Van Haght and Dantu heirs, and thus entitle them to demand the Falcidian fourth claimable by heirs in cases where more than three-fourths of the estate of the deceased would be exhausted in the payment of legacies. They then proceeded to aver the insufficiency of the estate to pay the legacies and to deny the plaintiff's right to any greater sum than that mentioned in the liquidation account. To which plaintiff's replication was general.

The facts having been admitted, as above stated, the Court heard the argument on the pure point of law.

Reitz, for plaintiff. In the first place, it is necessary to point out what plaintiff takes to be the import of the words " sole and universal heirs of the residue and remainder of my estate," according to the ordinary rules of construction; and secondly, to ascertain what the intention of testatrix was with regard to the defendants. As to the construction, defendants must either read the sentence as it stands, or claim that the word "residue" should be expunged as superfluous. The tendency of civil law under later Roman and Dutch legislation has been to make the rights included under the word " heir " indentical with those included under the word " legatee," so as to make these convertible terms; the question whether the said " heir " is to be read as legatee, or conversely, depending upon the circumstances under which the will is made or the co-relation in which the word stands to qualifying ones in the same sentence. *Van Leeuwen* (*R. D. Law*, book 3, pt. 4, §§ 1, 2, 3) lays down that a " legatee " on whom is conferred the administration of the entire estate is, in fact, the " heir." For proof that the use of the word " heir " no longer has any " instituting

*1868.
June 26.
July 13.*

*Dantu vs.
Widow Hart's
Executors.*

force," see *Van der Keessel, Th.* 290. If a testator erroneously calls a person to whom, by his will he has given only a *legacy*, the *heir* of such bequest, this will, not make such beneficiary the testator's heir, so as to entitle him to the Falcidian fourth. What little regard is now paid to the use of the word "heir" in a will is laid down by *Huber* in his *Præl. pt.* 3 *p.* 1326. The duty which formerly devolved upon the heir of paying the legacies, and administering the estate generally, now falling chiefly on executors, the absolute necessity of instituting an heir no longer exists. *Decker*, in his note to *Van Leeuwen's R. D. Law, bk.* 3, *pt.* 2, § 1, remarks that the detraction of the Falcidian is retained in Dutch law, for the benefit of the heir alone. A person, therefore, who has no right as against the testator *ab intestato*, but who claims simply on the ground that he is named "heir" in the will, should make out a strong case. It is perfectly clear that by "residue and remainder" testator refers to that part of his estate which shall be over after payment of both debts and legacies. If we are, therefore, to read the word heir in the technical sense that defendants ascribe to it, *i.e.*, "universal heir," then the words "residue and remainder" either directly conflict with such meaning, or else they must be taken as qualifying the word "heir" in such a manner as to make it signify nothing more, in this case, than a residuary legatee. The words "residue and remainder" can only be considered as superfluous in case they do not qualify "heir;" or the latter word has so overpowering a technical meaning as to force every other standing in the same sentence with itself into a position consistent with its own purport. But the arguments already used and authorities already cited, go to show that there is no ground for either assumption. The nearest approach in Roman law to residuary heirs are those "*ex re certa.*" The "*heres ex re certa*" under the old Roman law could claim the Falcidian, the fact being that he was not in reality an heir "*ex re certa*," as the whole inheritance might under certain circumstances devolve upon him. *Code* 6, 24, 13, declares *heredes* "*ex re certa*" to be nothing more than legatees; and *Huber* in his *Præl. pt.* 3, *p.* '290, cites a case in which this is laid down as the law in Holland; and suggests, as the ground for this decision, that restricting the heir to a part is an indirect way of forbidding him to take the Falcidian. As to what was testator's intention with regard to defendants, there is no positive, but some negative evidence,—*e.g.*, the "heirs" are not appointed joint executors, which, though not absolutely necessary, is customary. And an intention to benefit the legatees rather than the "heirs" is apparent in the previous part of the will.

Porter for the defendant. The heirs named in the will are heirs entitled to the Falcidian portion. The words appointing them are large. They are made sole and universal heirs of all the residue and remainder of the estate and effects. If the heirs so named be not lawful heirs, then the writing is not a will, but a codicil; and the heirs *ab intestato* of Mr. Hart, whoever they may be, are entitled to the Falcidian. (*Dwyer vs. Executors of O'Flinn*, 28th February, 1857.) The testatrix has instituted heirs, and if so, they take the Falcidian; but as there is no prohibition to deduct the Falcidian, either the heirs named in the will or the heirs *ab intestato* must be entitled; and this will be an answer to the action under the general issue. The words "residue" and "remainder" are, in law, surplusage. All our colonial wills give legacies first, and then proceed to institute heirs, and no heirs can, as far as the language of the will is concerned, take more than what remains after legacies are paid; so that the maxim applies, *Expressio eorum quæ tacite insunt nihil operatur*. No doubt, the chief Roman reason for granting the Falcidian was to induce the heir to adiate. But a presumed intention to benefit the heir as the principal objects of the testator's bounty is also to be considered. Had Mrs. Hart been asked whether she preferred her legatees to her heirs, she would have answered that she did the very reverse. The heirs here were not heirs *ex re certa*, but of the whole estate; but even the heir *ex re certa* was entitled to the Falcidian. *Code* 3, 36, 10; 6, 50, 11; *Dig.* 35, 2, 47, § 1; *Leyser's Meditations*, spec. 391, sec. 17. Perhaps, this right in the heir *ex re certa* was connected with the civil law rule that no man could die partly testate and partly intestate. The Dutch law, no doubt, allowed that a man could do so. *Grot. Int.* 2, 18, 38; *Voet* 28, 1. 1; *Groen. De Leg. Abr. Inst.* 2, 13, 9. In certain cases it is admitted that a testator may prohibit the deduction of the Falcidian to all heirs except children in the first degree. *Voet*, 35, 2, 11. And *Voet* in this passage states that the prohibition need not be in express words, but may be made by equivalents. But there must be express words, or else a necessary implication. In making certain persons sole and universal heirs to "the residue and remainder" of the testatrix's estate, there is no necessary implication that all the legacies should be paid without any diminution. *Sande's Decis.* 4, 7, 9. In this case, the testator instituted A B as his heir in fifteen florins, and distributed the rest of his estate in legacies, adding a clause that any contravener of his will should forfeit what was left to him. The question was whether A B was thereby prohibited from deducting the Falcidian? And the Court held that he was not. It is laid down, no doubt,

1868.
June 26.
July 13.

Dantu *vs.*
Widow Hart's
Executors.

that no heir can deduct the Falcidian except an heir who adiates under benefit of inventory. *Van der Linden, p.* 147. *Cen. For.* 3, 16, 10; *Voet,* 28, 8, 22. But by the law of this Colony, under Ord. 104, every heir has the benefit of the inventory framed by the executor. Looking to the will, an inference of intention in favour of the heirs may fairly be drawn. They are made substitutes to certain legatees in case the latter should die, and " the inheritance " of one of these heirs is made *fidei commissum.* The testatrix mistook the value of her estate, but she plainly meant to leave inheritances to her heirs; and to give them nothing would defeat her intention.

Cur. adv. vult.

Postea (13th July) the Court delivered judgment.

CONNOR, J., said: The question in this case arises upon the will of a Mrs. Hart, dated 4th October, 1865, by which she directed her executors to sell the whole of her estate and effects, except some articles specifically bequeathed, and then left to the plaintiff £250, to be paid to him at twenty-one years of age, and the interest in the meantime to be applied by the executors in his maintenance and education, and if he died before twenty-one, the interest was to go to his mother for life (one of the residuary legatees), and after her death the capital to go to her children. The testatrix made several other pecuniary bequests, and finally, by the clause which raises the question in the case, she did " declare to nominate and appoint as the sole and universal heirs of all the residue and remainder of my estate and effects, the said Solon van Haght and Magdalena Johanna Dantu, born Hendriks, in equal shares and proportions, burdening, however, the inheritance of the last mentioned with the entail of *fidei commissum,* the interest only being received by the said Magdalena Johanna Dantu, and the capital devolving, after her decease, to her children in equal shares and proportions." The testatrix then " nominates and appoints " the defendants heirs, and inserts codicillary and reservatory clauses.

The testatrix's property was not sufficient to pay all the legacies, and the executors having allocated to the two so-called heirs of the residue the Falcidian portion, this action is brought on behalf of the plaintiff, a minor, to have it declared that the Falcidian portion is not claimable by the heirs in question, one of whom is, as I have said, his mother. The sum in dispute being very small, it seems to be greatly to be lamented that the question in the case could not have been disposed of without the institution of an action. The Court has, however, now to decide the question raised by the action. The contention which that question involves is certainly at first sight a little alarming, as it amounts to this,—that persons who, for the purposes of this action, must be taken to have no claims against the testatrix's estate, except what her will gives them, and being only given under the clause of the will in question what shall remain after the payment of legacies, can, by reason of that gift, claim the payment of a sum which not only does not remain after the payment of the legacies, but which, if allowed, will lessen considerably the amount which would be otherwise applicable to their payment, and will increase by one-fourth the inadequacy of the testatrix's estate to pay the legacies expressly bequeathed by her. Some provisions of the Roman law in reference to wills are, I think, generally admitted to be unsuited to the requirements of more modern society; and I think that Courts are not only warranted, but bound, to avail themselves of any sufficient authority for rescuing the public from the inconveniences of being subjected to those objectionable parts of the old law. The case of *Simpson vs. Forrester* (1 *Knapp, P.C. Rep.* 231) before the Privy Council, and which I have on more than one occasion lately referred to, is, I apprehend, an ample authority for our applying to the construction of wills the well-known testamentary principle of election, viz., that if any person avails himself under the will of any benefit which the will might have disposed of otherwise, he cannot prejudicially affect or insist upon any claim which will so affect provisions of the will in favour of other persons. This is a principle which commends itself so much to all men's instinctive sense of justice that it ought not, I think, if once established by authority, to be allowed by us to be subverted by verbal refinements or subtleties. And the principle appears to me to be in this case fatal to the defendants' contention. As, however, the case was but little argued with reference to this principle, I proceed to consider it further with respect to the points more particularly discussed.

It was argued here, on the part of the defendants, that the residuary clause in question is, in truth, an institution as heirs of the persons named in it, and that the law is that persons instituted as testamentary heirs are, by reason of such institution, entitled under the *Lex Falcidia* to deduct from their testator's estate one-fourth of the whole. to the loss, if need be, of the legatees; and that the Court is bound by this law until it be repealed by the Legislature. On the other hand, it was argued, on behalf of the plaintiff, that this law only applies to the strict Roman law heir, and that the residuary clause here did not constitute the legatees such heirs.

1868.
June 26.
July 13.

Dantu *vs.*
Widow Hart's
Executors.

1868.
June 26.
July 13.
―――
Dantu vs.
Widow Hart's Executors.

The heir of the Roman law was a successor to the whole rights, the *universum jus*, of the deceased. In the *Dig.* 50, 17, 62, (*et Id.* 50, 16. 24), it is laid down, "*Hereditas nihil aliud est quam successio in universum jus, quod defunctus habuerit ;*" and Huber, referring to these passages (*Prælect.* 2, 14 [a]) says: " An heir is the successor to the *universum jus* which the deceased had ;" and that hence the institution of an heir is, " the surrogation into the *universum jus* which the deceased had at the time of death." *Van Leeuwen* (Rom. Dutch Law, 3, 6, 1) says : " The leaving of an inheritance is an institution, by which any person transfers the management of his estate to another after his death ;" and he cites the *Dig. ubi supra*. And (3, 6, 3) a little farther on he speaks of the principal difference between the institution of heirs and the giving of legacies, as being that the former consists in the full management of the estate, and the latter in a mere bequeathing, which has no consequence but the enjoyment of the bequest, without any further management. I need hardly say that, according to this passage, the residuary clause in the will before us, taken with what we know to be the law of the Colony as to executors, was a *bequest*, and not an *institution of heirs*. There seems, however, to be no doubt but that in the Roman law, partly from what was known as the *jus accrescendi*, partly from a rule that a person could not die intestate as to part of his property only, and partly from the necessity of the appointment of an heir to the validity of a will, the institution of *one* person as an heir, even for a specified quantity, was held to constitute him a general heir. *Huber (De Cas. Enucl. Quæst*, 8, 2) explains this: " Since inheritance is nothing else but succession into the *universum jus* which the deceased had, as the jurists define it, it seemed that *prima facie* we should say that an institution of the usufruct, or of the bare property, was not valid ; because then no one is successor of the *universum jus*."

Add to this the perpetual nature of heirship, by which he who is once made heir never ceases to be heir, while, on the contrary, a fructuary has only a temporary legal character, which remains to the end of life, but is extinguished by death. But these reasons are not of so much weight that they hinder the institution of an heir from an usufruct. For there exists a firm rule of law that a testator cannot die testate as to part, and intestate as to part (*Dig.* 50, 17, 7), the force and power of which is, that the whole inheritance (*assem*) need not be disposed of by the form of institution. For if any person have written one man heir, for instance, of half, the whole inheritance will be in the half (says *Cæsar, Inst.* 28, 5, 5); that is, whoso has been instituted by express words of half, shall by the *jus accrescendi* take the whole inheritance. In like manner, a will is valid, when the person is nominated in it heir of certain things (*Inst.* 2, 17, 3); for the nominated heir of a thing certain, as of a farm, or other the least thing, is understood to be heir of all (*ex asse*), the mention of the thing being omitted. (*Dig.* 28. 5. 1. (4.) But if the heir of a thing certain have received a co-heir of some part of the whole, he is deemed a legatee, and, certain things being specified, it behoves him to deliver all other things to the other appointed *simpliciter*. Huber writes of this as then the *lex Frisica*; but that system adopted the Roman law more strictly than was done by the law of Holland proper, as appears from *Huber* himself in his *Dissertatio de Authoritate Juris Romani in Frisia*, where he says : " *In nulla terrarum orbis parte constanti gravitate et religione, juris Romani Legis æque florere ac in Frisia patria mea dulcissima.*" And, again, in his book *De Cas. Enucl. Quæst*, 20. 2. 7., in reference to a mother's appointment of a guardian, having stated that *Groenewegen* spoke of the Roman law on the subject as being abrogated, he proceeds : " Whatever it may be in the forensic use of the Batavi and other neighbours, I strongly doubt whether in Frisia, *which most religiously venerates Roman law*, this abrogation extends so far." Sande also refers to the same fact, *Decis. Fris*, 2. 7. 1. and 3. 1. 1. (*vid. et Groenewegen De Leg. Abrogat. Inst.* 2. 13). *Voet*, 28, 5, 23, states the Roman law to the same effect as *Huber*; namely, that if but one person be instituted heir, though for a limited quantity, or thing certain, he was still heir of the whole ; but, further on, *Ib.* s. 26, he says : " But since in present practice it has generally prevailed that any one can die testate in part, hence a person instituted of a thing certain, or of half, or a third, there being no co-heir, takes nothing but the thing or part assigned to him by the will ; the rest goes to the heirs *ab intestato*, if another evident intention of the testator to the contrary should not appear ;" and after referring to *Groenewegen* and to *Paul Voet*, and many others cited by them, he proceeds : " And hence also the *jus accrescendi* among testamentary heirs has not at present place further than the probable intention of the testator introduces it." *Groenewegen*, in the passage cited, *De Leg. Abrogat. Inst.*, 2, 14, 9, bears out *Voet*, and adds : " So, also the scrupulous subtlety of the Roman law being exploded, that *jus accrescendi* which draws its origin not from the context of the words and the likely intention of the testator, but from the law's power, is not received in our practice." (*Vid. et V. d. Keessel, Th.* 322.) This passage from *Groenewegen* has also a bearing upon a principle which I have already referred to, that where the Court has warrant of authority

1868.
June 26.
July 13.

Danta vs.
Widow Hart's
Executors.

<small>1868.
June 26.
July 13.

Dantu vs.
Widow Hart's
Executors.</small>

for it, it ought gladly to get rid of any subtlety or harshness of the Roman law, which sacrifices the intention of testators to the tyranny of words, and involves in the sacrifice men's instinctive principles of justice and fair dealing.

In a recent case (*Oosthuysen vs. Oosthuysen*, 1, *Buch. Rep.* 51) I went at length into what appeared to me to be grounds for holding that here, and now, the question of institution of heirs in a will, and adiation of the inheritance, stands on a wholly different footing from what it did in the Roman law. I refer, therefore, at present to that subject very shortly, and rather for the purpose of adding to the authorities which I referred to in the case which I have mentioned, this *Thesis* of *V. d. Keessel* which was cited in the argument (*Th.* 290): " At present a testament is valid, wherein an heir is not instituted, not so much by the help of the codicillary clause, as on account of the use of and reason for the *Lex* 7 of the *Dig.* 50, 17, ceasing." This *Lex* of the *Digest* is one declaring that the Roman law did not suffer the same civilian person to have departed both testate and intestate. This *Thesis* of *V. d. Keessel*, as we see, asserts that a will is valid without the institution of an heir, and that this is so independently of the codicillary clause, and implies that any necessity for such institution had its origin in a law which is abrogated, namely, that a person cannot die testate as to part, and intestate as to the remainder. *Christinæus*, too, in several places of his *Decisiones*, lays down the same proposition (1, 304, 16, and 305, 17, and 4, 10, 3); and having (1, 305, 17) cited *Gudelin*, that the institution of an heir was not necessary by the then practice, and that a testament scarcely differed from a codicil, he adds : " That an heir must necessarily have been instituted arose from the Roman law that no one should die partly testate and partly intestate, against *Dig.* 50, 17, 7, which subtlety is neglected among us. . . . Wherefore this is by our practice admitted, as the same learned *Gudelin* says, that that may be, and be called, a testament in which legacies only being left, no institution of an heir is made : for thus the laws *Parisiensium, Aurelianensium, Gandanensium, Ostracensium,* and very many other States, declare that the institution has not place in a testament; and the laws of other places consent at least in this, that the institution of an heir is not necessary to the substance of a will." We have it therefore, I think, sufficiently supported by authority, that a limited institution of heirship is not to be extended beyond the expressed limitation, and that any occasion for the institution of an heir to the validity of a will had reference to a law no longer in force, and is not now to be deemed essential to such validity.

It was argued by Mr. Porter that every institution of an heir contained an implied exception that the legacies were to be deducted from what he was to receive, and that, therefore, the express restriction of the heir to the residue was inoperative, on the principle of the maxim *Expressio eorum quæ tacite insunt nihil operatur.* But the argument for the defendant's contention was necessarily one which, as I have already intimated, urged on the Court that it was under a necessity of carrying out the behests of a strict, stern *protestas legis*, to use *Groenewegen's* expression, the effect of which would be to enable persons deriving any right they had, solely under the will of the testatrix, to defeat the same testatrix's intentions expressed in that very will; and the Court must, therefore, be astute to require claimants under such circumstances to bring their claim clearly and strictly within the express terms of the law on which they rely. They are not to be surprised if to the cry " I'll have my bond," they are met by the question, " Is it so writ in the bond ? " But, again, as an heir under the Roman law was one who had the *universum jus* of the deceased, every legacy was in fact left *from* him, and every *fidei commissum* was imposed as a burden on him; and this, I need not say, is the language of the Roman law and of the jurists always in reference to the subject. But in the case of the will before the Court, the legacies are not left from the so-called heirs; they are not given an interest, and they have no interest, in any part of the fund for paying the legacies. Again, the term *residue* refers to what remains after payment of debts, as well as legacies; but the heir of the Roman law was liable to the debts, and the inheritance, before payment of the debts, went to him.

With reference to the *Lex Falcidia* itself, there was a case cited in the argument from *Sande, Decis. Fris.*, 4, 7, 9, where it was held that a person instituted heir for fifteen florins, the remainder being given away in legacies, was entitled to deduct the Falcidian portion, though there was a clause that a contravener of the will should be deprived of that whereby he was benefited. This decision appears to me to have clearly proceeded upon the strict Roman law doctrine that a single person instituted an heir, though only of a thing certain, was to be regarded as an heir general. *Sande,* however, with reference to the clause as to contravening the will, adds that the decision " was in accordance with the opinion of those who hold that an express prohibition was necessary to prevent the Falcidian deduction; although the greater part teach that a tacit prohibition is sufficient." It is clear, therefore, that *Sande* was of opinion that a clause imposing a penalty upon any one contravening the will

1868.
June 26.
July 13.

Danta vs.
Widow Hart's
Executors.

contained a prohibition against a deduction which would lessen the fund for the legacies. It appears to me that this implied prohibition is stronger when the person claiming the Falcidian portion is not by the terms of the will to get anything until after the legacies, &c., have been paid. In addition to that, however, I repeat here what I have stated in another case (*Trustees of Blignaut vs. Cilliers*, 13th July, 1868, vide *post*), that the case of *Simpson vs. Forrester* before the Privy Council is an authority warranting the Court to adopt a principle which appears to me to be in itself a desirable and reasonable one, that the necessary result of the provisions of the will, as affected by any act, is to be deemed prohibited by the testator as effectually as if an express prohibition were contained in the will ; and that, therefore, with us the Falcidian portion can be tacitly prohibited.

I ought to mention, lest it should be thought I had overlooked it, that a case in this Court, that of *Dwyer vs. Rutherford*, was referred to by Mr. Porter as an authority in the defendants' favour. It is, however, I think, sufficient to observe that in that case there was no question of election ; and that the plaintiff claimed as the heir *ab intestato*, so that no question arose as to the form of the institution of heirs. This appearing from the statement of the case in the argument, I have not had occasion to consider the case more fully. The decision, as I understood, was to this effect : That a will, insufficiently attested as a will, may operate in certain cases as a codicil, and its provisions will then bind the heir *ab intestato*, but he will be entitled to the deductions which the Roman law gave to such an heir, burdened with an universal *fidei commissum*. This, as I have said, does not embrace the points which appear to me to decide this case, though no doubt it may imply, under the like circumstances, certain rights in an heir *ab intestato*.

In *Oosthuysen vs. Oosthuysen* I cited a case before this Court, that of *De Smidt vs. Burton* (*Menzies' Rep.* 222), in which the Court held that upon the true construction of the will, the surviving spouse, instituted universal heir of the firstdying, was entitled to an usufruct of the estate until the only child of the marriage should attain twenty-one. But we find that no allusion to any right in such an heir, though burdened with an universal *fidei commissum*, to the Trebellianic, or any other portion. Nor, again, in *Hofmeyr vs. De Wet*, also before this Court, and cited in *Oosthuysen vs. Oosthuysen*, do we, I think, find any such claim recognized. And if in later times there has, from, it may be, a love of the antiquities of learning, or of the archæology of law, or otherwise, been any resuscitation on such points of the old Roman law, which, its subtlety exploded and its arbitrariness reproved, has been allowed to die and to be buried, it is, I think, a wise and benefical act to reconsign it to the grave; and for one's justification, if any be needed, to point to the headstone erected over it after the lapse of ages, and now itself moss-grown; but which, upon examination, is found to have been long ago inscribed by authority with the epitaph *jam obit*. I cannot but think that there has been some confusion between the Roman-Dutch law in favour of children and other heirs at law, and the Roman law in favour of testamentary heirs. To the children and to certain other heirs at law was given, as superior to and overruling testamentary power, their legitimate, and it may be, other like portions; but surely in all *a priori* principle and right, and except in subservience to some technical rule, the occasion for which is long lost, those who have no claim except under the provisions of the will ought to be limited to the benefits which the will purports to give them. I doubt not but that there may be found in Roman-Dutch jurists statements antagonistic in appearance to some of the above propositions. But when those statements are scrutinized to their foundation, and you distinguish between their author's expositions of the theory of the Roman law, and what was their then practice, and when you select those who, being admittedly authorities of weight, are not prejudiced to what is obsolete, and if, moreover, and to some extent above all, we avail ourselves of the decisions of the Privy Council,—for us, I may say, equivalent to a legislative declaration of the law,—we shall be able, I believe, in a great degree to rescue the public from the more glaring inconveniences of the antiquated (all that is old is not antiquated) portions of a grand system of jurisprudence.

1868.
June 26.
July 13.

Dantu *vs.*
Widow Hart's
Executors.

It was stated in the argument that the present was the first case of the kind which, as far as was known, had occurred for decision. I have, therefore, gone into the questions involved at greater length than I probably otherwise should; and, on the whole, I have come to the conclusion that there ought to be judgment for the plaintiff.

The costs ought, I think, to be borne by the testatrix's estate. The words which she used in the will occasioned the difficulty; the point involved was new, and the plaintiff's success is to the benefit of the legatees generally.

BELL, J.: I concur very much with my brother Connor's views, considering them in the abstract. Doing so, I have not felt it necessary to deal with the arguments presented by the counsel on either side so much at large as I otherwise would have felt it my duty to do; but the difficulty I feel is, while agreeing with my brother's positions in the abstract, to apply them in the concrete.

That the institution of an heir is necessary to the constitution of a will has been not only the reading of the text, but the tradition of the Elders in Roman-Dutch law ever since I have had the honour of a seat on this Bench. I should, therefore, hesitate before disturbing that doctrine, unless in a case in which I felt called upon to do so, and to say whether I would uphold a rule, which in my own opinion and, so far as at present advised, seems to me to be effete and inapplicable to the present state of society. In this case I am not so called upon. Were I placed in such a position, I should probably not hesitate to enter upon the disquisitions raised by my brother; and possibly I would draw the same conclusion as that at which he has arrived; but I could only do so after the matter had been more fully discussed and more forcibly presented than the present case has afforded an opportunity for doing. Mr. Reitz did every justice to his client's case, his argument discovered much learning and research, and was delivered with a clearness and precision that showed he was master of the subject he was handling, and gave promise of his being a valuable acquisition to the Bar; but it was not necessary, in my opinion, to go so far as he seemed to think necessary, although it was convenient for the defendant to say that he must do so or fail.

The case of the plaintiff is admitted to be *sui generis*, and of the first impression, and in its circumstances it does not suggest cases in which to ignore the rule as to the necessity for the institution of an heir, and with it the right to the Trebellianic and Falcidian portion, might conflict with the natural law, so far as the rule as to them has its foundation in natural law. Both of these deductions from the estate of the testator have their origin, partly at least, in the assumption that the testator, at the time of framing his will, had not present to his mind the natural claims of his natural heir. Where the heir instituted happens to be the natural heir, and the disposition of the testator's estate by his will is such that, after they are satisfied, nothing will remain for him, there is both reason and justice why the claims of nature should be satisfied by the allowance of the Trebellianic or Falcidian portion, as the case may be. Nay, where the heir instituted may not be the natural heir, and, without his institution, there would not be any one to carry out the provisions of the will, if such a case could now occur, it might be expedient that a temptation, in the shape of an allowance of the Trebellianic or Falcidian portion to the person instituted as heir, should be held out to induce him to undertake that burden.

But it is not necessary in the present case to enter into any of these considerations. Assuming the institution of an heir to be necessary to the constitution of the will, without which the testator would have died intestate, and in which case the heir at law would have come forward, there is by this will the institution of an heir in the terms of the residuary gift, making the defendant " sole and universal heir of all the residue and remainder of my estate," and the only question to be decided, in my opinion, is, whether these terms do or do not deprive the person so instituted as heir of any right to claim either the Trebellianic or the Falcidianr portion.

1868.
June 26.
July 13.

Dantu vs.
Widow Hart's
Executors.

It is, no doubt, true that where the party is instituted heir without more,— as I think is the more general practice in wills,— he is entitled to deduct the Trebellianic portion, and if the estate be exhausted by legacies, he is entitled to deduct the Falcidian portion. Nay, if the heir be left something by the will, if he be made heir *ex re certa*, he may still be entitled to the Falcidian portion, according both to *Voet* and *Pothier* in the passages cited for the defendant, if the legacies, as in the present instance, exhaust the estate.

But it was admitted for the defendant that, if deduction of the portions were expressly forbidden by the will, the prohibition must receive effect, except, in the case of near descendants. On the other hand, it was argued, and properly too, perhaps, that the prohibition, in order to receive effect, must be precise and definite. In illustration of this, the case from *Sande*, 4, 7, 9 was referred to. There the party was instituted heir in fifteen florins, and the will contained a declaration that anyone contravening the will should be deprived of everything which, by the terms of the will, he was to take. The question was, could the heir instituted to the fifteen florins, and, as such, clothed with the general inheritance, take this special bequest, and at the same time claim to deduct the Falcidian portion from the general estate of the testator ; and the decision was that he could, the fact of claiming the portion not being considered to be a contravention of the will. In other words, the clause was held not to be a prohibition expressed in such definite and precise form as to entitle it to receive effect ; *Sande's* own opinion, however, being that an implied prohibition was enough.

I am quite willing to accept the argument of the defendant as a true exposition of the law, and the instance as confirmatory of it, and yet, and in some degree because of that exposition, I am of opinion that the judgment of the Court ought to be for the plaintiff, finding that the defendant is not entitled to deduct either the Trebellianic or the Falcidian portion, and for this reason, as I threw out in the course of the argument, the defendant is not at the outset of the will instituted heir without more, the institution being followed by specific

1868.
June 26.
July 13.

Dantu *vs.*
Widow Hart's
Executors.

gifts to others; neither after disposition of the estate by gifts to others is he instituted heir to a definite, specific part of the estate, as in the case in *Sande*, but the estate is first disposed of by legacies, without mention of an heir, and thereafter, and not till then, the defendant is instituted, not generally as heir, without saying more, or to the general inheritance, as the law would infer in such circumstances, but he is instituted heir " in all the residue and remainder" of the estate. This, as I read it, is as good as an express definite prohibition against the party taking, as heir, more of the estate than shall remain after payment of all the legacies given before his institution as heir in this remainder. It is impossible in such a case to give effect to the presumption on which the allowance of the Trebellianic or the Falcidian portion is founded, viz.: that when disposing of the estate the right of the heir was not present to the mind of the testator; for in the very terms of the institution, the right of the heir to something is recognized, and is at the same time limited as to its extent.

I am of opinion that upon this ground the judgment of the Court should, as I before observed, be in favour of the plaintiff, for payment of his legacy so far as the estate, without deduction either of the Trebellianic or the Falcidian portion, is equal to such payment.

Judgment was given for plaintiff accordingly; costs out of the estate.

[Plaintiff's Attorney, *Van Zyl.*
Defendants' Attorney, *De Korte.*]

MCLEOD & CO. *vs.* DUNELL, EBDEN & CO.

Sale and Purchase.—Broker's Note, Interpretation of, by Extrinsic Evidence.—Custom of Trade.

1868.
June 14.
„ 23.
July 13.

McLeod & Co.
vs. Dunell,
Ebden & Co.

This was an action to compel delivery of a promissory note for £228 4s. 3d., payable at Cape Town on the 13th July, 1868, or payment to the plaintiff of the said sum of £228 4s. 3d.

The declaration stated that on the 10th January, 1868, the defendants were indebted to the plaintiffs in the said sum, as the price of twenty-five hhds. of Cape brandy (together with charges of coolie-hire, shipping, freight and primage) sold and delivered to defendants, it being agreed at the time of sale that the promissory note prayed should be taken in settlement, which note, however, the defendants had neglected and refused to deliver, &c.

The defendants having pleaded the general issue, pleaded specially: That they were merchants trading in Port Elizabeth, and that the defendants are merchants trading at Cape Town; and that the plaintiffs, on the 10th January, and at Cape Town, sold to the defendants twenty-five hhds. of Cape brandy, warranted by the plaintiffs to be, as regarded the strength of the said brandy, fully nineteen degrees of Cartier's hydrometer. That the plaintiffs shipped and defendants received twenty-five hhds. of Cape brandy, of which number the defendants, relying on the representations of the plaintiffs, involved in the warranty aforesaid, did, without testing the strength of the brandy, immediately after its arrival, sell and dispose of nine hhds., which nine hhds. defendants admitted for the purpose of this action to have been of the strength warranted by the plaintiffs. That shortly after the sale and delivery by them of the said nine hhds., they caused the remaining sixteen hhds. to be carefully tested, when they discovered that none of it was of the degree of strength warranted, but that it was of considerably less strength, to wit, eighteen degrees of Cartier's hydrometer; of which fact the defendants did, within a reasonable time from their receipt of the brandy, give the plaintiffs notice, and apprise them that they would not accept the sixteen hhds., but would hold the same for plaintiffs, at their disposal, which had been accordingly from that time hitherto done. That for the value of the nine hhds. sold, defendants had always been willing to give a promissory note, but the plaintiffs had refused it, averring that the whole of the twenty-five hhds. were of the strength by them warranted, namely, nineteen degrees by Cartier's hydrometer. The plaintiffs' replication was general.

The Court heard evidence, directed, amongst other points, to the usage of trade in Cape Town in testing the strength of brandy sold, when it appeared that no allowance was made for temperature either on the Cape Town market or among private dealers, and that glass Cartiers were in general use, and not brass Cartiers with thermometer and scale attached. The leading points of the evidence on which the Court laid weight will be found more fully given in the judgments below. It was agreed at the Bar to confine the case to the nineteen hhds. undisposed of by defendants, leaving all questions as to the other nine hhds. out of the case.

Postea.—The Court heard the argument, when *Cole*, for plaintiffs, maintained that the contract had been fulfilled by plaintiffs, who having undertaken to supply brandy full nineteen degrees by Cartier, had, on the evidence, supplied brandy of that strength as tested by the glass Cartier in general use on the Cape Town markets and

1868.
June 14.
" 23.
July 13.
———
McLeod & Co.
vs. Dunell,
Ebden & Co.

1868.
June 14.
" 23.
July 13.

McLeod & Co.
rs. Dunell,
Ebden & Co.

among dealers in brandy both in Cape Town and Port Elizabeth. That on the evidence of Bolus, the broker through whom the sale was effected, he had never known a brass Cartier to be used in the Colony, and at the time of sale thought that the measurement would be by the glass Cartier in ordinary use, and thus bound the defendants, as his principals (*Story on Contracts, ed.* 1856, *vol* 1, *pp.* 396-7). As to the interpretation of " full 19 ^{o}" in the broker's note, that must be guided by the general rules for interpretation of words in contracts by custom and usage of trade (*Addison on Contracts*, p. 851, 4*th ed.*).

Porter for defendants.—On the question, what was the contract, there can be no controversy ; the brandy was to be full nineteen degrees Cartier. That is common cause, although the broker's note is silent. But that contract has not been fulfilled. Warranty must be not substantially, but strictly kept (*Smith's Merc. Law*, 4*th ed.*, p. 460). The Cartier should have been a true brass Cartier, such as the defendants use, and not a glass one, as the evidence shows is in use by all besides them. The glass Cartier may be in use on the Cape Town market, but there is no proof of any custom in Cape Town by which the strength of brandy not bought upon the market is, irrespective of the voluntary consent of both parties, to be determined by the market-master with a glass Cartier. It might as well be determined by the marketmaster's palate. The custom of the market, to bind the purchaser in it, must be a good custom. (*Hibbert vs. Shee*, 1 *Camp.* 113 : *Yates vs. Pym*, 6 *Taunt*. 446 : *Taylor on Evidence*, 2 *vol.*, §§ 1064-5.) When a purchaser stipulates for an article, the strength of which can be scientifically ascertained by a certain instrument, any custom of trade which shows that the strength has been not ascertained by the proper scientific instrument, scientifically applied, is not admissible. It is a vicious custom, and against express contract. Dunell, Ebden & Co. could not have contracted to buy the brandy on any understanding that temperature was not to be taken into consideration in testing its strength, when at the date of contract they had in their possession a true brass Cartier with thermometer.

Cole in reply.
Cur. adv. vult.

Postea (13th July).—The Court delivered judgment.

HODGES, C.J. : In January last the defendants, merchants at Port Elizabeth, through their brokers there, caused a message to be sent, by telegraph, to Mr. Bolus, a broker in Cape Town, requesting him to quote the price of Cape brandy. Bolus thereupon made an application to the plaintiffs, who are extensive dealers in brandy, and afterwards sent a message in reply to the effect that he could purchase of the plaintiffs, " McLeod & Co, brandy, full 19° strength, at £21 per hhd." Another message was then sent, directing him to purchase twenty-five hogsheads for the defendants at that price. Bolus bought according to his instructions, and the following brokers' note was drawn up :

1868.
June 14.
" 23.
July 13.
McLeod & Co.
vs. Dunell, Ebden & Co.

" Cape Town, 10th January, 1868.

" Sold on account of Messrs. Wm. McLeod & Co., to Messrs. Dunell, Ebden & Co., 25 hhds. of brandy, good quality, full 19° strength, at £21 per 127 imperial gallons, including wood. To be shipped per *Majestic* (at 10s. per ton), freight and shipping charges added to invoice, but not to be insured. Payment—promissory note six months from date payable here; seller to pay brokerage.

" A. B. HARRIES & Co., Brokers.
" Per H. BOLUS."

The brandy was shipped by the *Majestic*, and received by the defendants at Port Elizabeth, who on the 12th February, 1868, sent the following letter to the plaintiffs :

" By to-day's post you would have received a settlement for the brandy per *Majestic*, had it proved equal to what we purchased by, 19° Cartier. But it falls far short of this, being only just $17\frac{1}{2}°$."

By return of post, the plaintiffs replied as follow :

" We are in receipt of your favour of the 12th instant, the tenor of which we are much surprised at. We sell here according to our market standard, and the brandy having been the full strength of 19° according to that proof when shipped."

To this letter the defendants, in reply, say (*inter alia*) :

" You harp upon the Cape Town standard, with which we have nothing to do, and which we understand to mean a test by a Cartier hydrometer, irrespective of the temperature of the brandy at the time."

A long correspondence was then carried on, but the parties not being able ultimately to come to any satisfactory arrangement, the result was, the present action brought by the plaintiffs, to compel the defendants to give the promissory note referred to in the brokers' note, or to pay the amount claimed. Evidence has been given to show that a great reduction in the value of brandy took place at about the

1868.
June 14.
" 23.
July 13.

McLeod & Co.
vs. Dunell,
Ebden & Co.

period of the correspondence, but that circumstance cannot affect our decision. The whole question has turned on the meaning of the words "full 19 strength" as used in the note. It appears by the correspondence already referred to that the defendants insisted that the brandy must be full 19 strength as denoted by a Cartier hydrometer used with a thermometer and scale, whilst the plaintiffs contended that it meant 19 Cartier, as that instrument was invariably used in the Cape Town markets and in the various wine stores there, without reference to the heat of the liquid, and without any use of a thermometer or scale. Without discussing the abstruse, scientific and very interesting evidence which has been brought before us, it is sufficient to say, for the purpose of my judgment, that it was clearly demonstrated that by the use of a Cartier, without reference to the state of the atmosphere, a greater degree of strength was indicated by the instrument in warm weather than when it was used in cold weather. But the evidence was overwhelming to show that for upwards of twenty years the strength of brandy had been ascertained in Cape Town by the use of Cartier's ordinary instruments, formed of glass, without any reference whatever to temperature. The marketmasters of the two markets, where brandy is sold in large quantities, proved that at the time they submitted the liquor to auction, they invariably immersed the instrument in a tin cup, in which a portion of the liquor to be sold was placed, and then the apparent strength which the instrument indicated was marked on the cask, and it was sold and purchased as of that degree of strength. Several experienced merchants likewise informed us that in their experience they had sold and purchased brandy in the same manner, and in no other, and although it was not proved that the instruments used by the marketmasters were treated as standards by which all other instruments should be regulated, yet it was shown that in several instances when new instruments had been purchased at the chemist's shops, the marketmasters were applied to by the purchasers to test their accuracy. They were, in fact, in universal use among the persons in the trade. One witness proved that he had sold these glass Cartiers by hundreds, and it was also shown that they were used in the stores as well as on the markets, and no doubt can be entertained that for very many years the comparative degrees of strength of the brandies bought and sold in Cape Town were thus ascertained. Indeed, the evidence was, in the language used by Tindal, C. J., in *Lewis v. Marshall*, 7 Man. and G. 745, "clear, cogent and irresistible." There is nothing morally wrong in this mode of ascertaining the strength of the brandies, neither is it an unreasonable usage. Indeed, I am not sure that, under the circumstances, it was not the best way in which the farmers from the interior, and the buyers of brandy in Cape Town, could arrive at a tolerable notion of the comparative merits of the article brought to the market. If the marketmasters had used an instrument of a more scientific character, with a scale adapted to the thermometer, adjusted at so many degrees of heat, I doubt if it would have given as much satisfaction to the vendors as the use of this much more simple test. It was, as one of the witnesses described it, a rough-and-ready way of ascertaining the comparative strength of the brandies submitted for sale. And it is a singular fact that the witnesses were, with one or two exceptions, quite ignorant that the state of the atmosphere had anything whatever to do with the indication shown by the instrument when it was used. No doubt a Sykes or Cartier used with a thermometer and scale would have denoted the actual strength with more perfect accuracy; but I cannot come to the conclusion that the usage or custom so proved is so objectionable as to make it illegal. Assuming, then, that the defendants are bound to accept this brandy, if it was put on board the ship in Table Bay at a full strength of 19, indicated by Cartier used without a thermometer, is the evidence sufficient to show that this condition was fulfilled? I think that no doubt can be entertained on that point. The plaintiffs proved that their Cartier had been tested with the instruments of the marketmasters before the contract was entered into; that the shipment was made of brandy which answered the description of full 19, when tried by their thus previously tested instrument; that when the dispute as to strength had arisen, they tested a sample bottle of the brandy sent to the defendants with the instruments used by the marketmasters, and it was found to be full 19 Cartier, applied according to the usage. But there are other points deserving of notice. First: Was all this evidence of usage admissible to explain the contract as it was expressed in the broker's note? I apprehend that it was. Without extrinsic evidence the note would be unintelligible. What is the meaning of "full 19 strength?" It might mean strength by Sykes' hydrometer, which is the standard required to be used in the Colony, for the purpose of ascertaining the strength of spirits, for purposes of revenue by the Act No 1, 1855. We all know that this hydrometer cannot be used without ascertaining the heat of the liquor at the time; this is done by immersing a thermometer in the spirits, and then the scale set, I believe, at 60 Fahrenheit is referred to, and thus the actual strength above or below proof, and not the apparent strength, is ascertained. But the defendants did not contend

1868.
June 14.
„ 23.
July 13.
McLeod & Co.
vs. Dunell,
Ebden & Co.

1868.
June 14.
" 23.
July 13.

McLeod & Co.
vs. Dunell,
Ebden & Co.

that Sykes' hydrometer, which acts on a totally different principle from Cartier's, was to be used. They admitted that it was by the use of one of Cartier's instruments that the full 19 strength was to be ascertained; but they contended, further, that a thermometer must be used and a scale applied, as in the case of Sykes' instrument. Now it is not unimportant to remark that no instrument of Cartier's fitted up with a thermometer and scale was ever seen in Cape Town, until the arrival of the Cartier instrument, made in London, was produced for the purposes of this cause, and which had also been previously used by the defendants to test the brandy at Port Elizabeth. The expression "fully 19 strength," therefore, required extrinsic evidence to explain its meaning, and Bolus, the broker, and many other witnesses, deposed that it meant full 19 strength as denoted by Cartier's instrument, used without a thermometer, and irrespective altogether of the state of the atmosphere. The rule as to the admissibility of such evidence is accurately laid down in the note to *Wigglesworth vs. Dallison, Smith's Leading Cases*, 530: "With respect to contracts commercial it has been long established that evidence of a usage of trade applicable to the contract, and which the parties making it knew, or may be reasonably presumed to have known, is admissible for the purpose of importing terms into the contract, respecting which the written instrument is silent. The words 'usage of trade' are to be understood as referring to a particular usage to be established by evidence, and perfectly distinct from that general custom of merchants which is the universal established law of the land, and which is to be collected from decisions, legal principles and analogies, not from evidence in *pais*, and the knowledge of which resides in the breasts of the judges." And in *Myers v. Earl*, 30 *Law J.* (*Q B*) 9, Mr. Justice Blackburn says on the same subject : " The decision of this case turns simply upon the point that the words of a written contract are to be understood in that sense which the phrase has acquired in the trade with regard to which it is used. It is the *prima facie* presumption that it was the intention of the parties to use it in that sense, and having expressed themselves in a written contract making use of the phrase, it is *prima facie*, as a matter of construction of the contract, to be taken that they use the phrase in the peculiar and limited sense which it had acquired in the trade. That peculiar and limited sense—if such an one had been acquired—must be shown by parole evidence, and this having been shown, then the presumption is that that was the sense in which the parties making the contract used it. I do not think that in order to introduce this extrinsic evidence it is necessary that the phrase itself should be at all on the face of it ambiguous." Then referring to the rule laid down in *Smith's* *Leading Cases* already referred to, the learned Judge says : "That, I take it, is the true rule of law upon the matter, that in each case of a contract, where it is shown that the term or phrase has acquired a peculiar meaning in the trade, it is *prima facie* to be taken as used with that meaning unless upon construing the whole contract you can see, either in express terms or by necessary implication, the parties intended to use it in a different sense." Then, secondly, did the defendants know or may they reasonably be presumed to have known the usage at Cape Town to test the strength of brandies by a Cartier, used without a thermometer? On this point there is the evidence of one of the plaintiffs (Mr. McLeod), that he had on a former occasion sold brandy to the defendants with a warranty as to its strength, and that they received it without objection at Port Elizabeth, after he had used a Cartier in the usual way to ascertain the strength. There is also the evidence of Mr. Haupt that he had consigned parcels of brandy to the defendants with warranty as to strength, ascertained by a Cartier in the usual manner, and that no objection was ever made. Lastly, it is stated by Bolus, who purchased the brandy, that he had full knowledge of the usage, and also that he had on various occasions purchased brandy of the plaintiffs, with a warranty as to strength, which he had himself ascertained and approved of after testing it with a Cartier used without a thermometer. It is not necessary to say that the defendants were irrevocably committed by the knowledge of Bolus (although *Sutton vs. Tatham*, 10 *A. and E.*, 27, and *Bayliffe vs. Butterworth*, 1 *Exchequer R.*, 415, are strong authorities to show that they were), but it seems to me an irresistible conclusion that when Bolus, in answer to the telegram, replied, " I can buy brandy of Messrs. McLeod & Co., 19 strength, at £21 per hogshead," they would undoubtedly have made inquiry as to the meaning of the expression, if they had not perfectly understood what it meant. I think that their silence on the matter, taken in addition to the other facts, is a clear indication that they were well informed that brandies were tested in Cape Town by a Cartier, used without the thermometer. This case, therefore, is quite a different one from *Kirchner vs. Venus*, 12 *Moore's P. C. Cases*, 399, where it is said that "where evidence of the usage of a particular place is admitted, to add to or in any manner to affect the construction of a written contract, it is admitted only on the ground that the parties who made the contract are both cognizant of the usage, and must be presumed to have made their agreement with reference to it. But no such presumption can arise where one of the parties is ignorant of it." For these reasons I am of opinion that

1868.
June 14.
„ 23.
July 1 3.

McLeod & Co.
vs. Dunell,
Ebden & Co.

judgment should be for the plaintiffs for £228 4s. 3d., with costs.

BELL, J.: The transaction between the plaintiffs and defendants, out of which this action has arisen, was as follows: The defendants, Dunell & Co., merchants in Port Elizabeth, applied to mercantile brokers in that town to learn on what terms Cape brandy could be bought in Cape Town. These gentlemen telegraphed the inquiry to Messrs. Harries & Co., of Cape Town. Mr. Bolus, the managing clerk of Harries & Co., applied to the plaintiffs, McLeod & Co., and telegraphed to their correspondents in Port Elizabeth that the plaintiffs had brandy to the strength of 19 to dispose of at the price of £21 per hhd. The brokers in Port Elizabeth communicated this to the defendants, and thereafter, by their desire, the brokers telegraphed to Harries & Co., to buy of the plaintiffs 25 hhds. at the price mentioned. Harries & Co. performed their duty by making the purchase, and passing bought and sold notes to the buyer and seller, in which the strength of brandy was stated at "full 19," without further addition. McLeod & Co. filled up 25 hhds. from vats in their cellars, and drew from each hogshead a certain quantity which they tested by their Cartier hydrometer, and then they filled a quart bottle with the samples taken from each cask. The 25 hhds. were shipped in Table Bay in a vessel which sailed some time in January, I suppose, as the plaintiffs wrote the defendants on the 16th of January, advising them of the shipment, and of their having debited them with the amount as due on the 13th July, or six months from the date of the bill of lading, in conformity with the brokers' note: and I suppose the brandy would reach Port Elizabeth late in January or early in February, though, singularly enough, there is no evidence, so far as I can see, of the particular day on which the defendants got delivery. On the 12th February, Dunell & Co. wrote to McLeod & Co. that they would have forwarded them a settlement of the brandy "had it proved equal in quality to what we purchased, to wit, 19 Cartier, but it falls far short of this, being only just $17\frac{1}{4}$." The letter concluded with saying, "a few casks were sent away, unfortunately, before the low strength was discovered." It will be observed from this letter that without anything said in the letter of McLeod & Co., of the 19th January, about "Cartier," Dunell & Co. themselves construed the expression in the brokers' note, "full 19 per cent. strength," to mean not 19 certain, but "19 Cartier." On the 15th Febuary, McLeod & Co. wrote Dunell & Co., expressing their surprise, at their letter of the 12th, and continued, "we sell here according to our market standard, and the brandy having been the full strength of 19 deg., according to that proof, when shipped, we must insist upon a settlement according to invoice." On the 18th February, McLeod & Co. again wrote Dunell & Co., enclosing certificates from their own produce clerk, showing that the strength was as invoiced, and continued, " as to the brandy being only 17½ by our Cape standard, it is simply impossible, as we never buy brandy under 19." On the 24th February, Dunell & Co. wrote McLeod & Co.: " You harp upon the Cape Town standard, with which we have nothing to do, and which we understand to mean a test by a Cartier hydrometer, irrespective of the temperature of the brandy at the time. We decline to accept of the parcel, which (save the nine hogsheads unfortunately sent away before we discovered the weakness of the spirit, and for which we are quite prepared to settle), we hold at your disposal." On the 27th February, McLeod & Co. wrote Dunell & Co. that they had " requested Mr. Masters to test the strength of the brandy, and we have also requested him to take a sample and get the same tested by Sykes's hydrometer. We regret you do not mention the strength by Sykes, as tested by yourselves, as had you done so, we might have tested the sample we have here, and thus have arrived at the true strength. However, we prefer having a certificate from a disinterested party, and if on receipt of that we find ourselves to be in error, we shall willingly relieve you of the remainder of the parcel." On the 2nd March, Masters sent McLeod & Co. a certificate, by one of the Custom-house officers of Port Elizabeth, that the strength of the brandy—the heat being 74 and the indicator 68·4—was equal to 21·6 per cent. under proof by Sykes. On the 4th March, Dunell & Co, apparently assenting to the report of Masters, wrote McLeod & Co.: " His report will, we imagine, convince you of the poorness of the brandy." On the 7th March, McLeod & Co. wrote Dunell & Co.: " As the certificate of Masters gives 21·6 under proof by Sykes, while the landing-waiter here gives 19 degrees Cartier, as equal to 22·6 under proof, it follows that the former must be stronger by 1 of Sykes than the latter, and, therefore, *over* the strength of 19 degrees Cartier, and, consequently, in accordance with the strength stipulated for in the brokers' note. We are confirmed in our opinion that you have no ground for complaint, and we must insist upon a settlement as per invoice rendered. We may state that 17½ Cartier—the strength given by you of our brandy—would be equal to 33 under proof of Sykes, whereas by Mr. Masters' certificate it was only 21·6 under proof." On the 11th March Dunell & Co. wrote: " Setting aside the tests by Sykes's hydro-

1868.
June 14.
„ 23.
July 13.

McLeod & Co.
vs. Dunell,
Ebden & Co.

1868.
June 14·
22.
July 13.

McLeod & Co.
vs. Dunell,
Ebden & Co.

meter altogether, the strength of the spirit by our Cartier, than which there is none better in the Colony, being a well and expensively made metal instrument, not one of glass as commonly used, is under 18, which you will at one perceive when we tell you that the instrument, being adjusted for a temperature of 60, indicated only 18 with the temperature at 67." On the 17th March McLeod & Co. wrote, accepting an offer of reference contained in Dunell & Co.'s letter of the 11th March, and proposing as the referees the two marketmasters of Cape Town, " to and by whom such disputes here are invariably referred and settled." On the 24th March Dunell & Co. objected to these referees, " for the simple reason that we do not consider either of them competent to decide the question in dispute, for if they test spirit in the way we believe, viz., without reference to a thermometer, it is impossible for them to arrive at the correct strength." The correspondence ended here, and the result has been the present action, which was preceded, however, by a letter from the attorneys of the plaintiffs to the defendants. On the 6th April the defendants answered that letter, saying ; " We saw no chance of our taking the brandy *as being quite unsuited to our trade* (underscored); it would only suit us to become the proprietors of it by a very large reduction in price, larger, we knew, than McLeod & Co. would consent to." I have taken out these extracts from the correspondence because, in my opinion, they go two-thirds of the way in deciding the case. I shall recur to them by-and-by ; meanwhile, let me make these observations in passing. The words of the brokers' note are, " strength full 19·per cent." Nothing in that instrument, or in the letters of McLeod & Co., previous to Dunell & Co.'s letter of the 12th February, explained what these expressions meant; but that letter of Dunell & Co., of 12th February, explains them to mean " 19 by Cartier." Nothing in the brokers' note, or in the letters of McLeod & Co., previous to the letters of Dunell & Co. of 24th February and 24th March, explained what " 19 by Cartier " meant, but the letter of Dunell & Co. of the 24th of February shows that these gentlemen understood " 19 Cartier " to mean, in the market to which they had come to buy, " a test by Cartier's hydrometer, irrespective of the temperature of the brandy at that time," and the letter of Dunell & Co. of 24th March showed that they believed that the marketmaster of Cape Town tested spirits " without reference to a thermometer, and it is impossible for them to arrive at the correct strength." If the plaintiffs, instead of entering upon correspondence with the defendants as to the strength of the brandy, had stood upon the facts that the defendants had not only taken delivery, but kept delivery for a time, and had also broken bulk by selling nine of the twenty-five hogsheads before they made any complaint, and had insisted that the defendants were not entitled after this, to repudiate the sale upon any question as to the strength of the brandy, I am rather disposed to think their position would have been a good one ; but in the first place, the evidence does not, as I before observed, inform us of the day on which the defendants got delivery of the brandy, nor consequently of how long they kept possession before complaining of the deficiency in strength ; and inasmuch as the plaintiffs gave up that stand-point by going into the question of deficiency of strength raised by the defendants, I am disposed to think that the argument for the defendants is good, that they cannot, in these circumstances, be precluded from going into the inquiry what was the strength of the brandy at which the defendants bought, and whether the plaintiffs performed their part of the contract by delivering what was so purchased. I am not sure how far the defendants intended to push this argument, and therefore, in the course of it, I inquired whether they relied upon the correspondence in proving a new contract, a contract that the brandy in question should be of 19 strength certain. This the defendants repudiated, and, in doing so, they were undoubtedly right, for the letter of the plaintiffs, in which they speak of taking the brandy back if it should prove not to be 19 by Cartier, was written still in ignorance that Cartier without a thermometer was comparatively useless, and in innocent confidence that even if it were used in that way, it would show that the brandy was 19, as had been shown when it was tested before shipment, and that the use of a Sykes would show nothing else ; therefore the case between the parties is, in my opinion, narrowed to what the defendants have urged, viz.: what was the strength of brandy they bought, and have the plaintiffs given them brandy of that strength ? The defendants do not rely upon the terms of the brokers' note, to the effect of alleging that they were entitled by it to brandy of the certain strength of 19, howsoever ascertained, though what they insist for may, in the result, amount to that they admit that the strength they were to have was 19 by Cartier. They admit that " 19 by Cartier " is the meaning of the brokers' note, but they argue that the meaning of that expression is 19 by Cartier used with a thermometer, which, if they are right, is 19 certain, as Cartier so used will show the certain strength. The scientific evidence adduced for the defendants proved conclusively that without the use of a thermometer, the Cartier hydrometer cannot afford any precise test of the strength of any given

1868.
June 14,
  „ 23,
July 13.

McLeod & Co.
vs. Dunell,
Ebden & Co.

parcel of spirits, because that instrument is adapted to be used on the assumption that the atmosphere is 60 of Fahrenheit, and, therefore, unless the atmosphere should, at the time of testing, accidentally be 60 of Fahrenheit, the test will be fallacious, inasmuch as a higher state of the thermometer gives a strength which is apparent and not real, by how much the temperature may be above 60, the effect of heat being to expand the spirit, and this increase of apparent strength the evidence showed to be in the proportion of one degree of strength to every five degrees of heat; the spirit therefore which, with the temperature at 60, would be 19, would, with the temperature at 65, be 20; and, *vice versa*, the spirit with the temperature at 55 would be only 18, and so on. Although *in rerum naturâ*, this is undoubtedly the case, as proved by the scientific evidence, yet the unscientific evidence proved, as conclusively, that the dealers in brandy throughout the Colony, with the notable exception of Corbet, the deceased partner of the witness Dyason, have been wholly ignorant of the effect of the temperature to raise or depress the apparent strength of spirits, and have been in use to buy brandy and to sell brandy tested by a Cartier, without using a thermometer. According to this the buyers and sellers have supposed that the strength indicated by Cartier, thus used, was the real strength, whereas it indicated the strength only approximately. This, no doubt, is a very loose and ignorant way of doing business. If the day of sale happened to be a warm one, the seller would sell brandy at a strength apparently greater than the spirit possessed; and the buyer would buy at this disadvantage. If the day of sale happened to be a cold one, the seller would sell at a strength apparently below what the spirit really possessed, and the buyer would buy at this disadvantage. But if the buyer on the warm day resold on a cold day, the disadvantage of his purchase might be adjusted; and the buyer on the cold day, if he resold on a warm day, might have his advantage adjusted. In the long run, therefore, this happy-go-lucky or " rough-and-ready " way of dealing, as the witness Steytler termed it, might, in its results, not do much injury either to buyer or seller. This is the more probable from this circumstance, that the records at the Observatory show that the mean temperature throughout the last fourteen years has been 61·71, or 1·71 above the temperature at which Cartier is set. This information I obtained from the usual readiness to communicate information of our worthy Astronomer Royal. At all events, till this action arose, ignorance was bliss—he who gained did not know it, and he who lost did not know it. The only evidence by which the defendants attempted to negative this universal ignorance was that of the witness

Dyason. According to him, his deceased partner, Corbet, had made a determination that he would never buy under 19, tested by Sykes—that is to say, he would never complete a purchase of brandy, whether made on the public market or by private bargains, unless satisfied by the test of Sykes's hydrometer on his own premises that he had got spirit of the strength of full 19. This witness admitted, however, that the spirit was bought, whether on the public market or by private bargain, of the strength tested by Cartier, used, of course, as has been proved, without a thermometer; and that if Corbet found by Sykes that the spirit was above 19, he did not make any allowance to the farmer for this increase. On the other hand, Dyason sold the brandy so bought, and said, " If I send brandy ordered at 19 under 19, it was at my risk, " and he added, on cross-examination, " When I said I never sent brandy under 19, I meant 19, not by Sykes, but by Cartier. " This witness, therefore, so far from displacing the evidence as to the general and ignorant use of Cartier, in fact confirms it. All that his evidence shows, beyond that, is that he and Corbet were more enlightened than their neighbours, and used the light to their own advantage, how far creditably it is not necessary to say. This mode of buying and selling by an instrument which gave only an approximation to the strength of the spirit, cannot perhaps be called a custom of trade in the sense in which that expression is used to designate something exceptional from the general law, but given effect to by Court of Law because of its universality, though perhaps it approaches to that; neither can it perhaps be called a usage of trade, in a particular locality, as distinguished from the general rules as to trade observed elsewhere, and sanctioned by law. It was neither the custom nor usage, but it was the trade itself; and what is more, the general trade of the Colony, until the year 1858, was conducted in the same loose and ignorant way that brandy was dealt in, and seems still to be dealt in. In the year 1858, I had the honour to be President of the Legislative Council. In the session of that year an Act was passed to regulate the weights and measures of the Colony, and during the progress of the Bill through the House, I had an opportunity of getting an insight into these matters. The expression so much per hundred weight is used. What does that mean—100 bales or grains? No, it meant 112 lbs. English and 120 lbs. Dutch, according to a supposed English and Dutch standard, which, in fact, had no existence. Nay more, the Dutch weights had been in use for hundreds of years, and in course of time, whatever correspondence they might generally have had with any conceivable standard, they had by tear and wear long lost it, and were almost

1868.
June 14.
" 23.
July 13.

McLeod & Co.
vs. Dunell,
Ebden & Co.

universally deficient. The English weights had not been so long in use, and being made of iron, had not suffered so much by tear and wear, but they also were almost universally deficient. On the supposition that the weights—Dutch and English—had continued of the weight originally intended, it was known to those acquainted with such matters that the Dutch hundred weight was 8 per cent. heavier than the English. The boer, ignorant of this, weighed his produce before leaving home by the Dutch weights, and after selling it, bought from the merchant coffee, sugar, and other imported goods, weighed over to him by the English weights, thereby getting 112 lbs. instead of 120 lbs., as he had given. So matters went on, and had gone on for centuries, until somehow the difference in the weights and the faultiness of all of them became known, and hence the origin of the Weights and Measures Act of 1858. In the same way the Dutch sold and bought by the ell, and the English sold and bought by the yard; that is to say; the one used a stick of a certain length divided into certain proportions, and the other used a shorter stick also divided into certain proportions. But in many instances the parties were ignorant of this difference, and in many instances the same price was paid by whichever of the sticks the material might have been measured. But not only did the two sticks differ from each other, but there was no evidence that either of them corresponded with any standard ell or any standard yard. The story was the same as to liquid measures, and yet trade went on happily and contentedly enough, all being equally ignorant until enlightened by the inquiries which produced the Act of 1858. The present case has revealed the same state of things in regard to the strength of spirits, and revealed, further, that this case is an omission from the Act of 1858. The Cartiers which have been used were not more fallacious, if so fallacious, as the weights and yards and ells which have for centuries regulated the trade of the Colony. I speak of the Cartiers used before the introduction into the Colony by fraudulent dealers of those trash which the activity of the defendants in the conduct of this case have brought forward, but which were not used in this transaction, and do not form any part of the evidence on which my judgment will rest. No doubt, any one as astute as the defendants might have raised questions in other trades than that of spirit-dealing, as to whether, in any given transaction, they had got the right weight or measure; and, in the absence of fraud in the transaction, it might have been difficult for the Court to come to any determination without any standard of weight or measure to go by; but no such difficulty presents itself in this case, as the evidence shows that the defendants were aware of the fallaciousness of the test by Cartier without a thermometer, and neverthless bought according to that test. Whether viewing the dealing with a Cartier without the concurrent use of a thermometer as a custom or usage of trade or ignoring it as either, the evidence of that general mode of dealing is most material to be considered, when endeavouring to arrive at a meaning of a contract made in a particular instance; for the prevalence of any general course of dealing raises a presumption that the parties to the contract in the particular instance intended to conform to the general practice, and justifies the Court in construing what they have put into their contract by the aid of this light. The sold note here is for 25 hhds. of brandy " full 19 strength." Taken by themselves these words have no meaning. Introduce the evidence of the witnesses as to the course of dealing, and the letter of the defendants of 12th February, and they mean " 19 by Cartier." Apply, again, the evidence of the witnesses as to the course of dealing, and the letters of the defendants of the 24th February and 24th March, and " 19 by Cartier" means 19 by Cartier used without a thermometer. Apply still further the evidence of the general course of dealing, and the letters of the defendants of the 24th of February and 24th of March, as showing their knowledge of that course of dealing, at the time they bought the brandy in question, and they establish satisfactorily to my mind that the defendants bought the brandy at 19 by Cartier, used without a thermometer. And unless I am to disbelieve the evidence of the Custom-house officers here, of the two marketmasters, and of Bolus, the brokers' clerk, which I see no reason to do, I am satisfied, from the evidence of McLeod and Arnold, that the brandy when it left Cape Town was of the strength of 19 Cartier, used without a thermometer. Being so satisfied, I do not think it necessary to scrutinize the evidence as to the testing of the brandy at Port Elizabeth and of the sample at Cape Town, with the view of seeing which is the most to be relied on. I say so not only because of the evidence of testing at the time of shipment, but because De Villiers, Volsteedt and Bolus all concur in stating that when the sample sworn to by McLeod and Arnold as having been taken by them from all the twenty-five hogsheads at the time of shipment, their intruments each and all showed the strength to be as nearly as possible 19, and De Villiers, Volsteedt and Schmieterloew concur in stating that when their respective instruments were compared at Hull's office, by being applied to a sample of spirit produced for that purpose, they one and all gave the strength at $20\frac{1}{2}$. It is true that it must have been impossible for the defendants, if they doubted the plaintiffs' statement that the

1868.
June 14.
" 23.
July 13.

McLeod & Co.
vs. Dunell,
Ebden & Co.

1868.
June 14.
,, 23.
July 13.

McLeod & Co.
vs. Dunell,
Ebden & Co.

brandy was 19 by Cartier, without using a thermometer at the time he shipped it, to test it by a Cartier, used in the same way on its arrival, because the two testings could only correspond if the temperature at the time of each testing happened to be exactly the same. But inasmuch as the defendants knew when they bought, as their letters show, that the brandy would be sold and tested in this way of using Cartier, I can only conclude that they meant, as all other dealers in brandy did mean, to be content with an approximation of strength, and to take the chance of the brandy showing a higher or lower strength, according to the accidental state of the atmosphere, and intended to regulate their dealings with their own customers accordingly by selling it in the same way. I am warranted in saying so, because they sold nine of the twenty-five hogsheads, more than one third of the parcel, without having applied any test as to strength. The witness Leibbrandt, a large dealer, swore that he sold all his brandy in December, because he was aware the crop of grapes was to be a large one, and he anticipated a consequent fall in the price of brandy. In the absence of any information from the defendants to account for why they were led to test the spirits, after having sold the nine hogsheads without having done so, I am forced to conjecture that the information as to the largeness of the incoming crop of grapes, which had reached Leibbrandt in December, had got the length of Port Elizabeth by February, and had been confirmed by the incipient fall in the price of brandy. I am forced to conjecture that this led the defendants, Dunell & Co., to bring into play their knowledge of the unscientific way in which brandy was dealt in in Cape Town, which their letters of 24th February and 24th March, as I have observed, showed they possessed, and then, and not sooner, to avail themselves of their knowledge of Sykes's instrument, by using it in order to discover whether the spirit was in fact below 19, the strength mentioned in the brokers' note, or below 19 by Cartier used with a thermometer instead of without one, as they knew had been done by the plaintiffs, McLeod & Co., in selling to them, and was done universally in Cape Town. The fall in price, and not any unexpected discovery of deficiency in the strength of the spirit, I must assume, was what induced the defendants to endeavour to get rid of the purchase. The evidence shows that a fall in the price of brandy began in February, and continued until what was sold in February at £21 could be bought at £10 10s. That this is what induced the defendants to repudiate their purchase is confirmed by the terms in which they uniformly declined to entertain the plaintiffs' offer of a deduction from the price, corresponding to what might be proved to be the deficiency in strength. If the brandy was 1½ degrees weaker than what it was sold for, as alleged by the defendants, nothing was easier than to cure the defect by the addition of the requisite quantity of alcohol, the price of which was easily ascertainable and could not have been great, not more, I should think—dividing the price £21 among the degrees (19) of strength, than a little over £20. But the defendants wrote that nothing but such a reduction as they were sure the plaintiffs could not allow would induce them to retain their purchase. What could that mean but that the price had fallen so low that nothing but a deduction corresponding to that fall was what they would entertain, and this, in their own breasts, they knew they had only to state to have rejected by the plaintiffs? The expession in their letter of the 6th April, described the brandy as "quite unsuited to our trade." How is that reconcilable with the fact that they had already sold more than one-third of the parcel without objection by the purchaser? At least if he made any objection we have not heard anything of it. How is it reconcilable, moreover, with the fact that they were willing to become the purchasers at such a deduction as they thought the plaintiffs would hardly accede to. A deduction from the price would not have altered the nature of the article or make it more suitable for the trade. Some years ago a wiseacre sent a cargo of skates to Hongkong, or some equally warm place. It is intelligible how the skates could not be suited for trade where ice is not known; but how brandy could be said to be not suited for the trade of Port Elizabeth because it was one and a half degree below the strength at which it was sold for, while this could be immediately cured by the introduction of the requisite quantity of pure alcohol, is unintelligible. But it is quite intelligible that the price of the article having fallen considerably, probably much below what it would have cost to repair the deficiency in strength, supposing it to exist, the defendants should desire to get rid of their purchase by representing the article to be such as they could not deal in, so as thereby to induce the plaintiffs either to take back the brandy or to make a deduction from the price greatly beyond what could be necessary to supply the alleged deficiency of strength. It is observable, moreover, that the letter of the defendants of the 12th February, which said "a few casks were sent away unfortunately before the low strength was discovered," gives no explanation of what led to this discovery. If it were not their own inquiry, suggested by the fall in price, what was it? Refusal of an intending purchaser to buy from them? If so, surely it would have been mentioned. We heard a great deal from the scientific witnesses about the

June 14.
23.
July 13.
McLeod & Co.
vs. Dunell,
Ebden & Co.

trumpery instruments sold as Cartiers, and how much the one differed from the other; that evidence I hope the dealers in brandy will for the future make a due use of. But it has little or nothing to do with the case. What we have to do with is the Cartier used by the plaintiffs; that corresponded with the two instruments used by the marketmasters, and with Mr. Schmieterloew's, when they were compared together at the office of Mr. Hull, and it seems, moreover, to have corresponded with the Sykes used by the Custom-house officer of Cape Town. No doubt, the witness Gibb swore that he took one and the same sample of brandy to the marketmasters, separately and consecutively, and that they gave certificates of strength which showed that their instruments differed from each other. But that mode of proceeding will not induce me to disbelieve the much fairer and opener comparison and correspondence of the instruments at Mr. Hull's office. That evidence and some parts of the other evidence show me that the Cartier used by the plaintiffs was a reasonably fair one, and, if used with a thermometer, would have given a true indication of the strength of this brandy. I say so, because, if the instrument had been one of those lately introduced by fraudulent dealers, giving altogether a fallacious indication, the case might have been different. But the instrument being in my opinion a reasonably good one, and such as had been in use in the Colony among honest dealers, it was equal to the purpose for which it was used, viz., to give the real strength, if the atmosphere should happen at the time of its use to be 60, and an approximation to the real strength, should the atmosphere happen to be above or below 60—a use which, as frequently before observed, the defendants were cognizant of at the time they made their purchase. The judgment of the Court, in my opinion, ought to be for the plaintiffs, with costs.

CONNOR, J.: As the rest of the Court have come to their decision on the main question involved in this case, it becomes unnecessary for me to express any decided opinion on it, and I am disposed to avail myself the rather of that position, not only because the only ground on which I could have concurred in the judgment for the plaintiffs is one to which substantially no part of the mass of evidence in the case was directed, which was also, I think I may say, hesitatingly urged on the part of the plaintiffs, and which it was insisted on the part of the defendants it was not competent for the plaintiffs to set up, but also because, on grounds other than the latter, I have not been able to satisfy myself that even on this subordinate point the law is in the plaintiffs' favour.

It struck me from an early period in the case that the justice of it, at least in fact if not in strict law, would be best met by leaving the defendants to bring their action against the plaintiffs for any difference in value between the brandy which had been contracted for and that which was supplied. The purchase had been made here in Cape Town. The brandy had been shipped for Port Elizabeth, sent there, and received by the defendants, and out of twenty-five hogsheads they had sold as large a proportion as nine, without, as far as we know, any loss to themselves or any complaint from those who purchased from them. They have, therefore, prevented themselves from returning the subject-matter of the contract to a large extent; the brandy which they received is clearly not unsaleable (*Voet* 21, 1, 5, citing *Grotius* 3, 15, 33, 34); according to the evidence, the difference in value, at least in Cape Town, would have been very slight. The defendants, according to the evidence, have received, and, I presume, disposed of, many thousand pounds worth of brandy under like circumstances. The right to rescind a contract is, I think, *stricti juris* (*Cujac ad Cod.* 4. 45, *Van Leeuwen, C. F.*, 1, 4, 40, 9); the inconvenience to the plaintiff must be considerable at a distance from his place of business; and the defendants have, by their own act, disabled themselves from returning a large proportion of the consignment. *Voet*, 18, 5, 20, speaking of the action to rescind a sale, says: "This seems settled, that the injured buyer cannot obtain this legal remedy if he have sold and delivered the thing bought to another, because now, by his own will and act, he has brought the business to that state that there no longer remains to the seller the power of choosing, given by law, whether he prefer to dissolve the sale, or to amend the inequality of price." So, also (4, 1, 22), in reference to *restitutio in integrum*, he says that whatever comes to the person obtaining restitution, from purchase or sale, or other contract, this he ought to restore. It appears from *V. d. Kees., Th.* 901, that the rescinding of a contract was in practice brought under the *restitutio in integrum;* and *Huber* (*Prælect.*, 4, 1, 2), citing the definition of *restitutio*, as being *redintegratio amissæ causæ*, adds: "It is not in vain called *redintegratio*, because all things are reduced on each side into the original state, so that every restitution may be reciprocal." So in an American Book on Contracts (*Story*) it is said, citing several cases (*S.* 844 *a*): "When either party would rescind a contract, he must return, or offer to return, to the other all the subject-matter of sale, and must, in as far as he is able, restore him to the position in which he was before he made the contract." On the other hand, there seems to be much ground for holding that the *actio redhibi*-

1868.
June 14.
„ 23.
July 13.

McLeod & Co.
vs. Dunell,
Ebden & Co.

toria lies for the purchaser in respect of any separable part of the subject-matter of the contract (*Voet* 21, 1, 4; *Murray v. De Villiers*, *Menz.*, 366), and it is to this redhibitory action, rather than the rescissory or restitutionary, that I apprehend the defence in this action most corresponds.

It was urged, on behalf of the defendants, that the effect of the correspondence between the plaintiffs and the defendants in reference to the case, before the action was commenced, was that the plaintiff could not now object to the defendants' rescinding the contract, the sale of the nine hogsheads. This point in itself appears to me to be very important, and to be new; that a proposal made when the parties are discussing the question whether or not the contract has been broken, and how that question is to be ascertained and an action avoided, and when the proposal falls through, and the action proceeds, that this proposal is to bar the party making it of some defence to the whole action which he would otherwise have had. I have gone through the whole correspondence, and had it been necessary for me to come to a conclusion upon it, I should, I apprehend, have deemed it out of the question to hold that it bound either party to the waiver of any right in this action. There have been two very recent cases in England, before Courts of Appeal, one before the Exchequer Chamber, *Ogle vs. Vane* (37 *L. J.*, *Q. B.*, 77 *and* 36, *ib.*, 175); and the other before the Court of the Lords Justices of Appeal, the *Prudential Assurance Company vs. Thomas* (37, *L. J.*, *Ch.*, 202), in which the effect of a correspondence before action brought was discussed, and both of which are, I think, confirmatory of the view which I have expressed. Supposing, however, the law to be (these points were not argued, and I therefore avoid expressing any positive opinion, it not being necessary to do so),—the law, I say, to be, that the seller has a right to say to the buyer,—" If you insist on my taking back any, I shall insist upon your giving back all;" still there might be much ground for saying that if he does not make this election expressly, either before the action or in it, but with knowledge of the fact of the sale of part, he makes throughout no objection on that ground, then that such an option is not open to him, under the general issue.

It will be gathered from what I have said that I am little disposed, so far as facts are concerned, to regret that judgment should here be for the plaintiff. I should, however, have had great difficulty in upholding such a usage of trade as has been contended for on behalf of the plaintiff. An usage of trade ought, it has been decided, to be in the cognizance of both parties to the contract. (*Kirchner vs. Venus*, 12 *Moore P. C. C.*) But one peculiarity of this usage is that no one was cognizant of it; for we cannot be said to be cognizant of anything whose existence is in its operations, and as to the effect of whose operations we are wholly ignorant or mistaken. It is clear from the plaintiff's letter of 27th February to the defendants, that he was confident that the Sykes hydrometer, in the experienced hands of the Custom-house officers, would confirm the uncorrected indications, or rather the (unknown to him) fantastic freaks of his unscientifically constructed Cartier, but which, even if perfect in its construction, would only profess to indicate correctly at a temperature of 60° Fahr. Nor is there, I think, throughout the correspondence, certainly not at its outset, or until after experiments had been made, any intimation that either party to it conceived that the one had been selling or the other buying by a fictitious scale. And I cannot but think it going too far to attribute to the defendants at Port Elizabeth a knowledge or cognizance of an usage which was not, in any real sense, known to the plaintiff himself at Cape Town. Customs, to be valid, must be certain, and must not be unreasonable (1 *Stephens's Comm.* 59). And it is well settled that the unreasonableness of an usage of trade may be resorted to to rebut its effect in an action. In a very recent case in which judgment was given in the Court of Common Pleas, in January last, *Grissell vs. Bristowe* (37 *L. J., C. P.*, 89), in which, in a sale of shares, an usage of the Stock Exchange was in question, Bovill, C. J., in giving the judgment of the majority of the Court, says (101): " This usage or custom, even if proved, as well as the practice of settlement between the members of the Stock Exchange, is, as it seems to us, so entirely unreasonable for the purpose of affecting the rights of principals who are not members of the Stock Exchange, that we should be disposed to refuse to give any effect to it on that ground also." That such usages must be reasonable, it is only necessary to refer to the case *Bottomley vs. Forbes* (6 *Bing. N. S.*, and 1 *Smith, Lead. Cas., Notes, Wigglesworth vs. Dallison*), and the case of *Sweeting vs. Pearce* (30 *L. J., C. P.*, 109), which last case was also before the Exchequer Chamber; there is, too, the case *In re Brooks* (33 L. J., C. P., 246), to the like effect.

1868.
June 14.
" 23.
July 13.
McLeod & Co.
vs. Dunell,
Ebden & Co.

I have not succeeded in picturing to myself any usage for the purpose, which is to my mind in some respects so uncertain as that contended for here. Suppose, as was suggested during the argument, it was the usage that each merchant, instead of a Cartier of his own, had, for testing, a taster of his own; or suppose the degree of strength was by usage decided by the cast of the dice-box, the uncertainty and unreasonableness of such modes could hardly be doubted;

1868.
June 14.
" 23.
July 13.

McLeod & Co.
vs. Dunell,
Ebden & Co.

but such an usage would have this superiority over that in question,—those who knew this usage would know of its uncertainty. To take a leap in the dark is proverbial of uncertainty, but it is certainty itself compared to the usage before us. For they who take the leap know that it is in the dark they go; but the victims of this usage had their organs of vision inverted, and took the darkness into which they plunged to be the blaze of day. When one exhausts oneself in heaping terms of contempt, ridicule and almost disgust on the fantastic absurdity of this usage, what does one but express in strong terms one's sense of its uncertainty and unreasonableness, or, in other words, one's conviction of its invalidity? It has been suggested that it is a mistake to call this practice an usage of trade,—that it is the trade itself. I am afraid that I hardly understand the distinction. I certainly fail to perceive its soundness. I am aware of but two systems governing in any trade—the law of the country and the valid usages of the particular trade. The law of the country certainly does not say that a Cartier hydrometer is to be read against its own rules—that when its principles are that allowance is to made for temperature above or below 60° Fahr., its indications are to be taken without any such allowance being made. If such a practice can prevail, it must then, I apprehend, be under an usage of the trade.

It has been also said that in an average of cases it would come to the same thing, in all probability, to buyers and sellers, whether the Cartiers were used according to rule, or according to this usage. I cannot, however, think that such an average result would obviate the objection of uncertainty and unreasonableness, with reference to any particular transaction before the Court. Whist-players, I think, tell you that one's gains and losses at whist neutralize each other in the long run, and, for all I know, those who use the dice-box may say the same. It is said (1 *Steph. Comm.* 59) that apparent uncertainty in a custom will be remedied if the maxim *id certum est quod certum reddi potest* applies; but here the means of rendering the usage certain would be a correction by the thermometer, which is what the defendants contend for, and the plaintiffs oppose.

Tedious as in many respects the lengthened evidence in this case was, there was this great satisfaction, that it seemed to be given by all the witnesses with the most perfect fairness. The plaintiff, Mr. McLeod (I call him so, though nominally the plaintiffs are McLeod & Co.) had learned before he went into the witness-box, what, as I have said, he does not seem to have known at the date of the contract, that his Cartier, or any other the most perfect, only indicated truly when the temperature of the spirits was 60° Fahr., and that at a higher temperature the apparent strength exceeded the true. He admitted this variance with complete candour, and indeed he put it as high against himself as did any one else who gave evidence, and higher than some others; higher, too, I am disposed to think, than is correct, viz. : 1° of alcoholic strength for every 10° of temperature Fahr., inversely on either side of 60°. Others put it at 1° for every 14° of temperature. The graduated ruler of the defendants' Cartier by Long showed that at a temperature of 74° Fahr., an indication of 19° strength was equivalent to 18° true. Mr. De Villiers, the senior marketmaster, gave his evidence with, of course, not the least bias either way, and admitted that he would have used the long narrow tin cylinder, which he was in the habit of filling with brandy for testing, though the heat of the weather had made it hot to the touch, without doubting the accuracy of the uncorrected indication of the Cartier. Another witness takes a sample bottle to be tested, walking some distance on a Cape Town summer afternoon, and carries the bottle under his arm as he walks along, to submit it to a crucial experiment. We had the advantage of the evidence of Mr. Orpen, the Sub-Collector of Customs at Cape Town, and he told us that the 21°·6 Sykes below proof, which it is admitted the brandy in question was, was equivalent to 18°·41 Cartier true. Mr. Orpen was good enough to explain to us the process by which he arrived at that conclusion, but there was, I think, a difficulty in our following him, for this reason, that we had not had it fully explained what the 21°·6 meant. I understood it to mean that the brandy was such in strength that at a temperature of 60° Fahr. it would show by Sykes' hydrometer 21°·6 below proof, and if this were so, and if approved tables, such as Redwood's, purported to give the equivalents in Cartier at 60° Fahr. to Sykes at the same temperature, I found it difficult to understand why these figures 21°·6 Sykes should require any manipulation in order to obtain from the table their equivalent in Cartier. The tables purporting, apparently, to give as the equivalent for 21° Sykes, 17°·80 Cartier ; and, of course, 21°·6 Sykes would have a lower equivalent in Cartier than that of 21° Sykes. On the other hand, there are many reasons for supposing that Mr. Orpen's results were correct. There are first his own considerable experience, and his confidence in his results. Then that Mr. Gibb, eminent here, I believe, as a chemist, evidently supposed some such manipulation requisite, though he hardly hoped to convey it to the Court, and it led him to a different result. Then another chemist, who adopted the tables without what I have called manipulation, failed, I thought, in reconciling his results

1868.
June 14.
" 23.
July 13.
McLeod & Co.
vs. Dunell,
Ebden & Co.

with his observations. No one, however, has put the true alcoholic and strength of the brandy at higher than 18°·41 Cartier ; and I certainly am not prepared to say that one who contracts for full 19° Cartier is bound to take 18°·41.

Judgment was then given for plaintiffs with costs.

[Plaintiffs' Attorney, *Mr. E. Hull.*
Defendants' Attorneys, *Messrs. Fairbridge & Arderne.*]

BLIGNAUT'S TRUSTEE *vs.* CILLIERS'S EXECUTORS AND OTHERS.

Mutual Will.—Legitimate Portion.—Trebellianic Fourth.— Inofficious Sale and Bequest.—Fidei-commissum.—Lex hac edictali.—Ord. No. 6 of 1843, section 48.

Where the husband of a testator's daughter surrendered his estate in insolvency before the testator's death, the testator can, by subsequent will or codicil, impose on the daughter's legitim certain fidei-commissa which will prevent the absolute property in the legitim vesting in the daughter or her husband, to whom she was married in community, and will, to some extent, preserve it for the children of the marriage.

Where two co-heirs under a testator's will prevailed upon a third co-heir to sign a document during the testator's lifetime, but unknown to such testator, whereby the third co-heir surrendered or modified his right of inheritance to accrue under the will. SEMBLE *that such document or consent paper is void, and cannot bind the party signing.*

1868.
Feb. 14.
June 4.
" 5.
" 8.
July 13.
Blignaut's Trustee vs. Cilliers's Executors and Others.

This was an action to have the rights of an insolvent estate declared and asserted, and for other purposes.

The plaintiff, as trustee of one Blignaut, claimed certain rights as against the estate of P. G. Cilliers, deceased, the father of the insolvent's wife,—the plaintiff urging claims which he contended the insolvent Blignaut could himself have urged in respect of his rights under the law of community of goods, and of his wife's rights as a child of the first marriage of the deceased. A principal part of the plaintiff's claim was rested on this, that the deceased Cilliers and his wife, the defendant, Mrs. Cilliers, had partly sold and partly bequeathed the farm Driefontein to the defendants, L. A. Visagie and P. J. Pienaar, sons of Mrs. Cilliers by former marriages, for the sum of 26,000 rds. (£1,950), subject to a life usufruct and certain other rights, to Mr. and

Mrs. Cilliers and the survivor ; that this price was greatly below the value of the farm, and affected the legitimate portions of the children, and must therefore, so far, be deemed inofficious.

P. G. Cilliers was married first to the mother of Mrs. Blignaut, and of that marriage there was issue Mrs. Blignaut and another daughter, a Mrs. Aswegen. After his first wife's death he was married to the defendant, Mrs. Cilliers. She had been married first to a Mr. Visagie, by whom she had three children, one of whom is the defendant, L. A. Visagie. She was married a second time to a Mr. Pienaar, by whom she had two children, one of whom is the defendant, P. J. Pienaar. She was then married to the father of Mrs. Blignaut, P. G. Cilliers ; and of this marriage there was no issue. At the time of making the mutual will and the codicils in the case, and also at the death of P. G. Cilliers, the husband, there were either living, or represented by their children, two children of the husband and five of the wife. The husband died in April or May, 1859. His son-in-law, the insolvent Blignaut, surrendered on the 23rd February, 1858. The deceased, Cilliers, and the defendent, Mrs. Cilliers, made a mutual will, dated 2nd August, 1852, in which they declared that they have provisionally sold the farm Driefontein to the wife's two sons—the defendants, L. A. Visagie and P. J. Pienaar—in the manner already mentioned; and they directed that the 26,000 rds. should, after the death of them both, be divided in two equal parts,—one-half for the husband's children, and the other for the wife's,—the farm not to be appraised on the death of the first-dying, nor any part of the value thereof disbursed or paid to the heirs of the first-dying by way of inheritance or otherwise. Each testator then appointed the other spouse, with the testator's children, universal heirs, except as to the farm Driefontein, and the surviving spouse was appointed executor.

In a joint codicil of the 14th April, 1857, the testators directed that the 26,000 rds. for the farm should not be inherited by the two sons of the wife, to whom the farm was devised, but that the sum was in advance awarded to the other five heirs, and should be divided among those five as a legacy. Then the father alone, by a codicil of 4th February, 1859, purported to burden the inheritance of his daughter, Mrs. Blignaut, after deduction of four promissory notes due by her husband, so that after the death of the daughter, and her husband, the property should go to their children or descendants, and he instituted the daughter and her husband as heirs of the usufruct during their lives, and declared that this fidei-commissary disposition is to secure the daughter and her husband and children, in case of misfortune or going

1868.
Feb. 14.
June 4.
" 5.
" 8.
July 13.

Blignaut's Trustee *vs.* Cilliers's Executors and Others.

1868.
Feb 14.
June 4.
„ 5.
„ 8.
July 13.

Blignaut's Trustee *vs.* Cilliers's Executors and Others.

backwards in money matters, insolvency, or other accidents, maintenance and the means of livelihood; wherefore he declared that the interest and usufruct should not be paid to anybody else than to his said daughter, or after her death to her husband; and he revoked the annual interest, if the creditors of the daughter or her husband should seek to enforce their claims, and gave these interests over to P. J. Joubert, a son-in-law of his wife. The same testator again, alone, by a codicil of 11th April, 1859, stated that he thought it better to modify the fidei-commissary disposition of 4th February, by authorizing his executors to award to the "present creditors of the estate" of Blignaut, if they wish it, one-third of Mrs. Blignaut's inheritance, on condition that they do not interfere with the administration of the estate. By the liquidation account filed by Mrs. Cilliers, as executrix of her husband's will, the creditors of Blignaut, as in compliance with the codicil of 11th April, 1859, are given one-third of Mrs. Blignaut's inheritance, less the £141 5s., the debt due by Blignaut; and the whole balance is given to the children. This codicil did not, however, direct the £141 5s. to be deducted from the one-third which the creditors were given, nor did it take away the usufruct given by the codicil of 4th February, 1859. On the 16th June, 1859, Mrs. Cilliers, as executrix, transferred to each of the sons his share of the farm, subject to the conditions already referred to.

The declaration prayed that the sale of the farms may be declared to have infringed on the legitimate portion claimable by the insolvent in right of his wife, out of the estate of her father, P. G. Cilliers; and that such sale may be so far set aside; and that L. A. Visagie and P. J. Pienaar may be condemned to make up the legitimate and Trebellianic portions claimable by the insolvent in right of his wife; these two portions amounting to £2,330 13s., less the insolvent's debt of £141 5s. Or if the Court should reject the claim of the Trebellianic portion, then the legitimate alone, amounting to £1,553 15s. less the £141 5s. debt; and that the farm be declared to have been worth £12,000 at the time of the death of P. G. Cilliers, and at the date of the contracts of sale; and that the liquidation account may be corrected accordingly, and for interest; or if the sale be not held to be inofficious, then that the plaintiff may be declared entitled to the *legitim* and Trebellianic portion on the surplus estate, £830 13s., over the £141 5s., and also to one-fifth of the 26,000 rds. on their becoming payable, on the ground of this sum being a legacy, and not entailed in the inheritance; also one-fourth of the usufruct to the farm during the life of Mrs. Cilliers under the *lex hac edictali*.

To this the defendants at first pleaded only the general issue; but on February 14th, *Cole* for defendants (with him *Reitz*) moved for leave to plead specially and to re-open a commission which had taken evidence *de bene esse* at Colesberg, on the grounds that during the evidence so taken it had come out that, in 1849, the insolvent had, in the testator's lifetime and before his own insolvency, signed a document which defendants wished to plead in bar.

1868.
Feb. 14.
June 4.
„ 5.
„ 8.
July 13.

Blignaut's Trustee *vs.* Cilliers's Executors and Others.

Leave having been granted accordingly, the defendants subsequently pleaded specially and set up a writing of 13th June, 1849, signed by, among others, the insolvent, consenting to a bequest of the farm to the defendants, L. A. Visagie and P. J. Pienaar, in substance according to the terms of the sale to them and of the will of the 2nd August, 1852. The plaintiff to this special plea replied the general denial, and further that this consent of June, 1849, had been waived and abandoned by the common consent of all concerned. No further evidence was, however, taken for defendants, on the re-opened commission; but on the 4th June, the insolvent and his wife were called by plaintiffs, in Cape Town, and examined as to the circumstances under which the document in question was signed. The Court then desired the argument to proceed generally, and not merely on the legal effect of the document pleaded in bar.

Porter for plaintiffs. As to the document of 1849, the replication is borne out by the evidence of abandonment. As to the effect of such a document, he cited *Voet*, 23, 2, 112; *V. d. Keessel, Th.* 484; *Voet*, 2, 14, 6, *and* 5, 2, 52. This is the first time, it is believed, that the question of inofficious donation, or of sale amounting to it, has come before the Court. The protection of the law in favour of children extends equally to both. (*Burge, vol.* 2, *p.* 148; *Voet* 39, 5, 37, *licet autem, et* 38; *Grotius*, 3, 2, 19, *with Schorer's note; Huber's Prelections*, 39, 5, 6; *Perez. ad Cod.*, 8, 56, 3, *and* 3, 29; *Leyser Med. ad Pand., Specimen* 91, and the decision there quoted.) It is true the period of prescription in regard to inofficious donations is five years; but, independent even of the fact that all statutes of limitation should be specially pleaded, which has not been done here, this is an action to supplement as much as is necessary to make up the legitimate; and such *actio ad supplementum* is not prescribed until the lapse of thirty years. (*Voet*, 39, 5, 39 *Cessat tamen*; *Voet*, 5, 2, 67; *Cens. For.*, 3, 4, 34; *V. d. Keessel, Th.* 491.) And the codicil of 1859 having established a *universal fideicommissum*, this gives the right to claim the Trebellianic. (Also, *Cens. For.*, 3, 9, 8; *Voet*, 36, 1, 52, 54; *Grotius*, 2, 20, 8; *Perez ad Cod.*, 6, 49, 17. *Gail Observ.*, 133, 2, 4; *Voet*, 23, 2, 112.)

P

1868.
Feb. 14.
June 4.
" 5.
" 8.
July 13.

Blignaut's Trustee vs. Cilliers's Executors and Others.

Cole for defendants (with him *Reitz*) first went into calculations to show that there was no inofficious donation in the case, as the legitimate of Mrs. Blignaut had, in reality, not been prejudiced (and so it proved). There must therefore be judgment for Visagie and Pienaar. He also cited *Voet*, 39, 5, 38, and 36, 1, 37; *Sandar's Institutes of Justinian*, 2, 23, 9, with *Sandar's* explanation of the text, to show that the Trebellianic prayed by plaintiff was not claimable; for if there is sufficient left *quovis modo*, whether *titulo institutionis* or *titulo legati*, which will give the heir, over and above the legitimate, more than he would claim for the Trebellianic, if thereto entitled, that is enough to bar the Trebellianic.

Porter in reply.

Cur. adv. vult.

Postea, 13th July, the judgment of the Court was delivered by

CONNOR J., who, after stating the facts as above given, said: The claim against Mrs. Cilliers under the *lex hac edictali* is rested in the declaration solely on the ground that the bequests to Mrs. Cilliers exceed those to the two children of her husband by the usufruct given to her in the farm Driefontein. But in making this claim, no notice is taken of the fact that each of these children is given one-fifth of the 26,000 rds., in which Mrs. Cilliers takes nothing.

In the course of the trial, it was agreed that the farm Driefontein should be taken to be of the value of £7,500, and it was ascertained that at that value, in which we may mention no deduction was made for the widow's life usufruct, the surplus estate of the testator, P. G. Cilliers, left available for Mrs. Blignaut more than her legitimate portion, without even taking into account her interest, under the will and the first codicil, in the sum of 26,000 rds., the price paid or to be paid by the defendants Pienaar and Visagie for the farm. There is, therefore, no ground for setting aside or otherwise interfering with the sale of the farm, so far as the two defendants L. A. Visagie and P. J. Pienaar are concerned, and there must be judgment for them in the action.

There remains the question, whether the plaintiff, as trustee of Blignaut's insolvency, is bound by the provisions of the codicils of 4th February, 1859, and 11th April, 1859, without any right to the Trebellianic portion; and whether he is entitled to the benefits of the *lex hac edictali* as against Mrs. Cilliers. The plaintiff's rights depend on the provisions of section 48 of the Insolvent Ordinance, which vest, *inter alia*, in the trustee, all estates which may after the order of sequestration be purchased or acquired by, or may revert, descend, or be devised, or come to the insolvent, during the insolvency and before the confirmation of the plan of distribution; and also, in reference to Mrs. Blignaut's *legitim*, upon the question, as to how far a father may pretect his daughter's *legitim* from the creditors of her insolvent husband.

The *whole* of the wife's *legitim*, or other such property, devolving to her during the marriage, clearly does not in the terms of the Insolvent Ordinance come to the husband, even though solvent. He is but entitled to it in common with his wife. If, however, it be subject to his debts, it would be a mere question of form as to how it should be made available by the trustee of the insolvency for the creditors. When, then, the husband of a testator's daughter has surrendered his estate in insolvency before the testator's death, can the testator by a subsequent will or codicil, impose on the daughter's *legitim* certain *fidei-commissa*, which will prevent the absolute property of the *legitim* vesting in the daughter or her husband, and will to some extent preserve it for her children? Merula (*De Controvers. Juris*, 17, 43, 2), says that the jurists commonly teach (and he cites a host as confirming his statement) that *Novell*, 115 (3) (which relates to the disinheriting of children), was introduced for the children's benefit and utility, and, consequently, ought to cease in that case in which it is expedient for the child to have been disinherited, lest that which was introduced to his favour be turned to his disfavour against the rule in the *Code de Legibus*, 6. Then *Van Leeuwen* (*Cens For.*, 1, 3, 4, 18 and 19) says: "Some burden can be imposed on the *legitim* itself for the advantage of the heirs themselves, but a child can be even disinherited by his father *bonâ mente*, and from a provident and prudent purpose; suppose for puerility, least the goods be committed to an unsure guardianship or care; or for prodigality, great debt, or other just cause, as in the text *Dig.*, 28, 2, 18, and *ib.*, 38, 2, 12 (2) and 27, 10, 16, (2). Which rights are not contrary to *Novell*, 115, which is only concerned with disinheriting, which is done *ex mala mente* and by angry parents, with a mark of ignominy" (and he cites several authorities); " and it is not opposed to our practice (*moribus*), in which nothing is more frequent than that a father disinherits a son, who has been prodigal of his goods in the greatest part and has contracted great debt, and the father fearing lest his goods also be wasted by him, disinherits him, and institutes as heirs the children born of him. Parents' disposition and provision of which kind, notwithstanding that every condition or burden must be removed from the *legitim*, is valid

P 2

1868.
Feb. 14.
June 4.
„ 5.
„ 8.
July 13.

Blignaut's Trustee *vs.* Cilliers's Executors and Others.

and effectual by law and custom." And he refers to *Sande Decis.*, 4, 2, 3, who is also referred to by *Voet*, 5, 2, 22. The case in *Sande* thus referred to is as follows : " N., the mother, disinherited her son Vincentius and her daughter Anna for their prodigal habits, as they who had been prodigal of their father's goods in the most part ; wherefore the testatrix, fearing lest her goods should be also wasted by them, professed in her will that she, from affection toward her children, ‚disinherited them, and instituted the children lawfully begotten by her son and daughter, yet so that she left the usufruct to her son and daughter. The question was whether this disinheriting may stand. Which was so held by the Senate (8th May, 1627, *Jacobs vs. Jaspers*). Because a child can be disinherited *bonâ mente*, and from a provident and prudent purpose, suppose from puerility, lest the goods be committed to an unsure guardianship or care, or for prodigality, or for some other just cause for the advantage of the children." " For many, " says *Ulpian* in *Dig.* 28, 2, 18, " disinherit children not for the sake of a mark (of ignominy), but that they may be prudent for them." The same *Ulpian* in *Dig.* 38, 2, 12, (2) says : " If any be disinherited, not by his parents, *mala mens*, but for another cause, the disinheriting is not hurtful to him." And *Paulus* answers, *ib.* 47, " that the disinheriting of a grandson (*nepotis*), which is done not for the sake of a mark, but for another purpose, does not necessarily hurt him." And the text is almost in our terms in *Dig.* 27, 10, 16, (2), where *Tryphonius* speaks thus : " A father could also provide otherwise for his grandchildren if he have ordered them to be heirs and have disinherited his son (*i.e.*, a prodigal), and he have bequeathed to him from them a certain quantity, which would suffice in the name of subsistence, the cause and necessity of his determination being added. Those rights are not corrected by *Novell*, 115, because it spoke of disinheriting, which is done *malâ mente*, and the question of a mark enters " (and he cites several authorities). " Hence also it is laid down that though every condition, burden, delay, must be removed from the *legitim*, yet if some burden be imposed on the *legitim* for the children's advantage, a disposition and provision of this kind of parents is by law valid and effectual, as *Prætis* discusses at length. Moreover, it can be gathered by putting this and that thing together (*or* from circumstances *conjecturis*), that the disinheriting can be done *bonâ mente*. In fine, it is to be noticed that one is presumed a prodigal whom his father or mother has called so by will." *Huber Prælect*, 5, 2, 19, says : " A mother instituting her grandson, disinherits her daughter lest her prodigal husband should waste her goods ; the disinheritiug was *bonæ mentis*." Then Van Leeuwen (*Rom. Dutch Law*, 3, 5, 9), referring *inter alia*, to Sande *ubi supra*, says: "But in case any incumbrance or obligation be charged thereon (the *legitm*), for the benefit of the children, or if they have been disinherited, not with the view of disiuheriting them, but for their own benefit and good motives ; for instance, as when to a son who is deeply involved in debt, the fruits only are bequeathed for his maintenance, and the property itself is left to his children, or to others who would certainly give him the fruits for his maintenance,—it would in such case remain effectual."

There can therefore be no doubt upon the authorities that a parent can, when the husband of his daughter has surrendered his estate as insolvent, leave the *usufruct* of the *legitim* to the daughter for life, and after her death, and that of her husband, to the children. It was urged that the cause which actuates the parent in imposing the *fidei-commissum* must be expressly stated. We find, however, it laid down by Sande that the *bona mens* may be gathered *ex conjecturis*; and as we know that the sequestration of the testator's son-in-law (Blignaut's) estate had taken place some months before the date of the codicil of the 4th February, 1859, and that *insolvency* of Blignaut is expressly referred to in the codicil, as are also his creditors, and that the codicil of the 11th April, 1859, which refers to the codicil on the 4th February previously, expressly provided in respect of the " present creditors in the estate of Blignaut," there can be no doubt but that the cause is here sufficiently stated to show the *bona mens* of the testator, and to support the limitations. We may add, too, that the case of *Simpson vs. Forrester* (1 *Knapp, P. C.*, 231) is an authority that the necessary construction of the provisions of a will, or a necessary result from them, is equally binding on the legatee or child of the testator, as an express statement in the will. In that case there was no express statement that the testator's child should elect between the provisions for her in the will and her *legitim;* but the Privy Council held nevertheless that she, having accepted under the will what the testator was not bound to have given her, must be deemed to have adopted the will, and relinquished the *legitim*. Such a construction, too, appears to be a desirable one, and that the insisting on a testator's inserting express technical clauses is in effect to lay a trap for testators, rather than to maintain a principle which recommends itself on its substantial merits. As, however, there are passages in Roman-Dutch authorities to a different effect, it may be well to state the case of *Simpson vs. Forrester* at some length. It came before the Privy Council on appeal from Demerara. Mr. Cook, the

1868.
Pub. 14.
June. 4.
, 5.
8.
July 13.

Blignaut's Trustee *vs.* Cilliers's Executors and Others.

father of a Mrs. Knight, had directed by his will all his property to be sold after the death of his wife, and the money arising therefrom to be deposited in the Bank of England, and the interest to be paid to Mrs. Knight for life, and the principal to be wholly at her disposal at her death; but in case the daughter died before his wife, the property to be at the disposal of his wife, whom, however, the daughter survived. She (Mrs. Knight) was married in community of goods to Mr. Knight; and a creditor of his after the death of his wife's father and mother, obtained judgment against him, and procured an order authorizing execution against the debtor's property. In two months after this Knight and his wife petitioned the Court to have an administrator appointed to carry out the provisions of the will of the father. This was done. And when the creditor seized part of the property in execution, the administrators opposed the execution, on the ground that one-half belonged to them in trust for Mrs. Knight, and the Court in Demerara gave judgment in their favour, in respect of one-half, interdicting the creditor from further proceeding in his levy. The creditor then appealed. The Privy Council affirmed the judgment of the Court below. The judgment was delivered by Lord Wynford, who says (242): " The property is affected with a trust or *fidei-commissum*; it is to be sold and the proceeds of the sale are to be placed in the Bank of England. . . . . Whether when the trust shall have been executed by the sale of the property, and by investing the proceeds in the bank, the husband's creditors may get hold of the dividends, is not now to be decided. They can only be entitled to the fruit; they have attempted to cut down the tree which is to bear it; and this attempt has been very properly frustrated in the Court below. Then another point has been ingeniously made at the bar, that the testator could not annex this trust to the whole of the property bequeathed by his will, because his daughter was entitled to the third part of that property as her legitimate share, or *legitim*; but in the very chapter of *Van der Linden*, to which we were referred as supporting this objection, it will be found that a parent may put his child to an election whether she will take her legitimate share of his property unfettered, or the whole of it subject to a *fidei-commissum*. This will subject the whole of the testator's property to a *fidei-commissum*. The daughter could only take the whole property under this will subject to the *fidei-commissum*. She has taken the whole property, and she must therefore be presumed to have adopted the will and to have relinquished the *legitim*." It may not be satisfactory to our ideas to have a question of the kind decided on a reference only to *Van der Linden*. But this, probably, shows more clearly how strong on principle the proposition appeared to the Privy Council to be. It had before it, too, *Van der Linden's* proposition contemplating an express putting to election, but the Privy Council is not prevented thereby from applying the principle to the will before it, in which there was no such express putting to election. Nor can it, of course, make any difference that the usufruct in the whole property was given to the daughter (after the mother's death). The question is, is anything given by the will to the child which the testator might have given away from her? If what is so given is accepted, then according to the decision of the Privy Council, the well-known principle of election prevails, and the provisions of the will are binding on the child.

1868.
Feb. 14.
June 4.
„   5.
„   8.
July 18.

Blignaut's Trustee *vs.* Cilliers's Executors and Others.

Then there remains the question whether the plaintiff is, in right of the insolvent, entitled to claim the usufruct during Mrs. Blignaut's life. Is the liquidation account to be corrected so as to give this usufruct to the plaintiff? We think not. The plaintiff by the declaration claims Mrs. Blignaut's share in the legacy of the 26,000 rds. That is something which, in the whole, we apprehend, but certainly in part, the testator might have given away from Mrs. Blignaut; and of course, from her husband, in whose right the plaintiff claims for her creditors. The plaintiff therefore, accepting a benefit under the will, must be bound by its provisions (*Simpson vs. Forrester*); and these provisions exclude the creditors from absorbing the wife's interest. They can receive no more out of the inheritance than the codicil of the 11th April, 1859, gives them. It may be that they have forfeited any rights under this codicil by their institution of this suit, or otherwise, but no defence to that effect is set up on the part of the defendants.

In a very recent case before the Privy Council, from Canada, *Renand vs. Guillet* (37 *L. J., P C.* 1), in which the Privy Council, reversing the decision of the majority of the Court below, gave no judgment, but simply adopted the judgment of Mr. Justice Meridith, one of the judges of the minority below, we find this passage in his judgment there reported: " It may, however, be answered that a testator may, by an express provision to that effect, bequeath property so as to be free from seizure for the debts of the legatee, and that property left expressly *pour aliments* (as the authors say) is not liable to be brought to sale for the debts of the legatee;" and in accordance with this we find in *Voet*, 2, 4, 51 : " Favour towards *alimenta* seems also to have effected this, that they when due *in futurum* to any one be not burdened by arrest; for no one seems to be easily defrauded of his daily aliment, and so killed, according to *Dig.* 25, 3, 4 ;" and further on,

1868.
Feb. 14.
June 4.
„ 5.
„ 8.
July 13.

Blignaut's Trustee *vs.* Cilliers's Executors and Others.

" to which we may add that so the last desires of the dying would be subverted, who bequeathing *alimenta* to a certain person, would be unwilling that they should be otherwise diverted; which was also the reason why the laws forbid there to be a compromise (*transigi*) concerning these without a decree, nor permitted a decree to be interposed unless the intention of the deceased should remain unhurt." The *Dig.* 42, 3, 6, in reference to *cessio bonorum*, is in accordance with this passage : " If he who has made *cessio bonorum* have acquired, after the sale of his goods, some *modicum*, his goods are not sold again ;" and then in the term *modicum* are included these, " if anything have been left to him *misericordiæ causâ*, suppose something monthly or annual *alimentorum nomine*, his goods must not be again sold for this, for he is not to be defrauded of his daily aliment. It is the same also if an usufruct be granted or bequeathed to him, from which there is only received as much as is sufficient for him, in the name of aliment." We refer to these propositions more as illustrations of the main questions before us here, than as directly applying to them ; the legitimate portion was not involved there, but the *alimenta* are taken to have been acquired from any person. We may add that, according to the authorities, the term *alimenta* includes house, food and clothing (*Brissonius, ad verbum*), and the authorities which we have cited help to show that the plaintiff cannot claim Mrs. Blignaut's usufruct, which is not averred or proved to be more than sufficient for the allowable purposes of aliment.

A case, *in re Zeederberg*, was before this Court last year. There the testator had imposed a *fidei-commissum* upon his son's inheritance, giving him a life usufruct ; and by a clause towards the end of the will he directed that the interests of his fidei-commissary heirs should not be liable to their debts, but should be exclusively for their and their children's maintenance. The Court held that the trustees of an insolvency of the son, occurring four years after the testator's death, were entitled to the son's life usufruct. In some sense this case is an authority for the conclusion at which we have arrived in this case, as it evidently recognizes the principle of election as binding on the trustees of the insolvency, who apparently were not supposed by any one to be entitled, adopting the usufruct, to claim also the son's legitimate portion, or the Trebellianic portion in respect of the *fidei-commissum* on the son's inheritance. The case is a direct authority only for this proposition, that if you give a life usufruct to a person, you cannot by mere declaration that it shall not be subject to his debts, bar the right to the usufruct of the trustee of a subsequent insolvency of the usufructary. For that proposition the case of *Renand vs. Guillet* is a direct authority; both decisions rest on this proposition, that such a declaration by a testator is not binding when there is no, or no valid, bequest over in case of the contingency happening. The case *in re Zeederberg* differs from the present in many respects; the question here is not in respect of an interest bequeathed to the insolvent; the insolvency here was in the lifetime of the testator, and was expressly referred to by him; and there is a bequest over on the happening of the contingency guarded against.

1868.
Feb. 14.
June 4.
„ 5.
„ 8.
July 13.

Blignaut's Trustee *vs.* Cilliers's Executors and Others.

We have already intimated that the liquidation account appears to us to be incorrect in some particulars. We do not find that the debts due by Blignaut and Aswegen are, as we apprehended they ought to be, included in the amount of the inheritance, and then the respective amounts deducted from the shares of each respectively. There is also no ground for deducting the debt of Blignaut from the creditors' one-third: it ought to be deducted from the whole share. And the parents' life usufruct ought not to be given to the children.

There ought, therefore, on the whole, to be judgment for the two defendants, L. A. Visagie and P. J. Pienaar, and a declaration that the plaintiff is entitled to one-fifth of the sum of 26,000 rds. when payable, and to one-third of Mrs. Blignaut's share of the inheritance; the debt of £141 5s. due by the insolvent being deducted from the whole of such share and not from the plaintiff's one-third; but that the plaintiff is not entitled to any part of the *corpus* of the remaining two-thirds of the inheritance of Mrs. Blignaut, nor in respect of the usufruct during her life.

With reference to the claim of the plaintiff against Mrs. Cilliers in respect of her life usufruct in half the farm Driefontein, the claim is founded upon the allegation that Mrs. Cilliers takes more under the will than either of her husband's daughters by his first marriage. But this way of looking at the case leaves, as we have said, out of consideration the bequest to the daughters of a share in the 26,000 rds., in which Mrs. Cilliers takes nothing; nor has any evidence been given to show that one-fourth of the usufruct of the farm is worth more than one-fifth of the 26,000 rds. And Mrs. Blignaut's share of this usufruct would, we apprehend, form part of her inheritance, and the plaintiff, therefore, be entitled to only one-third of it, *i.e.*, one-twelfth of the usufruct of the whole.

Then, again, the plaintiff is, as we have said, bound by the provisions of the will, and one of these is that Mrs. Cilliers shall keep for herself this usufruct. We are not aware of any sufficient reason why the principle of election, which it was decided in *Simpson vs. Forrester* by the Privy Council

1868.
Feb. 14.
June 4.
„ 5.
„ 8.
July 13.

Blignaut's Trustee vs. Cilliers's Executors and Others.

applied to the *legitim* (*vid. et Sande, Decis.* 4, 2, 4, and 4, 7, 2, *ad fin.*), should not also apply to the subject matter of the *lex hac edictali*. The provisions of this law are for the benefit of the children of the first marriage, but they, or those who claim in their right, elect to take what we must suppose is the greater benefit given by the will. The decision, too, in *Sande, Decis.* 2, 3, 6, seems analagous to this extent, that there the provision of the will by which, if the *lex hac edictali* was insisted on by the children of the first marriage, so much as the wife lost thereby was given from them to the children of the second marriage, was upheld by the Court. *Sande*, no doubt, objects to the decision; but he seems to have urged his objections on the Court, and to have been decided against.

The view which we take of the case renders it unnecessary to express any opinion in reference to the validity or subsisting effect of the consent paper of the 13th June, 1849, relied on by the defendants' special plea; we shall only observe that there seems to be much ground, on the authorities, for holding such an agreement, at least when made without the knowledge or consent of the testator, to be void. (*Van Leeuwen Cens. For.* 1, 4, (15); *Voet*, 2, 14, 6; *V. d. Keessel, Thesis* 479.; *Huber, Prælect.*, 2, 14, 3. *Sande, Decis.* 4, 2, 4). The plaintiff's claim to deduct the Trebellianic portion was, we understood, given up in the argument as being prevented by or merged in the legacy of the share in the 26,000 rds. However 'that may be, to allow the claim would be, so far, to defeat the will and codicils, by the provisions of which we hold the plaintiff to be bound.

[Plaintiff's Attorneys, Messrs. *Fairbridge & Arderne*.
Defendants' Attorneys, Messrs. *Hofmeyr, Tredgold & Watermeyer*.]

TRUBY'S TRUSTEE, APPLICANT; SWEMMER AND COETZEE, RESPONDENTS.

Taxation of Costs.—Circuit Court.

The Court refused to allow the reopening, for review in Cape Town, of a Circuit Bill of Costs taxed and allowed by the Registrar of Circuit; but gave liberty to apply before the next Circuit Court.

1868.
Aug. 31.

Truby's Trustee, Applicant; Swemmer and Coetzee, Respondents.

De Villiers, for applicant, moved on notice dated 6th August to the respondents, who were the joint attorneys for the defendant in an action of undue preference, "Truby's Trustee *vs.* Truter," heard at the George Circuit Court in April, 1868, before CONNOR, J. Judgment being then given for defendant, with costs, the bill of costs was duly taxed by Mr. Merriman, Registrar of Circuit at George; whereupon a writ of execution was issued on the 6th April, and an *alias* writ on the 12th May. The object of the present motion was to review the bill of costs, and strike out certain alleged overcharges.

1868.
Aug. 31.

Truby's Trustee, Applicant; Swemmer and Coetzee, Respondents.

Porter, for respondents, submitted that the case of " Truby's Trustee *vs*. Truter " is not at present in this Court, which cannot reopen for review a bill of costs in a case not before it. It may be regarded as, under the 185th Rule of Court, " removed " into this Court at the conclusion of the Circuit Court ; but that is then a " removal " of a case heard and bill of costs taxed ; for the removal is of the case as it stands at the rising of the Circuit Court. Rule 207 provides, it is also true, that the bill of costs taxed by the Registrar of the Circuit at which the case is tried " or by the Circuit Court which shall be held for the same district, or by the Supreme Court or any Judge thereof," &c. But then the notice must be upon the defendant himself, and not upon his attorneys : which is in itself a sufficient answer to this motion. The writ of execution was taken out in Truter's own name, and the motion should have followed it, and made him the respondent to this motion.

The Court refused to grant the motion and gave costs against the applicant, holding that the notice should have been upon Truter, and not upon respondents, but intimated that a proper motion could be heard at the ensuing Circuit Court for George.

[Applicant's Attorneys, *Tiran & De Smidt.*]
[Respondents' Attorney, *De Korte.*]

In " Truby's Trustee *vs*. Barrington," *De Villiers* then moved for a review of a similarly taxed bill of costs. Barrington was applicant's own agent at the trial of the case referred to *supra*, and it was urged the difficulty as to notice in the motion just disposed of did not exist in this. But the Court, as there was nothing to show clearly that Barrington, who made no appearance, had had notice of this application, intimated that this motion, also, could be heard with the other at George.

Truby's Trustee, Applicant; Barrington, Respondent.

[Applicant's Attorneys, *Tiran & De Smidt.*]

SUPREME COURT REPORTS.

1868.

PART IV.

PORT ELIZABETH DIVISIONAL COUNCIL, APPELLANTS, AND DEFENDANTS BELOW, *vs.* UITENHAGE DIVISIONAL COUNCIL, RESPONDENTS, AND PLAINTIFFS BELOW.

Main Roads Act, No. 10 of 1864.

Divisional Council: Action to recover Subsidy.—Error of Law: Action to recover Money paid under.

1868.
June 12.

Port Elizabeth Divisional Council, Appellants, *vs.* Uitenhage Divisional Council, Respondents.

This was an action heard at the Port Elizabeth Circuit Court, to recover £480, being the amount of subsidy alleged to be due under Act 10, 1864, from 1st July, 1866, to 1867, towards the maintenance and keeping in repair of the main roads in the division of Uitenhage.

The defendants, admitting their liability to pay to the plaintiffs this sum, pleaded that the plaintiffs were indebted to them in an equal sum, with interest; and that for several years before the taking effect of the Road Act of 1864, a toll-bar had existed at Rawson's Bridge, within the division of Port Elizabeth, over the Great Zwartkops River. That after the passing of that Act, defendants, in ignorance of their rights to the whole of the tolls collected at the said toll-bar, and without any intention to surrender such rights, and without any power in law so to do, suffered and permitted the sum of £907 5s. 6d., being one-half of the rent of the toll from 1st January, 1865, to 27th January, 1867, to be paid over to the plaintiffs, contrary to the provisions of the Road Act. And that the plaintiffs, well knowing the premises, and although often requested to repay the said sum, nevertheless detained the same, and neglected and refused to pay

1868.
June 12.

Port Elizabeth Divisional Council, Appellants, *vs.* Uitenhage Divisional Council, Respondents.

it over; the defendants being ready and willing at all times to deduct from such sum of £907 5s. 6d. with interest, a sum equal to the £480 now claimed by plaintiffs. Wherefore they prayed judgment, with costs. And for a claim in reconvention, the defendants claimed the same amount of £907 5s. 6d. with interest.

The plaintiffs, having first replied to the general issue, specially replied further, that they took and received the sum of money in the plea mentioned by and with the consent and authority of and under a contract with the defendants, and that such sum of money was in fact voluntarily paid in pursuance of such agreement. And as to the reconventional claim, plaintiffs replied to the same effect.

It appeared from the statement at the Bar, that at the Port Elizabeth Circuit Court held before FITZPATRICK, J., in October, 1867, another action by the Uitenhage Divisional Council *vs.* the Port Elizabeth Divisional Council was first heard; and that case involved the question whether the toll-bar on the Zwartkops was in the division of Uitenhage or Port Elizabeth. Judgment was given for the Port Elizabeth Council, with costs. And, as a consequence, a similar judgment was given in this second case. Appeals were noted from both decisions; it being agreed that the evidence taken in the first case should apply to both. In February term (*Pt. I., p.* 40), the appeal from the first action was heard, and the decision of the Court below reversed; and the present appeal from the decision in the second case was now proceeded with.

Griffith, A.-G., for appellants (with him *De Villiers*) maintained their right to retain the moneys claimed by respondents against the money paid by appellants, in mistake of law, and to claim *condictio indebiti* for what had been paid, under a common error, to the respondents. He admitted that if such an action had been brought in the English courts, appellants would be out of court; but maintained that by the law of the Colony there is a right to recover money paid under a mistake of law. There would, no doubt, be found to be a great conflict of authority upon the point; but, as favourable to appellants' claim, he relied upon the following: *Dig.* 12, 6, 29, and 40; 21, 6, 7, 8; 41, 3, 31; *Grotius* 3, 30, 6 (*p.* 421), and 3, 30, 18 (*p.* 424); *Van Leeuwen Cens. For.* 1, 4, 14, 3 (*p.* 397); *V. D. K. Th.* 796; *Dutch Consult. pt.* 4, *Consil.* 9; *Vinnius Selectæ Questiones, bk. I, ch.* 47 (translated in *Evans's Pothier*, 3rd *Am. ed.* (*vol.* 2, *p.* 372, *et seqq.*); *Dissertation on Mistakes of Law, by D'Aguesseau*, translated in the same work and volume, *p.* 347, *ed seqq.* All the cases referred to were cases in which there was a right to give away money, but a right restrained on account of legal incapacity ; whereas in this case divisional councils are absolutely incapable of making donations to each other.

Porter, for respondents (with him *Cole*). The respondents are not said to have acted in bad faith, or knowing that by law they had no right to do what they did. The difficulty has only arisen from the oversight of the Legislature in not applying to the case of a bridge connecting two divisions the principle of half-share which they applied to the case of a ferry plying between two divisions. Then, as to the contract respondents rely upon in their plea, on the 11th November, 1864, the civil commissioner of Port Elizabeth, as chairman of the divisional council, sent to the civil commissioner of Uitenhage, as the chairman of that divisional council, a letter, arranging for the joint repair of the bridge and the collection of the toll moneys ; and the evidence in the case shows that accordingly, at the periodical letting of the tolls, and the repairs of the bridge, the action of the two councils was joint. The respondents might have established opposition tolls, but were lulled to sleep by this contract. As to the authorities on the right to recover, there is a great conflict. Favourable to the respondents are *Voet*, 12, 6, 7, and 22, 6, 5 ; *Domat*, 1, 18, 1, §§ 13-16, *Burge* 3, 733. It has been a principle in this Court in cases of such conflict of authority among the civilians to follow *Voet*, as in *Blatchford vs. Blatchford*, decided in this Court on the 10th December, 1861. And it has been another principle that where there is such conflict among the civilians, and one of the conflicting doctrines is the doctrine of the courts of law in England, this Court favours the doctrine which so coincides with the English law, rather than that which contradicts. And a reference to the English law authorities shows that *Voet*, on this subject, writes like an English lawyer. (*Brisbane vs. Davies*, 5 *Taunt*. 143 ; *Marriott vs. Hampton*, 7 *Term R.* 269; *Story's Equity Jurisprudence, vol.* 2, *ch.* 5, *sect. III.*)

Griffith in reply.—There has been no compromise of disputed right in this case, for at the time of the letter, in 1864, no dispute had arisen. Every case of *condictio indebiti* is, more or less, a case of injustice. But in this case neither considerations of injustice nor morality can apply to defeat right. Mere conflict of authority furnishes no ground for rejecting the Roman-Dutch law, and having recourse to the English law. *Voet's* authority in this Court must rest upon his arguments, and not upon his name ; and in this case *Voet* only repeats the arguments of *Cujacius*, which are all met and answered by *D'Aguesseau* in his *Dissertation* cited.

The Court, after consultation, gave judgment for respondents.

1868.
June 12.

Port Elizabeth Divisional Council, Appellants, *vs.* Uitenhage Divisional Council, Respondents.

1868.
June 12.

Port Elizabeth Divisional Council Appellants,
vs. Uitenhage Divisional Council, Respondents.

HODGES, C. J.—It seems to me that the evidence shows that for a period of three years there was an arrangement between the two councils, which might have been, and may still hereafter prove, a very proper understanding to which to come, that the tolls of the bridge should be equally divided between the two councils. In virtue of such division, made by Mr. Campbell, civil commissioner of Port Elizabeth, the chairman of the divisional council there, and acceded to by the Uitenhage council, in good faith on both sides, and acting upon the arrangement so made, the tolls were remitted by the civil commissioner to the Uitenhage council. The bridge was from time to time repaired, under the joint superintendence of the two councils, and everything went on in a friendly way till the question arose which brought about this action. We are not made acquainted with the reasons which induced the civil commissioners and the members of the councils to agree to this arrangement. Some doubts may have perhaps been entertained whether the toll-house was entirely or in part in either division. For anything I can see, there is no reason to suppose that the agreement on which the two councils acted was not a proper one, and it would be a very strong proceeding now if we were to compel money paid under these circumstances to be repaid to a party who made that payment voluntarily and with a full knowledge of all the circumstances of the case. The Port Elizabeth council claimed from the Uitenhage council, and the Circuit Court decided that the claim was good in law, that the whole of the tolls collected at the bridge should go to Port Elizabeth. That decision was, however, reversed by this Court; and it follows as a consequence that the learned Judge having decided that all the tolls should go to Uitenhage, it put a stop to the simultaneously pending action which we now have brought before us, which is an action brought by the divisional council of Uitenhage against the divisional council of Port Elizabeth, to recover the subsidy of £480 in respect that it was payable under Act 10, 1864; and as the Port Elizabeth council at that time set up a right to half the tolls, not the whole, there was a plea of set-off, to the effect that under the arrangement improperly made, as they said, at that time, and inadvertently, the £480 had been received. And then, as a claim in reconvention, they sought to recover the remaining balance of half the tolls. Although we have reversed the decision in the former case, we think the decision in the second case correct, and that the appeal should be dismissed, each party to pay his own costs of appeal.

BELL, J.—I concur that there is enough evidence to satisfy me that the two councils agreed between themselves, from motives which we are not bound to inquire into, nor is it necessary to inquire into them, that the tolls should be divided; and I am not disposed to interfere in any way by reversing the payment of money so made. It is wholly unnecessary, therefore, to go into the nice distinctions so learnedly argued on both sides.

1868.
June 12.
———
Port Elizabeth Divisional Council, Appellants, *vs.* Uitenhage Divisional Council, Respondents.

CONNOR, J.—We have to thank the Bar for the learning shown in the argument, and the assistance the Bench have received, and which may be useful at some future time. There is undoubtedly a great conflict of authorities upon the right to recover money paid under a mistake of law. During the short recess the Court took, I found two other authorities, one on each side: *Merula* against the *condictio indebiti* for *ignorantia juris;* and *Huber* (who is more modern than *Voet*), in favour of it. Yet whatever difference of opinion there may be upon that question, there is no difference on this, that there must be a natural equity on the side of him who claims the *condictio indebiti.* Well, if so, the *onus* is on him to show that natural equity; and I think in this case the respondent has failed in showing that there is any such natural equity on his side. The two councils came to a particular arrangement, acted upon that arrangement, and received and paid the money upon the basis of that arrangement; and certainly it would be a strong measure to say that either of them would have a natural equity as opposed to that arrangement, for we must assume that the money paid was laid out for the proper purpose. I concur that the appeal should be dismissed.

Appeal dismissed accordingly; but without costs of appeal.

[Appellants' Attorneys, *Reid & Nephew.*]
[Respondents' Attorney, *Tennant.*]

WALKER & CO., APPELLANTS, AND DEFENDANTS BELOW: BEETON'S TRUSTEES, RESPONDENTS, AND PLAINTIFFS BELOW.

One of two Co-trustees cannot sign a valid Power of Attorney authorizing the commencement of an Action; the Power, to be good, must be signed by both.

This was an appeal from a judgment of the Eastern Districts Court in an action of undue preference.

The declaration in the Court below set forth that "Joseph Walker, jun., of King William's Town, in his capacity as

1868.
June 2.
 „   12.
———
Walker & Co, Appellants;Beeton's Trustees, Respondents.

1868.
June 2.
" 12.

Walker & Co, Appellants; Beeton's Trustees, Respondents.

the surviving and liquidating partner of the firm of Joseph Walker, jun., & Co., heretofore trading under that style and title, at King William's Town,—of which partnership one Henry Maynard and one Charles Maynard were also partners, but are beyond the jurisdiction of the Court," had been summoned to answer the trustees of Beeton & Co., of Queen's Town, in an action for undue preference. The declaration then went on to allege the sequestration of the estate on the 1st February, 1863 ; and that between the 1st November, 1862, and 31st January, 1863, the insolvent firm had ceded, delivered, &c., to Walker & Co. certain promissory notes and open accounts, amounting to £3,629 16s. 9d. And this the declaration, after the usual averments of contemplation, &c., prayed might be declaied an undue preference under the 84th section of Ord. 6, 1843 ; " and that the defendant, in his said capacity, and heretofore trading as aforesaid," may be condemned to deliver to the plaintiffs the said promissory notes and open accounts, or to pay the value thereof, £3,629 16s. 9d., with interest from the date of delivery. And, further, forfeiture was claimed under the 88th section. The defendant pleaded the following exceptions and plea in abatement :

" First, that whereas Frederick Hall (in the plaintiffs' declaration erroneously called Frederick James Hall), one of the plaintiffs in this suit, is alleged, in and by a certain warrant or power to sue, filed by the plaintiff, Charles Ross Gowie, of record in this suit, to be beyond the jurisdiction of this Honourable Court, the said defendant has been summoned to answer the said Frederick Hall, and not Richard Shaw Smith, of Graham's Town, the duly constituted agent of the said Frederick Hall.

" Second,—That whereas the said warrant, or power, purports to be given by the said Charles Ross Gowie on behalf of the said Frederick Hall, the said Charles Ross Gowie has not filed of record in the office of the Registrar of this Honourable Court, or exhibited to the said Registrar, as by law required, any power constituting him the agent for the said Frederick Hall for such purpose. Wherefore the said defendant prays that the said plaintiffs' suit may be dismissed, with costs.

" And as and for a plea in abatement, should the above exceptions be overruled, but not otherwise, the said defendant says that the said Charles Maynard, in the said plaintiffs' declaration mentioned, now deceased, was a member of the said firm of Joseph Walker, jun., and Company up to the date of his decease ; and that the said Charles Maynard died on the 5th day of September, 1862 ; and that, thereafter,—to wit, at the date of the alleged transactions impeached by the said plaintiffs,--the said defendant and the said Henry Maynard were carrying on the business of the said firm for the benefit of themselves and of the estate of the said Henry Maynard, who, though at present in England, is the owner of considerable property in this Colony, and within the jurisdiction of this Honourable Court, and carries on business in Graham's Town, Port Elizabeth and King William's Town, within the jurisdiction of this Honourable Court, and has not been joined as defendant in this suit; and also that Robert Dunlop Buchanan, executor of the last will of the said Charles Maynard, and who has in his possession, custody and power considerable property within the jurisdiction of this Honourable Court, belonging to the estate of the late Charles Maynard, deceased, has not been joined as defendant in this suit; and this the said defendant is ready to verify. Wherefore the said defendant prays that the said plaintiffs' suit may be dismissed, with costs."

1868.
June 2.
" 12.
Walker&Co., Appellants; Beeton's Trustees, Respondents.

Then followed the general issue.

To this the plaintiffs replied : That the two first exceptions were informal and bad in law, being grounded on allegations of fact not set forth in the declaration, and which should have been specially pleaded or verified in pleas of statement by affidavit; and that the absence of Maynard and Buchanan was no sufficient ground for their joinder as defendants.

The Court below dismissed the two exceptions, and ordered the plea in abatement to stand as a special plea. And, on the 5th December, 1867, gave judgment for plaintiffs, with costs.

This day (June 2) the Supreme Court heard the argument on the exceptions.

Porter, for applicants.—The first exception is not so stongly relied on; but the second exception is a good one. It raises this question : whether it is competent for one of two trustees to file a warrant to sue, as required by the Rules of Court, for himself and his co-trustee without producing some specific authority, in writing, from the co-trustee, authorizing him so to do. There is no such implied power. (*Trustee of Dodds, King & Co. vs. Watson. Menzies' Rep., p.* 140.) That was, it is true, on a provisional case ; but in regard to the principle of the decision no distinction can be drawn between a summons on a liquid and an illiquid case. Perhaps Gowie might sue as an individual trustee, specially averring Hall's absence from the Colony ; but that is very different to what has been done here. The Court will also take judicial notice of its own proceedings, and observe that after this action now appealed from had been brought and decided, Gowie applied to the Eastern Districts Court to remove Hall from the trust, and he was removed accordingly ; and then a question connected with the election of a new joint trustee was raised before this Court (*vide Part* 2, *p.* 103). The ground of the Court below in overruling the exceptions was, according to the notes of FITZPATRICK, J., "that Walker's appearance had cured the defect." Now, from *Chitty's Practice*, heading " *Irregularities in Process,*" no doubt many irregularities could be cured by the defendant's appearance ; but under the heading " *Staying Pro-*

1868.
June 2.
" 12.
Walker & Co., Appellants; Boetou's Trustee, Respondents.

ceedings," it will be seen that where at any stage of the proceedings it is discovered that the attorney is proceeding without authority, the defendant may move to stay proceedings. It may be said, *contra*, that this must be done by motion, and not exception ; but our practice is the other way. To take exception is the right course of procedure, for it amounts to a particular exception specifically described, *i.e.*, *exceptio inhabilis procuratoris*. (*Van Leeuwen, Cens. Forens.* pt. 2, *lib.* 1, *ch.* 5, *sec.* 3.) And the policy of the rule is obvious : for there may be cases in which pleas in reconvention are filed, and judgment given for defendants, or an order for costs against plaintiffs, and then Hall, although *dominus litis*, would not in reality be before the Court granting such judgment or order. *De Haas*, in his annotation to *Van Leeuwen* (*ubi supra cit.*), shows that the exception may be raised at any stage of the proceedings, even up to execution. If one of two trustees present in the Colony refuse to join his colleague when so directed, the Court would make an order compelling him to join, if found desirable ; but this is not that case, for one of the trustees is *ex concessis* out of the Colony. Next, as to the plea in abatement. That is good also. Substantially, it is this—that Walker is improperly sued altogether, and in a character which is, in part of it, as described upon the pleadings, unknown to the law, and having no meaning. In what treatise on partnership will such a phrase as "surviving and liquidating partner " be found ? " Surviving partner " Walker certainly is not. He is one of two surviving partners, for Henry Maynard is the other. And as to the phrase " liquidating partner," that may have a popular, but it has no legal meaning. All the surviving partners should be sued ; and here there is, then, a good writ given by the plea in abatement, as against Henry Maynard. But it is said Henry Maynard has property here, but is not here in person. That might be a good ground for a motion to the Court to hold a service on Walker, within the Colony, good on Maynard, out of the Colony ; but it does not justify the dropping Maynard altogether out of the record. If the Court should give a judgment against the trustees *de bonis propriis*, all the trustees divide the consequent responsibility; but how could Henry Maynard—not on the record, and not a plaintiff to the suit—be compelled to discharge his share of such responsibility ?

Postea (June 3) —*Griffith, A.-G.* (with him *Cole*), for the respondents, argued in support of the judgment below. In point of fact, the defendants have not appealed on the exceptions or the plea in abatement, but on the merits. And secondly, even had they so appealed, this Court has no jurisdiction to try that appeal, inasmuch as the Eastern Districts

Court Act, 17 of 1864, section 25, provides for appeal to the Supreme Court only " against any final judgment, decree or sentence of the said Court, or against any rule or order made in any civil suit or action having the effect of a final or definitive sentence." Now, a judgment on exceptions is a judgment that the defendant *respondeat ultra*, which is not a final, but an interlocutory order. If the Court had allowed the exceptions and dismissed the case, that would have been a final order.

[CONNOR, J.—Was it not " finally ordered " that the defendant was to answer alone?]

That may have been the order on the plea of abatement; but the judgment on the exceptions was that defendant had not made a good exception.

[CONNOR, J.—Then you take away the right of appeal on exceptions altogether? That would lead to great inconvenience.]

This may be looked upon as a purely technical objection, but this objection *contra* is also a purely technical objection; and it is fair to meet it in the same way. Then, further, the defendant was ill advised in proceeding to the trial on the general issue. The defect was " cured by appearance," according to the Court below; and certainly under any circumstances it was cured by verdict. The defendant did not show previous ignorance of what he excepted, for he enters appearance to the plaintiffs on their summons, and admits, therefore, they are before the Court.

[CONNOR, J.—Is it a ground of exception? If so, the Rules of Court require entering of appearance before exception taken.]

It was not matter of exception. The proper course was, a motion to take the proceedings off the file. An exception is to the declaration, and not to the summons. If such motion were made, costs must go, if the one trustee appeared unwittingly, against the attorney who had misled him. There could be no order for costs in any other way. If the judgment on the exceptions had given costs against the plaintiffs, that would be giving costs against a person who, on defendant's own showing, was not before the Court. But the preliminary proceedings on motion would have obviated this inconsistency. Suppose the case of a single plaintiff to an action, and it appeared the attorney representing him had filed no power, and the objection raised on exception instead of motion, and judgment on exceptions against plaintiff with costs, no costs could be recovered, for the essence of such a decision would be, no plaintiff before the Court.

[CONNOR, J.—But there is one plaintiff in this case.]

Then, in such a case, the notice of motion to take proceed-

1868.
June 2.
" 12.

Walker & Co., Appellants; Berton's Trustees, Respondents.

ings off the file would be against the one plaintiff and the attorney; just as, in the case of a single plaintiff, it would be against the attorney alone. As to the authority of *Van Leeuwen*, cited *contra*, the Latin word "*exceptio*" used by him is of a larger signification than the technical "exception" in this Court. It means any objection to the proceedings in an action: whereas the exception of this Court is in the nature of a special demurrer. And that the safer mode of proceeding would be by preliminary motion follows from *Van der Linden*, p. 411. Then as to the case from *Menzies*, cited *contra*, that was a provisional claim, and there is a great distinction between liquid and illiquid cases in this respect. There is no appearance entered by defendant to the summons in a provisional claim, except in Court. And, further, the proceedings in a provisional case are very like a motion supported by affidavits. Then, again, if the defendants had a right of appeal, they were bound to have appealed before they went on to try the case on the merits; and hence, not having done so, the defect is cured by verdict. The order on the exception was on the 6th August, and the trial on the general issue on the 4th December; which would have allowed time for the prosecution of the appeal on the exceptions, if it existed. As to the plea in abatement, there was no ground for it; it being averred in the declaration that one trustee was dead, and the other out of the jurisdiction.

Porter, in reply.— The argument on the plea of abatement, *contra*, has been dismis·ed too summarily. No case will be found in which when a firm was sued, having partners both here and England, all the partners were not sued; although for the purpose of service it has been held that service in the place of business within the jurisdiction is sufficient to bind absent partners. But there is here no such service, and one partner has not been made a defendant at all. As to the exception "*inhabilis procuratoris*," *vide Voet*, 44, 1, 6. To proceed either by motion or exception was open. There is a close connection between the "*exceptio inhabilis procuratoris*" and the "*exceptio non qualificatæ*;" and the latter is competent as an exception. The initial proceedings by the trustee should have been, under section 52, Ord. 6, 1843, before the summons issued.

Cur. adv. vult.

Postea (June 4).—The Court desired to hear the case on its merits before deciding on the argument on exceptions.

Postea (June 12).—The case was heard on the merits accordingly.

Postea (June 19).—*Porter* inquired when the Court would

deliver judgment, whereupon HODGES, C. J., mentioned that their Lordships would deliver judgment shortly, having already agreed. *Porter* then inquired whether, as the mail was leaving for England that morning, there would be any objection on the part of the Court to mention whether their Lordships had found for plaintiffs or defendants.

1868.
June 2.
„ 12.

Walker & Co., Appellants; Boston's Trustees, Respondents.

HODGES, C. J., after consulting with BELL, J. (CONNOR, J., having already left for Natal).—The judgment will be for defendant, on the exceptions, with costs. We will deliver our written judgments in a few days. And I may add that our brother, CONNOR, agreed in the conclusion at which we arrived.

Owing, however, to the sudden and lamented death of His Honour the Chief Justice shortly afterwards, no written judgment was ever delivered by the Court in this case.

[Appellants' Attorney, *E Hull*.
Respondents' Attorneys, *Reid & Nephew*]

GRAHAM, N.O., *vs.* POCOCK & CO.

Customs Regulations.—Ord. 6, 1883, *Sec.* 32.

Where an Entry was passed at the Custom-house for three carriages and a package of glassware, and on seizure of the carriages by the Custom-house authorities they were found to contain 3,350 *gross of corks ; the Court ordered the forfeiture of the corks and carriages, but not of the glassware.—Intent.—The question of intent is immaterial under Section* 32 *of the Ordinance.*

This was an action for the forfeiture of certain goods or merchandise for breach of Customs Ordinance No. 6, 1853. The declaration stated that John Thomas Pocock and John Alfred Mathew, carrying on business together in co-partnership, in Cape Town, under the style or firm of John T. Pocock and Co., had been summoned to answer Robert Graham, the Acting Collector and Principal Officer of Customs in this Colony, in his capacity as such principal officer, the plaintiff in this suit, for the forfeiture of 3,350 gross of corks, 25 cases of glassware, and 3 carriages, landed by the defendants wrongfully, and in contravention of the provisions of Ordinance 6 of 1853, entitled "An Ordinance for the general management and regulation of Customs of the Colony of the Cape of Good Hope," on or about the 8th May last, from the bark *Loch Awe* then lying in Table Bay, without any valid or due entry thereof, and

1868.
Aug. 24.
Sept. 4.

Graham, N.O., *vs.* Pocock & Co.

1868.
Aug. 24.
Sept. 4.

Graham, N.O.,
vs. Pocock & Co.

without payment of the Customs duty legally payable on the whole of the said goods or merchandise. That the said goods were taken by and delivered to the defendants, the importers thereof, out of the *Loch Awe* by virtue of an entry, or pretended entry, made by the defendants, as importers, and lodged with the officers of Customs at Cape Town. That said goods were not properly described in such entry, or pretended entry, by the denominations, and with the characters and circumstances according to which such goods are charged with duty, and may be imported; inasmuch as the corks were omitted altogether. Wherefore the plaintiff submitted that the said entry, or pretended entry, ought to be deemed invalid, and the goods deemed to be goods taken without due entry thereof, and to be forfeited with costs of suit.

The defendants pleaded the general issue.

On the 25th August, the Court heard the evidence in the case, when it appeared that the corks were not included in the entry, the glassware and carriages being alone entered. The carriages were packed in cases, the interstices being filled up with the corks. It appeared that Pocock, the senior partner of the firm, being in London in the early part of the year, shipped, on consignment from merchants, to his firm at the Cape, three carriages and a parcel of glassware, and shipped on his own account a second parcel of glassware and a quantity of corks. To save freight, he filled up the carriage-cases with corks, and on the 7th March wrote from London to Mr. J. R. Moore, auctioneer, of Cape Town, who was to dispose of the consigned goods, as follows; "The cases are filled with corks, which, please, hand over to our firm, and Mathew will give you the duty on them. To suit your convenience, these corks can be put into our stores until you sell them, which, please, do without delay." He also wrote Mathew to the same effect. The *Loch Awe* arrived in Table Bay on the 8th May, when Mathew passed an entry for the glassware and carriages, having, as he alleged, forgotten all about the corks, the duty on which was £10 6s. 6d., being 10 per cent. on the invoiced value. The cases of carriages were subsequently seized by the Custom-house authorities, and found to contain the corks.

On the 4th September, *Griffith, A.-G.*, claimed the forfeiture of the carriages, glassware and corks, on the ground that the non-entry of the corks vitiated the whole entry from which they were so omitted. Under the 32nd section of Ordinance 6, 1853, intent was altogether immaterial.

Porter, for defendants, admitted that on the evidence the corks were liable to forfeiture; but contended that the forfeiture should not be extended beyond the articles omitted from the entry.

The Court (BELL, C. J., and DWYER, J.), held that the carriages and corks, forming together one case, or package, should be forfeited; but that the glassware, a distinct package, had been correctly described in the entry, and should not be forfeited. The question of intent was immaterial under section 32 of the Ordinance, and it was, therefore, unnecessary (it being clear that the corks had not been entered, and that the entry contained a misdescription of the carriage-cases, and, therefore, entailed, in the opinion of the Court, the forfeiture of both carriages and corks) to consider, in this case, whether there was an intent on the part of Mathew, in making the entry, to defeat the Ordinance.

1868.
Aug. 24.
Sept. 4.
Graham, N O.,
vs. Pocock & Co.

[Plaintiff's Attorneys: *Reid & Nephew.*
Defendants' Attorneys: *Fairbridge & Arderne.*]

GRAHAM, N.O., vs. POCOCK & CO.

Customs Regulations.—Ordinance 6, 1853, Sec. 50.

In order to make out a case under Section 50 it is essential to prove guilty knowledge and fraudulent intent.

This was a second action (between the same parties and arising out of the same transaction) for the treble value of the forfeited articles, under section 50 of Ordinance 6, 1853. The evidence in the last case was, by consent, taken to be the evidence in this case also.

Sept. 4.
Graham, N O.,
vs. Pocock & Co.

Griffith, A.G., for plaintiff, relied on the case of *The Crown vs. Sorey, sen., The Crown vs. Sorey, jun.,* and *The Crown vs. Van Zanten,* all decided in favour of the Crown, 24th June, 1867, and treble penalty awarded.

Porter, for defendants.—Although intent is admittedly immaterial in actions under section 32, in actions under section 50 intent is everything. Section 50 implies guilty knowledge in the persons brought under it, and applies to cases of smuggling. But the evidence in this case shows a mistake, or forgetfulness, on the part of Mathew, and no fraudulent intention to conceal or avoid the Customs law. The cases cited *contra* were clear cases of deliberate smuggling. Moreover, section 50 does not apply to the importers of the goods, but to third parties " assisting or being otherwise concerned in the unshipping, landing or removal, or in harbouring of such goods." As to the construction of the section, he quoted *Dwarris on Statutes, 2nd ed. p.* 621.

Griffith in reply.

1868.
Sept. 4.
Graham, N.O.
vs. Pocock & Co.

The Court gave judgment for defendants, with costs; holding that the 50th section applied only to cases of smuggling. The evidence in this case did not, in the opinion of the Court, show any such guilty knowledge or fraudulent intent on the part of Mathew to avoid the payment of duty on the carriages, as was essential to make out a case under section 50.

RE CERES MUNICIPALITY.

Public Bodies' Debts Act. Proceedings under.

Nov. 15.
Dec. 1.
Re Ceres Municipality.

This was the first proceeding under the Public Bodies' Debts Act, No. 11 of 1867.

Porter applied, under the 1st section of the Act, for a rule *nisi* calling upon the Commissioners of the Ceres Municipality to show cause why a rate should not be assessed on the immovable property within the said Municipality to make good the sum of £148 7s. 8d., being the taxed costs of a suit tried at the Tulbagh Circuit Court in October, 1867, before HODGES, C. J., between the Ceres Municipality, plaintiffs, and Adolph Arnholz, defendant. Judgment was given for defendant, with costs; for which costs a writ of execution was subsequently issued, the return thereto being an insufficient levy. By the 3rd section of the Act it is provided that " if such public body shall not satisfy the said Court by sufficient securities that it can and will fully satisfy such judgment, decree or order, with interest and all costs properly incurred in respect thereof, and also such other debts as are hereinafter mentioned, if any, with interest, within a reasonable time, to the satisfaction of the said Court, then the Court shall assess and impose such a rate or rates on the rateable property of which such public body is empowered to levy rates, to be levied at such time or times as to the said Court shall seem fit and necessary, to satisfy, either at once or by instalments, as to the said Court shall seem right, from and out of the net proceeds of such rate or rates, all moneys payable under or by virtue of such judgment, order or decree," &c. And it was now moved accordingly, that in the first instance a rule *nisi* should issue under the 1st section, to show cause why relief should not be given under the 3rd section.

The Court granted the rule *nisi*, returnable on the 1st December.

Postea (14th December), there being no appearance, the rule was made absolute, and a further rule *nisi* granted to show cause why an assessment of 1d. in the pound should not be made to cover the costs of the action.

[Applicant's Attorneys: Messrs. *Fairbridge & Arderne*.]

BASSON, APPELLANT, DEFENDANT BELOW; CIVIL COMMISSIONER, PAARL, RESPONDENT, PLAINTIFF BELOW.

1868.
Nov. 19.
" 20.
Basson, Appellant, Defendant below; Civil Commissioner, Paarl, Respondent, Plaintiff below.

Grant: Is a Quitrent Grant a liquid document of debt ?

Resident Magistrate's Court : Is it ground of objection to an Action by a Civil Commissioner, nomine officii, for arrear Quitrent, that he is himself the Resident Magistrate to try the case ?

This was an appeal from a judgment delivered by the Resident Magistrate of the Paarl.

The defendant in the Court below was summoned to show why he had not paid to the Civil Commissioner of the Paarl, acting for and on behalf of the Colonial Government, a sum of £21 12s., for eight years' quitrent, due 31st December, 1867, on a farm, " Caledon's Gift," together with £1 12s. for stamps required by law ; in all £23 4s.

The case was heard below on the 20th August, 1868, when the defendant took three exceptions to the summons. *Firstly*, that the amount sued for exceeded £20 and, according to section 8, Act 20, 1856, was therefore above the jurisdiction of the Court. The Court below overruled this exception, on the ground that it considered an action of debt for rent received on a grant to be on a liquid document; and that, therefore, the Court's jurisdiction in a case like the present extended to £40. *Secondly*, that by the second section of the Tacit Hypothecations Act, No. 5 of 1861, the tacit hypothec possessed by the Government for the arrears of quitrent is only claimable for the amount of three years' rent ; whereas here the claim was for eight years. Further, that, by section 9 of the same Act, defendant was liable only for the rent which had accrued during his own ownership of the farm ; and, that as a fact, defendant's ownership commenced in 1864. The Court below overruled this objection likewise. *Thirdly*, that the Civil Commissioner, who is the plaintiff, being the Magistrate who now sits on this case, is not competent to give judgment on the case, in which he is a party. The Court overruled this exception, on the 6th section of Ordinance No. 9 of 1844.

The defendant then tendered into the Court below £8 14s., quitrent for the last three years, from 1st January, 1865, to 31st December, 1867, the amount for which he considered himself liable, he having become possessed of the property about November, 1864, and received transfer 20th July, 1865 ; urging that the transfer should not have been passed without the arrears of quitrent being paid up, inasmuch as such transfer warranted the property transferred free from

1868.
Nov. 19.
" 20.
Basson, Appellant, Defendant below; Civil Commissioner, Paarl, Respondent, Plaintiff below.

all incumbrances and hypothecations. The plaintiff, however, declined the tender, and the case was proceeded with on the merits; when it appeared that in 1815 a grant was made by Government, to one Johan Meyer, of a piece of quitrent ground, " Caledon's Gift," measuring 30 morgen 362 square roods, and liable to an annual quitrent of £2 6s. 6d.; and in 1826 a grant was also made by Government, to Widow Van der Merwe, of a further piece of adjoining quitrent ground, also called " Caledon's Gift," measuring 229 morgen 128 square roods, and liable to an annual quitrent of £2 14s. Subsequently, both places came into the possession of one Ludeking, whose estate was surrendered. Basson bought both places out of the insolvent estate, on the 9th November, 1864, and went into possession immediately, and received transfer from the trustee on the 20th July, 1865, of both places in one day. Filed with the deed of transfer was a certificate by the Civil Commissioner, that the quitrent on " Caledon's Gift" (described the larger property of that name) had been paid up to 31st December, 1865. The action was brought to recover the quitrent on the smaller property; and judgment went for plaintiff, with costs.

De Villiers, for plaintiff —The first exception is not now relied on. The second was properly a plea to the action, and may be considered with the merits; but the third exception is good.

[DENYSSEN, J.—*Nemo potest judex esse in suâ causa*, it is true. But how can it be said that the cause here was *sua*?

[BELL, J.—What possible advantage could the Magistrate take?]

It is admitted he gains no advantage; but as Civil Commissioner he has already prejudged the case. The 6th section of Ordinance 9 of 1844 provides that "the Civil Commissioner may recover arrear rents according to law in some competent court." The Supreme Court is such " a competent court." Suppose one of the judges of this Court happened to be an executor dative, or a trustee, he could not sit during the hearing of any case connected with the estate of which he was executor dative, or with the fund of which he was trustee. It might be a ground of defence that arrear quitrent had already been received by the Civil Commissioner; and how could the Magistrate properly try that point impartially? Besides, there are some Resident Magistrates who are not Civil Commissioners, *e g*, Wynberg, Simon's Town, Knysna, Hondeklip Bay, &c. And in 1844 the Magistrate of the Paarl was not a Civil Commissioner.

Griffith, A.-G.—On the first exception. The Resident Magistrate can have no possible interest in the matter; he can always be recused if necessary. Section 12 of Ordinance No. 9, 1844, clearly contemplated that, in Cape Town at all events, where the offices of Civil Commissioner and Resident Magistrate have been, until very lately, filled by the same person, the Civil Commissioner could prefer and decide claims before himself as Resident Magistrate. And if the law allow it as desirable in one case, it is a fair inference that such a proceeding is also desirable in other precisely similar cases. In the case of Resident Magistrates not Civil Commissioners, the case is different. The present practice is undoubtedly more convenient, and less expensive, for all parties, than to bring such actions in the Supreme Court.

1868.
Nov. 19.
„ 20.

Basson,, Appellant, Defendant below ; Civil Commissioner, Paarl, Respondent, Plaintiff below.

The Court, before adjudicating on this exception, desired to hear the case on the merits.

De Villiers then maintained that it was the practice of the Deeds Registry Office, of which practice judicial notice might be taken by the Court, never to pass transfer without arrears of quitrent being paid up. If there had been a departure in this particular instance from that practice, and Basson was allowed to obtain transfer without a demand for the quitrent, he had been misled into supposing there were no arrears to pay, and was absolved accordingly by thus getting transfer.

[DWYER, J.—Should not a person taking transfer assure himself that all arrears of quitrent are paid? And if he does not do that, how can his taking a pure transfer, as he supposes, free him from liability for quitrent due by former owners?]

In England, the assignee of a lease is only liable for rent accruing while such assignee is in occupation. The remedy of the lessor is against the original lessee for arrear rents. (*Woodfall's Landlord and Tenant*, p. 104.) Quitrent lands in this Colony are held in emphyteutical occupation, and the same principle will apply, that all purchasers of land obtaining transfer are absolved from prior quitrent. This view is confirmed by the analogy drawn from the Land Registry Ordinance, No. 97 of 1833 (*Statute Law*, p. 227, *section 25, proviso*), which declares "that any person who shall have become liable to pay, or shall have incurred any such tax, duty, or quitrent, shall continue and be personally liable to pay the same, notwithstanding that the lands or houses in respect of which such tax, duty, or quitrent became due or was incurred shall by virtue of any such order as aforesaid have been enregistered as the property of any other person." But, under any circumstances, Basson is only liable for the three years he is willing to pay for. The claim of the Government *ultra* is prescribed by Act 5 of 1861.

1868.
Nov. 19.
" 20.

Basson, Appellant, Defendant below; Civil Commissioner, Paarl, Respondent, Plaintiff below.

Nov. 20.—*De Villiers* recurred to the first exception, and said he now thought, on reconsideration, it was a good exception. The claim of quitrent on the grant of "Caledon's Gift" was not a provisional claim; and, if not, the Magistrate had exceeded his jurisdiction under Act 20, 1856, inasmuch as he had jurisdiction for £20 only in cases founded "on any bill of exchange, promissory note, good-for, or other written acknowledgment of debt commonly called a liquid document," &c. Now there is no written acknowledgment of Basson's debt on his grant, for it does not bear his signature. There can only be provisional sentence on leases signed by the defendant lessee. The only case of provisional sentence not based directly on the defendant's signature is that of a taxed bill of costs, operating as a judgment. But even there the bill must have been taxed in the presence of, or after due notice to, the defendant. (*De Wet vs. Meyer.* Menz. 59.)

Griffith, A.-G.—It is evident the exception should first be disposed of. For if the Magistrate's jurisdiction falls away, there is no use proceeding further. In all cases of Government grant, the acceptance of the grant by the grantee and his occupation under it, on the terms of the grant, so bind him as to make him a defendant even on a provisional claim. His signature to the grant is assumed. He accepts the land subject to its incumbrances, among which are also former unpaid quitrents. In this case, moreover, transfer was received by Mr. I. H. de Villiers, Basson's attorney. And although, it is true, both vendor and purchaser have a common attorney in the transaction of the sale and transfer, and that transfer is given by the vendor, as a rule, still the vendor's attorney is made the attorney of the purchaser for the receipt of transfer, and accepts it accordingly.

BELL, C. J., said the first exception should, in his opinion, be allowed, and the judgment of the Court below reversed in respect thereof. What might have been the judgment of the Court under other circumstances, if the case had assumed such a form that he could ascertain what it really was based upon, was another matter. But here the plaint merely set forth that the defendant had been summoned for this arrear quitrent, without adding on what the quitrent had become due, whether the claim was made on a grant of land specifically described, or on the books of the Civil Commissioner's office, showing the arrear quitrent. If this had been done, perhaps the exception might not now be sustained; but in the particular insufficient form of this summons the exception was good, and must be allowed. At the same time, he refrained from giving any indication as to what would have been his opinion if the transfer or the Civil Commissioner's books had been sued upon and referred to in the summons.

DENYSSEN, J., said the claim was twofold—for quitrent and for stamps. Now, to prove the quitrent, it would be necessary to go to the books of the Civil Commissioner, or to the grant; aud to prove the stamps, it would be necessary to show the number of years' rent due, and how the stamps were payable. Here, however, the action was not on the grant, or transfer, for nothing concerning them was inserted in the summons. The grant would have to be made evidence to prove the amount due; and the transfer to show that defendant represented the original grantee. And this necessary recourse to extraneous evidence clearly, therefore, took the case out of the category of a provisional claim, where no extraneous evidence was required, but where the defendant's liability was apparent on the face of the document sued upon, as in all the ordinary examples of provisional claims, promissory notes, bills of exchange, signed conditions of sale, or leases, or taxed bills of costs operating as judgments.

DWYER, J., concurred, and only thought it necessary to add that judgment could not go against the defendant without virtually striking out the words "or written acknowledgment of debt," spoken of in section 8 of Act 20, 1856.

Judgment reversed accordingly, with costs.

[Appellant's Attorneys, *Fairbridge & Arderne.*]
[Respondent's Attorneys, *Reid & Nephew.*]

1868.
Nov. 19.
,, 20.

Basson, Appellant, Defendant below; Civil Com missioner, Paarl, Respondent, Plaintiff below.

NICHOLSON'S TRUSTEE *vs.* COETZEE.

Misdescription of Defendant in Summons.

In this case the summons called upon "Jasper Jacobus Coetzee" to pay to the plaintiff the sum of two promissory notes, both signed "Jasper J. Coetzee." The sheriff's return was one of personal service on "the within-named defendant," as described in the summons.

An affidavit was produced from Jasper *Johannes* Coetzee, simply setting forth that the summons, copy of which was annexed to the affidavit and corresponded with the summons served on Jasper *Jacobus* Coetzee, had been served upon the deponent; but that deponent's name was Jasper *Johannes*, and not Jasper *Jacobus*.

The Court, at first, on the ground of misdescription in the summons, refused provision against the defendant, intimat-

Nov. 16.
Nicholson's Trustee *vs.* Coetzee.

<small>1868.
Nov. 16.

Nicholson's
Trustee vs.
Coetzee.</small>
ing that it would reserve the question of costs until it ascertained whether the "Jasper Johannes Coetzee" of the affidavit was the "Jasper Jacobus Coetzee" of the summons, and whether, consequently, the present objection was purely technical. The plaintiff, however, electing to take judgment as prayed in the summons, taking the risk of execution on such summons, the Court gave judgment as against " Jasper Jacobus Coetzee, " with costs.

[And as to misdescription in summons, *vide Menz.* 124—5]

[Plaintiff's Attorney, *E. Hull.*]
[Attorney for Coetzee, *Nelson.*]

A. vs. B.

Provisional Sentence.—Costs.—Act 20, 1856, *Sec.* 35.

<small>Nov. 16.

A. vs. B.</small>
Provisional sentence was prayed against defendant, residing in the division of Port Elizabeth, by the plaintiff, residing in the division of Uitenhage, for the sum of £12 on a promissory note.

The Court, allowing the right of the plaintiff to sue defendant in the Supreme Court, they being resident in different divisions, were inclined, however, in the matter of costs, to allow only Magistrate's costs. But, on reference to the 35th section of Act 20 of 1856, the Court found that the Legislature had distinctly placed this beyond the discretion of the Judges, by enacting that Supreme Court costs should follow judgment. And ordered accordingly.

FICK & KARSTEL *vs.* BAARTMAN.

Breach of Contract.—Dropped Defence.

<small>Nov. 18.
„ 19.

Fick & Karstel
vs. Baartman.</small>
This was an action for damages for breach of contract to deliver certain cattle.

On the 18th November, all the plaintiffs' witnesses, with exception of one, were examined by *Porter*, for plaintiffs, and cross-examined by *Griffith, A.-G.,* for defendant.

On the 19th, *Griffith* mentioned to the Court that he was no longer instructed, the defendant being, he was informed, about to surrender. At the same time, if the Court wished the case to proceed, and desired to assign him as counsel for defendant, he would have no objection to continue to act.

Their Lordships, however, thought it better not to adopt that course ; and *Porter*, electing to proceed with his case, examined the only remaining witness. Whereupon the Court ordered the case to stand over until it should appear whether the defendant surrendered his estate, and whether the trustee in his estate would elect to continue the defence of the action.

1868.
Nov. 18.
" 19.
Fick & Karstel
vs. Baartman.

[Plaintiffs' Attorneys, *Berrange & de Villiers.*
Defendant's Attorneys, *Hofmeyr, Tredgold & Watermeyer.*]

RE GEORGE DIVISIONAL BANK.—*Ex parte.*

Joint-stock Companies Winding-up Act, 12, 1868. *First proceedings under. Practice.*

This was the first application under Section 12 of Act 12, 1868, the Joint-stock Companies Winding-up Act.
Porter presented the petition of Mr. M. W. Theunissen, of George Town, a shareholder, and, at the same time, only remaining trustee (his co-trustee, F. A. Swemmer, having resigned his trust) in and of a joint-stock copartnership trading as bankers at George, under the style of the George Divisional Bank. The petition set forth that the Bank was established on the 1st January, 1861, for a period of ten years, with a nominal capital of £12,000 in 2,500 £5 shares, of which only 1,216 were taken. That the Bank is in pecuniary difficulties, and unable to meet lawful liabilities due and becoming due, and had been summoned on overdue obligations and cheques lawfully drawn on them, and justly and legally payable by them, and which they were not and are not in a position to meet. The petition then recited divers instances, and added, that for these reasons it had become highly desirable and necessary, for the protection of shareholders as well as creditors of the Company, that it should be placed under the operation of the above-quoted Act, for the purpose of being wound up under the provisions thereof. An affidavit by Mr. Theunissen, verifying the statements of his petition, was also produced.

Nov. 15.
Dec. 10.
Re George
Divisional Bank

The Court thereupon ordered that a rule *nisi* issue, returnable 1st December next, calling on the Bank to show cause accordingly; and further directed that this rule be inserted in the *Government Gazette* and in the *George Advertiser,* and be served on the Directors and Cashier of the Bank, at the Bank Buildings, George Town.

Postea (Dec. 10). The rule was made absolute, no appearance being made.

1868.
Nov. 15.
Dec. 10.

Re George
Divisional Bank.

The Court then, on motion made, directed the appointment of Messrs. Biddulph and Vintcent joint liquidators to wind up the Bank, by the following order:

"Upon reading the petition of George Allman and others, shareholders and creditors of the said George Divisional Bank, and the petition of J. G. Aspeling and others, likewise shareholders and creditors of the said Bank; upon hearing also Mr. Attorney-General and Mr. Porter, of counsel for the respective petitioners,—it is ordered that William Burnet Biddulph, of George, and Joseph Vintcent, of Mossel Bay, be, and they are hereby, appointed liquidators provisionally, and until the further order of this Court, on their giving security, by the said William Burnet Biddulph, to be approved of by the Resident Magistrate for George, and by the said Joseph Vintcent, to be approved by the Resident Magistrate for Mossel Bay, each to the amount of three thousand pounds sterling; the liquidators to pay out nothing, but to proceed in the collection and realization of the assets, subject to the further order of this Court; a meeting of the shareholders and creditors to be held on the 15th day of January, 1869, at the court-house at George Town, for the recommendation to this Court of permanent liquidators, of which meeting the Resident Magistrate for George shall be chairman, and the votes to be taken for the different candidates for the office of liquidator, annexing to the names of each voter, whether shareholder or creditor, or both, number of shares, and the amount of debts held or represented by such voter, and whether the same is held or owned by him in his own right or in some special capacity, and if the same shares or debt shall be held or owned by any such voter in some special capacity, then in what capacity the same are held or owned respectively,—shareholders and creditors to be at liberty at such meeting to vote either in person or by proxy, and the proxies or copies thereof to be filed with the proceedings of the meeting, the chairman to be at liberty, if he shall think fit, to adjourn the said meeting, of which adjournment, if any, notice shall be given in the *Government Gazette*, and in such other newspapers or manner as the notice of this rule is hereinafter ordered to be given, provided the date of such adjournment, if any, shall permit of such notice being given, and the same shall in other respects be possible; and if such date shall not allow of such notice, or the same shall in other respects be impossible, then such notice thereof shall be given as the Resident Magistrate shall order; and the results of such original or adjourned meeting shall be, as soon after the holding thereof respectively as may be reasonably possible, certified by the said Resident Magistrate for George to this

Court. All actions against the said Bank to be restrained or stayed, unless by leave of this Court. The costs of Messrs. Biddulph and Vintcent, of their applications in this matter, to be paid out of the estate. This order to be forthwith published in the *Government Gazette*, and in the George newspaper, if any ; and if there be no local newspaper in George, then copies of this order to be printed and posted in the town of George and that of Mossel Bay, in the usual places for posting public notices in those towns respectively."

1868.
Nov. 15.
Dec. 10.
Re George Divisional Bank.

[Applicant's Attorneys, *Fairbridge & Arderne*.]

WOLLASTON, APPELLANT; WEHMEYER, RESPONDENT

Telegraph Act, No. 20, 1861. *First proceedings under.*

On the 26th October a rule *nisi* was granted, *in camerâ*, by DENYSSEN, J., on application of Wollaston, the manager of the Cape of Good Hope Telegraph Company, returnable this day, calling upon respondent to show cause why he should not be interdicted from interfering with the maintenance of the Electric Telegraph, and especially from destroying or removing any of the poles deposited on his land for the purpose of such maintenance ; or from hindering or obstructing any wagons, drivers, or line-men, who may be engaged by or on account of the Cape of Good Hope Telegraph Company in conveying poles over respondent's land.

Nov. 17.
Wollaston, Appellant ; Wehmeyer, Respondent.

Porter, for applicant, now moved to make the rule absolute ; relying on the 2nd section of the Telegraph Act, No. 20 of 1861, incorporating the 10th to 13th sections of the Road Act, No. 9 of 1858, as giving the applicant power to cross the respondent's grounds and deposit spare poles thereupon for the purpose of effectually maintaining the line.

The respondent's affidavits were intended to show an unreasonable use of respondent's ground. But, after hearing counsel, the Court were of opinion that there was no unreasonable user proved, and made the rule absolute accordingly, with costs.

[Applicant's Attorney, *E. Hull*.
Respondent's Attorney, *De Korte*.]

VON LUDWIG, APPELLANT; VAN REENEN, RESPONDENT.

Where Conditions of Sale stipulated that the article sold shall be taken by the Purchaser at his risk, and there is no clear evidence of a Warranty by the Auctioneer, such Auctioneer is not thereafter liable to the Purchaser.

1868.
Nov. 20.

Von Ludwig, Appellant; Van Reenen, Respondent.

This was an undefended appeal from a judgment of the Resident Magistrate for Namaqualand, whereby the appellant, an auctioneer, who had sold certain oxen at public sale to the defendant, was condemned to repay to the respondent the purchase price of those oxen, on the ground that they were sold under warranty, and were, in fact, diseased when sold, and had died from the effects of such disease.

Porter, for the appellant, read the evidence below, and submitted to the Court the importance of the question whether an auctioneer selling to A, under certain conditions of sale, oxen belonging to B, and being himself a third party to the transaction, and a stake-holder for both parties, having already paid to the seller the amount realized, should be condemned to refund the amount to the purchaser.

The Court reversed the judgment, with costs.

BELL, C. J., held that the contract between the parties, as contained in the conditions of sale, should regulate their rights; and on reference to these conditions it was to be seen that the articles sold were to be taken at the purchaser's risk.

DENYSSEN, J., concurred. If there had been a clear warranty by the auctioneer, it would have been different, and he would have been liable.

DWYER, J., concurred. Even supposing the auctioneer had warranted the cattle, there was no evidence to show their unsoundness at the time of the warranty. In the absence of such evidence, the purchaser was clearly liable.

[Appellant's Attorney, *E. Hull*.]

GLEESON, APPELLANT; DURRHEIM, RESPONDENT.
Seduction : Action of.

The Man's Oath is entitled to preference over the Woman's, if there is no aliunde evidence to support her statement.

Nov. 17.

Gleeson, Appellant; Durrheim, Respondent.

This was an undefended appeal from a judgment delivered by the Resident Magistrate for King William's Town, in June last, for £20 damages and costs, in respect that the appellant had, in July, 1867, debauched and carnally known the respondent, a virgin, who, on the 19th April, 1868, was delivered of a child, the fruit of the intercourse. *Bond*, for appellant, read the evidence taken in the Court below: (1) That of the respondent herself, a minor, assisted by her father and natural guardian. This witness, however, gave her evidence in a very unsatisfactory manner, both in regard to dates and otherwise. (2) Of the respondent's father, who, beyond deposing to the birth of the child and the respondent's statements to him, gave no other supporting evidence. For the defence, a number of witnesses were called, among whom was the present appellant, who, in the most unqualified manner, denied on oath the evidence of the present respondent. The other witnesses gave such evidence as went, in many important respects, to cast doubt on the girl's testimony,—to show, moreover, that according to their statements, her conduct and character were decidedly not of the most moral description.

The Court, without calling upon *Bond*, reversed the decision of the Court below.

BELL, C. J., said : The ground of the reversal of the judgment below must be the incredibility of the woman. There could be no doubt that when, in such a case as the present, a woman swore to her seduction by a man, and the man swore the opposite, and there was no evidence *aliunde* to lead the Court to doubt the man's oath, by the law of the Colony the oath of the man must be believed, and the oath of the woman disbelieved. But if there was evidence *aliunde* to support the woman's oath, and to lead the Court to give it credence over the oath of the man, then the Court must exercise its discretion by believing the woman, whose oath was thus confirmed. And so his Lordship had decided in a recent case, at the Swellendam Circuit, held in September, 1868, *Du Toit vs. De Wet*, where the woman's oath, being supported by *aliunde* evidence, judgment was given in her favour, although the positive oath of the man was the other way ; so also, in the present case, if there were any evidence to induce the Court to look with suspicion on the man's oath, and to give preference to that of the woman, supported by other testimony, the judgment must have been upheld. But it clearly was not so ; and the judgment must be reversed accordingly.

DENYSSEN, J., concurred in the reversal on the same grounds.

DWYER, J., was inclined to the opinion that the law which gave a preference to the man's oath over the woman's was, in some cases, a hard law ; but if it were the law, agreed that, with reference to this particular case, the judgment should be reversed.

[Appellant's Attorney, *E. Hull.*]

RE DREYER'S ESTATE.

Ord. 6, 1843, *Sec.* 48.—*Divisional Council—Trustees.—Liquidation Account, Amendment of.*

The Trustees of an Insolvent Estate are liable to be sued for Road and other Rates, inasmuch as, by the 48th section of Ordinance 6, 1843, *the Estate has become vested in them, and, by section* 41 *of Act* 9, 1858, *Divisional Councils are entitled to recover from the Owners of Property on which Assessments have been levied.*

1868.
Nov. 19.

Re Dreyer's Estate.

Porter moved for the confirmation of the liquidation account in the insolvent estate of J. H. Dreyer.

Bond, for the Cape Divisional Council, objected that an item of £6 0s. 7d., being for assessment for railway sub-guarantee and road rates, had been omitted from the account by the trustees, although a judgment for the amount had been recovered by the Council against the trustees, in the Resident Magistrate's Court of Cape Town. The assessment was made after the insolvency, and while the trustees were in possession of the property; and, by section 41 of Act 9, 1858, the Council might proceed " against the owner or occupier, either separately or both of them, in one and the same case, each for the whole rate, in any competent court," &c. The trustees, being the owners at the time of the assessment, were therefore liable under the section, the Council having elected to proceed against them.

Porter, for the trustees, said this was a case of the first impression, and intended to raise the question whether trustees in insolvent estates are owners liable for municipal and road rates within the scope of the Municipal and Road Acts. And submitted to the judgment of the Court.

BELL, C. J., said, immediately the order of sequestration was granted, the owner of the property ceased to be the owner; but, under the 48th section of Ordinance 6, 1843, the trustee took possession of the insolvent estate, and was clothed with all rights and obligations thereto appertaining, and was liable, accordingly, in the present case. It was difficult to see how there could be a doubt on the matter.

DENYSSEN, J., concurred that this was the effect of the 48th section.

DWYER, J., concurred, on the ground that there had been a decision in favour of the Council by a Court of competent jurisdiction, which decision had not been appealed against or set aside, and should therefore have effect given to it.

The item was ordered to be inserted in the account accordingly.

[Applicant's Attorneys, *Reddelinghuys & Wessels.*]
[Respondent's Attorney, *E. Hall.*]

JOSEPH'S EXECUTOR, APPELLANT, DEFENDANT BELOW;
PEACOCK, RESPONDENT, PLAINTIFF BELOW.

Contract: *Specific performance of.*

Sale of half of a farm to a third party—contrary to an agreement between the joint owners of the Farm stipulating for the right of pre-emption—set aside.

Pre-emption: *Right of.*

Transfer: *Unconditional transfer to a third party, contrary to the agreement between the joint owners, stated supra, set aside.*

This was an appeal from a judgment delivered by DENYSSEN, J., at the Port Elizabeth Circuit, in an action for the specific performance of a contract, or for damages.

1868.
Nov. 19.

Joseph's Executor, Appellant, Defendant below; Peacock, Respondent, Plaintiff below.

The plaintiff's declaration in the Court below set forth that on the 1st June, 1843, the plaintiff, then the owner of the whole of the farm Pavo Park, otherwise called Prinsloo, in the division of Somerset East, sold to the late George Edward Joseph a half share of the said farm, for £1,173 15s., upon a written agreement, which contained, amongst others, the following condition : " That should at any time one or other, that is to say, the said George Edward Joseph or Walter Peacock, wish to dispose of his half share, or any part thereof, it is agreed and declared, and by these presents we severally agree, that such party wishing to sell shall first be obliged to offer his share of the said farm to the holder of the other half, or share, for the amount of the original cost of such half share (£1,173 15s.), together with such amount of costs and full value of improvements as may be agreed upon; or should the parties not agree between themselves, then the same to be settled by arbitration. That no sale without such previous offer, and answer in writing, can be made or held to be good, or transfer effected of any share, part, or parcel thereof, to any other party, without such knowledge and consent in writing from the party interested and holding the other half share or portion of the said farm Pavo Park." That the plaintiff hath hitherto continued to be the owner of the other half of the farm not sold by this agreement. That the meaning and effect of the agreement and condition above quoted was and is that neither the said Joseph nor the plaintiff, nor their legal representatives, either before or after their death, or the death of either of them,

1868.
Nov. 18.

Joseph's Executor, Appellant, Defendant below; Peacock, Respondent, Plaintiff below.

should be entitled to have the right to dispose of or sell the half share belonging to either of them, respectively, to any stranger or other person whatsoever, without having previously offered the same to the holder of the other half, as in the agreement set forth, at and for the sum therein mentioned. That George Edward Joseph died on the 26th July, 1866, being still the owner and holder of the half of the farm within the meaning of the agreement. That, thereafter, the defendant, who was appointed executor testamentary, did wrongfully and unlawfully, and in violation of the agreement and condition above cited, sell, on the 25th January, 1867, his father's half share to one J. A. van Niekerk, without having previously offered the same to the plaintiff for £1,173 15s., *plus* the value of improvements, although the defendant well knew that the plaintiff was and still continued ready and willing to purchase the said half share under the agreement. That the sale was effected privately, and not at public auction, for £3,000, being £1,000 less than the real value of the said share. And that the half share so sold still stands enregistered in the name of George Edward Joseph. Wherefore the plaintiff prayed delivery and transfer of the said half share, tendering to pay £2,500 on receipt thereof. Or otherwise, that the defendant should pay to him the said sum of £2,500, as damages, with costs of suit.

To this the defendant pleaded, first, the general issue; secondly, that an unconditional transfer of the half share claimed was made to the late George Edward Joseph, by the plaintiff, on the 16th September, 1857, by which unconditional transfer the condition of the agreement was waived and abandoned; thirdly, that the agreement, except in so far as carried out by the said transfer, was binding only on the parties thereto, and not on their representatives, wherefore the defendant was not bound thereby; fourthly, that on the 3rd March, 1863, the said late George Edward Joseph gave and presented to the defendant, in his individual capacity, by way of *donatio inter vivos*, the said half share now claimed, which donation the defendant duly accepted. But that on the 30th of September, 1865, during the lifetime of the said George Edward Joseph, the defendant, in consideration of his father's inability to satisfy the claims of his creditors, consented to give up his right to such half share, which was then sold for the benefit of the creditors of George Edward Joseph's estate.

To which the plaintiff replied by a variety of replications, setting up, *inter alia*, as a replication to the third plea, that during the lifetime of George Edward Joseph, on the 31st October, 1865, the said George Edward Joseph had, by his duly authorized agents in that behalf, tendered and offered to sell to the plaintiff the half share of the farm referred to, by the following letter :

1868.
Nov. 19.

Joseph's Executor, Appellant, Defendant below; Peacock, Respondent, Plaintiff below.

"Loan, Trust and Agency Company of South Africa (Limited),
31st October, 1865.
" W. Peacock, Esq., Farm Prinsloo, Somerset East.

" SIR,—As the duly authorized agents of Mr. George Edward Joseph, we beg to bring to your notice that application has been made to us for the sale of the farm Prinsloo ; and therefore wish to give you an opportunity of stating whether you are willing to make an offer for the same.
" Soliciting the favour of an early reply,
" We are, &c.,

" W. SELWYN,
" E. P. AMYOTT,

" Trustees Insolvent Estate Perkins, Ogilvie & Co.
And agents for Mr. G. E. Joseph."

To which the plaintiff replied on the 4th November, 1865, as follows :
" Pavo Park, 4th November, 1865.

" Messrs. SELWYN & AMYOTT,
Agents for Mr. GEORGE EDWARD JOSEPH,
Port Elizabeth,

" GENTLEMEN,—In answer to your letter of the 31st October informing me that an application has been made to you for the purchase of the farm ' Prinsloo,' or rather the half share belonging to Mr. G. E. Joseph, I have to inform you that I am quite willing to purchase the same at the original price, viz., £1,173 15s., as per agreement existing between Mr. Joseph and myself, dated Somerset, 1st June, 1843.

" I have, &c.,
W. PEACOCK."

By reason whereof the plaintiff became entitled to claim the half share claimed in the summons.

The Court below gave judgment for plaintiff for £1,500, with costs.

De Villiers, for appellant.—The unconditional transfer of the half share to Joseph, sen., by Peacock, on the 16th September, 1857, was a waiver, by Peacock, of the rights under the agreement of 1843. The correspondence relied on in appellant's replication was after the unconditional transfer. And, besides, the letter of the 31st October alluded to no agreement, but was a mere *aliunde* offer by one ordinary co-proprietor to the other. The mention of an agreement in the matter only occurs in the reply of Peacock. Under any circumstances, such a prohibition of sale as is contained in the agreement does not interfere with a donation *inter vivos*. (*Voet*, 18, 3, 10.) And here it is sworn

1868.
Nov. 19.

Joseph's Executor, Appellant, Defendant below; Peacock, Respondent, Plaintiff below.

in the evidence that Joseph, sen., donated his half share to Joseph, jun., as he had a legal right to do, notwithstanding the prohibition. Moreover, the agreement was only a personal agreement between Joseph, sen., and Peacock, which, if performed at all, should have been performed in the lives of both parties thereto. Therefore no action lies against the executors of Joseph, sen., for a breach, by them, after his death, as the *commoda* of such an agreement as that of 1843 must descend to the heirs, but not the *incommoda*. (*Voet*, 3, 18, 8.) The agreement was one which required registration to bind the property. (*Voet* 18, 3, 8.) But here there was an unconditional transfer.

The Court desired to hear the argument *contra* only on the question whether the agreement of 1843 bound only the parties to that agreement, or whether obligations therein contained descended to their heirs also.

Griffith, *A.-G.* (with him *Porter*), confined himself accordingly to this point. The general principle of our law is, that heirs are bound, unless specially exempted. The benefits and obligations of such agreements must be mutual and correlative. (*Voet*, 18, 3, 8.)

De Villiers in reply.

The Court affirmed the decision of the Court below. But, in respect that the Judge below had intimated that the question was one which might well be appealed upon, gave no costs of the appeal.

[Appellant's Attorney, *Van Zyl.*]
[Respondent's Attorney, *Hull.*]

RE ESTATE A. B.

Ordinance 6, 1843, Section 52.—Practice.

Dec. 8.

Re Estate A. B.

The Master reported that owing to the absence from the Colony of the trustee in this estate, his removal had become necessary under the provisions of section 52 of Ordinance 6, 1843. In answer to the Bench, the Master added that he produced no supporting affidavits, but grounded his application on certain letters sent in to him by creditors, notifying the absence of the trustee, and that his usual practice was to report in this way to the Court, the section of the Ordinance requiring that the removal should be " on cause shown by the Master."

But the Court was of opinion that such removal should be asked by the Master on cause shown on motion from the Bar, in the usual way; and ordered that that should be the future practice accordingly.

LAUBSCHER *vs.* BASSON'S EXECUTOR AND ANOTHER.

Will set aside for nonconformity with the provisions of Ordinance 15, 1845; which requires that Wills shall be signed or acknowledged by the Testator in the presence of two competent Witnesses, present and subscribing thereto at the same time.

This was an action to declare invalid a certain will made by one J. P. Basson, in which will the first defendant was declared appointed executor, and the second defendant, Mrs. Lambrechts, sole heiress. Plaintiff, who was a nephew of the testator and an heir *ab intestato*, prayed that the will might be set aside for nonconformity with the provisions of Ordinance 15, 1845, section 3, as to attestation; and further that the letters of administration already granted to the first defendant might be revoked.

From the evidence led by *De Villiers*, for the plaintiff, it was conclusively proved by the two witnesses to the will that they had neither signed in the presence of each other nor of the testator, although they had signed in the same house and on the same day. Whereupon the Court, without requiring argument, at once gave judgment for plaintiff. Costs to come out of the estate.

1868.
Dec. 9.

Laubscher *vs.* Basson's Executor and Another.

[Plaintiff's Attorneys, *Redelinghuys & Wessels.*
  Defendants' Attorney, *Dickson.*]

MATTHEWS' TRUSTEES, APPLICANTS; STEWART, RESPONDENT.

The 48th section of Ordinance 6, 1843, vests in an Insolvent's Trustees not only the Landed Property itself, but also all Title Deeds and Muniments of Title connected therewith, which must therefore be surrendered to him by the possessors thereof at the time of Insolvency.

This was a motion to compel the delivery up by respondent of certain title deeds and deeds of transfer of four farms duly made in favour of insolvent, whose estate was sequestrated on the 15th of May, 1866, during his absence from the Colony. In July in that year, the insolvent, being then in London, had entered into an agreement to sell to the Natal Land and Investment Company the four farms in question. In August the Company procured the title deeds, &c., from the insolvent, and in the course of certain business transactions between them and the Standard Bank, of which the respondent is the General Colonial Manager, transferred

Dec. 10.

Matthews' Trustees, Applicants; Stewart, Respondent.

1868.
Dec. 10.

Matthews' Trustees, Applicants; Stewart, Respondent.

them to the respondent, in whose possession they now were. The Natal Company's estate was subsequently put under liquidation.

The Court held that the 48th section of the Insolvent Ordinance—6, 1843—vested in the applicants not merely the landed property in the estate, but all deeds and muniments of title connected therewith; and ordered the delivery up of the documents, as prayed.

[Applicants' Attorney, *Hull.*
Respondent's Attorney, *Van Zyl.*]

VAN WYK *versus* VAN WYK.

Witnesses' Expenses.—Act 4, 1861, *Section* 8.

Parties to a case are allowed Witnesses' Expenses where the Court is of opinion they were " necessary Witnesses."

Dec. 13.
" 14.
" 15.

Van Wyk *vs.* Van Wyk.

This was an action for the cancellation of a mortgage bond, on the ground of satisfaction by payment. One of the chief witnesses for the plaintiff's case was the plaintiff himself; and for the defence, the defendant himself. There was a direct conflict between their testimonies on the point of the payment of the bond.

The Court gave judgment for the defendant, with costs.
Upon application, by *Porter,* for defendant, the Court allowed defendant's expenses as witness, under the 8th section of Act 4, 1861; he having been, in the opinion of the Court, " a necessary witness;" and it being principally on his evidence the case was decided.

[Plaintiff's Attorney, *Van Zyl.*
Defendant's Attorneys, *Tivan & De Smidt.*]

RE DE KOCK'S ESTATE.

Trustees' Charges.

The Court refused to allow a Cape Town Trustee his Travelling Expenses to Worcester, the present, and Malmesbury, the former, seat of the Insolvent's Business.

Dec. 15.

Re De Kock's Estate.

Porter moved the confirmation of the liquidation account in this estate. The Master had objected to three of the trustee's charges, viz.: " Travelling expenses, Cape Town to Worcester, £2 2s. Agency at Worcester, £9 9s. Travelling expenses to Malmesbury, £11 3s. 3d." It appeared from the trustee's affidavit that the insolvent, last before his insolvency, carried on business at Worcester, and prior to that at Malmesbury. Most of the creditors were resident in Cape Town, and, on the appointment of applicant, had exacted from him a promise (of which nothing, however, was on record) to visit Worcester and Malmesbury, in the interest of the estate. Applicant had made visits accordingly, and arranged for the gradual realization of the Worcester estate through an agent. All the items charged were actually expended, and with due economy. If these charges were not allowed, the trustee's commission would be only £12 on an estate where the balance for distribution was £892.

1868.
Dec. 15.

Re De Kock's Estate.

The Court, however, refused to allow the charges, and confirmed the account subject to their deduction; holding that the trustee accepted the appointment knowing the position of affairs, and nothing short of a formal resolution of creditors specially authorizing the trustee to undertake the journey, or to employ a Worcester agent (no proof of which appeared in this case), would justify the Court in allowing trustees more than their regular commission.

[Applicant's Attorney, *E. Hull*.]

J. O. SMITH & CO. *vs.* THE STANDARD BANK OF BRITISH SOUTH AFRICA (LIMITED).

Contract: *Action for damages for breach of.*

Pleading: *Ultra vires must be specially pleaded.*

This was an action to recover £354 18s. 4d., with interest, as damages for the breach, by defendant, of a certain contract.

The plaintiffs' declaration set forth that the Standard Bank of British South Africa (Limited) are a corporation incorporated in England with perpetual succession, trading in this Colony through certain managers or agents duly authorised to act for and on behalf of the said corporation, and to bind the same. That in the course of such trade, in April, 1865, the Bank became and was creditor, to a considerable amount, of certain merchants trading at Port Elizabeth under the firm of Kirkwood, Holland & Co, which firm, having become involved in difficulties, summoned a meeting of their creditors at Port Elizabeth on or about the

Nov. 26.
" 27.
" 28.
" 30.
Dec. 1.
" 2.
" 3.
" 4.
" 5.
" 7.
" 8.
" 15.

J. O. Smith & Co. *vs.* The Standard Bank of British South Africa (Limited).

1868.
Nov. 26.
" 27.
" 28.
" 30.
Dec. 1.
" 2.
" 3.
" 4.
" 5.
" 7.
" 8.
" 15.

J. O. Smith & Co.
vs. The Standard Bank of British South Africa (Limited).

4th of May, 1865, and gave notice of such meeting to the defendants, amongst other creditors, through their agent and manager, duly authorized in that behalf, one James Tudhope, who, on their behalf, duly attended such meeting, representing himself, as in fact was the case, as authorized to act on behalf of the said defendants in all respects in the matter to be laid before such meeting. That at the said meeting the said James Tudhope, on behalf of defendants, proposed to offer to the creditors of Kirkwood, Holland & Co. a composition of 10s. in the pound, in consideration that the said creditors should assign to the defendants their claims, respectively, upon the firm, and release it and the members thereof; and that the firm should assign to the defendants the assets belonging to it. But the creditors, believing, for the most part, that better terms would be offered by other persons, adjourned the meeting, by resolution, in order that the accounts of the assets and liabilities of the firm might be fully examined and ascertained by the persons intending to propose a compromise on behalf of the said firm. The adjourned meeting was held on the 6th May, 1865, when defendants again attended, by Tudhope, their duly authorised agent, and formally tendered to the creditors there assembled a compromise, or composition, on behalf of the said firm, which was accepted and agreed to by all the creditors then present or represented, among whom were the plaintiffs, and subsequently by all the creditors of the firm, and was embodied in a minute made at the time. The tender of composition, so accepted, was to the effect that, on condition that the creditors of the firm should cede to the defendants their claims, respectively, upon the firm, and release it and the members thereof from liability to the creditors in respect of such claims, the defendants would guarantee to the said creditors the sum of 15s. in the pound on the amount of the debts due to them by the firm, in four equal instalments, at six, twelve, eighteen and twenty-four months. That all the payments which the firm was then liable to make at a future date should be reduced to a ready-money value, by treating them in account as if discounted on the 1st May, 1865 ; and that on the footing of an account so stated, the said composition, or the instalments thereof, should be secured by the acceptances of the defendants being given for the amounts thereof, respectively, to the said creditors. And, further, that the defendants should release the firm from all liability to them, upon its handing over and ceding to them all the assets then its property. The plaintiffs were, at the time of such tender, creditors of the firm to the amount of £473 3s. 4d., and have not since been paid or satisfied for any portion thereof. The tender, so accepted, was acted upon by many of the parties thereto for some time thereafter, and particularly by the defendants and the said firm; and moneys were from time to time paid into the hands of the said defendants in respect of certain of the claims so ceded, or agreed to be ceded, to the said defendants by virtue of the agreement completed by such tender and acceptance, which moneys the defendants placed to their own credit, or applied to their own purposes. In the month of July following, the defendants, believing that the arrangement of compromise or composition would not be so profitable to them as they had at first supposed it would, became desirous to evade the obligations thereby entailed upon them, and cast about the means of escaping the same, and, with this view, privately and fraudulently suborned and procured one of the said creditors of the said firm, one Isidore Sigismund Gordon (who had already assented to the said arrangement of compromise or composition, and had subscribed the minute of the said meeting in the name of the firm under which he traded, viz., Gordon & Co., in token of his assent thereto), to sue the firm of Kirkwood, Holland & Co., in respect of a debt appearing to be due to him, or his firm, on a promissory note made by the firm and endorsed in blank (which note, however, was not in reality the property of the said Gordon or his firm, or, if so, had been given to or procured for him or his firm by the defendants, and was, or had been, the property of the defendants), and was sued for by Gordon at the cost and by the direction of the defendants, or under a contract of indemnity to him made by the defendants. Having thus procured Gordon to sue the firm, in fraud of the other creditors, parties to the arrangement of composition, the defendants obtained, in Gordon's name, judgment on the said promissory note, and thus compelled the surrender of the firm's estate as insolvent, which surrender was accepted by this Court on or about the 1st day of December, 1865, in ignorance of the true state of the case. Whereupon the defendants refused to perform their part of the arrangement of composition, pretending that by reason of such surrender the performance of the terms of the said arrangement had become impossible; and the plaintiffs and the other creditors seeking the performance by defendants of the obligations undertaken by them by such arrangements of composition had great difficulties thrown in their way in compelling such performance. The plaintiffs, however, did not for a considerable length of time after the surrender come to the knowledge of the collusion by the defendants in procuring it; but they never acquiesced therein, and never proved their debts thereunder; always insisting and informing defendants that they held them

1865,
Nov. 26.
„ 27.
„ 28.
„ 30.
Dec. 1.
„ 2.
„ 3.
„ 4.
„ 5.
„ 7.
„ 8.
„ 15.

J. O. Smith & Co.
vs. The Standard Bank of British South Africa (Limited).

1868.
Nov. 26.
" 27.
" 28.
" 30.
Dec. 1.
" 2.
" 3.
" 4.
" 5.
" 7.
" 8.
" 15.

J. O Smith & Co.
vs. The Standard Bank of British South Africa (Limited).

liable for the amount before stated, with interest on each instalment from the day on which it should have fallen due had the arrangement been performed on the part of defendants. But the defendants have always neglected and refused to pay the same or any part thereof. The plaintiffs, moreover, commenced an action in the Court of the Eastern Districts, virtually against the said defendants, for the recovery of the same moneys, on or about the 1st March, 1866, upon which certain proceedings were taken; but doubts having arisen as to the form in which such action had been brought, they ultimately determined to abandon the same, and did so abandon it, and commenced the present action in lieu thereof. The plaintiffs have always been ready and willing to do all acts necessary on their part to the due fulfilment by all parties to the said arrangement of the terms therein contained; and they submit that by the act and fraud of the defendants they have been prevented from compelling the performance specifically by the other parties to the said arrangement (if any of such parties other than the defendants were unwilling to perform their respective parts therein, which the plaintiffs, however, deny), and submit that they ought to be placed, so far as the defendants are concerned, in the same position, as nearly as may be, as if the said arrangement had been carried into full effect by all the parties thereto. The plaintiffs, therefore, prayed that defendants might be compelled, by the order of this Honourable Court, to pay to them the said sum of £354 18s. 4d., together with interest as due on the four several instalments, to be calculated at the rate of six per cent. per annum; and that the plaintiffs might have such further or other relief as the nature of the case may require, with costs of suit.

The defendants pleaded, first, the general issue. And, for a further plea, they said that the proposal made by Tudhope at the meeting of the 6th May, 1865, was intended to be, and was, a proposal to the whole of the creditors of Kirkwood, Holland & Co., and not to a portion of them only; and that such proposal was not, and is not, binding upon the defendants unless each and every one of the creditors shall assent thereto. That some of the creditors did, in fact, refuse or decline to assent to such proposal; in consequence whereof the same was withdrawn by or on behalf of the defendants, as it lawfully might be for the cause aforesaid. And, thirdly, as a further plea, defendants said that the true intent and meaning of the said proposal of Tudhope was, and is, that any of the creditors of Kirkwood, Holland & Co. who might hold collateral securities in respect of their claims should cede and deliver up the same to, or on behalf of, the defendants, for the purpose of the same being realized by them, or on their behalf; and that the defendants should pay a dividend of 15s. in the pound sterling to each of the creditors of the said firm only upon the basis of the defendants possessing and realizing all the assets and claims of the firm, whether actually in their possession or power, or pledged or ceded by them to any of their creditors. But that divers of the said creditors who held such pledges refused to cede or make them over to or on behalf of defendants, but maintained their right to hold and retain them, and to realize them for their own benefit, and, after deducting the amount so realized, to call upon the defendants to pay them a dividend of fifteen shillings in the pound sterling upon the balance which might still be due to them from the said firm. That the said creditors did accordingly hold and retain these collateral securities for their own benefit, and, although often requested to do so, did neglect and refuse, and still neglect and refuse, to deliver them up to defendants, contrary to the true intent and meaning of the said proposal, and in derogation of the just rights of the defendants in respect thereto. (4) And for a further plea, defendants said that the proposal of Tudhope was, to the knowledge of the plaintiffs, based upon the representations of the firm of Kirkwood, Holland & Co. as to the amount of their assets and liabilities, respectively ; and that, in particular, the said firm represented certain promissory notes made by third parties in favour of the said firm, and certain shares, mortgage bonds and landed property, to be *bonâ fide* assets of the same, and that such promissory notes, shares, mortgage bonds and landed property would be assigned, transferred and made over to or on behalf of the defendants for the purpose of being realized by them or on their behalf towards payment of the dividends to be by them guaranteed. But so far from such promissory notes, shares and mortgage bonds being actually assets in the possession or power of the said firm, a great portion of them had been pledged and made over to several creditors of the firm, and could not, therefore, be assigned or given up by the firm to or on behalf of the defendants for realization. And, so far as the said landed property is concerned, it had not then, nor at any time since, been transferred to the firm, and could not therefore be transferred as an asset of the firm's estate to or on behalf of the defendants for realization. They have hereto annexed a list or schedule, marked A, of the promissory notes, shares, mortgage bonds and landed property so represented by Kirkwood, Holland & Co. to be their assets, but, in fact, already pledged and assigned to divers of their creditors. (5) And for a further plea, defendants said that at a meeting of the creditors of the firm of Kirkwood, Holland & Co., held

1868.
Nov. 26.
,, 27.
,, 28.
,, 30.
Dec. 1.
,, 2.
,, 3.
,, 4.
,, 5.
,, 7.
,, 8.
,, 15.

J. O. Smith & Co.
vs.-The Standard Bank of British South Africa (Limited).

subsequently to the meeting of the 6th May, 1865, to wit, on the 29th August, 1865, the withdrawal of the said offer made by Tudhope on behalf of the defendants was distinctly notified to and acknowledged by the said creditors; and it was thereupon (amongst other things) resolved by the said creditors that the estate of the said Kirkwood, Holland & Co. be at once placed in liquidation under the management of certain persons, and subject to certain conditions then and there mentioned and agreed upon, and that should any of the creditors refuse to sign the deed of assignment (meaning thereby the deed of assignment to be prepared under the said resolution of the said meeting of the 29th day of August) within fourteen days, the estate should be at once surrendered. That the greater part of the creditors having refused to sign within fourteen days, the firm, on the 1st December, 1865, in terms of the said resolution, surrendered their estate as insolvent; and the defendants were and are thereby released from all liability in respect of their said offer. And this they were ready to verify. Wherefore they prayed judgment with costs.

Plaintiffs replied to all these pleas, the general issue.

On the 26th, 27th, 28th and 30th November, and the 1st and 2nd December, the Court heard the evidence.

December 3, 4, 5, 7, 8.—The Court heard the argument.

Griffith, A.-G. (with him *De Villiers*), for plaintiffs.—The argument *contra* will be that the agreement of the 6th of May was *ultra vires* of Tudhope, the local manager of the Standard Bank at Port Elizabeth, *ultra vires* of Stewart, the general manager of that Bank in this Colony, and *ultra vires* of the Standard Bank itself, even if the London board of management had authorized it expressly by resolution. But the defendants are not entitled to raise the question of *ultra vires* on the pleadings as they now stand. There should have been a special plea; the general issue pleaded being a traverse that any such contract as the plaintiffs rely on has been made. The general issue puts in issue the fact of the contract, and not the power of the parties to enter into it. (*Whelpdale's Case*, 3 Co., 119; *Mestayer vs. Biggs*, 1 Cr. M. & Rosc. 110; *Edwards vs. Brown*, 1 Crompt. & Jerv., 307, especially the judgment of *Baron Bayley*, 311-12; *Hill vs. Manchester and Salford Waterworks Co.*, 5 B. & A. 866; *Royal British Bank vs. Turquand*, 5 E. & B. 248, and *Lord Campbell's Judgment*, 259—61; Do. do., 6 E. & B. 327; *Agar vs. Athenæum Life Ass. Co.*, 3 Com. B. Rep. N. S. 725.)

[The Court desired the argument to proceed generally on the merits.]

Griffith.—There had been no misrepresentation on the

part of Kirkwood, Holland & Co.; and even were misrepresentation proved, it is essential that the misrepresentation should have been fraudulent. As to the collateral securities, there was no contract on the face of the proposal on the 6th May that these should be given up. And such contract is necessary. (*Thomas vs. Courtnay*, 1 *B., & A., p.* 1.) There is no distinction in this Colony between contracts under seal; and therefore, however necessary a seal might be to a contract entered into by the Bank in England, it is unnecessary here. The *locus solutionis* is the *locus contractus*. Here the *locus solutionis* is South Africa, and therefore the contract must be governed by the law here. The contract of the 6th May was a contract within the Articles of Association of the Company (*Arts.* 4, 89, 101), and was merely the purchase of rights of creditors to secure to the Bank the efficient realization of an estate also indebted to itself. This is not a case of composition. It is a case of the purchase of an estate by one creditor, and a compromise by him with the other creditors, by pledging his own security for the composition. The only person who could set the arrangement aside was a creditor who was dissentient from the commencement. But no creditor has moved here. If a release were not given by any creditor, that might be a ground of action by Kirkwood, Holland & Co. against the Bank, but such dissentient creditor's claim would not be against the Bank; for he never had rights against the Bank. All his rights were against Kirkwood, Holland & Co. But it will be said, there is an insolvency of Kirkwood, Holland & Co.; and then the question is, whether, under Ordinance 6, 1843, the arrangement of the 6th of May could have been set aside, as an undue preference, by any dissentient creditor. It could not. For a *bonâ fide* sale of an insolvent's whole assets for a valuable consideration is not an act of bankruptcy. (*Whitwell vs. Thompson*, 1 *Esp.*, 72, 73, *side paging*, 1st ed.; *Rose vs. Haycock*, *A. & E.* 460, *note.*) The signature of all the creditors was unnecessary. As each creditor signed, it became a contract between the Bank and the signing creditor, and would, as between them, have been valid even if all the other creditors had not signed. (*Small vs. Marwood,* 9 *B. & C.,* 300 . *Juta, Thooft & Co. vs. Glynn, decided in this Court,* 15th *Oct.,* 1863.) Creditors lying by, and making no active dissent, are held to be assenting parties to the composition. (*Ex parte Bayly,* 1 *Mon. & McAr.* 438.) Time was not of the essence of the contract; and any creditor might therefore sign before the Standard Bank became liable to pay. (*Whitmore vs. Turquand,* 3rd *De Gex, F. & J.* 107.) The signatures to the deed made by trustees of insolvent

1868.
Nov. 26.
„ 27.
„ 28.
„ 30.
Dec. 1.
„ 2.
„ 3.
„ 4.
„ 5.
„ 7.
„ 8.
„ 15.

J. O. Smith & Co.
vs. The Standard
Bank of British
South Africa
(Limited).

estates without special authority of creditors to compound are, nevertheless, valid as between the estate and the party with whom the contract is made. The object of the 97th section of our Insolvent Ordinance, No. 6 of 1843, corresponding with the 153rd section of the English Bankrupt Act of 1848, is merely to protect the trustee from personal liability for the consequences of his act. (*Griffith on Bankruptcy, vol.* 2, p. 1141; *Lee vs. Sangster,* 2 *Com. B., N.S., p.* 1.) The contract of the 6th May was not a contract beyond the powers of such a corporation as the Bank. (*Hill vs. Manchester and Salford Waterworks Co., ubi sup.*; *Royal British Bank vs. Turquand, ubi sup.*; *Agar vs. Athenæum Life Ass. Society, ubi sup.*; *Prince of Wales Ass. Society vs. Athenæum Ass. Society,* 3 *Com. B., N. S.,* 76; *Payne vs. Mayor of Brecon,* 3 *H. & N.,* 572.) A contract which may not have been good as between a company and its own shareholders may yet be good as between the company and strangers. (*Mayor of Norwich vs. Norfolk Railway Co.,* 4 *E. & B. Judgment of Erle, C.J.,* 417. *In re Overend, Gurney & Co, ex parte Oakes & Peek,* 3 *Law Rep. Eq.* 576; *Eastern Counties Railway Co. vs. Hawkes,* 5 *H. of L. Cas.* 345; *Bank of Australia vs. Breillat,* 6 *Moo. P. C. C., p.* 152; *Simpson vs. Westminster Palace Hotel Co.,* 8 *H. of L. Cas.,* 712; *Taunton vs. Royal Ass. Co.,* 2 *Hem. & Mill,* 135.)

Jacobs, S.-G. (with him Bond), first referred to the 46th section of the Charter of Justice constituting this Court (*Rules of Court,* p. 23), and argued that the declaration did not with sufficient preciseness disclose the cause of action, whether it was the breach by the defendant of the alleged contract of the 6th May, or an alleged wrongful act by the defendants in the subornation of Gordon to procure the surrender of Kirkwood, Holland & Co. But assuming the cause of action to be the former, the conditions of the document of the 6th May have not been complied with. It is a mere proposal, unaccepted even at the present time, and certainly unaccepted at the time the Bank receded from it on the 29th of August, inasmuch as the creditors of Kirkwood, Holland & Co. have confessedly not ceded over to the Bank their collateral securities. Those securities should have been given up. (*Stock vs. Mawsom,* 1 *Bos. & Pull.,* 286, *Judgment of Eyre, C.J.*; *Cowper vs. Green,* 7 *M. & W.,* 633; *Forsythe on Composition,* 2nd ed., p. 126; *Chitty on Contracts,* 8th ed. 771.) Next, as to the effect of the non-signature of some of the creditors and the specific refusal of one or more to sign. The contract of the 6th May was not a contract with each creditor, but with the whole of the creditors. (*Atherton vs. North,* 1 *Dick.,* 375; *Latch vs. Wedlake,* 11 *A. & E.* 959; *Reay vs. Richardson,*

2 *Cr. M. & Rosc.*, 422, *Judgment of Lord Abinger*, 429; *Boyd vs. Hyde*, 25 *L. J. Exch.*, 246, *Judgment of Pollock, C. J.*; *Forsythe on Composition*, 30; *Voet.* 2, 14, 23.) Trustees of insolvent estates have no authority to sign without the express assent of a meeting of creditors. (*Ord.* 6, 1843, § 97; *Griffith on Bankruptcy*, vol. 2, p. 1849.) The document of the 6th May was not a contract, but a mere proposal for a contract. The subsequent deed was to be the contract; and where a written contract is contemplated, then a previous parol contract is of no force unless reduced into writing. (3 *Burge*, 517; *Chitty on Contracts*, 8 ed. p. 71.) The Bank had a right of withdrawal at any time before the proposal was accepted by all the creditors; and on the 12th August, when it did withdraw formally, Lock and Hitzeroth, two of the creditors, had not assented. The plaintiffs had not at that time lost their rights upon Kirkwood, Holland & Co., their debtors, and the Bank had still a *locus penitentiæ*. (*Payne vs Cave*, 3 *Term Rep.* 148, commented on in *Whitmore vs. Turquand*, *ubi sup*; *Pothier on Obligations*, 3 *Evans Am. ed.* 1, p. 4.) Next, as to the effect of the misrepresentation by Kirkwood, Holland & Co., with the knowledge of the plaintiffs, of the assets of the estate. This was a contract between three parties,—the creditors of Kirkwood, Holland & Co., Kirkwood, Holland & Co., and the Bank. The Bank was really acting as surety for the debtor, and is entitled to be relieved against misrepresentation. (*Stock vs. Mawsom*, *ubi sup.*; 2 *Burge*, 501; *Chitty on Contracts*, 630.) Any contract to bind the Bank should have been under seal, and provision is made to facilitate the affixing of seals to such cotracts in the colonies. (27 *and* 28 *Vict. Ch.* 19; *Thring on Joint-stock Companies*, 237.) Next, as to the question of *ultra vires*. It is open to the defendants, under the general issue, to dispute the power of Tudhope, Stewart, or the Bank itself, to enter into such a contract. (*Bateman vs Borough of Ashton-under-Lyne*, 27 *L. J., Exch.*, 458; *Ridley vs. Plymouth Company*, 2 *Exch. Rep.*, 711; *Hamboro vs. Hull Company*, 28 *L. J., Exch.*, 62; *Balfour vs. Ernest*, 28 *L. J., C. P.*, 170.) Tudhope had no authority from his principals, the shareholders of the Bank, to enter into that contract. And his authority must be proved by the plaintiffs. (*Grant on Corporations*, 13 *and* 291; *Lindley on Partnership*, 2nd ed., vol. 1, 256-7.) The contract was, moreover, *ultra vires* the Bank's Articles of Association, and *ultra vires* its powers under the ordinary law. (*Pothier on Obligations*, vol 1, p, 142; *Story on Agency*, §§ 14, 15; *Coleman vs. E. C. Railway Company*, 16 *L. J., Chanc.*, 73; *Ridley vs. Plymouth Company*, *ubi sup.*; *Bateman vs. Borough of Ashton-under-Lyne*, *ubi sup.*;

1868.
Nov. 26.
" 27.
" 28.
" 30.
Dec. 1.
" 2.
" 3.
" 4.
" 5.
" 7.
" 8.
" 15.
─────
J. O. Smith & Co.
vs. The Standard Bank of British South Africa (Limited).

1868.
Nov. 26.
" 27.
" 28.
" 30.
Dec, 1.
" 2.
" 3.
" 4.
" 5.
" 7.
" 8.
" 15.

J. O.Smith & Co.
vs. The Standard
Bank of British
South Africa
(Limited).

Ernest vs. Nicholls, 6 H. of L. Cas., 408 ; *Athenœum Life Assurance Society vs. Pooley,* 4 *Jur., N. S.,* 371 ; *Hutton vs. Scarborough Company,* 34 *L. J., Chanc.,* 643 ; 12 *Jur., N. S.,* 899 ; *Clinch vs. Financial Corporation,* 5 *Law Rep., June No., Eq., Cas.,* 450 ; *Kernagan vs. Williams,* 6 *L. Rep., Oct. No., Eq. Cas.,* 228.)

Griffith, in reply, on the point of *ultra vires*, cited *Evans vs. Smallcombe,* 6 *L.Rep.,Appel.Ser.,p.*249,*Houldsworth vs.Evans do. do.*, 263, and maintained generally that all the cases cited on this point *contra* were not cases between corporations and creditors, but between shareholders and directors, in restraint.

Cur. adv. vult.

Postea(December 15).—The Court, by majority (BELL, C.J. and DENYSSEN, J. ; DWYER, J., *diss.*) gave judgment for plaintiffs, with costs.

DWYER, J., said : In this case, the Court not being unanimous, it devolves upon me, as the junior member of it, first to express my opinion. The action is brought by Messrs. Smith and Christian, trading under the style or firm of John Owen Smith & Company, against the Standard Bank of British South Africa, which is a company incorporated and registered under the Joint-stock Companies' Acts in England, and having a registered office in London, and also registered under the Joint-stock Companies' Act passed in this Colony. The objects for which the Company is established are, as set out in the Memorandum and Articles of Association, " the transacting of every kind of banking business, under the general superintendence and control, and in co-operation with, a principal establishment in London." Provisions are contained in such articles also for the appointment of a board of directors in London, and the management of the business by them. The Bank had one of its branches at Port Elizabeth, of which, in May, 1865, Mr. Tudhope was, and for some time previously had been, local manager. A Mr. Stewart was the general manager of all the branch banks of the Company throughout the Colony. In May, 1865, trade became very much depressed at Port Elizabeth. Stewart refers to this state of things in a letter addressed to the London Board, bearing date the 2nd of May, 1865, in which he says : " Several stoppages have taken place, and such, in consequence, is the amount of distrust prevailing, that trade is almost at a complete standstill ;" and among the stoppages he mentions the firm of Messrs. Kirkwood, Holland & Co., and states that their liabilities were £40,000, and their assets £51,000 ; their liabilities to defendants, as acceptors and endorsers, being something under £20,000. Messrs. Kirkwood, Holland

& Co. carried on at Port Elizabeth the trade of auctioneers; they also discounted bills and dealt in shares. The firm consisted of only two persons, Holland and Kirkwood, and the latter carried on a separate business on his own account. He had several shops in the country, and speculated largely, and there seems to have been a system of drawing upon each other, and upon others, accommodation bills, the only consideration being the giving similar accommodation acceptances in exchange; and the whole system of trading was built upon such a false foundation, that when one prop gave way, the whole of the rotten fabric tottered to the ground. Kirkwood's separate business failed, his liabilities being something like £50,000; and the failure of the firm of Kirkwood, Holland & Co. immediately followed. They then endeavoured to make some arrangement with their creditors; and with that view they laid a statement of their affairs, and especially of their assets and liabilities, before the Port Elizabeth Bank, of which Mr. Christian (one of the plaintiffs) was and is chairman, and which statement or statements (admitted by Mr. Christian to be substantially the same) were laid before meetings of the creditors of Messrs. Kirkwood, Holland & Co., to which meetings I will now refer. On the 14th May, 1865, the first meeting of creditors was held; and at that meeting Mr. Tudhope was present on behalf of the defendants, who were the largest creditors. He offered to pay a composition of 10s. in the pound, which was not accepted, and the meeting was adjourned to the next day but one, in order to enable Mr. Tudhope to examine into the statements laid before the meeting. It appears that Messrs. Kirkwood & Holland, in the course of their trade, when property was given to them to dispose of, were in the habit of depositing with their customers bills and other securities as a guarantee for their duly accounting for the produce of the sales. Some of those securities, to a considerable amount, remained in the hands of various parties at the time of Messrs. Kirkwood & Holland's stoppage; and one of the principal questions in this case is, whether by the alleged contract, to which I am about to allude, those securities were to be given up to the Standard Bank, or whether the holders were to retain them and prove upon the estate only for such balance as should remain due after deducting the value of the securities? And upon this point a great deal depends upon the construction to be placed upon the evidence. In the written statements laid before the meetings at which Mr. Christian (who, as I before said, is one of the plaintiffs) was present, and at both of which he presided as chairman, those securities appear as assets, and no mention whatever is made of their

1868.
Nov. 26.
,, 27.
,, 28.
,, 30.
Dec. 1.
,, 2.
,, 3.
,, 4.
,, 5.
,, 6.
,, 7.
,, 8.
, 15.

J. O. Smith & Co.
vs. The Standard
Bank of British
South Africa
(Limited).

being in the hands of third parties. When a person states that his liabilities are £40,000, and his assets are £51,000, I think all ordinary persons would be led to believe that every shilling of the £51,000 was available to meet the liabilities, leaving a clear balance, after payment of all demands, of £11,000; and to put down as assets securities held by third parties, and which, as collateral securities, cannot be made available assets, is, in my opinion, a fraud. I don't say a moral fraud, because it may be unintentional, but such a legal fraud as vitiates a contract based on such written statements, and which form part of the contract. With respect to those collateral securities, Mr. Holland says that he went to Mr. Tudhope's office on the 5th of May; that they both went most carefully over the various statements; and that he told Tudhope that some of the securities appearing amongst the list of assets were held by third parties. Tudhope positively denies this. But, assuming that he is mistaken, and that Holland's account is correct, does it amount to more than that he informed Tudhope in whose hands the securities were; and that Tudhope was thus led to believe that upon applying to such parties and paying the composition agreed upon, the securities would be given up? Holland does not say that he told Tudhope that the securities would be retained or would not be given up. Some shares were held by Messrs. Blaine and Co., upon which they advanced some £2,600 to Kirkwood, Holland & Co. It appears to me upon the evidence that those shares were the only securities in the list of assets which Tudhope knew were to be retained; and Kirkwood saying to Tudhope: " Oh, the loss will be only 2,600 half-crowns " confirms me in this opinion. Why did not Kirkwood tell of the many other half-crowns which would be lost by creditors retaining such securities and obtaining 20s. in the pound upon their debts? Both Mr. Holland and Mr. Kirkwood gave their evidence very fairly; but it must be recollected that they are interested in this case, more, perhaps, even than the plaintiffs. If the plaintiffs be unsuccessful, Kirkwood and Holland cannot appear again as independent traders without coming to this Court to be rehabilitated, which, I have no doubt, they would rather avoid doing. Tudhope having investigated the accounts, came to the adjourned meeting on the 6th May, and proposed to that meeting to pay the creditors 15s. in the pound upon their debts, upon the terms contained in the minutes and the resolutions annexed thereto; and one of those terms or conditions is, that the firm of Kirkwood, Holland & Co. should make an absolute sale and cession to the defendants of the whole of the assets of the said firm. When a party contracts with another for the sale to him of an estate, it is an implied part of the contract that the vendor shall give a marketable title. Could Kirkwood, Holland & Co., after having committed an act of bankruptcy, give a marketable title to any portion of their property—to Mimosa Dale, for example—without the consent of every one of their creditors? There is no law in this Colony by which a majority of creditors can bind the minority; and it is therefore always in the power of any outstanding creditor to defeat any arrangement whatever entered into by the rest. In my opinion, therefore, it was requisite for the plaintiffs to show that a complete and indefeasible cession of the property of Kirkwood, Holland & Co. had been made to the defendants before the plaintiffs could call upon the defendants to pay one shilling under this alleged contract; and that when it came to the knowledge of the defendants that one of the creditors had absolutely refused, as Mr. Lock did, to sign the deed, it was competent for the defendants to withdraw from the arrangement; they were not obliged to wait until each refusing creditor was coaxed into signing or compelled to sign the deed. Nor was it enough for the plaintiffs to say, "It is true that all the creditors have not signed, but it lies upon you to show that they will not sign." I think that an actual or implied assent of every creditor must have been shown, and the defendants placed in a position to plead such assent in bar of any action by a creditor to compel compulsory sequestration. And this was the view taken by all the parties at the time of the transaction. The agreement left everything *in fieri*. A deed was prepared by Mr. Chabaud, upon instructions given to him by Kirkwood immediately after the meeting of the 6th May, and the greatest exertions were made to get it signed by all the parties. Holland says that "he thought Lock's refusal to sign created a difficulty." It is clear that the impression on Holland's mind was that the assent of all the creditors was requisite, as forming one of the conditions of the agreement. And that it was the opinion of the meeting of creditors, and amongst others of plaintiffs, is evident from the protest in September, where they say, "the deed is now complete by the signature of all parties;" and this also shows that the deed was the document relied on as the principal instrument, and not as a mere accessory, as appears also from the recitals it contains. The telegram also from Kirkwood, Holland & Co., to Lock, telling him that "if he did not sign, the arrangement would fall through," is evidence that they at least thought the signatures of all the creditors requisite. Besides which, there is a resolution at the meeting of creditors in August, to surrender the estate in consequence of all not signing. I now come to another point in the case, namely, the alleged adoption of the arrangement by the defendants, as evidenced by their alleged authority to Holland, as their agent, to wind up the business of the insolvent firm, and in opening a liquidation account in their own books. Holland says, in speaking of his interview with Tudhope, " he authorized me to go on winding up the business as usual." A new account was opened with the Standard Bank to the credit of Kirkwood, Holland & Co., " in liquidation ;" and, accordingly, as any portion of the estate was realized, the money was taken to the bank by Mr. Wimpory, the bookkeeper of Kirkwood, Holland & Co., and by him lodged to the credit of the account of "Kirkwood, Holland & Co., in liquidation," and a new pass-book was opened, in which entries of the deposits were made. It is alleged by the plaintiffs that this account was opened by the defendants themselves ; that Holland was their agent, and they, in fact, were realizing the estate, and had thus adopted the arrangement. But I don't think t' e evidence supports this view. A great point has been attempted to be made of the fact that upon the first deposit note appear the words " in liquidation," in a corner of the note, in different ink from the rest, and it is suggested that the words were added by the Bank clerk. I don't think it has anything to do with the case. If anything, it only amounts to this, that when Wimpory brought the money, intending to lodge it to the old account of Kirkwood, Holland & Co., which had not been finally closed, the clerk may have said : "You must lodge it to a new account ; an arrangement is being carried out, and it is as well to keep the original account and the account since the stoppage distinct." But what if every single deposit note had been filled up at the counter by the officers of the Bank ? Nearly every bank has a different form of deposit note ; and if you take a number of different cheques, bills, and other securities to a bank, you will find that, simple as it appears, a deposit note is not always such an easy document to fill up : and you will be glad to see the officer take up your deposits and at a glance fill up the deposit note and hand it to you to sign, as is very frequently done in very many, if not in all, banks. With respect to the alleged authority to Holland to act as agent of the Bank, is it likely that, after a failure to so large an amount, the Bank would place such confidence in the insolvents as to commit an estate to them to wind up ? Lay the evidence before a jury of commercial men, familiar with banking and other business (and before such a jury, I think this case should have been tried), and what view would they take of it ? It is, I think, indisputable that from the first Stewart disapproved of the arrangement entered into by

Tudhope, and was determined, if he could legally do so, to get rid of it. He refused to adopt the arrangement until it was legally carried out. McDonald confirms this. He says: "I saw Stewart about it (*i.e.*, a bill which he wanted to have passed) on the 20th June. I asked why the 15s. was not placed to my credit ; and he said the documents were not quite completed, but that I might look upon it as quite settled." The view I take of this alleged authorization and adoption, and the view which I venture to think a jury would take, is, that the estate requiring some one to look after it, the managers of the Bank said : "We cannot interfere until the arrangements are completed; go on as usual, and when everything is settled, we will take over the remaining assets, and whatever has been lodged to the credit of the liquidation account." There is no doubt that Stewart was determined to get out of the difficulty by repudiating the transaction if he could. It is alleged that he did so because of the depreciation of the assets by subsequent failures. I don't think so. He knew the state of Port Elizabeth at that time, as is very evident from his letter of the 2nd May. There was certainly a depreciation in the value of the assets subsequent to the 6th May ;·but that arose chiefly because neither party would take charge of them—both were afraid of committing themselves ; and there would have been a still further depreciation of assets if Stewart had not accepted Gordon's offer to compel a surrender of the estate. The conduct of Gordon and Stewart in this matter has been much commented upon ; but I think undeservedly. To compel sequestration of the estate was the very best course that could have been adopted in the existing state of things. The conduct of St.wart deserving of condemnation is his having made use of Tennant as a mere tool, by inducing or compelling him to refuse to sign the deed of composition ; such a refusal was a mere sham, and to it I attach no importance. A great deal was said in the course of the argument as to the difference between the agreement and deed ; but I do not think it is very material which is looked upon as the principal instrument, because if the agreement, although *in fieri*, were not carried out, or if the contract were not performed by the defendants through their own default, in either case the plaintiffs would be entitled to maintain this action. But, whichever be the contract, it appears to me that the plaintiffs have not fulfilled their part of it. All the creditors have not even now signed, because a qualified signature to which the defendants have not assented is no signature, and because, although Pearson and others, who are creditors representing insolvent estates, have signed, it does not appear that they

1868.
Nov. 26.
„ 27.
„ 28.
„ 30.
Dec. 1.
„ 2.
„ 3.
„ 4.
„ 5.
„ 7.
„ 8.
„ 15.

J. O. Smith & Co.
vs. The Standard
Bank of British
South Africa
(Limited).

have signed as representing the creditors in those estates; and it is conceded that some of such trustees had not, and have not, obtained the consent of such creditors to the composition, as is required by the Insolvent Ordinance, and which consent would be requisite to enable the defendants to plead such signatures in bar to an action. Of course, if it be good law that the contract was complete with each creditor the moment such creditor signed the contract, my reasoning falls to the ground; but the authorities which have been cited on this point, in my opinion, have no application to the circumstances of the present case. There are only two other points, to which I shall very shortly refer. It is alleged by the learned counsel for the plaintiffs that the powers of the defendants are so ample as to enable them not only to enter into this arrangement, but even to set up a grocer's shop. The objects of the Standard Banking Company, as pointed out by their Memorandum of Association, seem very extensive; but in no place do I find that they are empowered to take upon them the debts and liabilities of insolvent firms. It is contended not only that they can do so, but that their agent here, acting under their authority, can do so by parol agreement. In this Colony there is, unfortunately, no statute analogous to the English statutes requiring certain agreements or contracts to be in writing. Here, agreements for the sale of the most valuable property or contracts of the most complicated nature may be proved, though entered into only by word of mouth; and hence the frightful amount of contradictory swearing that we find in almost every contested case. But when parties enter into a contract with a company incorporated and registered under the English Joint-stock Companies' Acts and also under the Joint-stock Companies' Acts of this Colony, such parties are bound to take notice of those Acts and the articles and memorandum of association registered under them. And, as Lord Wensleydale has said in *Ernest vs. Nicholls*, "If they do not choose to acquaint themselves with the powers of the directors, it is their own fault; and if they give credit to any unauthorized persons, they must be contented to look to them only, and not to the company at large. The stipulations of the deed, which restrict and regulate their authority, are obligatory on those who contract with the company, and the directors can make no contract so as to bind the whole body of shareholders, for whose protection the rules are made, unless they are strictly complied with. The contract binds the persons making it, but no one else." If, therefore, a contract be of such a nature as that, under the articles and memorandum of association, it could only be made under seal, the board of directors could not validly contract in any other manner; and I do not see how they could delegate to another a power they did not themselves possess. Seals of corporate bodies are not unknown in this Colony. The "Public Library Company of Port Elizabeth," the "Simon's Bay Dock Company," and several railway companies have common seals to authenticate their acts. It is said that it would be attended with great inconvenience if public companies, before completing any contract, were obliged to send it to England to be passed under the common seal of the contracting company. But such a course would be altogether unnecessary. The second section of the "Companies' Seals Act" provides for the affixing seals to contracts made abroad; and it would altogether destroy public confidence in trading companies if shareholders were to be at the mercy of unprincipled persons, who might swear to contracts having been entered into which were not even reduced to writing. I think we ought, therefore, to construe with the utmost strictness the provisions of any statute intended for the protection of shareholders in this respect. The last point to which I shall refer is upon the pleadings. It is contended that we cannot enter upon the question of *ultra vires* because it has not been specially pleaded; but I think that the plaintiffs have put this question in issue 'upon the face of their own declaration. In this Court there is great latitude allowed in pleading; this case has been at hearing for several days, and the point has not taken the plaintiffs by surprise: it has been most ably argued on both sides. I therefore think we ought to afford every facility for the case to be fully discussed elsewhere, so that when finally decided it may obviate the necessity of future litigation. In this Court there are no very precise rules of pleadings to guide either the Bench or the Bar; and, in the absence of such rules, to attempt to confine the parties to forms of pleadings established for every case, as it comes before us, would tend to defeat rather than promote the ends of justice. I will not go further into the case. Were it not that my opinions are opposed to judges of such great learning and experience as the rest of the Court, I should say that I have no doubt as to what our judgment should be. As it is, I can only express, with great diffidence, my opinion that the plaintiffs have failed to make out their case, and that the judgment of the Court should be for the defendants.

1868.
Nov. 26.
„ 27.
„ 28.
„ 30.
Dec. 1.
„ 2.
„ 3.
„ 4.
„ 5.
„ 7.
„ 15.
—
J. O. Smith & Co.
sr. The Standard Bank of British South Africa (Limited).

DENYSSEN, J.: This is an action brought by the plaintiffs against the defendants for the recovery of damages by reason of the breach on the part of the defendants of a certain contract entered into between the said plaintiffs and the said defendants. There has been some argument as to the form in which this action has been brought. An objection has been taken to it,—and in my opinion not without reason,—as not in accordance with the rules and practice of this Court. The action should have been for the specific performance of the contract upon which the plaintiffs now rely, leaving it to the defendants to raise their defence either under the general issue or by way of special plea; and should by such plea any matters have been alleged which require a special reply, the plaintiffs might have done so in their replication. For instance, if the defendants had pleaded, besides the pleas now on record, that the estate had surrendered, in the replication the might have been admitted, but the defendants' right denied to avail themselves of it on the ground of fraud, collusion, or on any other ground. As the declaration, however, has not been excepted to, and comprises the real cause of action, we canno· take any notice of the objection. It has also been maintained that under the general issue the power of the company to enter into any such contract as alleged can be questioned. I am of opinion that it cannot; it should have been specially pleaded; and I think during the argument nothing has been adduced to satisfy me that I am in error. In the numerous cases quoted, the point has not been raised; except in one of *Batement vs. The Mayor, Aldermen and Burgesses of the Borough of Ashton-under-Lyne*, in which Baron Martin, in his reference to the point, confirms the view I have taken in this respect. Upon the facts of the case as they present themselves to my mind, I have no doubt. And here I must remark, that although I do not impute perjury, or anything like it, to any of the witnesses, I am impressed with the conviction, where the evidence of Tudhope and Stewart is in conflict with that of Holland, Kirkwood and McDonald, I must give the preference to the latter, as I have done. It is said that Tudhope is not interested. It may be so; but neither are the other parties, in so far as I have been able to discover. It appears, then, that about the end of April and beginning of May, 1865, the affairs of the firm of Kirkwood, Holland & C⁰., of Port Elizabeth, became embarrassed. They held a meeting of their creditors on the 4th May, at which the plaintiffs and other creditors, also Tudhope, as representing the Standard Bank, were present. Certain statements were submitted to the creditors relating to the affairs of the firm, and a proposal made on the part of Tudhope, which, however, was not accepted, and the meeting adjourned; not, however, without recording an opinion that a compromise of 15s. in the pound would be accepted, but without fixing a day for meeting again, evidently for the purpose of enabling any party desirous of making such an offer an opportunity of inquiring into the business, and of ascertaining whether he would be justified in so doing. On the 5th May, Holland was sent for by Tudhope, and, according to Holland, the statements were produced, excepting two, and gone over and explained item by item. That this was most likely does not admit of any doubt. Tudhope had received certain instructions from Stewart, which he would exceed by adopting the resolution of the 4th May, and offering 15s. in the pound; and to justify himself, therefore, to do so, and to deviate in other respects from the instructions he had received, it was necessary he should scrutinize the statements most minutely. Holland further says that in going over the liabilities and list of bills payable, "I explained that there were certain parties who held securities. I mentioned Pearson and Carpenter. When we came to the Standard Bank shares, I explained that besides the ninety-two in the hands of the Bank, there were fifteen in the hands of Blaine & Co. for sale, and that I had received advances upon them. There was another credit of £2,600 of Blaine & Co. in London, who held 235 shares of the Mortgage and Investment Company, and also thirty-six Standard Bank shares belonging to the private estate of Kirkwood, which did not figure in our assets." This evidence of Holland is confirmed by Kirkwood, who says that on the morning of the 6th, Tudhope referred to these collateral securities as an objection to his making the offer. Tudhope contradicts these statements; but he cannot deny that some of the Bank shares were in the hands of Blaine & Co., as appeared from the statement, and that some were held by the Bank. On the 6th of May, an adjourned meeting was held. At that meeting, Tudhope made an offer in writing virtually adopting the resolution of the creditors of the 4th May, and which, with an addition made to it by the chairman, was signed as his offer, and afterwards accepted and signed by the body of creditors. By this contract, Tudhope, as representing the Standard Bank, purchases from those credit rs their claim as against Kirkwood, Holland & Co. at the rate of 15s. in the pound, and releases Kirkwood, Holland & Co. from their liability in respect of the same, as well as from the claim of the Standard Bank, upon their making over to him all their present assets. The arrangement being thus completed, Godsman, the secretary to the Bank, communicates it to the general manager, then in Cape Town, who acknowledges, and certainly does not repudiate, it by his letter of the 9th May; and on the same day Tudhope communicates it to the London directors,

1868.
Nov. 26.
„ 27.
„ 28.
„ 30.
Dec. 1.
„ 2.
„ 3.
„ 4.
„ 5.
„ 7.
„ 8.
„ 15.

J. O. Smith & Co.
vs. The Standard Bank of British South Africa (Limited).

1868.
Nov. 26.
" 27.
" 28.
" 30.
Dec. 1.
" 2.
" 3.
" 4.
" 5.
" 7.
" 8.
" 15.

J. O. Smith & Co.
vs. The Standard
Bank of British
South Africa
(Limited).

informing them that "the assets had been carefully examined by ourselves, the Port Elizabeth bank, and others." Upon this a new account is opened in the books of the Bank, "Kirkwood, Holland & Co., in liquidation." The old pass-book is discarded, and a new one commenced under the above heading. Instructions are given to wind up the affairs; the payment of minor accounts is authorized; and accommodation notes are exchanged. There is nothing in the books to show that these payments and this exchange did not take place. Holland swears it was under the direction of Tudhope. When one of McDonald's bills had to be exchanged, he was referred by Holland to Tudhope, who declared he would not continue these exchanges. Tudhope, however, after referring to the terms of the agreement, agreed to pay McDonald 15s., less the discount; and when McDonald, a day or two afterwards, inquired why his account had not been credited with this amount, he was told the arrangement had not been quite completed,—he would have to wait a day or two longer; and seeing Stewart afterwards, it was said the document had not been quite completed, but that he might consider it as all settled. On the 5th July, Holland was sent for by Stewart, and a conversation took place between him, Tudhope, and Stewart,—the latter intimating he was determined to get out of the deed of composition (this is the first intimation of an endeavour to get out of the arrangement), and urging Holland to surrender, which was refused. On the 10th July, however, Stewart wrote to the London office that he felt considerable anxiety in the matter, and would now, if it were possible, withdraw from the arrangement. And not until the 29th July was a letter written to Kirkwood and Holland by the Attorneys Innes and Elliott, on behalf of the Bank, stating that on the ground of the collateral securities not having been surrendered, and all the creditors not having signed, the Bank declined to execute the deed of assignment. Carpenter, who held such securities, had on that day, for the first time, been asked whether he would give up the securities he held; but no such application had at any time been made to Pearson, who also held similar securities. In writing to the London office on the 9th August, Stewart refers to his endeavours to get out of the " foolish arrangement entered into by Tudhope with the creditors of Kirkwood & Holland," and on the 12th of August he meets certain of the creditors at the Bank, when Christian, Ebden, and some others were present, and he then tells them he would not carry out the agreement " because the estate had been misrepresented and deception used; that all the creditors had not signed, and that parties would not give up their collateral securities." Upon this Christian agreed not to insist upon the agreement being carried out if deception had been used; but finding such not to be the case, he commenced proceedings. On the 17th of August, Chabaud, on behalf of Kirkwood, Holland & Co., requested, in reference to the letter of Innes and Elliott of the 29th July, to be furnished with the names of the parties who had refused to sign, and in reply, on the 18th of August, Innes and Elliott gave the names of Hitzeroth, Tennant and Pinchin, stating further, as an additional ground for not carrying out the arrangement, that the assets which were submitted to Tudhope, and on the faith of which the offer was made, turned out to be incorrect. Stewart, in writing to the London office on the 28th August, says : " I have stronger hopes than ever that we shall be able to get out of this engagement entered into by Tudhope, without having recourse to litigation, as, apart from the question of misrepresentation as to the assets, the assignment is not yet completed, and one creditor positively declines becoming a party to it." This creditor is Tennant, who declined to forego any part of his claim. It, however, appeared of a rather doubtful character; and it further appeared that the letter had been written at the instance of a manager of a branch bank, and that Tennant was under heavy pecuniary obligations to the Bank. He had never before appeared as a creditor in the estate, and, when called upon, had shortly before paid a debt due to the estate of Kirkwood, Holland & Co. On the 29th of August, another meeting was held of some of the creditors, on the premises of the Bank, on which occasion Kirkwood explained that, in consequence of several creditors not agreeing to accept 15s. in the pound, the Standard Bank had refused to carry out their offer. At this meeting the plaintiffs were not present. Certain of the creditors, however, expressed their determination to hold the Bank to its contract; while others resolved upon another course. On the 19th September, a letter was sent to Kirkwood, Holland & Co., on behalf of certain of the creditors, including the plaintiffs, recommending them not to surrender their estate unless required by the Standard Bank, to whom they look for a settlement of this claim under the composition of the 6th May. On the 28th September, a meeting was held of certain of the creditors, at which the above letter was read; and at this meeting it was resolved not to surrender the estate except by force of circumstances. At the same meeting a suggestion was made by one T. S. Gordon, a creditor, to Stewart, to lend to him a bill for suing Kirkwood, Holland & Co. upon it, in order to compel a surrender, with a view of relieving the Bank from the

T

1868.	
Nov. 26.	
,, 27.	
,, 28.	
,, 30.	
Dec. 1.	
,, 2.	
,, 3.	
,, 4.	
,, 5.	
,, 7.	
,, 8.	
,, 15.	
J. O. Smith & Co. vs. The Standard Bank of British South Africa (Limited.)	

agreement. This suggestion was adopted by the manager; a bill given over to the party, upon which proceedings were commenced, which resulted in a surrender of the estate. It must be here remarked that Lock, a creditor in the estate of Kirkwood, Holland & Co., who had at first refused to be a party to the arrangement, did, on or about the 30th of August, give his assent, to which reference is made in the letter of the creditors of the 19th September, and that certain other creditors for small amounts, which had been paid, and a few others, had never signed the written offer. Upon these facts, the first question which has been raised is, has any contract been entered into at all as between Tudhope, representing the Standard Bank, and the creditors of Kirkwood, Holland & Co.? By the law of this Colony, a contract need not be under seal, nor, indeed, in writing, unless it is so stipulated. In this case it was in writing, and was, what it purports to be, a contract between Tudhope, as representing the Standard Bank, and the several parties thereto. This is its true construction, and was the construction put upon it by Tudhope and Stewart. 15s., even 17s. 6d. in the pound, left a handsome margin. So long as the signatures of the principal creditors had been severally obtained, the contract as regards them was completed. The express assent of the minor creditors was of no importance. The policy of the Court is to uphold such contracts, of which the parties concerned were aware. The intention to carry it out is equally clear. In the books a new account is opened, a new pass-book is furnished, and the deposit notes altered —no interest allowed, severally, to meet the altered circumstances. True, it is said that the entry in the ledger was the work of the bookkeeper, the new pass-book furnished at the instance of the depositor, and for the alteration of the deposit notes the clerk of Kirkwood, Holland & Co. is liable. But the manager of the Bank was not and cannot be held ignorant of what takes place in his office. And how explain the letters of Stewart to his secretary, and ot him and Tudhope to the London office, also the conversation between Tudhope, Stewart and McDonald, when the bill of £510 was to be exchanged? It is next said, admit the alleged contract to have been signed by certain of the creditors, the non-execution by certain other of the creditors rendered it incomplete, and authorized the Bank to repudiate or withdraw from the same. There was no intimation from the Bank to the creditors that it was not to be carried out until the meeting of the 12th August; and the Bank claims, therefore, to be entitled to the period which elapsed between the 6th of May and 12th of August for the purpose of repentance,—a doctrine I cannot assent to. But this contract did not stipulate, to render it effectual, that all the creditors should sign it; nor is it one of ordinary compromise between a debtor and his creditors; it is a purchase by one of the creditors of the claims of one or more of the others—the purchaser releasing the debtor from all liability in respect of such and all other claims, on condition that the debtor make over to the purchaser the assets he holds; and this contract of purchase and sale was effected by the agreement of the 6th May. When the plaintiffs accepted the offer, it was completed in so far as they were concerned. They lost their claim upon Kirkwood, Holland & Co., and Tudhope, representing the Bank, became responsible to them. It is not necessary in an ordinary composition between debtors and creditors that all the creditors should have signed. (See *Norman vs. Thompson*, and what Baron Martin says on *Boyes vs. Hind*, not necessary *a fortiori* in this case.) The defendants relied upon the non-signature of Hitzeroth, Pinchin and Tennant as entitling them to withdraw. Tennant's claim as a creditor is questionable. The fact that he paid a debt to the Bank at the time shows that he had no faith in his claim; besides which, the other circumstances proved in this case deprive the Bank of any right to make use of that claim. Hitzeroth's representative had signed, and Pinchin's claim was paid under the Bank's instructions. Pearson's signature has been challenged as of no value—upon what principle, as between the plaintiffs and defendants, I am at a loss to understand. He was legally vested with the estate he represented, and the creditors may call him to account; but certainly not the defendants in this suit. A number of other creditors, of more or less importance, were referred to during the trial, not before, of which the Bank is estopped from availing itself; and even if it could, it is not necessary, as before stated, that all should have signed in this case. Then it is said that the securities have not all been handed over; nor was it so agreed. (See the case of *Thomas vs. Courtney*.) Pearson's qualifications to his signature must have satisfied the defendants that he at least held certain securities which it was not his intention to surrender. He was never asked to do so. Carpenter was, on the 29th July, for the purpose of founding upon his refusal a ground for getting out of the contract, and for writing the letter of Attorneys Innes and Elliott of the same date. Besides which, it is evident from the evidence that the attention of Tudhope was called to the fact of these securities being held by Carpenter and Pearson. But, admit it was not, if the Bank were entitled to the same, they should have been recovered from Carpenter and Pearson: the non-recovery thereof cannot affect the plaintiffs. Mis-

1868.
Nov. 26.
„ 27.
„ 28.
„ 30.
Dec. 1.
„ 2.
„ 3.
„ 4.
„ 5.
„ 7.
„ 8.
„ 15.

J. O. Smith & Co.
vs. The Standard Bank of British South Africa (Limited).

1868.
Nov. 26.
" 27.
" 28.
" 30.
Dec. 1.
" 2.
" 3.
" 4.
" 5.
" 7.
" 8.
" 15.

J. O. Smith & Co.
vs. The Standard
Bank of British
South Africa
(Limited).

representation is the next ground upon which it is attempted to set aside the contract. When the meeting of creditors adjourned on the 4th of May, it was for the purpose of affording parties desirous of making an offer an opportunity of inquiring into the particulars of the estate of Kirkwood, Holland & Co. Tudhope did so ; and, considering that the resolution of the 4th May had fixed upon the sum of 15s. as the minimum the creditors would take,—his knowledge that some of the assets were in the hands of third parties,—that the Bank also held securities in respect of their claims,—can it be doubted that attention was not only directed to it, but that the matter was carefully inquired into, as Tudhope wrote to the London office by letter of 9th May ? Besides which, there is the positive evidence of Holland, both as regards the immovable property, the shares, and the securities. A right of withdrawal from the contract of the 6th May was founded upon the proceedings of the 29th of August, which has nothing to do with this case, as the plaintiffs are no party to it. They considered that the contract having been completed as between them and the Bank on the 6th May, the latter could not withdraw from it without their consent, and held the Bank responsible, as they had a right to do. The proceedings on and after the 28th September are equally unavailing. The Bank was anxious to get rid of its liability towards the creditors of Kirkwood, Holland & Co., and the means adopted—in one respect not very creditable—could not accomplish that object. There remains only the question as to the contract being *ultra vires* of the local manager and of the company ; and it may be questionable whether the Bank, in the exercise of its power under the Memorandum and Articles of Agreement, has the right of speculating in landed property or in the purchase and sale of shares of other joint-stock companies ; but if in the ordinary course of its business, as in this case, immovable or other property, shares, &c., come into the legal possession of the directors, their general or local managers, and with a right to dispose, as securities, and it is expedient for the interests of the Bank that they be held by them or disposed of, the directors or managers have a perfect right to do so, as it may seem expedient. The numerous cases to which reference has been made to establish a contrary doctrine do not apply. I found my opinion upon the Memorandum and Articles of Agreement. For the above reasons, my judgment is for the plaintiffs.

BELL, C. J. : I have no hesitation in concurring with my brother Denyssen that the judgment of the Court must be for the plaintiffs. As the parties, by the terms of their consent paper, intimated at the outset, not perhaps in the best taste, that there would, in any event, be an appeal from the judgment of this Court, it was deemed advisable to allow them to exhaust themselves in evidence and argument before indicating an opinion on any branch of the case, in order that the case might go elsewhere entire. In doing this the parties have consumed more time than I remember to have been occupied by any case during my experience in this Court; and yet I know not anything in the nature of the true case between the parties which should have made this necessary. It was argued for the defendants that the declaration did not disclose any ground of action. Though the form of the declaration may not be the best, there is enough in it to disclose that the plaintiffs allege the defendants to have agreed to pay them, as creditors of Kirkwood, Holland & Co., a dividend of 15s. per pound of their debt; that the defendants have failed to perform that agreement; and that the plaintiffs ask the Court to decree the defendants to pay them the amount of the dividend, as damages for non-performance of the agreement. At a meeting of Kirkwood & Co.'s creditors held on the 6th of May, Tudhope, the defendant's local manager, wrote out on a sheet of paper that he " informed the creditors of Kirkwood & Co. that on condition that they cede over to him the whole of their claims, and release Messrs. Kirkwood & Co. from all liability to them, he was prepared to guarantee the sum of 15s. in the pound, payable in four equal instalments, at six, twelve, eighteen and twenty-four months ; " that the liabilities of Kirkwood & Co. " be reduced to a cash basis on the first current, by the rebate of bills, &c., and the Bank's acceptances given for the amount of composition,"—*i.e.*, that everything should be calculated as if due on the 1st of May (six days previously), in order that that date might be assumed as the one from which the acceptances should run. This offer of the defendants had been preceded by one on the 4th of May, two days before, that Kirkwood & Co.'s estate " should be assigned to the defendants, in which case they would guarantee a dividend of 10s. in the pound, payable in six and twelve months." The offer of 15s. was, therefore, no first thought, but was made in substitution for, and in consequence of the rejection of, a previous offer of 10s. In drawing up the offer of the 6th May, Tudhope had not, as in his offer of the 4th May, made mention of an assignment of the assets of Kirkwood & Co. to the defendants, as the means wherewith to pay the dividend. On his suggestion, therefore, or on the suggestion of some one else at the meeting of the 6th, the following words were added to the offer by Tudhope : " The Bank releasing Messrs. Kirkwood, Holland & Co. from further liability on

1868.
Nov. 26.
„ 27.
„ 28,
„ 30.
Dec. 1.
„ 2.
„ 3.
„ 4.
„ 5.
„ 7.
„ 8.
„ 15.

J. O Smith & Co.
vs. The Standard Bank of British South Africa (Limited).

1868.
Nov. 26.
„ 27.
„ 28.
„ 30.
Dec. 1.
„ 2.
„ 3.
„ 4.
„ 5.
„ 7.
„ 8.
„ 15.

J..O Smith & Co.
vs. The Standard
Bank of British
South Africa
(Limited).

their handing over their present estate." Immediately below this addition to what Tudhope had written, Tudhope signed as defendants' manager. There then followed these words: "We, the undersigned creditors, agree to the above proposal," followed by the signature of the plaintiffs, and, a variety of other persons; and to the left of the plaintiffs' signature, appear these signatures: "Kirkwood, Holland & Co., J. A. Holland. J. S. Kirkwood." This document discloses two different independent contracts,—one whereby the plaintiffs and the other subscribing creditors cede to the defendants all claims they have on Kirkwood & Co., in consideration of which the defendants agree to give them 15s. in the pound of these claims, divided into four equal payments, by the defendants' promissory notes, dated 1st May, at six, twelve, eighteen and twenty-four months. This is the only contract made between the plaintiffs and the defendants, and execution of it by the plaintiffs was completed by their signature. From that moment they ceased to have any claim upon Kirkwood, Holland & Co., and, by necessary consequence, they ceased to have the power of attaching any assets of which Kirkwood and Co. might be possessed. Thenceforth they had nothing but a naked claim upon the defendants for their promissory notes for 15s. per pound, or three-fourths of the debt which had been owing to them by Kirkwood & Co. They had lost their debt owing by Kirkwood & Co., and by novation had acquired a new one owing by the defendants, to the extent of three-fourths of what had been owing by Kirkwood & Co. Acting in pursuance of this, the plaintiffs drew out a set of four promissory notes, which they sent to Tudhope, the local manager of the defendants, for signature by Stewart, their general manager. Performance of this contract by the defendants would have been completed by their signing the notes which the plaintiffs had sent them for that purpose. It was obviously immaterial to the plaintiffs what had induced the defendants to make this contract with them, or whether they had made any arrangement with Kirkwood & Co. to secure to themselves the assets of that firm. That was the defendants' affair. Being satisfied, in consideration of this agreement, themselves to sacrifice 5s. per pound, it was no part of the plaintiffs' duty to inquire how the defendants were to get the other 15s. which they promised to pay them. They might make Kirkwood & Co. a present of the 15s. per pound, for aught the plaintiffs or the other creditors, parties to the agreement, had to care. That this was the correct view of the plaintiffs' position would have been obvious, I think, to everyone if the offer by Tudhope had remained, as originally drawn up by himself in presence of the meeting of 6th May, and had been at once accepted in that form by the creditors. But, unfortunately, —I say unfortunately, because this seems to have formed the foundation of a great deal of the evidence which has been adduced, and of the argument which has been addressed to the Court,—argument and evidence which, in my apprehension, were equally immaterial and irrelevant,—unfortunately, then, before the plaintiffs and the other creditors of Kirkwood & Co. had closed with Tudhope's offer, as drawn by himself, it seems to have occurred to him or to some one else that the defendants would get into a false position, should the creditors at once close with them before the defendants had secured the assets of Kirkwood & Co. Tudhope's offer to the meeting of the 4th May was that the estate " be assigned to the Bank, in which case the Bank would guarantee 10s." In his offer to the meeting of the 6th, he had overlooked assignment of the estate. The creditors might nevertheless righteously have accepted the offer of the 6th; it was no part of their duty to protect the Bank, and even if the omission had crossed their minds, they might naturally have supposed that the Bank, who intervened as the friends of Kirkwood & Co., had taken care, by a private agreement with these gentlemen, to protect themselves. But, as I said before, this omission of assignment seems to have been mentioned in some way, and there were then added the words, " the Bank releasing Messrs. Kirkwood & Co. from further liability on their handing over their present estate." The signatures underneath of Kirkwood & Co., and of the two partners of that firm, could have reference only to these words, for neither the firm nor the partners had anything to do with the cession by the creditors to Tudhope of their claims against the firm, to which the offer of the 6th, as originally framed, was confined, and which had reference to the creditors alone. Nor, on the other hand, had the creditors any concern with the release of Kirkwood & Co. from " further liability" on their handing over their estate to the defendants : that was a matter entirely between Kirkwood & Co. and the defendants. This promise of a release by the defendants of Kirkwood & Co., on their handing over their estate to the defendants, and the signatures of Kirkwood & Co. assenting to the proposal, made the second of the two contracts to which I have before referred. This second contract between the defendants and Kirkwood & Co. was that the Bank, who by the first agreement had obtained from the creditors a cession of their claims, released Kirkwood & Co. of all liability, not only in respect of these claims, but in respect of the defendants' own claims against them; and in consideration of this, Kirkwood & Co. assigned to the defendants their whole assets. From the moment Kirkwood & Co., who were then perfectly *sui juris*, signed this document, they ceased to be *domini* of their assets. These became vested in right in the defendants, who could have procured an active title to such of the assets as a title was required to, by the common means known in law ; and from the same moment Kirkwood & Co. ceased to be liable to the defendants for their own debt, or for the debts of others, the claim to which was now vested in the defendants. The idea of the creditors, and also of the defendants, on the 4th May, as appears from the minutes of that date, was that Kirkwood & Co. should be allowed to realize the assets. Though not mentioned in the agreement of 6th May, this idea seems to have been retained, and to have been acted upon by the defendants ; for Kirkwood & Co. realized assets, which from time to time they paid over to the defendants, who entered them in a new account, headed " Kirkwood & Co. in liquidation. " By August (when Stewart repudiated the agreement), the deposits in this account amounted to upwards of £5,000, and the defendants treated these deposits as their own monies, for they did not credit the account periodically with interest, as they did after August, and they placed to the debit of the account the money which they had expended in this litigation, so extravagantly expended as to amount already to upwards of £600. The defendants, therefore, not only made the contract with Kirkwood & Co., but acted upon it by taking possession of the assets. It is mixing together the two contracts between the plaintiffs and the defendants, and between Kirkwood & Co. and the defendants, which I have mentioned, and treating them as one and indivisible, that has given rise to the supposed importance and difficulty of this case ; whereas the contract between the plaintiffs and the defendants is quite separable and distinct from that between the defendants and Kirkwood & Co., although it may be true that the one was inductive of the other. The first difficulty raised by the defendants to the plaintiffs' right to recover upon the contract with them was taken at the Bar, under the plea of the general issue, which, in terms, denies all the statements of fact and conclusions of law in the plaintiffs' declaration. Under this plea they objected, first, that Tudhope was not their duly authorized agent ; and second, that, even if he were, the directors of the defendants' company had no power to give him such authority. The first of these questions was the only one which, according to the rules of pleading, the defendants were entitled to raise at the Bar. There is a statement in the declaration that Tudhope was the authorized agent of the defendants,—this the general issue denied,—but there is no statement in the declaration that the directors had power to authorize Tudhope, and therefore the plea of the general issue does not deny that power. If it was intended to raise the question of power to authorize Tudhope, that question should have been raised by a special plea to that effect. But these objections, in my apprehension, would never have been taken, if attention had been paid to what alone they could be applicable. It was never in the course of the argument attempted to be disputed that Tudhope was authorized, or that the directors had power to authorize him, to buy up debts for 15s. in the pound, with a right to claim 20s. upon them, or anything between that and 15s. which Tudhope, as agent for the defendants, might think them likely to realize, without disturbing the defendants' right to claim 20s. per pound of their own debt of £10,000. But that is all that Tudhope had contracted with the plaintiffs. What was laboriously argued was, that Tudhope was not authorized, nor had the directors of a bank power to authorize him, to buy up landed property and shares of joint-stock companies, and so involve his constituents in speculations and liabilities foreign to the proper business of banking. That objection may or may not have something in it. It may be that Tudhope acted *ultra vires* if he did this, but that question is not *hujus loci*. It can have application only to the contract between Tudhope and Messrs. Kirkwood & Co. It may be that if these gentlemen had stood upon their rights under that contract, and, in respect of the assignment they had made by it, had, in its terms, claimed exemption from " further liability" to the defendants, and through them from liability to others, the defendants might have set up this question of *ultra vires* with effect, and have shown that Tudhope, having taken an assignment which neither he, nor even the directors, had authority to take, the assignment of assets thus failing, Kirkwood & Co.'s release from " further liability" fell with it. It is not necessary to consider that matter, because it has no reference to, nor does it create any interference with, the contract between the plaintiffs and the defendants. The objection, if taken successfully in any proceeding between the defendants and Kirkwood & Co., either by one or by the other,—for it might, if the assets had proved to have been undervalued, have suited Kirkwood & Co., instead of the defendants, to take it,—would, in the actual circumstance of an overvalue, only have shown that the defendants had not wisely and prudently secured the means out of which to make the payment of 15s. per pound which they had contracted with the plaintiffs to pay them. Such being the objections raised by the defendants, under

1868.
Nov. 26.
,, 27.
,, 28.
,, 30.
Dec. 1.
,, 2.
,, 3.
,, 4.
,, 5.
,, 7.
,, 8.
,, 15.

J. O. Smith & Co.
vs. The Standard
Bank of British
South Africa
(Limited).

the plea of the general issue, their first special plea was that their proposal to the creditors was not binding unless each and all of them assented to it, and to support this a number of cases of composition contracts were referred to ; but the research of the defendants failed to produce the case of *Harland vs. Binks*, to be found in 19 or 20 *Law Jo.*, I think. There Morley assigned his estate to Harland, as trustee, to pay a composition to such of his creditors as should come into the arrangement. Three creditors verbally expressed their assent to the arrangement, but the deed was not executed by one single creditor ; and yet the Court of Queen's Bench would not allow a creditor to sue Morley, the debtor, so soon as it appeared that Harland, who even had not executed the deed, had realized part of the estate, and so established the relation of trustee and *cestui que* trust between him and the creditors,—holding that the verbal assent of the three creditors, and their consequent refraining from suing execution against Morley's assets, was sufficient as against the other creditors to oblige them to come into the arrangement for the benefit of the creditors generally ; and the case of *Norman vs. Thompson*, referred to by my Brother Denyssen, is to the same effect. But were it otherwise, how is the fact here ? The defendants, when asked in August, 1865, by Chabaud, as the attorney of Kirkwood & Co., for the names of the creditors who had refused to assent, gave those of Hitzeroth, F. Pinchin and Tennant. Hitzeroth has since signed, Pinchin is a creditor for a small amount, and Tennant, if a creditor at all,—which is doubtful,—is a creditor who, being pecuniarily at the mercy of the defendants, they themselves unworthily, and in fraud of their contract with the creditors, induced to withhold his assent. The creditors, in fact, have all substantially assented. I refuse to notice those other names which were mentioned from the Bar, because the defendants are estopped by their own letter to Chabaud from giving any other names than were mentioned, unless they showed an omission by mistake, which they have not done. Refusal by the creditors to assent, therefore, did not entitle the defendants to withdraw, as their plea alleges. But I may observe that the present is not a case of composition contract ; it is the case of one large creditor buying up the claims of all the other creditors for 15s. per pound of their amount, and buying the estates of the debtor at the price of releasing him from all his liabilities. In a composition contract the debtor keeps his estate on condition of paying the composition. To him, therefore, it may be of the utmost consequence that all or none of his creditors should take the composition. The estate may not be more than equal to the composition. If so, some creditors might repudiate the composition, and sue for 20s. per pound of their debts; the debtor would be unable to pay the composition to the creditors who assented, and so the debtor would be in a worse position than if he had not offered the composition, and his sureties for the composition would be proportionally injured; consequently, it may be of importance to the debtor and his sureties to stipulate that if all do not agree, the composition arrangement shall fall. Here there was no such stipulation, because it was of no consequence to Kirkwood & Co. whether any creditor or none assented, for by their agreement with the defendants they were released from "further liability" on agreeing to make the cession of their estate, and that cession they had made; and to the assenting creditors it was equally immaterial. With regard to non-assenting creditors, —if any such there had been,—they might have sued Kirkwood & Co., leaving them to make good their relief from the defendants; but they could not have had any remedy against the assets, which, by the cession, made while Kirkwood & Co. were still *sui juris*, had become vested in the defendants. They might, by compulsory sequestration of Kirkwood & Co.'s estate, have attempted to bring back the assets from the defendants under the 84th section of the Insolvent Ordinance; but the success of such an attempt would have been dependent on showing that the estate was worth more than 15s. per pound, and that the cession to the defendants was intended to prefer them over the other creditors,—an attempt which, I need not say, would, in the actual circumstances, have been utterly hopeless, and, in any event, could not have affected the plaintiffs or the other assenting creditors who were to be paid their 15s., not out of the assets of Kirkwood & Co., but out of the pockets of the defendants. The next special plea of the defendants states that "the meaning of Tudhope's proposal" was that creditors who held collateral securities should deliver them up to the defendants, but divers creditors claimed a right to retain them, though "the basis" of the defendants' paying 15s. per pound was that the defendants should have all the assets of Kirkwood & Co., and this, by the plea, is stated to have been done "in derogation of the rights" of the defendants. But the plea, if plea it can be called, does not say what defence this gives them against the plaintiffs' action, nor is the expression "in derogation of rights" very intelligible,—it may take in everything or nothing. The short answer to any defence that could be raised on this statement is, that the plaintiffs are not one of these creditors, and that whatever others may do cannot affect the plaintiffs or their contract with the defendants. These other creditors may be bound to deliver over the securities, and may not be entitled to the 15s. till they do so; but that cannot affect the plaintiffs. The next special plea contains an averment that, to the knowledge of the plaintiffs, the proposal of the defendants was based upon the representations of Kirkwood & Co. as to their assets, but they have discovered that a great portion of these assets had been pledged and made over to creditors of the firm. This plea, as in the other instance, does not say what defence this gives the defendants against the plaintiffs; it leaves this to be inferred. The defendants expressly exonerate Kirkwood & Co. from any imputation of fraud, and confine themselves to an allegation of accidental misrepresentation of the amount of the assets. If the defendants had been fraudulently induced to make their offer, there might have been something in their averment, even as against the plaintiffs; but what have the plaintiffs to do with what occurred between the defendants and Kirkwood & Co. in the way of accidental mistake? The defendants chose to content themselves with the statements extracted by Kirkwood & Co. from their books, instead of verifying these statements with the books themselves, which were carefully written up. Whose fault was that but the defendants' own? But I do not believe the averment of this plea; and if it were necessary for this case—which, in my opinion, it is not—to form an opinion upon the evidence, I have no hesitation in saying that I believe both Holland and Kirkwood, that all the particulars of the assets, and the possession of certain of them by certain creditors as collateral securities, were disclosed to Tudhope at the meeting of the 5th May, the day before the offer was made. The concluding plea—if plea it can be called, which, like the others, pleads nothing—is a statement that the estate of Kirkwood & Co. has been put under sequestration. Be it so. But at whose instance? Why, at the instance of the defendants themselves, acting through Gordon, their tool. The only effect of the sequestration is, that the assets which, by the defendants' agreement with Kirkwood & Co., were to be handed over to the defendants, which, to a certain extent, the defendants had taken possession of, and which but for this sequestration, of their own procuring, would all have come to their hands, have passed into sequestration. I dare say the defendants would have little difficulty in getting that sequestration recalled; but, if not, this matters nothing to the plaintiffs, who must none the less be paid their 15s. per pound whencesoever the defendants may get them. If Stewart really repudiated Tudhope's offer when communicated to him,—of which I see no evidence,—his duty was, in his letter of the 9th May, distinctly to have said so, and to have desired Tudhope forthwith to communicate this to all concerned. *Locus penitentiæ* in such a case, exercised immediately, would have been open to him. But he lay by till the 12th August, and even then did not communicate with the plaintiffs and the other creditors, but with Kirkwood & Co. alone. On the whole the conduct of the defendants throughout has been most unbecoming, and unworthy of a large corporation. In the event, it has turned out that Kirkwood & Co.'s assets, instead of being equal to 17s. 6d. of their debts, as Kirkwood represented to Tudhope and the defendants' creditor, Craik,—which these gentlemen were credulous enough to believe, notwithstanding their presumed experience as men of business, and which Stewart, the defendants' manager, took from the 9th of May to the 12th of August to make up his mind whether to believe or disbelieve,—have turned out not to be equal to paying even 15s. per pound of Kirkwood & Co.'s debts. But suppose the event had been the other way. Suppose the assets had proved equal to 17s. 6d., or even more, and the plaintiffs, acting like the defendants, had repudiated their contract with the defendants, and had sued Kirkwood & Co., and having obtained judgment against them, had sued out execution against the assets, can it be doubted that the defendants would have interfered, and effectually, by asking this Court to restrain the plaintiffs' execution because of the assignment of these assets to the defendants? If so, can there be a doubt that, in the actual circumstances, the defendants must be as effectually bound by the contract as in the supposed case the plaintiffs would have been? My opinion, as I intimated at the outset, is that the judgment of the Court should be for the plaintiffs, with costs.

1868.
Nov. 26.
„ 27.
„ 28.
„ 30.
Dec. 1.
„ 2.
„ 3.
„ 4.
„ 5.
„ 7.
„ 8.
„ 15.

J. O. Smith & Co.
vs. The Standard Bank of British South Africa (Limited).

[Plaintiffs' Attorneys, *Fairbridge & Arderne.*
Defendants' Attorneys, *Berrange & De Villiers.*]

TRUBY'S TRUSTEE, APPLICANT; SWEMMER AND COETZEE, RESPONDENTS.

[See Part III., p. 218.]

Postea (October 1).—Both bills of costs were reviewed before BELL, C. J., at the George Circuit accordingly.

Oct. 1.
Truby's Trustee, Applicant; Swemmer and Coetzee, Respondents.

RE HENRY HAWKINS.

[See Part I., p. 23.]

Postea (December 29).—The Master reported favourably to the application, and it was ordered accordingly.

Dec. 29.
Re Henry Hawkins.

MOSTERT *vs.* SOUTH AFRICAN ASSOCIATION & ANOTHER.

Confession of Judgment.—Res Judicata.—Adjudication of Sequestration.—Mutual Will.

Where a power of attorney to confess judgment was drawn up for the defendant by or in the office of the plaintiff's attorney, judgment absolute obtained thereupon, and the defendant's estate compulsorily sequestrated thereafter,—HELD: that such confession was invalid, and that the judgment and all subsequent proceedings thereupon should be set aside as informal.

1868.
June 25.
„ 26.
Aug. 26.
„ 27.
„ 28.
„ 29.
Sept. 2.

Mostert vs. South African Association & Another.

This was an action to have an order of sequestration set aside, and to declare rights under a mutual will.

The plaintiff's declaration stated that on the 31st August, 1849, the said plaintiff, who is a farmer residing at Valkenburg, near Cape Town, was married in community of property to Isabella Petronella Hester Mostert, one of the daughters and heiresses of the late Cornelis Mostert. That on the 31st August, 1860, the said Cornelis Mostert and his spouse, Elizabeth Jacoba Mostert, executed their last will and testament, by which, after giving certain prelegacies to each of the heirs under the said will, they instituted as such heirs: 1st, the survivor of the testators; 2nd, their son, Cornelis Mostert; 3rd, the children of their daughter, Elizabeth Christina Mostert; 4th, their daughter, Maria Carolina Mostert, married to Jan Fredrik van Reenen; 5th, their son, Adriaan Sybrand Mostert; 6th, their son, Tobias Cornelis Mostert; 7th, their son, Johannes Andreas Mostert; 8th, their daughter, the said Isabella Petronella Hester Mostert, married to plaintiff; 9th, their daughter, Jacoba Anna Mostert, married to Jacobus Johannes Meintjes; 10th, their son, Jan Frederik Mostert—in equal shares; And, in case of predecease of one or more of them, their lawful descendants by representation *per stirpes*, subject to the following stipulations: *First*, That in computation with the inheritance of each of the instituted heirs, being children or grandchildren of the testators, shall have to be brought all that he or she respectively shall be found to be indebted to the estate of the said testators. *Secondly*, That when and where such debts should happen to exceed the amount of the inheritance from the estate of the first dying, the heir or heirs whom it may concern shall not be required to pay the excess immediately, but that it shall be sufficient for them to remain indebted to the survivor for such excess of debt above the inheritance from the estate of the first dying, to be afterwards, at the death of the survivor of the testators, brought into computation with his, her, or their inheritance from the estate of the latter. *Thirdly*, That, in so far as the inheritance from the estate of the first dying falling to the share of one or more of the instituted heirs might exceed the amount of his, her, or their debts to the estate, the excess of inheritance above debts may and shall be paid out to him, her, or them respectively free and unburdened. *Fourthly.* That all that shall fall to the share of the aforesaid instituted heirs of the testators as inheritance from the estate of the survivor of the testators (and in case and in so far as the said heirs may have remained indebted to the survivor of the testators for surplus of debts above the inheritance from the first dying, then after deduction of such debts) shall be and remain burdened with the entail of *fidei commissum. Fifthly.* That if it should come to pass that one or more of the aforesaid instituted heirs of the said testators is or are indebted to the estate of the survivor of the testators in more than the amount falling to his, her, or their share as inheritance therefrom, in such case any excess of debts above the inheritance falling to the share of such heir or heirs, shall be remitted to him, her, or them ; and such excess of debts above inheritance shall not be allowed to be taken in the computation of the inheritance of the respective heirs ; and the inheritance of the respective heirs shall be diminished in proportion to the joint amount of the excess of debt above inheritance. And the testators nominated and appointed, as executors testamentary, administrators of the estate, and guardians of the minor and fidei-commissary heirs, to wit : the testator, his wife, the present testatrix, together with the South African Association ; and the testatrix, her husband, the present testator, alone.

1868.
June 25.
" 26.
Aug. 1.
" 25.
" 27.
" 28.
" 29.
Sept. 2.

Mostert vs. South African Association & Another.

Plaintiff further declared that the said Cornelis Mostert, sen., died on the 15th December, 1862, when his widow and the said Association took out letters of administration; and that they have ever since acted as the executors and administrators under the will ; the Association being the administering executors and administrators. That on the 21st January, 1863, the widow informed the Association that she would not accept the prelegacy bequeathed to her by the will by the following letter :

Cape Town, 21st January, 1863.
To the Board of Directors of the S. A. Association for the Administration and Settlement of Estates, Cape Town.

GENTLEMEN,—With reference to the will of my late husband, Mr. C. Mostert, sen, I hereby declare that I do not accept the prelegacy made to me of the garden or estate called " Welgedaan," situated at the upper end of St. John's-street, with all the movable property, trinkets, and cattle which are therein, and request you to sell the same publicly, for account of the estate, in the month of March. I shall supply you with a list of articles which I wish to keep out for myself.

1868.
June 25.
„ 26.
Aug. 1.
„ 25.
„ 27.
„ 28.
„ 29.
Sept. 2.

Mostert *vs.* South African Association & Another.

With respect to the piece of land, with the buildings thereon, situated in Breda-street, now occupied by Mr. J. J. Meintjes, I desire that the same be without delay transferred to my daughter, Jacoba Anna Mostert, married without community of property to the said Meintjes, to whom the same was sold by my late husband for £1,500, when a mortgage bond must be passed by my said daughter for the full amount of the purchase money, £1,500, bearing interest from ——— ———, in favour of the estate of my husband. All the expenses of this transfer and of the mortgage bond to be passed by my daughter, also transfer dues, expenses of diagram, and all other expenses in connection with the said transfer and mortgage bond, must be paid out of the estate of my husband.

With regard to the different shares in companies which have been found in the estate and are set forth on the inventory, it is my desire that the same be sold as advantageously as possible for the estate, with the exception, however, of one share in your Association, with regard to which my desire is that the same may be taken over by my son, Jan Frederick Mostert, at the value now set upon it in the books, without any premium ; and as it will be necessary to take the opinion of the members of the Association upon this subject, I request you will employ your influence to have this my wish gratified.

I am, &c.,

Wid. C. MOSTERT, born LOUW.

And that on the 18th September, 1863, after having, as plaintiff alleged, adiated her inheritance under the said will, she informed the Association that she had resolved to claim only the net moiety of the joint estate, renouncing all legacies bequeathed to her, as also the child's portion devised to her by her husband; and requested the Association, as the administering executors of the estate, to liquidate the said estate as speedily as possible, and to pay her the half share due to her in cash, as she was not inclined to take in payment any bonds due by her children. This letter ran thus :

Cape Town, 18th September, 1863.

To the Board of Directors of the South African Association for the Administration and Settlement of Estates, Cape Town.

GENTLEMEN:—I have resolved to claim only the net half of the joint estate of my late husband and myself, and which, by virtue of the community of property which has existed between us, belongs to me by law, and to forego all legacies, and also the child's portion, bequeathed to me by my late husband. I now kindly request you, as the administering executors of the said estate, to liquidate the same as speedily as possible, and to pay me the half share due to me, in cash, as I am not inclined to take in payment any bonds due by my children.

I am, &c.,

E. MOSTERT.

I, the undersigned, Elizabeth Jacoba Louw, widow of the late Mr. Cornelis Mostert, senior, in my capacity as co-executrix testamentary with the South African Association,&c.,of my aforesaid husband,Cornelis Mostert, senior, do hereby declare to ratify and approve of everything which has already been done and performed by the aforesaid Association in the administration of the estate of the said Cornelis Mostert, senior, and which shall hereafter be done and performed ; and also hereby to grant full power and authority to the said Association, in their own name, and also (*as acting for me*) in my name, to make transfer and conveyance to the respective purchasers of immovable property from said estate, and such transfer shall be considered by me as having been made with my concurrence and knowledge, under obligation of my person and property, according to law.

E. MOSTERT.

1868.
June 25.
„ 26.
Aug. 1.
„ 25.
„ 27.
„ 28.
„ 29.
Sept. 2.

Mostert *vs.* South African Association & Another.

Cape Town, 28th August, 1863.

That, prior to the execution of the said will, to wit, on the 11th December, 1859, plaintiff passed a mortgage bond in favour of the said Cornelis Mostert, for the sum of £3,750, in payment and on mortgage of the said plaintiff's farm Valkenburg, by which bond plaintiff's father, Sybrand Jacobus Mostert, sen., bound himself as surety and co-principal debtor for the due payment of the said sum of £3,750. And that after the death of the said Cornelis Mostert, the Association, in framing the liquidation account of his estate, brought up, as one of the assets, the said mortgage bond for £3,750. That thereafter, to wit, on the 6th October, 1864, the Association, by two of their directors, William Smith and Johannes Tobias Jurgens, without the knowledge or consent of plaintiff, privately sold and transferred, or purported to sell and transfer, in their one capacity as administering executors of the said estate, to themselves in their other capacity as such Association, on their own behalf and for value received, the said mortgage bond, of which they thereupon claimed to be the lawful holders in their own right. That the Association, as such administering executors, have prepared and rendered eight several accounts of their administration, but that the liquidation account of the said estate has not yet been closed ; and that the several instalments or sums from time to time awarded to plaintiff's wife out of her father's estate, as one of his heirs, amount altogether, exclusive of her prelegacy of £300, to the sum of £660 1s. 3d., up to the 3rd of March, 1866, when the last of the said accounts was rendered, which said sum of £660 1s. 3d. does not represent the whole of her inheritance. That no part of his wife's prelegacy or inheritance has been paid to him, the same having been carried by the Association to account of the debt due for capital and interest under the said mortgage bond. That by payment made to the Association by his father, as surety under the bond, and by the credits aforesaid, the original capital of the bond has been reduced to £3,008 9s. 8d.; but that plaintiff, who has recently suffered from the late bad seasons, recently fell into arrear with his

U

1868.
June 25.
" 26.
Aug. 1.
" 25.
" 27.
" 28.
" 29.
Sept. 2.

Mostert vs. South African Association & Another.

interest, and the Association sued him, on the 7th November, for £361, being two years' interest (less £59 19s. 10d., a further instalment of the inheritance accruing due since 3rd March, 1866), and £43 4s., for premium of insurance paid by the Association on the buildings of the farm " Valkenburg." That the Association having obtained judgment on plaintiff's confession for £361, proceeded to place his estate under sequestration; and it was finally adjudicated as insolvent on the 28th November, 1867. That he confessed judgment upon the advice of the attorney of the Association, merely with the view of preventing his name from being called out in open court; and that at the time he was under an entire misconception of his rights under the will, and in total ignorance of the fact that the purchase of the bond by the Association was a mere private bargain, and not a purchase at public auction.

Plaintiff further submitted to the Court, as matters of law: 1, That the widow of the late Cornelis Mostert had not the right, after adiation, or even before adiation of her inheritance under the said will, to act in entire opposition to the agreement and joint disposition contained in the clause which directs that wherever the debts of any of the heirs should happen to exceed the amount of the inheritance of such heir from the estate of the first dying, the heir or heirs whom it may concern shall not be required to pay the excess immediately; but that it shall be sufficient for them to remain indebted to the survivor for such excess of debt above inheritance from the estate of the first dying, to be afterwards, at the death of the survivor of the testators, brought into computation with his, her, or their inheritance from the estate of the latter. 2, That inasmuch as the said mortgage bond was a debt due by one of the heirs under the will, it was not competent for the Association to bring up that bond, or any interest due thereon, as an asset in the liquidation account; but that, notwithstanding the renunciation on the part of the widow, it was the duty of the Association to follow the directions of the testator and testatrix in regard to debts due and owing to the estate by any of the heirs. 3, That the cession of the bond by the directors in favour of the Association was illegal; and consequently the Association are not the lawful holders thereof in their own right, nor as such entitled to sue for any interest due thereon. 4, That inasmuch as plaintiff, when he confessed judgment for the interest, was in total ignorance of his rights in respect of the bond, and of the facts on which his rights are founded, the said confession cannot prejudice his rights under the will, nor prevent him from having any subsequent proceedings based upon that judgment set aside. Lastly, That inasmuch as the Association, who were the only petitioning creditors, petitioned for the sequestration of plaintiff's estate at a time when no debt was legally owing by plaintiff to the Association, either in their individual capacity or in their capacity as the administering executors under the will, the order for sequestration ought to be set aside and all subsequent proceedings taken thereon annulled. Wherefore plaintiff prayed that the said Order of Court, dated the 28th November, 1867, by which his estate was finally adjudicated as insolvent, might be set aside, superseded, or otherwise revoked, and that all subsequent proceedings (including the appointment of a trustee of the said insolvent estate) taken by virtue of the said order might be annulled; that his estate might be placed in the same position in which it was immediately before such Order was made ; and that it be declared that the excess of the amount of the bond above the inheritance of his wife, or any interest due thereon, is a debt which cannot be legally claimed from him until the death of the said widow of Cornelis Mostert; and that he may have such further and other relief as to this Honourable Court shall seem meet, with costs of suit.

1868.
June 25.
„ 26.
Aug. 1.
„ 25.
„ 2 /.
„ 28.
„ 29.
Sept. 2.

Mostert vs. South African Association & Another.

Defendants pleaded, first, the general issue ; and further pleaded that the Court did, by its judgment or decree pronounced upon the 28th November, 1867, adjudge the estate of plaintiff to be sequestrated as insolvent. That the said judgment or decree was obtained in due form of law; and that the alleged facts and grounds set forth by plaintiff in his declaration as entitling him to have it set aside were all and each of them well known to him before and at the time said judgment or decree was pronounced and should then have been adduced by him, and cannot now be relied on by him as grounds for setting it aside. Wherefore they opposed to this action the plea of *rem judicatam*. They further pleaded that the South African Association, in their capacity as executors of Cornelis Mostert, prepared and rendered eight several and successive liquidation accounts of the estate. That all these accounts were so framed as to show that the widow had rejected all benefits conferred upon her by the mutual will, and had elected to claim her half of the joint estate as her own free property. That due notice was given by the Association, by advertisement in the *Government Gazette*, to all the heirs of the deceased, including the plaintiff, that the accounts were framed and lay at the office of the Association ready for inspection, and that unless objected to within fourteen days they would be considered as approved of and be acted upon by the Association as such executors. That the plaintiff did, in or about July, 1864, repair to the office of the Association for the purpose of inspecting the

U 2

1868.
June, 25.
26.
Aug. 1.
„ 25.
„ 27.
„ 2h.
„ 29.
Sept. 2.

Mostert vs. South
African Association
tion & Another.

first of the said eight accounts, which was then lying there for inspection, and did then and there inspect the same, and became and was then (if not before) fully aware that it stated and showed that the said Elizabeth Jacoba Mostert had elected, as aforesaid, not to take under the mutual will aforesaid, and not be bound by its provisions ; and that plaintiff had, in consequence, been debited with the amount of his mortgage bond for £3,750, with interest thereon from 16th February, 1861, and the joint estate was credited with the said capital and interest. That afterwards, and after the inspection and examination of the said account by plaintiff, and after he had been furnished by the Association with an extract from it on the 24th March, 1865, he repaired to the office of the Association, and there produced a receipt in the handwriting of the said Cornelis Mostert, purporting to be a receipt for interest on the bond up to the 16th February, 1862, and requested the Association to amend the account by giving him credit for interest up to that date. That certain of the heirs in the estate objected to the said receipt as not being genuine, and instructed the Association not to admit it; which instruction being communicated to plaintiff he withdrew his claim upon or under the alleged receipt, and agreed not to claim credit for any interest to a date later than 16th February, 1861. Whereupon, seeing that the said claim upon or under the said alleged receipt was the only thing in the nature of an objection that was lodged by any of the heirs against the said account, the Association treated it as unobjected to and paid out to certain of the heirs the inheritance awarded to them by the said account, and gave credit to plaintiff for his inheritance as so much money paid off by him from the bond and interest aforesaid by him due and owing. That although plaintiff had full notice and knowledge of each of the other seven accounts successively framed by the Association, he made no objection to any of them ; whereupon the Association paid out to the heirs the several sums awarded as their inheritances, and duly credited to the plaintiff the sums from time to time awarded to him as such heir. That the Association having, as executors, given credit to the joint estate of the said Cornelis Mostert and surviving spouse for the whole sum of £3,750, the capital of the bond, and interest thereupon from 16th February, 1861, till the date of the first of the eight accounts aforesaid, and having settled with the surviving widow and the heirs of the deceased out of the funds of the Association, precisely as if the Association had already received the capital and interest in full, the said Association did, as it lawfully might, cede in its capacity as executors of the deceased and agents of his surviving spouse, the said bond, with interest from 16th Febuary, 1861, to the same Association in its own right, whereby the Association became in his own right the creditors of plaintiff for the said capital and interest. That plaintiff became, not later than the latter end of 1865, fully cognizant of the fact that such cession had been made, and that the Association was the lawful holder of the bond, and was very frequently applied to for payment of interest upon it; but that he never at any time before the first meeting of creditors in his insolvent estate, held on the 11th December, 1867, raised any doubt or question regarding the right of the Association to the bond or interest, or to the manner in which the estate had been administered and settled. That the plaintiff having allowed the interest due upon his bond to fall largely into arrear, the Association was compelled to summon him provisionally for such interest, together with certain premiums of fire insurance paid by the Association for his account, amounting together to £344 4s. 2d.; whereupon plaintiff having in court confessed the debt, judgment absolute was given for that sum, with costs of suit, on the 15th November, 1867. And the matters of this plea the defendants were ready to verify. Wherefore they submitted that plaintiff was now estopped and precluded from disputing or questioning the principle or manner in which the joint estate aforesaid had being administered, or the title of the Association to be considered the lawful holders of the bond; and prayed that his claim be rejected with costs.

The plaintiff's replication was general.

Evidence having been heard on the 26th June, the case stood over till the 14th July; when it was arranged by consent that the Widow Mostert should be called upon to intervene, defendants paying costs of the day.

Postea(August 1).—(*Coram* HODGES, C.J., BELL, J., and CONNOR, J.)—It was intimated to the Court that the widow had declined to intervene, and that the other heirs, who had also been served with notice, had likewise declined.

De Villiers was then heard for the plaintiff on the whole case generally. He first referred to the fiduciary relation between the Association and the plaintiff, since by mutual will it was provided that the defendants should be co-guardians of the minor and fidei-commissary heirs. As to the confession of judgment of the 15th November, 1867, he maintained that it was made under a mixed ignorance of law and fact, and ·therefore was not binding. To meet the objection that such a confession of judgment was *res judicata*, he cited *Voet*, 4, 1, 1, and 4, 1, 26, where among the *justæ causæ* entitling to *restitutio in integrum* is "*justus*, *error."* (*Burge's Comm., vol.* 3, *p.* 1022; *Dig.* 4, 1, *ll.* 1 and 2; *Van Leeuwen, Cens. For.*, 2, 1, 4, 40; *Story's Equity Jurisprudence, vol.* 1, §§ 122—4; *Van Leeuwen's Rom.-D. Law, bk.* 5, 21, 1, *Eng. ed., p.* 604; *Evans's Pothier on Obligations, vol.* 2, *p.* 276.) He next maintained that the South African Association were not the lawful holders of the bond, inasmuch as, being executors under the mutual will, they could not buy assets from the estate of the deceased. (*Story's Equity Jurisprudence, vol.* 1, §§ 321—2.)

[BELL, J.—This is only a transfer of the bond for full value from themselves in one capacity to themselves in another. How can you make that a sale?]

It has all the requisites of a sale. *Steytler vs. Norden's Trustee*, decided in this Court November 24, 1853, is also an authority for the same position. Also *Voet*, 18, 1, 9; *Burge's Comm., vol.* 2, *p.* 465. He further referred to the peculiar form of the cession, which ran thus: " We, the undersigned, directors of the South African Association for the Administration and Settlement of Estates, also acting for the co-executrix of said estate, do hereby cede and transfer to and in favour of the said S. A. Association or order, the contents of the mortgage bond bearing date the 11th Nov., 1859, passed by J. J. Meintjes, jun , *q. q.* Sybrand Jacobus Mostert, jun., originally for the sum of £3,750, now amounting per balance to £3,111 18s. 1d. sterling, with the interest thereon from the 1st July, 1864, less the sum of £44 3s. 4d. received on account of interest, for value received. Cape Town, Church-square, 6th October, 1864. William Smith, J. T. Jurgens, Directors." Proceeding next to the question : had the widow a right to repudiate the provisions of the mutual will? he relied strongly on *Oosthuysen vs. Oosthuysen* (*S. C. Reports, Part. II., p.* 51), quoted passages from the different judgments then delivered, and argued that the widow, by taking out letters of administration, and by having acted in that capacity and taken executor's commission, had precluded herself from repudiating the will. He then went into figures to show that even were it held that the widow had a right of repudiation, there was sufficient in the estate to pay her her full half, without prejudicing the rights of the children.

Postea (25th August).—HODGES, C. J., having died in the interval, the case came on for re-argument before BELL, C. J., and DWYER, J., when *De Villiers* was re-heard for plaintiffs.

Before the case proceeded further, upon the suggestion of the Bench, the proceedings were so amended as to shape the action on the record against the South African Association simply as cessionaries of the bond, and not in their representative capacity as the executors. This was done on account of the non-intervention of the widow, the other co-executor, and the desire of the Court to prevent future difficulty on the ground of *res inter alios acta.* The Court also expressed its wish that the case should be separated into its two branches, and that the effect of the plaintiff's confession of judgment on the 15th November, 1867, should be re-argued before coming to the question of the widow's right to repudiate the mutual will.

1868.
June 25.
„ 26.
Aug. 1.
„ 25.
„ 27.
„ 28.
„ 29.
Sept. 2.

Mostert *vs.* South African Association & Another.

De Villiers was accordingly re-heard upon the first point; adding to the authorities already cited by him *Damhouder's Judicieel Practyk,* p. 286.

Porter, for defendants, maintained that the plaintiff was stopped by two distinct judgments—one which he confessed upon the 15th Nov., 1867, and the other the adjudication of sequestration upon the 28th Nov., 1867, which he allowed to go by default. Taking the latter first, he maintained that an adjudication of sequestration is a judgment of the Court according to the terms of §§ 17, 18, Ord. 6, 1843. [*De Villiers, passim,* admitted this.] In England, if no objection were raised within a limited number of days, it became a judgment on the lapse of that time. (*Griffith on Bankruptcy,* vol. 2, p. 1,130.) And by the Scotch Sequestration Acts, a period of forty days was in the same way fixed. But there are no such limits fixed in the Colonial Ordinance, so that immediately upon sequestration being adjudicated it becomes a judgment of the Court. Here, then, was an estoppal wholly irrespective of the merits of the case. And as to the scope and effect of *res judicata,* he cited 3rd *Burge,* 1014 and 1022; *Van Leeuwen's Cens. For., pt.* 2, 31, 5, *and* 2, 32, 2; *Pothier on Obligations, pt.* 4, ch. 3, § 1, pp. 559 *and* 563, *vol.* 1, 3rd Am. ed.; *Voet,* 42, 1, 29; *Perezius ad Cod.,* 7, 52, 2; *Van der Linden,* p. 262; *Voet,* 42, 2, 3, " *Nisi error juris,*" &c.; *Voet,* 42, 2, 7, " *Denique effectus,*" &c. *Voet,* 4, 1, 26, cited *contra,* he maintained must be taken to refer to *error juris,* not *error facti.* (*Dig.* 4, 1, 2, *and* 42, 2, 2.) The construction of the mutual will in this case could not be looked upon as " *error juris.*" Ignorance of its existence might have excused the plaintiff. Referring to English law on the subject of non-relief against *error juris,* he cited *Best's Principles of Evidence,* p. 46; *Marriot vs. Hampton,* 7 *T. R.,* 269, quoted in 2nd *Smith's Leading Cases,* 4th ed., p. 325; *Huffer vs. Allen and Another,* 12th *Jurist* (1866), p. 930; *Story's Equity Jurisprudence,* vol. 2, pp. 894-5 *and* 1572. *Botheroe vs. Forman,* 2nd *Swanston Rep., p.* 232. And, as to the Scotch law: *Erskine's Institutes of the Law of Scotland,* bk. 4, tit. 3, § 1, p. 1052; *S. S. Bell's Dictionary of Deci-*

sions, vol. 2, *p.* 1074, *citing McAllister vs. McAllister Trustees.* According to *Voet*, 42, 1, 28, relief against a judgment must be founded upon *res noviter veniens ad notitiam*, which the evidence shows was not the case here; for the plaintiff had full knowledge when he consented to judgment on the bond. Against " willing condemnation," by which term is described such an act as the present plaintiff did here upon the confession, relief cannot be afforded for mere mistake. (*Van Alphen's Papegaay of Formulier Boek, pt.* 1, *p.* 439; *Merula's Judicieel Practyk, p.* 186-7 *in notis*; *Van Wassenaer's Jud. Prac., de eod.*)

(August 26.)—*Porter* continued the argument by citing *Lindley's Introduction to Jurisprudence, pp.* 24-6; *Young vs. Keeley*, 16 *Ves., pp.* 348, 351.

[DWYER, J.—Must not a great distinction be drawn, in considering the question of *res judicata*, between cases solemnly argued at length in the court and a mere warrant of attorney to confess judgment given by a defendant to a plaintiff's attorney?]

Of all judgments, judgments by confession are the most conclusive. And, again, the practice in the Colony among attorneys has always been to do what Wessels in this case did with a view of saving expense to defendants who do not desire to contest an action. Had Wessels known that Mostert had rights under the will, or had that been intimated to him by Mostert, the case would have been very different. The question is, did Mostert, on the day of confession, when he went to Wessels, mean to raise any question of right, or the contrary? It is proved that Geyer, the sheriff's officer, had first advised him to confess, to save the calling of his name in court, and then he went to Wessels, and arranged accordingly.

[Bell, C.J.—Supposing Mostert, instead of confessing through Wessels, had gone to Mr. Fairbridge or any other attorney of the court, and told him what may reasonably be supposed to have been known to Redelinghuys & Wessels, namely, the history of the bond and the provisions of the will, and Fairbridge had advised him to confess judgment, would he not have been liable in an action of damages?]

No. The position and rights of surviving spouses, and especially when females, is a question of great difficulty; and if Mostert had stated the facts of the case to Fairbridge, and asked him, " What do you think I should do,—contest or confess judgment?"—and if Fairbridge had advised the latter, no action would lie, and it would be proper advice, on the strength of *Scorey vs. Scorey, Menz.*, 260. Besides, Smuts, who drew the power, though employed in the office of Redelinghuys & Wessels, was an independently admitted attorney of this court. *Blake vs. Foster*, 2 *Ball and Beat., Irish*

Reports, p. 461, and *Story's Equity Pleadings*, § 404, are also supporting authorities. Moreover, even if there had never been a judgment operating as an estoppal of the plaintiff, his acquiescence would have bound him, viewed in its relation to its effects on the status and position of the defendants, whose condition was changed by such acquiescence. (*Leyser's Meditat. ad Pand., Specimen* 289, § 4.) The defendants became cessionaries on the 6th October, and after the accounts of June, 1864, had been therefore seen and acquiesced in by the plaintiff. (*Story's Equity Jurisprudence, vol.* 1, 125, *note, and* 138 *d.*) The plaintiff is contending for a gain, but the Association is contending against a loss of £4,000, which amount they have paid out among the heirs on the strength of the plaintiff's acquiescence in the different accounts.

1868.
June 25.
„ 26.
Aug. 1.
„ 25.
„ 27.
„ 28.
„ 29.
Sept. 2.

Mostert *vs.* South African Association & Another.

[BELL, C.J.—Would not the *res judicata* doctrine applied to the confession cover merely the interest of the bond? Can it be contended that the insolvent confessed judgment on the bond itself?]

It is because the bond was due that the interest on it was due also; and the acquiescence would cover both. (*Greenleaf on Evidence,* § 534, *p.* 666.)

The Court, after consultation, set aside the confession of judgment made by the plaintiff on the 15th November, 1867, with all proceedings growing out thereof, on account of irregularity.

BELL, C.J.—As the case has been so very recently argued, it is not necessary for me to go into all the facts. The short question the Court has to decide now is, whether it shall grant the prayer of the declaration, that a judgment of the Court, obtained on confession of the plaintiff as to interest on a bond, should, or should not, be set aside; and whether, also, the adjudication of sequestration which followed on the return of *nulla bona* upon that judgment, should, or should not, be also set aside. The facts, in regard to the first, seem to me to be these, that this son-in-law of the original mortgagee having been reduced in circumstances,— how does not appear,—was called upon by the executor of his father-in-law's estate to pay a sum of £364 as interest upon a bond he had given to his father-in-law,—secured by the suretyship of his own father, for the payment of a principal sum of £3,750,—in consequence of his mother-in-law, the mother of his own wife, having chosen to renounce the benefits of, and to repudiate the mutual will of her husband and herself, and to insist upon the payment of the capital from her children. The Association served the son-in-law with a summons to pay the interest, and the case would have

1868.
June 25.
" 26.
Aug. 1.
" 25.
" 27.
" 28.
" 29.
Sept. 2.

Mostert *vs.* South African Association & Another.

come on as a provisional case in the terms of the mortgage bond. The defendant received the summons, and kept it in his pocket till the morning of the day on which the case would be called on in court. That morning he met Geyer, the sheriff's officer, who had served the summons, and some conversation took place, in the course of which he expressed to Geyer his apprehension of his name being called in court, and Geyer said : " Why don't you confess ?" The plaintiff proceeded from Geyer to the office of Messrs. Redelinghuys and Wessels, solicitors to the Association, and there met Mr. Wessels coming out of the door of the office as he was going in, and entered into some conversation with him on the subject of the summons, and repeated to him what he had already said to Geyer about his disinclination to have his name called in court. Further conversation took place, in consequence of which Mostert, the son-in-law, acceded to Wessels's proposal that he should make a confession, who suggested, as he was in a great hurry himself, going into court, that Smuts, a clerk in the office, should attend to the matter; and a power to confess, usual in these cases, was made out in the name of Smuts the clerk, under the supervision of Wessels, was altered by Wessels in some respects, and was signed then and there by the present plaintiff. With that in his possession he was taken into court, and the counsel who now appears for him in this action appeared on that occasion to confess judgment. Now, it is said such a proceeding is nothing out of the common course : that it is the common practice to make confessions in that way. I do not know how that is. This is the first time I ever knew that it was so, and I do not mean to make any observations as to whether it is regular or irregular beyond this, that any attorney who does it, does it at his peril. It may be all very well where a summons is issued in an ordinary or provisional case, or on a copy of a promissory note whereby a man undertakes to pay, thirty days after date, a sum of £50 for value received. I say it may be very kind and very considerate for the plaintiff's attorney to say to the defendant in such a case : " Oh, you had better confess ; you will save expense in that way by only paying a guinea to the counsel confessing." It is very pleasant to hear that that is the way in which attorneys conduct business, and that they show so kindly a feeling towards defendants. But if any case occurs such as this, the attorney has himself to thank that he has done that which may be worth nothing. In my opinion, the confession in this case must go for nothing. If the defendant had gone to Mr. Fairbridge, who is now his attorney, or to any other attorney, and had mentioned the matter to him, it would have been the duty of that attorney to have asked the circumstances under which he proposed to make the confession. If the attorney had not done so he would have been wanting in his duty to his client. But it was said, if he had so gone to another attorney, the case is of such a nature that in all probability the attorney would have given him the same advice to confess. That may be so, but I very much doubt whether an attorney giving such advice, without consulting counsel, would not be subject to an action for damages for giving such an opinion, if that opinion had been attended with such serious consequences as this confession has brought upon this poor client. I say nothing casting any reflection upon Mr. Wessels.; quite the contrary. I am sure he did nothing but what he meant should be well. But we must take the circumstances of the case independently of the parties to those circumstances; and, as the late Chief Justice said during the earlier part of this case heard before him,—said with the kindliness and gentlemanliness of feeling which always characterized him,—the Court cannot refrain from expressing its opinion because it may hurt the feelings of anybody. He expressed disapprobation of what Mr. Wessels had done, and I repeat that disapprobation. I think it was not becoming in him, knowing, as he must have known from his acquaintance with this estate, of the cruel circumstances under which the widow was acting to the ruin of her children. I must think, if Mr. Wessels had reflected at all, he would have thought twice before he took the confession, and he would not have taken a power to himself virtually through a third person, a clerk in his office. I say again, I do not cast any reflection upon him. It was because he believed he was acting on an acknowledged custom that he did not reflect; but that does not alter the case. The least he could have done would have been to say, "No, I will follow out the instructions of my client, but one step beyond them I will not go. You had better go and consult other attorneys." And if the plaintiff had then gone to an indifferent attorney, and that attorney, neglecting his professional duty, as I think he would have been neglecting it, had advised him to confess, and he had confessed accordingly, that would have been a good confession, and the only relief the client could have had in the case would have been possibly an action of damages against the attorney who had taken such a confession. But Mr. Wessels did not do so. Mostert never had an opportunity of going to another attorney; and, in fact, as the counsel for the defendants himself put it, he came into court not to contest any right, but to confess, to save his name being called in court. In the language of *Voet* (42, 2, 3) he acted "*per fervorem quendam*

1868.
June 25.
" 26.
Aug. 1.
" 25.
" 27.
" 28.
" 29.
Sept. 26.

Mostert *vs.* South African Association & Another.

præcipitatum." He never considered his rights, but rushed into court to save the calling of his name. It would be a gross abuse of justice if this Court were to sustain such a confession; it would be an abuse of its proceedings to take such a confession without inquiry into the character of the circumstances under which it was made. I think Wessels acted inconsiderately, and according to what he thought was a received practice; but, any way, it would sanction an abuse of practice if this Court were to say that it will take this as a good confession, or that what followed upon it must be viewed in the light of *res judicata*. I have never seen the Court so flooded with books of authorities as it is in this case, and it would indeed be cruel that a man should be taken to have in this way confessed rights which will require an elaborate discussion of two or three days to ascertain. I, for one, should be sorry indeed to hold that. It might be that if he had consulted others and confessed, I might have felt it my duty, notwithstanding the hardship, to declare him bound by that confession, and by the decree upon it as *res judicata*; but I am relieved from that painful duty by the circumstance that this was not a confession, and that there was no judgment following on it. Then it is said, moreover, that the adjudication of sequestration was another judgment, and the counsel for the plaintiff incautiously admitted during the argument that it was so. But the word "adjudication" must have misled him. It is not a judgment. It is a mere administrative order. Anyone who reads the Ordinance can see that. A distinction is made between the adjudication of sequestration and the confirmation of a liquidation account. The latter not only is a judgment, but in the language of the Ordinance is declared to have that effect. . But the mere adjudication, I repeat, is in my opinion, upon a just consideration of the Ordinance, a mere administrative order, part of the machinery of the Act, and even the petitioning creditor's debt is liable to be investigated into during the sequestration, and, it may be, be set aside. And another proof is that the Ordinance as to the sequestration declares that after everybody is paid, the remainder of the estate goes to the insolvent. Is there any similarity between that and a judgment? A judgment is between litigant parties, and decrees a certain thing to be done by the one to the other. Adjudication of sequestration is a mere administrative order, which, creating a recourse on the insolvent's property, so to say, continues living and open to revision during the insolvency. The judgment on the confession, and the adjudication following on it, will both be set aside. The ground, therefore, may be considered clear for the son-in-law contesting with his mother-in-law whether she had a right to repudiate the mutual will.

DWYER, J.: I am also of opinion that the power of attorney of the 15th November, 1867, was null and void, and that, therefore, all proceedings arising out of the confession obtained thereupon must be set aside. I quite concur with what has been said by my brother BELL in his judgment, as to what is the proper definition and effect of an adjudication of sequestration. Now, in this case it is evident, and was indeed conceded on both sides, that the present plaintiff, the defendant in the former action, was anxious that his name should not be called in court, and for that purpose he gave this power to confess. But has he avoided the notoriety? Look at the dates. On the 15th November he gave the power, and confessed judgment on the 22nd. The return of *nulla bona* is dated the same day; and soon after this follow the proceedings in sequestration, which give that very notoriety he wished to avoid. There is something here looks like bad faith in this respect; and that alone would be a ground for setting aside a confession which was really made through the plaintiff's attorneys in that action, and by them, acting as attorneys for the Association, through a clerk in their office. I quite concur, moreover, that if this be the practice of attorneys here, to make confession for defendants although acting for plaintiffs, the sooner such a practice is upset the better. If attorneys—and respectable attorneys such as Redelinghuys and Wessels—choose to adopt such a practice, they must be prepared to accept as the consequence of the act that a man to whom they no doubt meant kindness should afterwards succeed in overthrowing the confession by showing an apparent ingratitude. The great fallacy in the defendant's argument was the attempt to call the confession a *res judicata*. One of the cases—and I am satisfied to rest my judgment upon that—cited by Mr. Porter was *Blake vs. Foster*, 2 *Ball & Beatty, p.* 461, an Irish case. That case was decided in 1813, and was five days before a full Court; and even then there was an application to file a supplementary bill, and the Court took time to consider from the 28th February to the 7th March. It is impossible to contend that a judgment obtained against a defendant on a confession sued out by the plaintiff's attorney is *res judicata*. I quite agree with Mr. Porter in his able argument, showing so much learning and research in the case, that if this were *res judicata* it would be utterly impossible to set it aside. But it is not a judgment made regularly and in due form. I was not aware, till the circumstance was just now mentioned by my brother BELL, that the late Chief Justice had expressed a similar opinion as to the nullity of this confession, and the importance of attending better to the way in which such confessions are made. And when we were, more or less,

1888.
June 25.
„ 26.
Aug. 1.
„ 25.
„ 27.
„ 28.
„ 29.
Sept. 2.

Mostert *vs.* South African Association & Another.

1868.
June 25.
„ 26.
Aug. 1.
„ 25.
„ 27.
„ 28.
„ 29.
Sept. 2.

Mostert vs. South African Association & Another.

cautioned by Mr. Porter against interfering with the landmarks of the law and practice, on the strength of the great Roman-Dutch authorities cited to us from that Roman-Dutch law we are bound to administer, it is a consolation to me to find that with reference to that learned Judge who presided so long as the head of this Court, I can decide this case quite in accordance with the sentiments he expressed. My brother BELL has gone so fully into the matter that it is unnecessary for me to add more than that I fully concur that the power of attorney dated 15th November, 1867, must be set aside, and also all subsequent proceedings thereupon.

Postea (August 27).—*De Villiers* was heard on the second branch of the case : the right of the widow to repudiate the provisions of the mutual will, and to fall back upon her half in community. He first laid down the following five heads, or propositions, for argument : 1. That the defendants are not lawful holders of the bond in their own right. 2. That if the Court shall hold that they are, then the whole of the bond is subject to the same equities as the estate from which the Association purchased it. 3. That the bond, while in the estate, was subject to the second stipulation in the will ; and that payment of the bond could not therefore be claimed from the plaintiff. 4. That if the Court hold that the widow had a right to repudiate after taking out letters of administration and acting under the will, then her renunciation cannot deprive the plaintiff of the benefit conferred on him by the will as long as the widow gets one-half of the net assets of the estate, and the other heirs are not deprived of their legal rights. 5. That there has not been such an acquiescence on the part of the plaintiff in the acts of defendant as to deprive him of his rights under the will, whatever they may be. On the first point, he argued, as he had done on the 25th August, that there had been a purchase of the bond by the executors from the estate they administered, and that this was illegal (*Lewin* on *Trusts, p.* 360), and was proceeding to quote other authorities to show that trustees cannot deal with the property of their *cestui que* trusts, when he was stopped by the Court giving an intimation of its opinion that it regarded the transaction not as a sale, but as a mere transposition of creditors on the bond, for full value. As to the second point, this needed no argument. Notice must be taken for granted ; and then the purchase of the bond, after such notice, would subject the cessionaries to all the equities of the cedent. The third was the main point in the case. Had Mrs. Mostert the right to repudiate ? The testator died 15th December, 1862. Mrs. Mostert and the Association took out letters of administration on the

23rd December following. On the 21st January, 1863, Mrs. Mostert, by letter, renounced her prelegacy; but it was not until the 18th September that she repudiated, eight months after the testator's death. *Oosthuysen vs. Oosthuysen, S. C. Reports, pt. II, 50 ; Dufour vs. Pereira, 1 Dick. 419, referred to in* 1 *Williams on Executors, 5th ed., p.* 109.) The enjoyment of executor's commission by Mrs. Mostert was the acceptance of a benefit under the mutual will, the commission having been paid out of the whole joint estate. The will itself directly referred to the commission of the executors, and stipulated that it should be taxed. The mere taking out of letters of administration without any enjoyment of benefit was virtually adiation and adoption of the mutual will ; after which adiation and adoption the survivor could not recede from the terms of the will. In *Ashburne vs. Maguire,* 2 *White & Tudor's Leading Cases, 2nd ed., p.* 229, it is laid down that a legacy of interest and bond is a specific legacy, and therefore no argument can be founded *contra* to show that the bequest in *Oosthuysen vs. Oosthuysen* having been a farm, there was any distinction in principle, on that ground, between the two cases. *(*1*st Roper on Legacies, 3rd ed. p.* 199.) *Scorey vs. Scorey, 2nd Menz.,* 231, which will be relied on *contra*, was not the case of a mutual will. As to the fourth point (the Court having intimated that it was unnecessary now to go into accounts, as they could better be ascertained by a reference to the Master), he assumed that, subject to such finding by the Master, the widow would get her half and the children their legitimate if the £1,200 which had, after the testator's death, been paid into the estate by the plaintiff's father, as surety on the bond, were taken as an asset in the estate. In order to find out what the parties were entitled to, all money paid into the estate, whether rightly or wrongly, must be taken, for the purpose of this computation, to be part of the assets. And if the widow could so get her half, without interfering with the dispositions of the will, then all the provisions of the will may stand, being *jus tertii,* and of other heirs than the plaintiff. But if the heirs could not be fully paid their legitimate, then he admitted that the bond must be diminished by so much as would be required to make up the legitimate. As to the sixth point, acquiescence can only bind where the party acquiescing had the fullest knowledge of what he was doing, and of its legal consequences to himself. (*Lewin on Trusts, pp.* 661-3 *; Fox vs. Macraith,* 1 *W. and T. Leading Cases, p.* 141, *note, and authorities there cited.)*

(Friday, August 28.)—*Porter* argued for defendants, following, substantially, the same divisions as those marked out for the plaintiff. As to the first point: There was

1866.
June 25.
„ 26.
Aug. 1.
„ 25.
„ 27.
„ 28.
„ 29.
Sept. 2.

Mostert *vs.* South African Association & Another.

1868.
June 25.
" 26.
Aug. 1.
" 25.
" 27.
" 28.
" 29.
Sept. 2.

Mostert *vs.* South African Association & Another.

no sale of the bond, but a transfer for full value, according to the useful and proved practice of the old Orphan Chamber, and also of all executorial boards in the Colony. Further, it does not lie in plaintiff's mouth, suing, as he does, as a debtor and not as an heir, to raise a question which only the *cestui que* trust can raise. As to the second point, that principle is admitted. As to the third point: It is said, *contra*, that if a surviving spouse takes any benefit from the deceased spouse, and the will of the deceased spouse is of such a nature as to show that that benefit was made contingent upon the carrying out of the will as regarded some of the property of the surviving spouse, then the surviving spouse is bound and cannot refuse to allow his or her property to go in the conditional way. Admitting that that is the principle, has this surviving spouse received a benefit? No doubt she drew commission as the executrix; but that is not such a benefit under the will as can have any effect upon her right, if she had a right, to repudiate the will and claim her half. And this for two reasons. Firstly, commission is not, in contemplation of law, a benefit derived from the estate of the deceased, but is a mere compensation of work and labour. Secondly, under the circumstances of this case the widow has drawn no commission out of the half of the estate belonging to her deceased husband. Ord. No. 104, § 37 (*Cape Statute Law, p.* 277) and Shedule C, p. 280, leave it discretionary with the Master to fix an executor's recompense. He may, if he sees cause, give none at all, although, for convenience sake, there are no doubt certain usual recognized allowances. Really and truly, however, it may be formally, the widow received no commission in her husband's estate. It is common to speak of the executor of the joint estate, but that is an impropriety of speech. It should be the executor of the will of the first dying; for the surviving spouse can have no will or executor, since *nemo est hæres viventis*. The executor sells the joint estate, therefore, as executor of the deceased's half, and as agent of the survivor as to the other half. In this case, the whole joint estate was realized, and the commission charged on the assets of the whole estate; and by its division equally between herself and the Association she in reality only drew commission on her own half. Whatever be the form of account, it would lead to too much subtlety to hold otherwise. Nor can the mere joint proving of the will be taken as an adoption of the will; it is a mere act of piety and duty to the deceased. It might be that the will contained something inconsistent with the legal rights of the party proving. There next comes the great and important question as to the right of surviving spouses, being widows, to repudiate a mutual will. This point has never been decided in this Court; the decisions given having been uniformly in cases where the husband was the survivor. Can it be laid down that a mutual will must be so construed that it shall bind by its own force the survivor, either before or at the moment of the death of the first dying, so as to preclude that survivor from freedom of disposition afterwards? It is a great principle of every system of jurisprudence where wills are allowed, that until the last gasp every one has the power to make or change his will as he thinks fit. *Pacta successoria* contracts regulating the succession of living persons, are void. (*Voet*, 2, 14, 16.) No agreement can by law be made by A and B, both living, that B shall make C his heir. (*Voet*, 28, 3, 10.) A mutual will, in theory of law, is two different wills in one paper writing, but having no different effect than if separately made. There are two estates growing out of the community of marriage, and two wills; and all general principles as to a separate will apply, presumptively at least, to the case in which the will is mutual as well as one in which it is separate. It is usual for spouses to make a mutual will, but it is not universal; and even where a mutual will is made it is by no means uncommon to appoint different executors for each spouse. Then as to the revocability of the mutual will once made, this depends on the general question, can a husband and wife married in community contract? There are no doubt authorities which seem to go to the extent of saying that they are entitled to contract, as long as they do not infringe upon the prohibition to donate to each other. (*Voet*, 23, 2, 63 ; *Voet*, 24, 1, 8 ; "*Licet enim*," &c.) But there is this distinction, that not one case put in *Voet*, or that can be found elsewhere, will go to the extent of saying that any contract between husband and wife will bind the wife to make a will in a particular manner if she happen to be the survivor. No two spouses married in community could go this day into the office of a notary public and say that it is agreed between them that neither of them shall make a will, whether during the subsistence of the marriage or after the termination thereof, except a will in favour of C D, as sole and universal heir, Such a contract would be waste paper, involving the *pactum successorium*, contrary to principle and law. It is very important to look who in this case is the survivor. The husband is the guardian for the wife ; he is presumed to exercise authority over her, and she to act under his coercion. It might be that the husband would be bound, if he proved the survivor, by the contract made with his wife; but it cannot be that the wife is bound when she proves the survivor. (*Groenewegen, De Leg. Abr.,*

1868.
June 25.
„ 26.
Aug. 1.
„ 25.
„ 27.
„ 28.
„ 29.
Sept. 2.

Mostert *vs.* South African Association & Another.

x

1868.
June 25.
„ 26.
Aug. 1.
„ 25.
„ 27.
„ 28.
„ 29
Sept. 2.
Mostert vs. South African Association & Another.

ad Cod. 4, 29, 11; *Beucher's Fris. Decis., ch.* 182; *Scorey vs. Scorey,* 2 *Menz. Rep., p.* 234.) In Scorey's case, although it is not stated in the report, it is found on reference that the widow was not the executrix. It is said, *contra,* Scorey's is not the case of a mutual will; but it is an *a fortiori* case, for a mutual will is only an implied contract to give up rights under community; but in *Scorey vs. Scorey* there was express contract. The only principle which prevents a surviving spouse both altering her own will and taking the benefits of the husband's will is, that, by presumption of law, the deceased is understood to have been allowed to make a will of the survivor by the survivor's consent. But that can never benefit a surviving widow who rejects the benefit and claims. (*V. d. Berg's Advys Boek, vol.* 2, Cons. 210, *p.* 578; *Voet,* 29, 2, 23, "*Plane si mulier ;*" *Huber's Prælec., bk* 2, *tit.* 17, § 3; *and bk.* 28, *tit.* 3, § 4.) The views of *Huber,* it is true, are general, irrespective of sex; but the previous authorities have reference specially to the case of a surviving widow. Unless *Scorey vs. Scorey* be overruled, it is impossible to hold that expressly and still less by implication, can a woman deprive herself of the right of afterwards saying, " I now fall back upon my primary rights, which I now find would be interfered with if I am to carry out the mutual will." There may, no doubt, be a *pactum de non revocando* entered into, but it must be express, and not implied from the effect of the mutual will. (*Leyser, Med. ad Pand., Specimen* 43, § 7, *and Specimen* 351.) The doctrine of a contract is untenable, for if such contract commence from the moment the will is made, then neither party could alter that contract during life, except with the consent of the other. But if it be shown that, by our law, not only without the consent, but against the will, and even without the knowledge of the other, either party can alter the will during lifetime, then all notion of a contract is exploded. (*V. d. Keessel, Th.* 298, *Latin ed.*) It is curious to notice that in the first edition of the valuable translation of this Thesis by Mr. Lorenz, the translation is the opposite of the original; but that has been corrected in the second edition, issued in 1868.

[Bell, C.J.—Does not *Van der Keessel,* then, lay down that it is open to one of the spouses to commit fraud upon the other?]

It may not be thought a strictly honest mode of action; but it is in deference to the great principle that no such contract between the spouses can legally tie the hands of either; for the right to change is common to both. No authority can be produced *contra* to show that in the case of a mutual will neither party can revoke except openly and with the concurrence of both. *Van der Keessel* is a clear authority for the contrary position. Moreover, in the will before the Court there is nothing like a contract. There is only a common testamentary intent, expressed at a particular moment, in regard to a particular part of the joint estate, that is, in regard to the debts due by the children. On general principles, if A and B leaves C £1,000 upon the death of the first dying,—or, suppose a mutual will, in which A B and C D, before a notary, institute their children sole and universal heirs, and stop,—then, one dies, the children are heirs of the property of the one who is dead, but not of the one who is living. By our law, marriage is a community, or partnership, and the same general principles apply. (*Vinnius Select. Quæst., bk.* 2, *ch.* 26 ; *Voet*, 30, 1, 28.) In the leading cases on mutual wills decided in this Court, there was an adiation and acceptance of benefits. Neither *Britz vs. Britz*, in 1842 (*vide Appendix, post*), nor *Neethling vs. Neethling*, in 1853 (*vide Appendix post*), nor *Oosthuysen vs. Oosthuysen*, in 1868, can be taken as authorities for holding that it is the mere contract in the mutual will that binds the survivor, altogether irrespective of the adoption or repudiation of the will.

(August 29.)—The principal authorities for the doctrine that surviving spouses may be bound are *Grotius*, 2, 15, 9 ; *V. d. K., Th.* 283 ; *Van Leeuwen R. D. Law*, 3, 11, 7. In all of them perception of benefit is made the test, and not the technical adiation simply. As to *Dufour vs. Pereira*, relied on *contra*, it will be seen from the judgment of Lord Loughborough, in *Walpole vs. Awford*, 3 *Ves.*, 416, that there was enjoyment of benefit in that case, and that it amounted pretty much to our *Neethling vs. Neethling*. As to the widow's clear right to repudiate, see the following authorities : *V. d. Berg's Advys Boek* 2, *Cons.* 210 ; *Dutch Consultations*, 2, 272 ; *do.*, 4, 43 ; *do.*, 1. 50 ; *do*, 3, 3, *n.* 4 *and* 5 ; *do.*, 2, 102 ; *V. d. B.'s Adv. Bk.* 32 ; *do.*, 1, 50 ; *do.*, 1, 210 ; *do.*, 3, 65 ; *Utrechtsche Consultatien* 1, 61 ; *Coren, Obs.* 11 ; *do., Obs.* 12 ; *V. d. Linden's* note to p. 142 of his Dutch translation of *Pothier's Obligations*. *Voet*, 28, 3, 11, is rendered clear by a reference to the Dutch *Cons. pt.* 2, *Cons.* 275, cited by that author, which was a clear case of enjoyment of benefits. As to the fourth point : if the £1,200 paid by plaintiff's father, as his surety, into the joint estate is not taken as an asset,— which it should not be, the surety having made a wrong payment,—then there is not enough to give the widow her half and the children their legitimate, and yet let the will stand. And with reference to the " debts " forgiven in the will, it cannot be said that they include a mortgage bond with a solvent surety. If that did not continue due, together with its accruing interest, there might be nothing for the widow to live upon, which could not be the testator's intention. No doubt the account of the joint estate framed by the Association on the testator's death should have been made up on the principle of allowing the widow to claim one-half only of the bond, and regarding the other half as a legacy by the first dying of so much as was not covered by the inheritance; but that account can in so far be corrected. As to the fifth point, the evidence of the plaintiff's acquiescence is strong. Certain payments were made on the strength of that acquiescence; and where it is a question whether the Association should lose, or the plaintiff, the acquiescence of the latter should make the loss his

(September 2.)—*De Villiers*, in reply, dwelt chiefly on the third point. The wills in *Oosthuysen vs. Oosthuysen* and in the present case are of the same effect. For although in *Oosthuysen vs. Oosthuysen* the survivor was appointed sole and universal heir on condition of educating and supporting the children, and in the present case the survivor and children are instituted joint heirs, yet it has been held in this Court, in *Oosthuysen and Du Toit vs. Mocke*, 19th September, 1865, that in both cases the survivor is joint heir with the children. The second clause in the will in this case amounts to *legatum liberaticnis*. (*Voet*, 34, 3, 1; 34, 3, 5.) By our law, husband and wife can contract. (*Voet*, 23, 2, 63.) And on the fifth point he cited *Marker vs. Marker*, 9 *Hare's Rep.*, p. 16; *Cochrell vs. Cholmley*, 1 *Rus. and Myl.*, 419; and *Burrows vs. Walls*, 5 *de G., McN. and Gord.*

[DWYER, J., on this point also referred to *Reis vs. Executors of Galloway*, Menz., 186.]

Cur. adv. vult.

[Plaintiff's Attorneys, *Fairbridge & Arderne*.
Defendants' Attorneys, *Redelinghuys & Wessels*.]

MAGISTRATES' REVIEWED CASES.

ACT 17, 1867, § 2.

Imprisonment with Hard Labour.—Spare Diet.

DWYER, J., said that a case had come before him as Judge of the week, in which a Magistrate had sentenced a prisoner to twelve months' hard labour and spare diet. Now, in the 2nd section of Act No. 17 of 1867, it was provided that when a person was sentenced to more than three months' imprisonment, spare diet could not be inflicted. The sentence, therefore, would be quashed, as far as the spare diet was concerned.

1868
Nov. 16.

ACT 17, 1867, §§ 7, 8.

DWYER, J., said there was another case, in which the prisoner was indicted for receiving a certain portion of the carcase of a sheep, and sentenced to twelve months' imprisonment. Now, from a case mentioned in *Buch. Rep.*, p. 141, it appeared that this Court had decided that the Magistrate could not exceed his ordinary jurisdiction in a case of receiving a portion of the carcase of a sheep; and therefore the prisoner should only have received a sentence of three months. The sentence passed must, under the circumstances, be quashed.

Nov. 16.

ACT No. 16, 1864.

Bell, C.J., said that among the cases which had come before him recently, as Judge of the week, was that of *The Queen vs. Schwart and others*, charged with the theft of a sheep. The prisoners were sentenced to receive twenty-five lashes each, and to be imprisoned with hard labour, until the proceedings were returned from the Registrar of

Nov. 17.

1868.
Nov. 17.

the Supreme Court. So far as the imprisonment with hard labour was concerned, the sentence was illegal, and he sent it back with a recommendation that it should be amended by omitting the hard labour. The papers afterwards came back to him, and he then found that the sentence was so altered as to be made a new sentence altogether; for in this instance the prisoners were ordered not only to receive the twenty-five lashes, and to be imprisoned till the proceedings were returned as confirmed by the Supreme Court, but the prisoners were also sentenced among them to pay the sum of 10s., or a sheep of the value of that they had stolen. The Act authorized the Magistrate to inquire into the value of the sheep stolen, to condemn the prisoners to pay the value, and to hand it over to the proper party after a certain course of proceedings. But that was not the course which the Magistrate had taken. He had fined the men 10s., and ordered the money to be paid to the order of the owner of the sheep. That was wrong altogether; because the provision of the Act required that the value of the sheep stolen should be paid into the Treasury. So far as the fine was concerned, therefore, the sentence must be sent back; but the papers must again be returned, because there were other irregularities, of which he must take notice in another way.

Dec. 14.

DENYSSEN, J., said that a Magistrate's Court case had come before him, in which Harvey Ross and Susan Ross were charged with receiving stolen goods at Papendorp, on the 1st instant, knowing the same to have been stolen. They pleaded not guilty, but were sentenced to three months' imprisonment, with hard labour. Upon the record there was no evidence that any theft was committed at all to begin with, and, moreover, the evidence of a police officer was very meagre, and, although somewhat suspicious, was not such as to convict the parties of the crime of which they stood charged, namely, receiving stolen goods knowing them to have been stolen. The sentence must, therefore, be quashed.

ACT 17, 1867, § 2.

Dec. 29.

DENYSSEN, J., said that among the Magistrates' cases which had come before him was one from Namaqualand, in which the prisoner was charged with the theft of a goat, and, being convicted, was sentenced to four months' imprisonment; the first month with spare diet on alternate days, and the remainder with hard labour. By the provisions of Act No. 17 of 1867, section 2, spare diet could not be given when the imprisonment was to exceed three months; and the sentence, therefore, must be so far amended.

1868.
Dec. 29.

DWYER, J., said that amongst the Magistrates' cases which had come before him, was that of *The Queen vs. Lehmkuhl*, in which the prisoner was charged with destroying a packet of letters by throwing it into a well. The letters were, in the first place, alleged to have been destroyed by a man named Lee, who was convicted and sentenced to three months' hard labour; but something which was said by him at his examination led the Attorney-General to order proceedings to be taken against Lehmkuhl, Lee having said that Lehmkuhl told him to destroy the letters. Lehmkuhl kept a post office, and for some reason or other certain parties chose to send their letters to another post office, instead of allowing them to pass through Lehmkuhl's hands; and Lee's statement was that Lehmkuhl, in consequence of this, induced him to destroy the letters. The letters were thrown into a well, but they were afterwards taken out, and were not actually destroyed. Of that there could be no doubt; but then, Lee's was almost the only evidence against Lehmkuhl, and the evidence altogether, both for the prosecution and the defence, was very contradictory. Lee, in fact, contradicted himself on most material points, and, under the circumstances, it was the opinion of his learned brother (DENYSSEN, J.), as well as his own, that the conviction must be quashed. There was one point, in connection with this case, to which he wished particularly to direct the attention of Resident Magistrates. It appeared from the proceedings that the Resident Magistrate refused to allow the prisoner's agent to cross-examine the witnesses at the preliminary examination. His Lordship could hardly believe that it was so, for it was very important that there should be a full cross-examination of witnesses, both for the sake of the prisoner himself and also for the sake of the country, in order to prevent the expense of sending cases to Circuit Courts which might fail there, and which might never have been sent for trial at all if there had been a proper cross-examination at the preliminary examination. It ought therefore to be known to Resident Magistrates, that in all cases a full cross-examination of witnesses for the prosecution should be allowed to prisoners.

APPENDIX.

MUTUAL WILLS.

[For convenience of reference, the following two leading cases on the right of surviving spouses to make wills in conflict with the prior mutual wills of such surviving and their predeceased spouses (viz., *Brits vs. Brits's Executors*, decided 28th February, 1842, and *Neethling vs. Neethling's Executors*, decided 9th August, 1853), are given as an Appendix to this number. [*Et vide Oosthuysen vs. Oosthuysen, pt. II, p. 51*; and *Mostert vs. S. A. Association, pt. IV, p. 286.*]

BRITS vs. BRITS'S EXECUTORS.

Mutual Will: Will by Survivor contrary to terms of, set aside, and Transfer of a Farm ordered under the Mutual Will.

Husband and wife executed a joint will, whereby they made the survivor sole and universal heir or heiress of all the property of the first dying, movable or immovable, to be enjoyed as sole and own property, with the qualification that the survivor should educate and support the children of the marriage until majority, marriage, or other approved state, and then pay to them such amount of money as legitim as the survivor should conscientiously, and according to the state of affairs, find to be due. The will also contained a reciprocal appointment of the survivor as executor or executrix of the predecessor, and administrator of the estate, and the usual reservatory clause. Further, a clause which directed that in the event of the survivor remarrying, such survivor should, before such remarriage, have the whole estate valued. In respect of one-half of the whole estate, the predecessor nominated the children of the marriage his or her heirs in such half or equal portions; and special provision was also made that in case of remarriage the survivor should, nevertheless, enjoy possession of the property until the time fixed for paying the legitim in case of no remarriage. The estate was meanwhile to be converted into money, but from the sale was to be exempted the farm Doorn Kraal, which the survivor might take possession of for the sum of 11,000 guilders,

*under an obligation to make it devolve on the son of the
marriage, Hans Jacob Brits, or his children, if he should
predecease the surviving spouse. The wife died first; and
the husband, after a term, remarried, and made a will
whereby he revoked the first will of himself and his first
wife so far as Doorn Kraal was concerned, and directed
the farm to be sold, and the proceeds applied to the purposes of his sole will. The son of his first marriage had
died, leaving a son, who, after the death of his grandfather, brought this action against the executors appointed
by the grandfather's sole will, praying that they might be
decreed to give him possession of the farm Doorn Kraal
on his paying the 11,000 guilders ; and that the will of his
grandfather, so far as it revoked the bequest of the farm
aforesaid, might be set aside as null. The Court gave
judgment in terms of the prayer of the declaration, thereby
affirming that a joint will dealing re* singulari *was not
revocable by the survivor, as subsequently in Neethling's
case* (post.) *it affirmed that a joint will was not revocable
by the survivor where it dealt* universitate.

This was an action to cancel a testamentary disposition, and to compel transfer of a farm.

The declaration stated that Cornelis Jacob Brits, and his then wife, Judith Odendaal, both deceased, did by their mutual will and testament, bearing date the 25th November, 1808, declare it to be, *inter alia,* " their joint will and desire that they appointed each other reciprocally, that is, the first dying the survivor of them, as their sole and universal heir or heirs, and the same in all the property to be left by them, movable and immovable, both such as they are already or may in future become possessed of, without any exception, to be possessed by them for ever, as free and own property, without the gainsay of any person ; everything with this understanding, however, that the survivor remains bound and obliged to educate the children already or still to be procreated in this marriage, honestly and in the principles of the Christian religion, and to maintain them until they shall attain their majority, be married before that time, or come to other approved states, when to each of them shall have to be paid, as paternal or maternal inheritance, such an amount as conscientiously, and according to the condition of the estate, shall be found to be proper, which the survivor may fix at the legitimate portion ; they being, however, obliged in case of remarriage, and before the consummation thereof, to prove at the hands (*aan handen te bewyzen*) of two good men of irreproachable character, to be chosen as superintending guardians, the exact moiety of the whole of

1842.
Feb 28.

Brits *vs.* Brits's Executors

the joint estate on behalf of the joint children procreated by the testators in this marriage, as the first dying (if his or her child or children should be alive at the time of the remarriage of the survivor) in that case calls and appoints as his or her sole and universal heirs, his or her said surviving child or children, or the same in equal portions in all his or her property, nothing in the world excepted; and in case of predecease of one or more of them, their lawful descendants by representation. The survivor, however, shall remain in the full possession of their inheritances until the aforesaid time, in order to be the better enabled to maintain and educate them from the usufruct thereof, for which purpose the whole of the joint estate is to be sold by public sale, and according to the proceeds thereof the shares of the inheritance of the children are to be regulated. From this sale, however, are to be exempted, 1st, the place of residence of the testators, the farm Doorn Kraal, situated at the Duivenhok's River, of which the survivor may take possession for a sum of 11,000 Cape guilders; being obliged, however, to cause the said place to devolve on the child at present procreated by the testators, named Hans Jacob, or, in case of his predecease (if he shall leave children), on his eldest son, for the same sum."

And the plaintiff further said that the said Judith Odendaal having departed this life on or about the 17th October, 1829, she did by her death confirm the said last will and testamentary disposition touching the farm or place named Doorn Kraal. That the testators did by their said joint will appoint each other to be executor or executrix thereof, and did, moreover, by a certain private or underhand paper writing, signed by them, and without a date, appoint their only son, Hans Jacob Brits (the plaintiff's father), and one Johannes Odendaal, to be joint executors of the said will. That upon the decease of the said Judith Odendaal, wife of the said Cornelis Jacob Brits, and in the winding up and liquidating their joint estate, it was mutually agreed by and with the said Cornelis Jacob Brits and the said Hans Jacob Brits and Johannes Odendaal, in their capacity as joint executors of the said joint will and testament, that the place or farm Doorn Kraal should devolve upon the said Hans Jacob Brits at the decease of his father, in the terms of the joint will, and that they did, in consequence of such agreement and understanding, allow the said Cornelis Jacob Brits to remain in possession of the whole of the joint estate, without selling off the same, in terms of the said joint last will of the said Cornelis Jacob Brits and Judith Odendaal. That the said Hans Jacob Brits (the plaintiff's father) has since departed this life on the 15th April, 1841, and that plaintiff is his eldest son, and by virtue of the said joint will of his grandparents, and of the premises, is entitled to the possession and succession of Doorn Kraal. That the said Cornelis Jacob Brits entered upon a second marriage with one Christina Frederica Steyn, then being a widow of Matthias Pieter Taute, and, being so married, did, on the 29th January, 1839, make and execute a private or underhand last will and testament, whereby he revoked and annulled the aforesaid legacy of Doorn Kraal, made to the plaintiff's father or (in the event of his predecease) to the plaintiff, out of the joint estate of his late grandfather and grandmother. But the plaintiff said that such revocation is illegal, and of no effect at law to deprive him of the right of claiming the possession of Doorn Kraal in the terms and upon the conditions set forth in the said last will of Cornelis Jacob Brits and his then wife, Judith Odendaal, bearing date 25th November, 1808. Wherefore plaintiff claimed that defendants, in their above capacity, may be decreed to give him possession and legal transfer of the said place or farm, named Doorn Kraal, upon his paying to the defendants, in their said capacity, the sum 11,000 Cape guilders, or £275, in terms of the joint will and testament of the said Cornelis Jacob Brits and his first wife, Judith Odendaal; and that that part of the will of the late Cornelis Jacob Brits, deceased, bearing date the 29th of January, 1829, in so far as it revokes the legacy of Doorn Kraal, may be set aside and annulled, and that the defendants, in their aforesaid capacity, may be condemned in the costs of suit.

Defendants—admitting their capacity; the mutual will and testament of the 25th November, 1808; the death of Judith Odendaal at the time mentioned in the declaration; the appointment of executors, as therein stated; the death of Hans Jacob Brits at the time therein alleged, and the averment therein made that the plaintiff is his eldest son; and the second marriage and last will of Cornelis Jacob Brits, as in the said declaration more particularly mentioned,—as to all other allegations pleaded the general issue. And the plaintiff replied generally.

Cloete, for plaintiff, put in the will of old C. J. Brits and Judith Odendaal, dated the 25th November, 1808, and the appointment of Hans Jacob Brits and Johannes Odendaal as executors thereof; and the will dated 29th January, 1831, mentioned in the declaration; and called

Johannes Odendaal, who deposed: I live now near Cradock. I was the brother of the late Judith Odendaal, Brits's first wife. She died in 1829. I then lived in the district of Swellendam. I was one of the executors of the mutual will of herself and husband; and Hans Jacob Brits, their only child, was the other executor. He was then past the age of majority. After his death, there was no sale made, either by the executor or by the surviving husband of the general estate, before his second marriage. Seven or eight years after my sister's death, Brits remarried. Before his second marriage, I and Hans, his son, made a sort of valuation of his estate. We found that according to that valuation the whole estate, with the exception of Doorn Kraal, was worth 90,000 guilders. Doorn Kraal was excluded from the valuation, and remained as it was, because nothing could be done with it until after old Brits's death, in consequence of the provisions of the will. No value was put upon it. It was never brought into account. I apportioned 30,000 guilders to Hans, by awarding to him the farm Krans River for 24,000, and the slave girl Flora, with her children, for 6,000. The value of 90,000 guilders was a moderate valuation. Brits remarried soon after this. His wife's estate was then insolvent, and he rehabilitated it by making an arrangement with the executors. Soon after the marriage, Brits wanted to sell Doorn Kraal. He advertised the sale of it. On hearing of this, I went to him and asked how he could do this, as the place was left to his son; and he said he would come down and present an application to the Court to know if he could sell it. He went, and on his return I found he had sold the place by private sale to one Dirk Odendaal. I objected to this. He had sold the place for 25,000 guilders, and he offered to put it out on interest, and he would get the interest during his life, and after his death his son Hans should get the capital. I did not consent to this, and told him I would take legal proceedings to stop the sale; and the agreement to sell to Dirk Odendaal was cancelled, after he had lived a year in it. [*Cross-examined:*] I only awarded to Hans 30,000 guilders instead of 45,000, because there were outstanding debts due by the estate. Hans was present with me at the valuation. Doorn Kraal was not valued in it 24,000 guilders. It was a year after the valuation that I spoke to Brits about his sale to Odendaal. I never told Van der Spuy that Doorn Kraal was valued in. Hans never received more than 30,000 guilders.

Cloete, for plaintiff, was not called upon.

Porter, for defendants, after quoting *Voet,* 28, 3, 11, *Denique,* and *Cens. For.* 3, 11, 7, gave up the case.

Judgment was given for plaintiffs accordingly, including the costs of an interdict heretofore granted in the matter.

[Plaintiff's Attorney, *Buissinne.*
Defendants' Attorneys,, *Truter & Meeser.*]

HOFMEYR, NEETHLING'S CURATOR, vs. DE WET, NEETHLING'S EXECUTOR.

Close Will. Mutual Will.

Close Will; What is included under.

All papers found in a close will by the notary, at his opening thereof, must, when such close will has been executed and superscribed with the required solemnities, be taken to form part of such will, leaving any contrariety or repugnance between the separate papers so enclosed for the consideration and construction of the Court.

Mutual Will: Action to set aside a separate Will and Codicil by a Surviving Spouse in opposition to the terms of.

Where spouses made a joint will, directing, as to the whole common estate, that the survivor should enjoy the usufruct thereof during life, and that after her death the common estate should, after the deduction of certain legacies, form a poor fund for the support of indigent relations, and where for twelve years the surviving widow enjoyed the usufruct accordingly.—HELD : *that by her adiation and acceptance of such benefits under the joint will, she could not after her husband's death make a separate testamentary disposition in opposition to the terms of the joint will aforesaid; wherefore her separate testamentary disposition so made was set aside accordingly.*

In this action, the defendants were summoned as executors testamentary of the will of the late Anna Catherina Neethling, born Smuts, widow of the late J. H Neethling, LL.D., to answer the plaintiff, representing minor and other heirs and legatees, beneficially interested under certain testamentary dispositions, executed by the late J. H. Neethling and the said A. C. Neethling, in the lifetime of the former,—in an action to set aside a will and codicil, made by the said A. C. Neethling after her husband's death.

The declaration set forth that the testator and testatrix had been married in community of property, and on the 18th March, 1794, executed the usual joint will, by which the first dying instituted the survivor and the children, if any, of the marriage sole and universal heirs. That no children having been procreated, the testator and testatrix, in virtue of the reservatory clause in the will, made and executed a joint underhand codicil, dated 17th April, 1836, whereby they directed that the debts due to them on that date by their brothers and sisters, and their children, should be

318

*1863.
Feb. 22—28.
March 1.
Aug. 9.

Hofmeyr, Neethling's Curator, vs. De Wet, Neethling's Executor.*

assigned for the creation of a poor fund, for the support of poor relations. That on the 27th April the testator and his wife executed a further testamentary disposition, in which they directed, after bequeathing certain legacies, that the joint estate should remain under the longest living in usufruct for life,—and should be appraised and properly secured, and remain inalienable, for the purpose of using the annual interest for the behoof and maintenance of poor relatives on both sides bearing the name of Smuts or Neethling, and appointed for the above purpose, as heir, in trust, after the death of the longest living, for the remainder of the estate and capital, H. J. Neethling, with reversion, &c., and as heirs to the interest arising and accruing thereon, their brothers and sisters them surviving and their godchildren,—bequeathing at the same time some annual legacies. Further, that on the 13th June, 1863, the testator and testatrix jointly executed a codicil, wherein they revoked nothing of, but referred specially to, the disposition dated 27th April, and made further direction respecting the estate in the possession of the survivor, viz., that the survivor should make an inventory, but should not be required to file any inventory with the Master. Further, that by a further deed of last will, dated 2nd June, 1838, the testator and testatrix, without revoking or altering any of their joint dispositions, declared that their joint will of 18th March, 1794, should be in full force, as far as the appointment of heirs was concerned, and that their several dispositions under date 17th and 21st April, 1836, and 13th June, 1836,—which latter refers to and includes the further testamentary disposition of 27th April, 1836,—should remain in full force in as far as the same should not be altered or revoked by the said will of 2nd June, 1838 : and further directing that the survivor should remain in full possession of the estate, without an inventory being required according to the codicil of 13th June, 1836, or an appraisement according to that of 27th April, 1836. In this will of 2nd June, 1838, the defendants are appointed executors, &c. The declaration further stated that on the 2nd June, 183*, the testator and testatrix appeared before the notary, A. G. L. Plouvier, and producing to him the deeds aforesaid, of 17th April, 1836, 27th April, 1836, 13th June, 1836, and 21st June, 1836 (and others not necessary for the purpose of this action to be referred to), declared the same to contain their last will and desire ; which documents, at the desire of the testator and testatrix, were covered and sealed in a packet by the notary, under a notarial deed of superscription.

On the 4th June the testator died, confirming by his death the several dispositions aforesaid as his will for the half of the joint estate, and for the half to the widow belonging, should she abide by the same, and take and enjoy the benefit of the usufruct and enter on and enjoy the whole estate.

1853.
Feb. 22—28.
March 1.
Aug. 9.

Hofmeyr, Neethling's Curator, vs.
De Wet, Neethling's Executor.

The declaration further stated that the widow did enter upon the whole estate, and continued in possession until her death, on the 24th January, 1850, and took all the benefits of the usufruct aforesaid,—whereby the joint estate of both became subject to be administered according to the joint will and codicillary deeds delivered to the notary in June, 1838; but that the widow, notwithstanding, made an underhand will on the 17th September, 1839, and an underhand codicil on the 29th November, 1848, unknown to the parties interested in the succession,—and which became known to them only after her death. It was further stated in the declaration, that in this will of 17th September, 1839, the widow, setting aside the disposition of 27th April, 1836, declared it null and void, and disposed of the joint estate otherwise than had been agreed upon between her and her husband, and in entire opposition to the agreement and joint disposition contained in the deeds of last will and codicils delivered to the notary and endorsed by him,—which the widow had no right to do, having taken and had the enjoyment of the usufruct of the whole estate; but that, on the contrary, she was bound to allow the entire estate, with all the fruits and increase thereof, to go, after her death, in conformity with the joint disposition of herself and her husband.

The plaintiff further stated that the defendants took out letters of administration under the will of 2nd June, 1838, on the 9th June, 1838, a few days after the death of the first dying, and being appointed also under the widow's will, took out letters of administration under the will of 21st January, 1850, and entered on the administration of the estates under both appointments, notwithstanding the adverse interests thereby existing,—as the plaintiff alleged,—and have framed an account of distribution of the joint estate solely according to the last will and codicil of the surviving spouse, in opposition to, and discarding altogether the directions in the joint wills of both spouses, which in law they were bound to do.

The declaration concluded with stating that for the protection and interests of the minor heir and heirs in expectancy, plaintiff had been appointed *curator ad litem* by order of the Court, and in that capacity claimed that the will and codicil made by the wife after the husband's death should be set aside, in as far as they deviate from the joint wills made and executed by the spouses, jointly, and respectively dated 17th August, 1829, 17th, 21st and 27th April, 1836, 13th June, 1836, 2nd June, 1838,—that the joint estate, as left by the surviving spouse, be administered in accordance with the directions in those joint wills and codicils, and that the defendants be condemned to pay the costs in their private capacity.

To this the defendants pleaded the general issue, and claimed, in reconvention, to the effect,

That on the 2nd June, 1838, when the testator and testatrix appeared before the Notary Plouvier, and delivered to him the several documents containing their joint testamentary dispositions, to be by him sealed in a packet, under a notarial deed of superscription, the document of the 27th April, 1836, was placed among the other documents in error,—it having been previously agreed between the testator and testatrix that it should be void and of no effect; and after the discovery that the said document had been so erroneously inserted, the testatrix made her last will, of 19th September, 1839, and the codicil of 1848,—which in no wise deviate from the joint testamentary dispositions of the 17th August, 1829, 17th and 21st April, 1836, and 13th June, 1836, in as far as the same are confirmed by the joint will of 2nd June, 1838; but, on the contrary, are expressly confirmed in her will of 19th September, 1839. Whereupon they claimed that this will and its codicil should be declared valid.

They further pleaded, in reconvention, that if the document of the 21st April had been inserted with the knowledge of the testator, it was inserted without the knowledge of the testatrix, and that she, not being bound by an insertion made without her consent, was entitled in law to make her separate will, disposing of her half of the joint estate, without reference to the document of the 27th April, 1836; that the sole effect of the document of 27th April, being so inserted, would be to give validity to it as a codicil, containing certain legacies payable out of the testator's half of the joint estate, but that in law the institution of heirs and fidei-commissary heirs therein made was null and void, inasmuch as by the joint last will of 2nd June, 1838, the institution of heirs is entirely changed.

They further pleaded in reconvention, that even if the Court should be of opinion that the defendants, as executors of the testatrix, are now precluded from maintaining that the document of the 27th April is null and void, as inserted without the consent of the testatrix among the documents delivered to the notary, yet that the institution of heirs and fidei-commissary heirs therein contained cannot co-exist with the direct institution of heirs in the will of 2nd June, 1838, wherein it is expressly declared that the institution of heirs in the will of 1794, viz. (there being no children), that the survivor should be heir of the first dying as of his or her free property, and that the document of the 27th April must be considered as nullified and set aside by the document of the latest date, that of 2nd June, 1838, with which it cannot be reconciled. They further alleged that the widow's will of September, 1839, and the codicil of November, 1848, are not in conflict with any of the testamentary dispositions enclosed by the notary in the cover, except with that of 27th April, 1836. Wherefore also they prayed that the will and codicil of 19th September, 1839, and of 29th November, 1848, might be declared valid.

<small>1853.
Feb. 22—28
March 1.
Aug. 9.

Hofmeyr, Neethling's Curator, *vs.* De Wet, Neethlings's Executor.</small>

Abstract of the papers enclosed by the notary in the closed will, in as far as important in this cause:

1. Mutual will of 18th March, 1794. The first dying institutes the survivor sole heir to the joint estate: to be for ever possessed as free and own property, without the gainsay of any one.

2. Codicil, 17th August, 1829 (has no reference to the case between the parties).

3. Joint codicil of 17th April, 1836, by virtue of the reservatory clause of the will of 1794, by which all debts due by the brothers and sisters and their children of the first degree at that date to the testators are assigned to them jointly for a poor fund; the division of the accruing interest to be in the discretion of the vestry of the Reformed Church. The enjoyment of the fund not to take effect until after the survivor's death. The further disposal of the capital and interest of the fund left to the husband, with whose directions concerning it the wife expressed herself *nunc pro nunc* satisfied.

4. 21st April, 1836.—A separate writing by the testator stating that " for many years my consort had agreed with me to constitute our whole estate a poor fund for the families of Neethling and Smuts (whereof deeds exists which are laid aside from ulterior considerations), I now dispose and declare that all the capital sums due to me by the family, &c., shall constitute a poor fund," to which nominal heirs are appointed, and the mode in which the interest is to be paid to the poor relatives settled.

5. " Further testamentary disposition and substitution with *fidei commiss.* by the undersigned married people, J. H. Neethling and A. C. Smuts, relative to that which, after the death of both, shall be done with the estate possessed by them in community," written in Mr. Neethling's handwriting and signed by both, confirming the will of 1794, except as herein altered, and further stating " that the joint estate remaining in the possession of the survivor of us shall be ascertained, and that care shall be taken by the aftermentioned executors that the same, as far as possible, shall consist in immovable property, and the capital be

Y

1853.
Feb. 22—28.
March 1.
Aug. 9.

Hofmeyr, Neeth-
ling's Curator, rs.
De Wet, Neeth-
lings's Executor.

secured against loss, diminution, or decay," &c., and then after some legacies " proceeding to the nomination of heirs, we declare that our estate shall never (or so long as is permitted by the laws of the Colony) be alienated or diminished; but that the same shall, after the compliance with our hereunder following dispositions, which shall all be usufructary, eventually serve for the support of the poor, limited to the own descendants of our respective father's bearing the name of Neethling or Smuts," appointment of nominal heirs of the capital and of heirs for the interest is there made, and the defendants are appointed executors and administrators of the joint estate.

6. Joint codicil of testator and testatrix, dated 13th June, 1836, in which the " testators by our mutual will of 1794, and our further will for the joint determination of our succession, made on the 27th April, 1836, referring by these presents to both of these wills and other special deeds of last will do declare"—among other things, that an inventory shall be made of the estate at the death of the first dying, but that it need not be filed with the Master of the Court.

7. 2nd June, 1838.—Joint will of the testator and testatrix, by which they declare that " we are desirous of directing and disposing further over the property we may leave at our death, as we hereby do,—but especially desiring that the will passed by us jointly on the 18th March, 1794, shall be and remain of full force and effect, in so far as relates to the institution of heirs therein mentioned, and that all further bequests made by us, either jointly or separately, by virtue of the reservatory clause contained in our said will, and respectively dated 17th August, 1829, 17th April, 1836, 21st April, 1836, and one of the 13th June, 1838, shall remain of full force and effect in so far as the same are not in this further and present disposition revoked, altered, or contain in themselves contradictory bequests."

Mrs. Neethling's will of the 19th September, 1839, repudiates the will of 27th April, 1829, solemnly declaring that this deed was " without the knowledge or consent of me, the undersigned, and contrary to my desire, erroneously enclosed in the notarial cover of 2nd June, 1838 ;" and further solemnly declaring "that she never was properly acquainted with the contents of the disposition of 27th April, 1836." She further confirms all the deeds enumerated in the will of the 2nd June, 1838, viz., the 17th August, 1829, the 17th and 21st April, 1836, and 13th June, 1836, and the mutual will of 18th March, 1794, on which the said dispositions are based. She further proceeds to bequeath legacies, unnecessary to particularize in this case. And the codicil of 1848 also gives legacies unnecessary to be now recited.

The parties in the cause admitted on the trial, "the

execution of all the different testamentary and codicillary dispositions in the plaintiff's declaration mentioned and referred to ; also the dates of superscription and opening by the notary, A. J. L. Plouvier.

"That the late Mr. Neethling and his wife were married in community of property, and died without issue. That the surviving spouse, after the death of her husband, enjoyed all the interest of the joint estate, save and except a certain sum of money invested in Holland, in Government securities. That after the death of Mr. Neethling, liquidation accounts of the joint estate were framed by the defendant in accordance with the mutual will of March, 1794, and joint codicils of 17th April and 13th June, 1836, and 2nd June, 1838, and codicils of 21st April, 1836, and that after the death of Mrs. Neethling, a liquidation account of the estate was made out in terms of the will of Mrs. Neethling, of the 19th September, 1839, and codicil of the 29th November, 1848."

1856.
Feb. 22—28.
March 1.
Aug. 9.
Hofmeyr, Neethling's Curator, vs.
De Wet, Neethling's Executor.

C. J. Brand, J. H. Hofmeyr, and *J. H. Brand* appeared for the plaintiff, and *Porter, A. G.,* and *E. B. Watermeyer,* for the defendants.

C. J. Brand, Hofmeyr, and *John Brand,* for the plaintiff, maintained the following argument: There are two questions: 1st, What is the joint will of Mr. and Mrs. Neethling ? 2nd, Could Mrs. Neethling make a will contrary to the disposition contained in the joint will ?

1st. The several testamentary papers of 18th March, 1794, 17th August, 1829, 17th, 21st, and 27th April, 1836, 13th June, 1836, and 2nd June, 1838, constitute the joint will of Mr. and Mrs. Neethling. It is admitted by the defendants that that of 27th April, 1836, was enclosed in the envelope. The testator and testatrix appeared before the Notary Plouvier, and handing over to him the seven documents, requested him to enclose them in the envelope. 27th April, 1836, is referred to in 13th June, 1836, to which reference is made in 2nd June, 1838.

2nd. It is true that, by the general rule of law, a joint will made by husband and wife, in one paper, is considered as two separate wills, which each is at liberty to revoke with respect to his or her share of the joint estate. But this general rule is subject to the following limitation : If the spouses have benefited each other, and have jointly and by common consent directed how the joint estate shall go after the death of the survivor, such survivor cannot, after the adiation of the estate and the enjoyment of the benefit, make another testament of his or her share of the joint estate

1853.
Feb. 22—28.
March 1.
Aug. 9.

Hofmeyr, Neethling's Curator,vs.
De Wet, Neethling's Executor.

contrary to the will of the first dying, unless it is directed by the joint will, that after the death of the survivor the remainder of the joint estate shall be divided into equal moieties between the relatives of the first dying and of the survivor. For in that case the survivor may revoke the mutual will for his or her one half of the joint estate. And this is the exception to the limitation above mentioned. (*Grotius II*, 15, § 9; *Dufaure vs. Pereira*, 1; *Williams on Executors*, p. 71; 4 *Burge*, 404; *Voet*, 28, 3 § 11, 30; 1, § 16, 23; 4, § 63; *Van der Keessel. Th.* 283; *Schorer in note to Grotius II*, 24 § 8, p. 267; *Bynkershoek, Quæst. Juris. Priv. III*, 10; *Coren., Dec.* 11, 12; *Van Leeuwen, Roman-Dutch Law*, 2, 3, § 4, and 3, 3, § 8; *Van Leeuwen, Censura Forensis*, p. 1, 1, 3, c. 2, § 16, and 1, 3, c. 21, § 7; *Christinæus Dec. Juris. Belg.* 1, 4, *Dec.* 12; 2 *Dutch Consultations, Cons.* 275; *Decision of the Supreme Court in Brits vs. Brits, 28th February*, 1842.)

Now the joint will of Mr. and Mrs. Neethling comes within the limitation before stated. For they disposed of the joint estate by common consent, as appears from the following expressions: "We have agreed to constitute our whole estate a poor fund," in 21st April, 1836; "further testamentary disposition of estate possessed by them in community," "jointly," "joint estate," "we" in 27th April, 1836; "our," &c. And Mrs. Neethling, it is admitted by the defendants, adiated the estate of her predeceased husband and had the enjoyment of the usufruct of the whole estate from 1838 to January, 1850. Therefore, according to the authorities above quoted, Mrs. Neethling could not revoke the closed joint will of 2nd June, 1838; and the estate must be administered according to that mutual will.

Porter, A. G., and *Watermeyer* for defendants.

There are two principal questions to be decided by the Court. The first is the document of the 27th April, 1836, a part of the close will of the testator and testatrix,—and the second, if it be a part of the joint will, had the wife, who it is admitted, adiated after her husband's death, the right of disposing anew, at least of her half of the common estate, differently from the disposition of the joint will?

On the joint question, they maintained—1st, that the document of the 27th April is not to be considered a part of the mutual will of the testator and testatrix, having been placed among the papers given to the notary through inadvertence or error. From the document of 2nd June, 1831, the paper of the latest date in this enclosure,—it is clear that deliberate attention was drawn to the testamentary dispositions intended to be confirmed as the will of the testator and testatrix. The very erasure and alteration in the enumeration, to which attention had been drawn by the plaintiff, shows this. All the papers containing testamentary dispositions intended to be confirmed are recited in chronological order,—and from them the paper of 27th April is excepted. It is clear that if the will of the 2nd June,—the paper of latest date,—had contained an express revocation of the paper of the 27th April, in apt words, and the paper of the 27th April had, nevertheless, been found in the cover, it would have been capable of averment that this paper had been placed in the cover by accident or in error. The same rule must apply in the case of a tacit revocation, which may be equally strong. There was, however, no necessity for any revocation, whether tacit or express, of the document of the 27th April in that of the 2nd June, 1838; because, not having been made by virtue of the reservatory clause in the testament of 1794, and in truth not being, nor purporting to be, a codicil at all, but a will, or testament, in its form and object, though valueless as such will through want of the proper solemnities, as the witnessing, it was a sheet of blank paper in contemplation of law, until its accidental enclosure in the cover, and through this accidental enclosure in the cover its only claim to being considered valid exists.

They maintained, 2nd, that by the paper of the 2nd June, 1838, the latest paper in the envelope, the codicil of the 21st April is clearly set up. The paper of the 27th April, which destroys and entirely swallows up that of the 21st, is not set up, but deliberately omitted. The two papers of the 21st and 27th having one object, but the latter amplifying and expanding the former, could not, and were not intended to work together. Both contain trusts, and the *cestui que* trusts are the same, and to be benefited in both deeds. Both trusts were to commence at the same moment. Both funds were under the same trustees. The difference—and a difference fatal to the supposition that they could work together—was in the fact that by the paper of the 21st April, the debts due to the joint estate at the survivor's death were to constitute a poor fund, and by the paper of the 27th the entire joint estate, after the survivor's death, was to constitute this poor fund. The two could clearly not work together. But the latter having been omitted in the latest documents in the envelope, containing a chronological recital of all the confirmed testamentary dispositions, in which recital the former is expressly set up, the inference is fair, and indeed cannot be gainsaid, that the latter was not intended to be enclosed among the papers in the envelope, together forming the entire joint will, but it must have been enclosed therein by mistake.

1853.
Feb. 22—28.
March 1.
Aug. 9.

Hofmeyr, Neethling's Curator, vs.
De Wet, Neethling's Executor.

3rdly. They maintained,—That the repugnancy between the document of the 27th April and that of the 2nd June, 1838, leads to the same conclusion. The will, for this it is, if it be anything, of the 27th April, changes the direct institution of March, 1794, into a fidei-commissary institution; the paper of the 2nd June, 1838, recurs to the direct institution of 1794. Both the papers of 27th April, 1836, and of 2nd June dispose of the whole estate; and the latter must be considered as completely in the stead of, and revoking, the former. (*Grotius' Introd.*, 2, 24, 9; *Van der Linden's Inst.*, p. 155; *V. D. Keessel, Th.* 329.) Both together could not form part of the mutual will. If there be any doubt whether the paper of the 2nd June, 1838, entirely reinstituted the heirship of the will of 1794, or intended a *fidei commissum*, the rule is, " *in dubio magis directa quam fidei commissaria institutio præsumitur.*" (*Voet*, 36, 1, 1.) The 27th April, 1836, was an entire revocation of 1794, and 1794, set up by 2nd June, 1838, is again an entire revocation of 27th April, and both could not have been intended to form the will.

4th. But if it be supposed that 27th April, 1836, had been inserted by design, can it yet be of value as part of the will? It is not a codicil, for it disposes of the entire estate and institutes heirs, which a codicil cannot do. Codicils purporting or alleged to be under the reservatory clause, at all events, cannot; although it is by some authors held that codicils made with the solemnities of wills can so institute. (*Van der Linden's Inst.*, p. 126; *Grotius' Introd.*, 2, 17, 2; *Van der Keessel's Thes.*, 289; *Voet*, 28, 5, 1; *Voet*, 29, 7, 5, *arguen.* 28, 1, 29; *Van Leeuwen Censura For.*, Pt. 1, 3, 11, 10.)

If therefore to be considered on the first supposition of the plaintiff as a codicil, it falls to the ground, for it does what a codicil cannot do, namely, institutes heirs; if, on the second supposition, it be taken as a testament, it is void, as being entirely revoked by the 2nd June, 1838. It has, indeed, been urged that the 2nd June, 1838, confirms, and does not revoke, the 27th April, 1836, because in one of the codicils, that of the 13th June, 1836, referred to in the 2nd June, 1838, the paper in question, of the 27th April, is referred to. But this reference (not confirmation) in its terms to 27th April, 1838, and to " other deeds of last will, " of which there probably existed a multitude; and is it pretended that these are also to be considered as confirmed? There is no confirmation of anything in the codicil of 13th June, 1838, and therefore, the confirmation in 2nd June, 1838, of the codicil of 13th June, 1836, cannot be taken as a confirmation of anything besides.

5th. If the 27th April were placed in the cover by design, and with the knowledge of both parties, it yet could not have effect on the wife's estate, being a will in the handwriting of the husband, in which *sibi vel suis quicquid adscripsit* contrary to law. (*Voet*, 34, 8, 3 ; *Ned. Adv. Boek, Vol. I, Cons,* 14—20 ; *Bynkershoek, Jur. Priv.,* 1, 3, *c.* 8 ; *Utrecht Consult.,* vol. 2, *c.* 64 ; *Van der Keessel, Thes.* 292.)

<small>1853 Feb. 22—28. March 1. Aug. 9. Hofmeyr, Neethling's Curator, vs. De Wet, Neethling's Executor.</small>

They maintained this general conclusion on the first question ; if the 27th April never was a part of the closed will, or in fact was revoked by the 2nd June, 1838, so as to be of no effect, then the separate will of the widow, which is clearly in accordance with and confirms all the documents enclosed in the cover, with the exception of the 20th April, does not deviate at all from the joint will delivered to the notary, excepting in as far as legacies, which it is clear the widow was entitled to make, are concerned.

On the second principal question, viz.; Had the wife, after adiation, the power to revoke as far as her share of the common estate is concerned ?

On this question it was maintained by the defendants that the plaintiff had wrongly relied on *Dufaure vs. Pereira* in *Dickens's Reports,* as exemplifying the principle that the wife, having taken property under a mutual will, was not entitled to change the disposition of the mutual will after the husband's death. In that case, however, it is clear from *Walpole vs. Walpole* (3 *Vesey,* 416), that the property the survivor had taken was the husband's, and therefore she was not entitled to change. The case is totally different from the present, where half of the property disposed of by the muual will was the husband's, and half the wife's.

By the law of the Colony, each spouse has one-half of the undivided estate in communion, and of this half each is entitled to dispose by last will. Mutual wills of spouses are two separate wills, on the same paper, of persons disposing each of his or her separate property. (*Van der Linden's inst.*) When in wills of this nature each institutes the other as heir, and directs what is to be done with the residue of the property after the survivor's death, then, although no change can be made by the survivor, with reference to the half share (in the common estate) of the predeceased, yet with respect to his or her own share, free liberty of testation, which is ambulatory until death, continues to exist. (*Bynkershoek Jur, priv.,* 1, 3, *c.* 10, *med.*) Adiation of the share of the predeceased does not take away this liberty on the part of the survivor with respect to her share. This is admitted in the authorities chiefly relied on by the plaintiff, viz., in the 11*th and* 12*th Observations of Coren on the Decisions of the High Court.*

1853.
Feb. 22—28.
March 1.
Aug. 9.

Hofmeyr, Neethling's Curator, vs.
De Wet, Neethling's Executor.

The principle is, that the one-half by law belongs to the survivor, and the predeceased could impose no burden on that, but could impose a burden only on that which the survivor enjoyed from him, viz., his half: he could not institute the survivor heir to his (the predeceased's) property with the condition that the estate of both should, after the survivor's death, go in a certain way. This would be depriving the survivor of the liberty of testation, or by contract taking from the survivor the power of testation. Inheritance, however, must in law be carried either by last will or *ab intestato*, but cannot be carried by contract. (*Voet*, 2, 14, 10.)

It is against law for the predeceased to institute the survivor his heir under the condition that the survivor shall, after his death, leave all her estate in a certain manner. (*Voet*, 36, 1, 11; *D*. 36, 1, 17.) And yet this is claimed by the plaintiff in this case. The utmost by the most liberal interpretation would be that a *fidei commissum* was induced for the amount left by the testator. The fullest power of revocation, on the part of the survivor for her share, therefore exists in a will thus made. Even in the antenuptial contracts (which are otherwise in all respects most irrevocable), where succession in a particular manner has been stipulated after the survivor's death, either party has full liberty of revocation as to such succession. (*Van der Linden's Note to Pothier on Contracts, vol.* 1, *p.* 146.)

The doctrine of election, it is granted, exists in our law as in English law and as in the " Approbate and Reprobate" of Scotch law. (*Voet*, 30; *Univ.* 26; *Story Equity Jur.* § 1078, &c.; *Erskine Inst.*, 3, 7, 10); but here there is no question of the kind. The survivor elected to take her husband's half under the burden to restore *it* (increased or diminished as the case might be, *Bynkershoek, Jur. Priv.*, 1, 3, *c*. 10, *med.*) according to his desire after her death; but her own half she had without reference to his will at all; it was her free matrimonial share, and remained at her disposal.

The error of the plaintiff's argument, that by adiation the widow has deprived herself of the power of testation with respect to her half, is founded on a misunderstanding of a passage in *Grotius' Introduction*; but which misunderstanding is corrected by *Voet*, and by *Boel's Commentary on the* 137*th Decision of Loenius.*

The passage in *Grotius* (*Introd.*, 2, 15, 9) is to the effect, that " where the first dying spouse has bequeathed any benefit in favour of the survivor, and afterwards has limited the disposal of the common property after the death of such survivor, then such survivor, if he or she accept the benefits, cannot afterwards dispose of his or her share by last will in any manner at variance with the will of the predeceased."

Voet (23, 4, 63) says, that if this passage is to receive a general interpretation, it does not rest on sufficiently good grounds in law. He says, that under such circumstances, the "*liberrima facultas testandi*" still exists on the part of the survivor for his or her half of the joint estate. The only supposable case in which this is taken away is, when each has disposed of the other's property, and each has expressly conceded to the other the power of so doing. Even when they jointly disposed as of one mass of the common property, the law still considers each a separate will revocable both before, and by the survivor after, the death of the first dying. (*Voet*, 23, 4, 63, *and* 28, 3, 11.)

1853.
Feb. 22—28.
March 1.
Aug. 9.

Hofmeyr, Neethling's Curator, *vs.* De Wet, Neethling's Executor.

From the cases quoted and the arguments in *Boel ad Loenium* (*Loenius*, *Cas*. 137) it is perfectly clear that adiation of the share of the first dying does not affect the right of revocation, as to the survivor's own share. There can be no stronger case on this subject than that of *Blydezin vs. Blydezin*, decided in the High Court of Holland, reported at considerable length by *Boel*; where, notwithstanding strict clauses of non-revocation in a mutual will, made by the spouses jointly, during their lifetime, in which will there was an express disposal, by both jointly, of the property of the joint estate, after the death of the survivor, the survivor, after having adiated and held possession of the entire estate for several years, was held entitled to dispose anew of his share of the community by will, the share of the predeceased being held to be governed by the provisions of the will made during the lifetime of both.

Van der Keessel (who and *Van der Linden* are the latest writers of authority on the Dutch-Roman Law) refers to the *Commentary of Boel on the* 137*th case of Loenius* as containing the law on this subject.

The true construction of the passage in *Grotius*,—as referring to singular things, not universal acquisitions like inheritances, is given by *Boel*; the true doctrine being that where, in a mutual will by spouses, some particular legacy is left to go in a particular manner after the survivor's death, the survivor cannot change this, even to the extent of the half interest which, by virtue of the community, he or she may have enjoyed,—but over *res singulares* only can such disposition be validly made, not over *res universales*. In accordance with this, the case of *Brits vs. Brits*, quoted by the plaintiff, was decided by the court; a particular piece of property of the joint estate having been left by way of legacy to a particular person after the survivor's death, the survivor could not change this disposition. In this view only is the rule laid down by *Grotius* not obnoxious to the answer given above, and reconcilable with the general principles of law. The same remark is applicable to the "*Consultations*" quoted by the plaintiff, and which are generally founded on the passage in *Grotius.* It was admitted by the plaintiff, and is clear from the authorities, that everything coming to the survivor after the death of the first dying, whether as fruits, legacies, or inheritances, must enter into the continued community. (*Bynkershoek, Juris. Priv. L.* 3, *C.* 10, *passim* ; *Van der Linden's Decisions, Decis.* 24.) If the plaintiff be entitled to say that with respect to the survivor's share of this continued community, she was not, after her husband's death, entitled to make a new will, he would deprive her of the liberty of testation, even with respect to future property, and by contract, which, as before stated, cannot be done. (*Vid. et Huber Prælect, Juris. Civil. l.* 28, *t.* 3, *passim.*) In no other way can this congeries of wills, forming the closed will, be read, than as one in which each spouse disposes of his own property, and therefore as two separate wills on the same paper, in which case it is clear that notwithstanding adiation for any period, the survivor is entitled to revoke his or her own will, though of course not the will of the first dying. (*Coren's Obs.,* 11 *and* 12.) It is not to be presumed that any one has given up the power of testation ; in fact, this is so difficult, that authors of repute think that by no form of words can it be done (*Huber Juris. Civil. Præl., b.* 28, *t.* 3, *med.*); but where it is intended, the intention must be most express, not implied, as in this case suggested (*Voet,* 23, 4, 63, *and* 28, 3, 11.) But it is evident that here there exists neither of the two cases put by *Voet,* in which he is of opinion that revocation by the survivor would not be permitted, viz. : 1st, the express concession of the one to the other of the liberty of disposing of the former's property ; and second, the disposal by each, by common consent, of the entire matrimonial estate.

Contract, apart from the question of its legality, was spoken of on the part of the plaintiff; but if there were really a binding contract, then repudiation (which it was admitted could take place by the survivor on the death of the first dying) could not be permitted to one of the contracting parties, it being impossible to obtain the other's consent to such repudiation. If repudiation be permissible, then the plaintiff must be driven to the conclusion that there was on contract, and, if no contract, then the plaintiff's argument entirely falls to the ground, it having been most clearly shown that adiation of the estate of the first dying does not take away the survivor's liberty of disposing of what is her estate, and not that of the first dying. The defendants' counsel concluded by maintaining, that not only on the weight of the authorities, but on the right interpretation of all the authorities, it was clear that the widow, by adiation of her husband's estate, and possession of the whole joint estate after his death, until her's, did not give up, and could not give up, the right of disposing of her share of the joint estate as she pleased.

1853.
Feb. 22 -28.
March 1.
Aug. 9.

Hofmeyr, Neethling's Curator, vs. De Wet, Neethling's Executor.

C. J. Brand in reply.—The allegation that 27th April, 1836, was introduced into the envelope by mistake, is rebutted by the act of superscription of 2nd June, 1838, which states that the several documents within the cover were enclosed at the request of the testator and testatrix, and by the silence of Mrs. Neethling, when the envelope was opened on the 7th June, 1838, and 27th April, 1836, read as part of the mutual closed will. She heard it read and made no objection. The 27th April, 1836, is part of the closed will, and is expressly mentioned in 13th June, 1836. There is no proof that the erasures were made *consulto*. (*Van der Linden's Decisions, Casus* 13, *p.* 77.) If there be any repugnance between the several documents, the latest must prevail. But the question here is not how the will is to be construed, but what is the will? It cannot be contended that 27th April, 1836, is invalid, because it does not expressly state that it is made in virtue of the reservatory clause. For *Bynkershoek, Quæst. Juris. Priv. II.* 16, § 4, merely says, "*vulgo fit.*" If 27th April, 1836, be taken as a codicil, it is not clear that it is vitiated because it contains *institutio heredis*,—for some authors hold that an heir can be instituted in a codicil. *Huber, Hedendaagsche Regtsgeleerdheid, II.* 12, § 5; *Voet*, 29, 7, § 5; *Van Leeuwen, Cens. Forens, p.* 1, 1, 3, *c.* 2, § 2.) The will of 18th March, 1794, having been *de facto* revoked by 27th April, 1836, is not revived by 2nd June 1838. (4 *Dutch Consultations Cons.,* 202; *V. d. Linden Institutes*, 155; *Van der Keessel, Th.* 329; *Voet,* 28, 3, 39.) It was intended that the 27th April should be part of the joint will, and that is sufficient. (*V. d. Linden's Decisions, p.* 181; *Bynkershoek, Quæst Juris. Priv., II,* 16, § 4, and *III,* 4.) The defendant's argument, that the 27th April, 1836, cannot affect the wife's estate, because it is a testamentary disposition in the handwriting of the husband, and in which *sibi vel suis adscribit,* does not apply. For it is not proved that it is in Mr. Neethling's handwriting. Neethling is not the survivor, and *suis* means *filii vel servi qui sunt in potestate patris vel domini.* (*D.* 48, 80, *l.* 10; *Van Leeuwen, Cens. Forens, p.* 1, *l.* 5, *c.* 2, § 5, *note* 2; *Voet,* 34, 8, § 3.) He pointed out the distinction between the Roman law and the law of Holland as to *pactum successorium* (*Voet,* 2, 14, § 16, *et quamvis nunc hactenus;* Voet, 10, 2, § 29; *Van der*

Keessel, Th. 235 ; *Voet,* 23, 4, § 63); and commented on the passage of *V. der Linden* cited by the defendants. The principle contained in the *Customs of Antwerp, Art.* 51, as to a *res particulares*, was adopted by the law of Holland, and extended to *res universales. Vide* the authorities. *Huber* cannot overrule the Dutch authorities and decisions, because he was a Professor in Vriesland, where the Dutch law of community does not exist. *Boel's* opinion and the judgment to which he refers apply to the exception of the limitation before stated. (2 *Dutch Advice Book, Cons.* 32 ; 2 *vol., Cons.* 165 ; *vol.* 3, *Cons.* 65.)

Cur. adv. vult.

The case was argued on February 22, 24, 25, 26, 28, and March 1.

Judgment was given on the 9th August, 1853.

WYLDE, C. J., observed that this was a suit between the relatives of the late Mr. and Mrs. Neethling, to determine under what testamentary dispositions their joint estate was to be liquidated and distributed. It appeared that the summons was issued on the 19th September, 1851, the plaintiff having been appointed a curator of the minor heirs, under an order of this Court of July, 1851. The pleadings in the case contained a very full statement of the facts upon which the question between the parties had arisen ; and it was only necessary to refer to them in order to ascertain what were the merits upon which the decision of that question depended.

By these pleadings it appeared that the defendants had executed not only the estate of the testator, Mr. Neethling, but also that of his widow, who survived him some years, under each of their wills. By the averments of the declaration, it appeared that the defendants took out letters of administration, under the joint will of testator and testatrix, on the 9th of June, 1838, and that they also took out letters of administration under the will of the surviving widow on the 29th of January, 1850; and the plaintiff avers that the said defendants were in duty bound, having accepted and taken the prior appointment and office as executors and guardians, under the joint will of the said predeceased husband, and surviving spouse as aforesaid, to carry out the directions therein given, in respect of the disposal of the joint estate, leaving it to the parties interested under the will of the surviving spouse, to object thereto, and, therefore, that the said defendants should be condemned to pay the costs and expenses of this action in their private capacity. It certainly seems rather unaccountable how the defendants could feel themselves at liberty to take the administration under such conflicting testamentary dispositions, and it will necessarily raise a question for the Court, whether or not this prayer as to costs on the part of the plaintiff should be complied with. The real question of the suit, in fact, is whether the testamentary disposition executed by the testator and his wife, under date of the 27th April, 1836, is to be taken as part of the mutual will executed so ago long as the 18th of March, 1794 ; this position being denied on the part of the defendant.

1853.
Feb. 22—28.
March 1.
Aug. 9.

Hofmeyr, Neethling's Curator, *vs.* De Wet, Neethling's Executor.

Admissions between parties have been put in and filed, under which most of the facts connected with the issue are admitted: for it is admitted as to the execution of all the different testamentary and codicillary dispositions, in plaintiff's declaration mentioned, as also the acts of superscription, and opening by the notary; that the testator and testatrix were married in community of property, and died without issue ; that the surviving spouse, after the death of her husband, until her death, enjoyed all the interests of the joint estate, save and except a sum of money invested in Government securities in Holland ; that after the death of the testator, certain liquidation accounts were framed by the defendants, in accordance with the joint will of 1794, and joint codicils of 17th April and 13th June, 1836, and 2nd June, 1838, and codicil of 2nd April, 1836, and that after the death of Mrs. Neethling, a liquidation and distribution account of the estate was made out in terms of the will of Mrs. Neethling, of 19th September, 1839, and codicil of the 29th November, 1848.

Under these admissions, it appears, also, that the testator died on the 2nd of June, 1838, and that, on the same day, he, in the presence of his wife, delivered a closed will to the Notary Plouvier, who thereupon executed an act of of superscription. On the 7th of June following after the death of the testator the act of opening the closed will took place,— and it may be fit to mention that such opening took place in the presence of the widow and several of the near relatives, when seven testamentary papers were found to have been so entered, and were read at length at such meeting of the widow and her relatives. Upon one of these seven papers the question in suit wholly arises, as it is contended, on the part of the defendant, that this paper ought not to be taken as intentionally inserted, as in conflict with the other testamentary papers found along with it.

This raises, therefore, the principle of what belongs to the construction of what is termed a closed will. There can be no doubt that all the papers contained in the enclosure of a will must be taken and read as forming the entire will, the same, indeed, as if all the writing had been contained— if it could be so—on one sheet; and the only question is,

1853.
Feb. 22.—28.
March 1.
Aug. 9.

Hofmeyr, Neethling's Curator, *vs* De Wet, Neethling's Executor.

whatever may be the conflicting parts of the papers, whether, upon the whole, the will of the testator can be ascertained. Whatever difficulties might occur as to the tenor of particular papers, the nature of the dispositions, or uncertainty as to purpose, the law requires that such a construction, if possible, should be given to the will as shall be considered to realize the intention of the testator, as may be best discoverable from the entire context.

The defendants' case rests wholly upon the presumption that the documents so enclosed are inconsistent and utterly repugnant, and that the Court cannot possibly find what was the will of the testator, except the paper dated the 27th April be laid aside and rejected. It is to be observed, however, that no such inconsistency or repugnance in the testamentary dispositions were objected until after the death of the widow in 1850. It is true that such objection is found to have been taken by the widow herself when her own closed will, of the 19th September, 1839, was opened on the 26th January, 1850, twelve years after the death of her husband, the testator. In her will she states, that the testamentary disposition dated 27th April, 1836, signed by her late husband and herself, should not be considered of any force or value, but as void, as having been without her consent or knowledge, and contrary to her desire, erroneously enclosed in the notarial cover of the 2nd June, 1838.

This objection is urged on the part of the defendants, not upon any extrinsic proof of the actual intention on the part of the testator and testatrix to exclude this paper from the will enclosure, but upon the terms of the testamentary disposition being inconsistent with other dispositions which were subsequently made by them. It is evident, therefore, that the defendants, as executors, administered the joint estate of the testator and testatrix, under what they now contend to be an objectionable will, for the term of twelve years, and gave therefore some countenance to the averment in the declaration, charging them personally with costs of suit.

Considering that closed wills may frequently contain several documents, it will be desirable, at least upon the opening of such closed wills, that the number of papers contained therein should be marked, as to number and dates, by the notary, in his act of opening. In this case, the numbers are not given, and it is only upon the admission of the parties that the Court comes to the conclusion that there were seven documents so constituting the closed will of the testator and testatrix.

Upon this principle, therefore, of taking every document contained in the envelope of the enclosed will as necessarily forming the entire will, it becomes requisite to refer to these testamentary papers, which made up the joint will of the testator and testatrix, at the time of his death, on the 2nd June, 1838. The case of the defendant, in fact, rests upon the assumption that thus a confusion will necessarily arise as to the intention of the testator and testatrix, and that no legal distribution can be made under such conflicting dispositions. But, after much consideration, I have become impressed, that no such confusion is attributable to the various testamentary dispositions, and that the intention of the testator and testatrix can be clearly ascertained from the tenor of the entire will. The Court has been assisted with all that legal knowledge and industry could bring to the task of justly construing the will in question, and I· am bound to acknowledge the considerable aid which has been afforded me, not only by the learned argument on the hearing of the case, but by the subsequent notes of that argument, with which the Bar has been so good as to furnish us. In respect however, of all that learning, and the able discussion upon it, I must be free to observe that the only great question with the Court is, how to apply it so as to come to a just and true construction of the real intention of the parties under their joint testament. There can be no doubt that upon the terms of these testamentary dispositions arguments have justly been raised as to their construction; and it has not been wholly without difficulty that I have been able to bring my mind to the conclusion that there is direct indication of the intentions of the testators, so as to make all the varying dispositions tend to, and agreeable with, those intentions.

Let me here remark, however strongly it has been urged as to the existence of this alleged inconsistency and repugnance, no such suggestion or idea arose until after the death of the widow, twelve years after the opening of the testator's will, under which will the joint estate had from the first been, and continued to be, administered by the defendants. It would seem rather strange that, upon the opening of the will, before such parties as were named to have been present, no such objection should have occurred, and that the estate should be administered for so many years without any supposition on the part of any one that any such conflict as to the testator's will could arise. Supposing the testatrix herself, instead of her husband, had died, would it not have been thought more than extraordinary that he could have taken any such objection as now maintained on the part of his widow? Could it have been argued on the part of the survivor, in such case, that it was intended that he, the testator, as the surviving spouse, was constituted the sole heir to the estate, and that the paper of the 27th of April, 1836, had been inserted by mistake in the envelope

1853.
Feb. 22—23.
March 1.
Aug. 9.

Hofmeyr, Neethling's Curator, vs.
De Wet, Neethling's Executor.

1853.
Feb. 22—28.
March 1.
Aug. 9.

Hofmeyr, Neethling's Curator, vs.
De Wet, Neethling's Executor.

of the closed will; Any such attempt, one may suppose, would have been, if not ridiculous, most certainly abortive and unsuccessful. But, however strangely, the objection is preferred in respect to the widow's suit, though she is present at the opening of the will, with so many of her relatives capable of forming good judgment upon testamentary dispositions. At her request, the act of superscription is made upon the notarial opening of it. She suffers the defendants, as executors, to conduct the administration of her estate, under the terms and upon the condition of the will as opened on the death of her husband, and she takes the full usufructuary estate during her whole life, thus confirming, by her act, for so long a time, the dispositions of the will, of which that of the 27th of April necessarily formed a part, for except it did so, she was entitled to the whole inheritance under the disposition of previous date; whereas she contents herself with receiving only the usufruct of the entire estate. It is among the facts of the case that she did make a private closed will on the 19th September, 1839, in which, it has been already said, the great objection was suggested. But leaving that closed will with the notary, she still continues to take the life usufruct only of the whole estate; thus acknowledging herself bound by the will, so confirmed as the joint will of herself and her husband. It does not appear that the defendants were aware of the secret will so made by the testatrix, or indeed, it would be wholly unaccountable how they could go on administering the estate as if no such objection had been made.

Now, referring to what should be found as the intention of the testator and testatrix, I think, upon reference to the documents themselves, it will sufficiently appear, that when they lost all expectation of having children of their own, the determination with each of them was that the survivor of either of them should have the enjoyment of the whole joint estate during his or her life, and that then the whole estate should be converted into a provision for the benefit of the relatives on both sides. We must now refer to the documents themselves, as to whether such can be justly maintained to have been the intention of the parties.

Under the will of the 18th March, 1794, the testators declared to institute each other respectively,—that is to say, the first dying the survivor of them, together with any child or children under their marriage, as heirs of the entire estate. This will remained unaltered for the long term of forty-two years. After this long time, when all hope as to children of their own expired, they both determined to have in regard a provision for their relatives, who took the place, in some degree, of children in their feelings. As far as can be collected from the terms of the testamentary dispositions, the testatrix entirely concurred with her husband in this intention; nor is there any evidence of the slightest suggestion of non-concurrence on her part, until after the testator's death, and then only secretly, in her closed will, made in September, 1839. It will be well to refer to an authority, as to what has been the rule of construction applied by courts of justice in determining what is to be considered as the will of a testator. In the case of *Lane vs. Earl Stanhope*, 6 *Term Reports*, 352, Lord Kenyon, Chief Justice, who is known to be a great equity lawyer, as well as skilled in common law, observes: " It is our duty in construing a will to give effect to the intention, as far as we can consistently with the rules of law; not conjecturing, but expounding, the devisor's will from the words used. Now, where certain words have obtained a precise and technical meaning, we ought not to give them a different meaning; that would be, as the judges have said, removing landmarks. But if there be no such appropriate meaning to the words used in the will,—if the devisor's intention be clear, and the words given be sufficient to give effect to it, we ought to construe these words so as to give effect to the intent, and not to doubt on account of other cases, which tend only to involve the question in obscurity."

It has been strongly contended that these papers, if constituting an entire will, contain within them serious ambiguities. " It is not," however, as observed in *Starkie on Evidence*, vol. 2, p. 926, " every degree of uncertainty appearing on the face of a will which will avoid it. Such a rule would be far too extensive for practical use; and where the ambiguity is not such as to avoid the instrument, but which cannot be removed merely by judicial construction of the will alone, the uncertainty must necessarily be removed by evidence to ascertain what is ambiguous by means of the context of extrinsic circumstances, and thus to confine expressions in themselves capable of different applications, according to the subject matter to which they are applied, to a certain and definite application to particular circumstances."

In this case no evidence has been given as to any such extrinsic circumstances;—but still, a case is not wholly wanting as to a knowledge of certain facts by the Court, which, in some degree, assume the character of such extrinsic circumstances. This intention of forming a fund for the benefit or relief of the relatives on both sides led the testator to make the codicil of the 21st April, 1836, signed only by himself, and therefore, of course, not binding at all upon the testatrix; but I refer to it merely to read that part which shows his full purpose of only leaving his wife, if surviving him, to enjoy a life estate, for he states: "I have to look upon my god-children as my adopted children, and my nearest kindred as the most entitled to my aid and assistance, and though these benefits must not prove any way detrimental to my widow *enjoying the whole of my property during her life*, yet my power, as husband, gives me the right to grant away any part of my property, which she has besides confirmed by her codicil of the 17th instant." Now looking back at that codicil of the 17th April, it will be found to have been executed by Mrs. Neethling, as well as the testator, and by it they both declare and order that certain debts due from certain relatives shall be made a poor fund for such relatives, as to the interest; whilst the further disposal of the capital and the interest of that fund is left with the testator, with which the testatrix declares herself, *nunc pro tunc*, to be satisfied.

The next deed to be brought under consideration is a document on which the main question is made on the part of the defendants, and which has been denominated by them as the will of the parties, but which, by the parties, is stated to be—"further testamentary disposition and substitution, with *fidei commissum*, by the undersigned, J. H. Neethling and A. C. Smuts, relative to that which, after the death of both, shall be done with the estate possessed by them in community. Having made our will of the 18th March, 1794, in the hope that our marriage may be blessed with children, but it not having pleased Providence to grant to us children, we are therefore *both of us* desirous, should we die childless, of directing jointly in what manner, in failure of children of our own, the remaining property shall devolve —at the same time, in separately confirming our former will, we do further direct as follows." Here certain bequests are stated; and then comes that which the defendants contend is a nomination of heirs to the inheritance, but which I must take to be only a name given to the *fidei commissum* trust of the poor fund to be created, inasmuch as the original will of 1794, appointing the survivor of each as the heir of the joint estate, is strictly confirmed in the terms of this very deed. "We appoint as heirs of the interest of the capital," certain parties named; and then " we appoint as heir of the capital of our estate, J. H. Neethling, for the term of his life." And the deed goes on to direct in what way that poor fund estate shall be regulated and distributed.

The constitution of this poor fund with the entire consent of the testatrix is fully proved under the next deed executed by both parties, dated 13th June, 1836, which states: "We, the undersigned, J. H. Neethling and A. C. Smuts, married people, testators by our mutual will of 10th March, 1794, and our further will for the joint determination respecting our succession, *made on the 27th of April*, 1836, referring by these presents to both these wills, and other special deeds of last will, do declare by this codicil to direct further, in manner following." It is clear from this language that the testator had no idea of altering, revoking, or changing in any way the appointment of heirs under the will of 1794, by that which was executed on the 27th April, 1836 ; and that whatever were the dispositions, therefore, under the latter will, they must be considered only as effecting an incumbrance upon the estate which would remain to the survivor as the heir under the will of 1794. In the deed of the 13th June, 1836, the testatrix reserves to herself the right of disposing of certain personal property belonging to herself, thus affording, on her part, the most perfect evidence of her entire consent at that time to their joint constitution of the poor fund to be created from the estate, after the life enjoyment of it by the survivor of them.

1853.
Feb. 22—28.
March 1.
Aug. 9.
Hofmeyr, Neethling's Curator, *vs.* De Wet, Neethling's Executor.

Thus the will remained until the 2nd June, 1838, two days .before the death of the testator. Referring to this deed, it thus commences: " We, the undersigned, J. H. Neethling and A. C. Smuts, married people, declare by these presents that we are desirous of directing and disposing *further* over our property we may leave at our death, as we hereby do; but especially desiring that the will passed and executed by us jointly on the 18th of March, 1794, shall be and remain of full force and effect in so far as relates to the appointment of heirs therein mentioned; and that all further bequests made by us, either jointly or separately, by virtue of the reservatory clauses contained in our said will, and respectively dated the 17th August, 1829, the 17th April, 1836, the 21st April, 1836, and the 13th June, 1836, shall likewise remain of full force and effect in as far as the same are not in this further and present disposition revoked, altered, or contain in themselves contradictory bequests ; and thus at present disposing further, we do declare." And then follow certain bequests ; after which it proceeds : " It being our further will that the survivor of us shall remain in the full possession of the estate, without being required to have the same inventoried, much less taxed." It further states : " Moreover, we declare that we reserve to ourselves the right and power to make such further bequests of legacies (the inheritance excepted) by a separate deed, under our respective signatures, as we may in time deem advisable."

I have now referred, so far as is necessary, to all the testamentary deeds, and it certainly seems clear to me that the will may be read so as readily to substantiate the construc-

z 2

1853.
Feb. 22—28.
March 1.
Aug. 9.
Hofmeyr, Necthling's Curator, vs.
De Wet, Neethling's Executor.

tion, that it was the intention of the testators that the survivor of each should enjoy, for life only, the entire estate; and that the estate should then be distributed among, and enjoyed by, the relatives of both their families. In respect of this interest it little matters whether the appointment of the heir shall be taken as made under the original mutual will of 1794 or under the testamentary paper of the 27th April, 1836. The only conflict as to this construction arises, as I have said, upon the terms used in the deed of 1836 as to the appointment of separate heirs to the interest and capital of the poor fund thereby created; but inasmuch as through the entire papers the will of 1794 is so specially confirmed as not to admit of any doubt of the intent of the parties to keep it as the declaration of their will with regard to the inheritance,—it seems to me that the construction to be put upon the terms of the deed of 1836, must be according to the principle referred to in *Starkie*, as quoted before, wherein he states : " As it may happen that on the face of the will the terms of devise may be such that would operate differently, and would give a different state according to extrinsic circumstances, such as the relation in which the devisee and the testator stood to each other." No such relation exists in this case; but, under the comparative statements of the testamentary dispositions, a similar principle of relation may arise as to the real intention of the testators, and the proper construction in respect to the terms adopted in their testamentary dispositions.

This brings me to the second point,—whether the widow was at liberty to dispose of her separate property by means of her will, or was bound, after the will, which was opened upon the decease of her husband, so as to fulfil its conditions. Many authorities were referred to at the Bar upon this question; but it seems to me satisfactory to refer to one authority, which places it as a settled point—4 *Burge, Conflict of Laws*, 404 : " A husband and wife may both make their testaments in one and the same paper writing; but the paper is considered to contain two separate testaments, which each of them may always alter separately, and without the knowledge of the other, as well as after the death of either of them. But if they have benefited each other reciprocally, and directed how their goods of the common estate are to go after the death of the survivor, if the latter has enjoyed, or wishes to enjoy, the benefit of it, such survivor can make no other last will or testamentary disposition of his or her share, unless he or she had rejected the benefit made and had ceded the same."

It is admitted that the widow, so far from repudiating the condition of her taking the inheritance subject to the burden of the *fidei commissum*, under the testamentary deed of the 27th April, 1836, at once received, and continued to receive, through and under the administration of the defendants, the usufruct of the whole joint estate during her entire life ; and I must again repeat, it is difficult to account for her thus so immediately consenting and abiding by the terms of the closed will, as opened upon the decease of her husband, if she had not willingly consented to the trust created under the deed of the 27th April, 1836. In this case there existed no antenuptial contract between the testator and testatrix, who were married in community ; therefore the principle connected with the *pactum successorium* does not apply. Under the conduct, too, of the executrix, she deprived herself of the benefit belonging to the *ambulatoria voluntas*.

It has been made a strong point, on the part of the defendants, that although the paper of the 2nd June, 1838, recites the dates of the various testamentary deeds which are to remain in full force and effect, the testamentary disposition of the 27th April, 1836, is not enumerated amongst such deeds. It is, certainly, not easy to account for this omission, but still, inasmuch as this document was one of the papers included in the envelope of the enclosed will, it must necessarily be taken as part of the joint will, and receive the like construction and effect as if included in that enumeration. For the Court cannot escape from the fixed legal conclusion, that whatever is contained in what encloses what is termed a closed will must be read, taken, and given effect to as a part of that will. Under these testamentary dispositions, it is quite clear that the testator never intended to take to himself greater benefit, or more of the estate, than what his wife would take if she proved the survivor. There is, therefore, a perfect mutuality of the conditions between the testator and the testatrix ; and if ever there was a case in which the doctrine of contract should bind the parties to the condition of a mutual will which has been confirmed by the death of either, and under which the survivor has taken the entire benefit of the whole joint estate--the testatrix in this case affords a most striking proof of the justice and equity of applying such a principle. For twelve years after the death of her husband she enjoys the interest of the whole estate, and those who now have an interest under that estate must be content to take it under the terms of the joint will as found at the death of the testator. It may be said that there may be some difficulty in the administration of the estate under that will. The Court, however, are not called upon to determine whether any such difficulties exist, or how they may be best removed. It has only to determine whether the testatrix was bound by the will she herself adopted at

1853.
Feb. 22—28.
March 1.
Aug. 9.

Hofmeyr, Neethling's Curator, *vs.*
De Wet, Neethling's Executor.

1853.
Feb. 22—28.
March 1.
Aug. 9.

Hofmeyr, Neethling's Curator, vs.
De Wet, Neethling's Executor.

the death of her husband, and, having found that she was so, must leave the administration of the estate with those in whose hands the will of the parties placed it, and who have undertaken that charge.

Upon this finding of the Court, in respect of the confirmation of the joint wills, as found at the death of the testator, it would seem that the administration of the estate by the defendants, under the will of the testatrix, can have been in no way beneficial to the interest of the parties taking under that will. The defendants, consequently, would not be entitled to charge any fees or expenses as for such administration after the death of the testator; no charge could, therefore, justly be imposed upon the parties taking under the joint will. As to the costs of the suit, however, considering such argument has been raised as would justify the defendants in opposing the construction of these testamentary dispositions as put on the part of the plaintiff, it would seem fitting that the costs of the action should be chargeable to and defrayed out of the joint estate.

BELL, J.—The very elaborate argument which we had in this case from both sides of the Bar, lasting for four days, led me to fear that there was more in the case than had met my ear in the course of the argument. I therefore went very carefully through the authorities, after having been furnished by the counsel on both sides not only with an arranged note of the authorities they had cited —which I had taken the liberty to ask—but with an epitome of their arguments, an excess of courtesy which I would not have ventured to ask, but for which I beg to return both gentlemen my best thanks.

After having carefully gone through the case, with this assistance, I have not been able to change the opinion which I formed in the course of the argument, that the case was not one of great difficulty when viewed in its proper light; nevertheless, as that does not appear to have been the view taken by others, I must now give the reasons why I have arrived at this conclusion, though I fear I may have to detain the Court much longer in doing so than I could have wished.

The case, as it was argued at the Bar, was said to resolve itself into two questions :

1st. Whether the testamentary disposition of the 27th April, 1836, should be read as part of the joint or mutual will of the testator and testatrix along with the other documents delivered by them to the notary, before witnesses, on the 2nd June, 1838, or should be set aside and disregarded as having been so delivered to the notary in error, and against the wish of the parties ?

2nd. Whether, supposing the first question to be decided adversely to the defendants, and the testamentary disposition of the 27th April, 1836, to be read as part of this joint will of 2nd June, 1838, there was anything in it, taken in conjunction with the other documents delivered to the notary on the 2nd June, 1838, which could in law prevent the widow from executing the wills in question?

1853.
Feb. 22.—28.
March 1.
Aug. 9.

Hofmeyr, Neethling's Curator, vs De Wet, Neethling's Executor.

In support of the plaintiff's case upon the first of these questions there was produced the deed made by the notary on the 2nd June, 1838, when all the testamentary documents were delivered to him, called the " deed of superscription." In this deed the notary states, in the usual form, that the testator and testatrix had handed to him " the herein enclosed documents and papers," with the information that they "contain their last will and desire, and the further codicillary disposition thereto annexed" (the meaning of these latter words is not apparent), and had requested him to seal them up. This desire, he says, was " complied with by these presents." The instrument then bears " *thus done* at Cape Town, &c. This is signed by the testator and testatrix, and then the notary affixes his seal and signature, and so do two witnesses mentioned by the notary.

The form here used is the usual one, according to the law of the Colony, for the making of what is called a " shut will;" and then we have the other usual form, a " deed of opening," as it is called, or instrument by the notary, certifying that he had opened the packet which had been sealed up by him on the 2nd June, after finding that the seals upon it were intact, and that he had found within various testamentary dispositions of Mr. and Mrs Neethling, and among the rest, the one in dispute, viz,, the will of the 27th April, 1836.

The argument of the defendants, for excluding this will of the 27th April from forming part of the final testamentary disposition of the parties, upon the ground that it had got into the sealed packet by inadvertence, and without the knowledge, of either of them, or, at least of the wife, was not based on any evidence of such inadvertence or want of knowledge; but rested entirely on an inferential argument, deduced from an alleged inconsistency of the will of the 27th April, with the other testamentary dispositions, and its repugnancy to some of their provisions.

Admitting such repugnancy and inconsistency to exist to a much greater extent than was attempted, their existence might occasion difficulty to the Court in ascertaning what was the wish of the testing parties, in regard to the matters embraced by the disputed document, and might ultimately oblige the Court to dismiss the contents of the document

1853.
Feb. 22.–28.
March 1.
Aug. 9.

Hofmeyr, Neethling's Curator, vs.
De Wet, Neethling's Executor.

from consideration, as much as if it had never been written. But when the question is simply, as it is under the first head of the argument, what documents are, or are not to be regarded as forming together the shut will of the parties, made on the 2nd of June, 1838, the Court must confine itself to the consideration of what was done upon that day. Now the evidence is clear and precise, according to the notary's instrument of enclosure or superscription, taken in conjunction with this instrument of opening, that the husband and wife delivered this will of the 27th April, along with the other documents, to the notary "'as their last will and desire."

Even if there had been direct positive evidence that they had done so by mistake or inadvertence, it is by no means clear to my mind that the Court could have taken such evidence into consideration. I am strongly impressed with the opinion that it could not, and for this reason:

By the law of this Colony, as of other places, there are varieties of evidence, both as to kind and degree, which, in the general case, parties desiring to prove anything may use according to their opportunities. They may use circumstantial evidence, or direct positive evidence, or parole evidence, or written evidence, or parole testimony by twenty witnesses, or by one or by two witnesses, or by notary and witnesses, or they may use all these kinds of evidence together. But when in any *particular* case the law says that a matter shall be valid *if* proved by *one* of these modes of evidence, it in effect says that it shall not be valid, *unless* proved by that particular mode. For as all the other modes of evidence would, but for the express law, be as good as the particular mode, saying that the use of the particular mode will give validity, is only repeating what was known before, and is doing nothing, unless all other modes are meant to be excluded. But a Court can never impute to any law such an ineption.

When, therefore, the law says that a particular matter will be good if done in a prescribed manner, what would, without the expressed law, have been a matter of *evidence* merely, becomes also a *solemnity*; and cannot be dispensed with, nor its place be supplied by equipollents. To allow either would be, not to administer, but to alter the law; it would be to say that what it has declared shall only be valid if done in one way shall be valid though done in any other.

The law of the Colony says that there are three modes of making a last will: 1st, by the testator signing it (originally in the presence of seven witnesses—and now) in the presence of two witnesses: 2nd, by the testator signing in the presence of a notary and two witnesses; and 3rd, by "shut will," made exactly in the way in which the one now in question was made, viz.: by delivering what is to constitute the will, as such, to a notary, in presence of two witnesses, and asking him to seal it up, and his complying with the request. And a will, *Van der Linden* (*p.* 125) says, " can take effect"—not when proper evidence is given of what was the will, these are not his words, but—" only *when the proper forms* are observed," and these forms are by *Voet* called " solemnities."

It is either proved or admitted in this case that all the solemnities necessary to make a shut will were observed, and that the will of the 27th April was among the documents delivered to and sealed up by the notary, as forming, together, that "shut will." It is, therefore, in effect, proved or admitted that the will of 27th April formed part of the shut will of the 2nd June, and that would be sufficient to dispose of the first question in the case, which is, simply whether the will of the 27th April is part of the will of the 2nd of June.

But then it is said—admitting that the will of the 27th April was properly enclosed on the 2nd of June, as part of the will of that date, so far as observance of all the solemnities is concerned, and that there is no direct evidence that such enclosure took place from inadvertence or want of knowledge—still it is not to be read as part of the shut will so duly made, because it is inconsistent with, and repugnant to, other parts of that will.

But the question at present only is whether it *is part* of the will, and this admission, in effect, though in other words, says that it *is* a part; for I have already shown that compliance with the solemnities makes everything enclosed part of the will. The admission in argument, therefore, also disposes of the first question; for if the will of 2nd June, instead of being composed of several testamentary papers, had consisted of one paper, and if all that is contained in the will of the 27th April had been embodied in that paper, it could never have been argued with any effect, in a question *to ascertain what constituted such single will* (which is all we are trying just now), that any matter indubitably to be found within the single testamentary paper was to be erased, because it was inconsistent with some other matters going before or after, yet that is, in effect, what is asked of the Court.

Every paper found within the notary's superscribed enclosure is as much part of the "shut will" as anything written in an "open will" is part of that open will. The repugnancy and inconsistency can receive effect when the will comes to be read and construed, for the purpose of administering the estate, or of considering whether the widow had power to alter or defeat the will of the 2nd June, but, in my opinion, cannot even be entertained when the question is limited to ascertaining of what part that will consists, not what the effect of those parts must be, when taken either collectively or distributively.

But then it was said the testamentary paper of the 2nd June confirms all the previous testamentary papers by their dates, which are given, with the exception of the will of the 27th April, all mention of which is omitted, and thence was argued an intention to revoke that will, and also evidence that it was delivered to the notary by mistake. If the omission to mention the will of the 27th April in that of the 2nd June could be carried to the height of working its revocation, the argument might avail the defendants; but they prudently did not attempt to go that length. And the conclusive answer is, that whatever might have been the effect of the will of the 2nd of June, had nothing else followed, it cannot have the effect contended for, of showing the intention of the parties to do away with the will of the 27th April; because *after* the will of the 2nd June had been executed, how long matters not, both husband and wife appeared before the notary, and gave him the will of the 27th April, and both signed his docket, declaring that what they had given him was their "last will and desire."

The will, therefore, of the 27th April, 1836, must, in my opinion, be taken to be part of the shut joint will made by Mr. and Mrs. Neethling on the 2nd June, 1838, by delivering it, along with the will of the 2nd June, 1838, and the other testamentary papers, as intended to constitute that joint will.

2nd. This brings me to the second general question raised by the defendants, whether, on the assumption that the will of the 27th April, 1836, is to be held as part of the shut will of the 2nd June, there is anything in the latter, so reading it, to prevent the widow from having made the wills which are called in question.

The solution of this depends upon several subordinate arguments which were raised by the parties.

For the affirmative, it was argued by the plaintiffs that the widow, by enjoying the whole joint estate for twelve years after her husband's death, adiated the joint will, and deprived herself of the right, which she otherwise would have had, at the time of her husband's death, to revoke the joint will, as to her own share of the joint estate, because by the joint will each spouse did not dispose of his half of the estate as a separate *unum quid*, among his own descendants or relatives; but each dealt with his own share and that of the other as one entire fund, of which they gave the benefit to the relatives of both, without distinction as to the number of persons or amount of benefit. The defendants answered, that the joint will could only be read as two separate wills, by two persons, written on the same paper, each disposing of his own estate, so that adiation could not have place to defeat the survivor's power to test on her own estate, and that even if read, as contended for by the plaintiffs, adiation had no such effect as that alleged, since it was impossible, by contract of any kind, for an individual to deprive him or herself of the power of making a will. The most, therefore, that could be said, was that the wife was bound to restore the husband's half after her own death, increased or diminished, as the case might be.

Upon a careful examination of the authorities, I can have no doubt that the decision of the Court, on the second question raised, should also be in favour of the plaintiff.

Grotius says, in somewhat general terms, that " if the predeceasing spouse has bequeathed any benefit to the survivor," the survivor, " if he accepted such benefits, " cannot revoke or alter the will of the deceased, by disposing of his or her share in variance from it. Though no mention is made here of spouses, it is evident from the expression, " his or her share," that the case of spouses is that which is being treated of. The vagueness of the expressions used by this author may be accounted for by the circumstance, to which *Schorer*, his editor (himself a person of authority) refers in his preface to the work, that the author wrote it in prison. This may or may not have been said with the pious fraud of an editor, to exalt the merit of his author; but at all events we have the fact from *Schorer* (incontrovertibly, I suppose), that *Grotius* gives no authorities for what he writes. " *Sed hæc*" (the imprisonment), *ratio est, cur dictis nullam adjecerit auctoritatem.*

Grotius, then, does not rest his doctrine upon the consent given by the surviving wife, nor upon the quality of benefit to the heirs of the two spouses, but solely on the benefit given by the predecessor to the survivor. That alone, he says, will be sufficient to prevent the survivor from disposing his, the survivor's share, in a manner at variance with the predecessor's " disposal of the property in general."

Peckius, whose commentary " *De Testamen. Conjug* " was written before 1646, says in I. 43, 4, " But since I shall in another place inquire how in the general case testaments are revocable, and what precautions must be observed, I shall postpone all these, and only adduce that one statute (*consultum*) against revocation when one of the spouses, with consent of the other, *alone* makes a will of the goods of both or a part of them for the common benefit of their children. *For then the disposition, though it be revocable on the part of the testator, yet on the part of the* SPOUSE CON-SENTING, *passes into a* CONTRACT, *and becomes irrevocable.*" This, he says, is to be supported by various authorities, showing that the case of strangers " *de meo tu potes testari me volente.*"

Here *Pechius* somewhat differs from *Grotius*. He agrees with him that the survivor cannot revoke; but he rests this apparently on the consent which the survivor had given to the predeceaser, and on the fact that the will was for the common benefit of their children.

So stand *Grotius* and *Peekius*, the earliest writers. Then comes *Van Leeuwen*, an admittedly high authority; and he, writing about the same time on the same subject, in his work on the Roman-Dutch Law—3, 3, 8—says a testator has not free disposal in three cases, the third of which he thus describes: " When two married persons have *reciprocally benefited each other*, and thereby directed how the goods of the common estate should devolve after the death of the survivor of them, such survivor *having enjoyed the benefit*, cannot dispose of his or her share by last will." This, in substance, is not very different from *Grotius*, and is expressed nearly in as general terms. The only variation from *Grotius* is that the benefit is required to be reciprocal. *Van Leeuwen* afterwards wrote on the same subject at greater length, in the *Censura Forensis*. This work he wrote with *Pechius* and *Grotius* before him, for he refers to both, and without apparently thinking that what he was writing was in conflict with either of them. He says in 3, 11, 7—" If two spouses in a joint will " reciprocally " institute each other heir *under the condition* that all the goods remaining at the death of the survivor shall be left to A and B, the survivor, *if he have adiated the estate of the first dying*, cannot afterwards dispose *even of his own share* in a different maner contrary to the mutual will; their estate having, as it were, *become consolidated, in which case only* the free revocation of testaments is prevented ; because the one has, with the consent of the other, made a will of the goods of both and a part of them (*parte eorum*), and that disposition, *which otherwise would be revocable on the part of the testator, passes into a contract on the part of the* ONE CONSENTING *to it, and becomes irrevocable.*"

After arguing why this should be so, he concludes in these words: " This limitation," *i. e.*, against revocation, " must be confined to the case where the one disposing the goods of the other by his consent, or both disposing reciprocally of the joint estate by consolidation, substitution, *fidei commissum*, or any other mode, institutes the other heir, or leaves him the usufruct *or any other benefit*, in which case it is the common opinion of the doctors that the other *having adiated the inheritance*, or *enjoyed the benefit of what was left*, cannot, even *for his share*, alter the disposition *because it is considered as only one disposition* made of the single joint patrimony, *consolidated by mutual mixture*; and this mode of making a testament is so common, especially between married people, that it cannot in any way be considered as departing from the law; provided it be certain that the one has disposed of the goods of the other, and that the other was instituted under this condition. And this is subject to less difficulty, because in this case it is not so much the free disposition of his own which is forbidden to either, as that the survivor is, *by adiating the inheritance*, burthened with a *fide-commis*. of the first dying to leave *even his own goods* after his death *to this or that person*.

1853.
Feb. 22—28.
March 1.
Aug. 9.

Hofmeyr, Neethling's Curator, *vs.*
De Wet Neethling's Executor.

"But if it be doubtful whether the one has disposed of the goods of the other by his consent,—for instance, if two spouses shall have disposed jointly of the goods of both, and instituted each other reciprocally as fiduciary heir *but in such a manner* that what shall remain, after death of the survivor, must come to the relations of both *in equal moieties*—in such case, and in any other less doubtful, from a liberal conjecture of intention, although two jointly, and in the same paper, reciprocally make a testament, there are considered as many testaments as there are persons bequeathing, which dispositions *each is at liberty to revoke as far as he is concerned*. For in doubt it is held, that each has disposed only of his own share, and not of the other's."

The same author (*Cen. For.*) *in* 3, 2, 16—after speaking of wills by several persons (not spouses, though they are given as instances) written in one paper, as being so many wills as there are persons, and each revocable—continues: "Unless by consolidation and mutual consent each shall have disposed of the goods of the other, in which case, though it be revocable on the part of the testator," (*ex parte testantis*), that is, the party dying first, "yet on the *part of the consentor it passes into a contract* and *becomes irrevocable*, according to what *Peckius* la s down. (*Tract. de Test. Conjug.*, 1, 43, 4—3, 11, 6.)

Van der Keessel, the latest writer of all, says in his *Thesis* 283, that the surviving spouse instituted heir to the predeceaser, may not alter a will of the joint estate as to that part which is to devolve on the substitute heirs of the predeceaser; but he or or she may, as to the part to go to his or her own heirs, "*unless both shall have disposed by mutual consent of the joint estate or a* (*his or her*) *part thereof*.

1853.
Feb. 22.—28.
March 1.
Aug. 9.

Hofmeyr, Neethling's Curator, rs.
De Wet, Neethling's Executor.

The only authority relied upon by the defendants to destroy the effect of those I have quoted is *Voet*, who (writing between 1699 and 1705) has laid down that the law is not to be taken as *Grotius* gives it in the passage I have quoted. The passage in *Voet* is in 23, 4, 63, where he says that if by antenuptial contract (and the same reason, he says, holds as to testamentary dispositions) the spouses contract that, after the death of the survivor, "the goods shall go *equally to the relatives of the two*. Then, he says, either of the spouses may alter this while both are alive, or the survivor may do it after the death of the other, to the effect of testing upon his own estate; and though, he says, it is otherwise laid down by *Grotius*, yet what he says "must be taken to apply to the case in which the spouses acted together, *testing the one upon the goods of the other*, and each giving to the other the power of so doing.

Now, it may be observed that *Grotius* has not apparently done that which *Voet* seems in this passage to assume that he had done. He does not speak of a will whereby the goods on the death of the survivor, " go equally to the relatives of the two," the case in which *Voet* says his doctrine would be invalid ; all *Grotius* speaks of is the incapacity of the survivor to revoke, created by acceptance of benefits from the predeceaser.

What, then, may be held to be established by a comparison of the whole authorities, taking the *Censuria Forensis* as the guide? In this work *Van Leeuwen* says if spouses have " reciprocally instituted each other heirs," under a condition that the estate, at the death of a survivor, shall go to A and B, the survivor cannot, if he have adiated the estate, dispose even of his own share. The reciprocal institution of heirs is the interpretation he puts on *Grotius's* expression, " bequeathed any benefit," and on his own expression in his Roman-Dutch Law, "reciprocally benefited." The adiation of this benefit, he says, cuts off the power of revocation, even though the estate do not go to children, but to third parties, such as A and B So far the *Censura* is supported by *Grotius*, who, as I before observed, does not limit his doctrine to the case of the estate dividing between the joint heirs ; and it is also supported by the *Treatise on Roman-Dutch Law* and by *Van der Keessel*. *Peckius*, the only other authority except *Voet*, does not destroy this. He says, that if one of the spouses, with consent of the other, make alone a will of the goods of both *for the common benefit of their children*. in such a case the survivor can not revoke. In this he does not slacken the cord in favour of revocation; he is drawing it tighter. He does not say that though revocation is not competent where the will is for the benefit of children, it is competent where the will is in favour of strangers, which is what defendants wish to establish. Not at all. Where the will is for the benefit of children, the presumption seems to be in favour of revocation, as we have seen in the passage from *Van Leeuwen*, where, speaking of what is to be done where there is a doubt as to whether the survivor gave his or her consent to the predeceaser to make the will, he says an instance giving rise to such doubt is where the will gives the estate to the relations in equal moieties. But *Peckius*, without going into the question of evidence of consent, says that even where the will is for the common benefit of the children, revocation is competent, if the will have been made by the predeceaser with the consent of the survivor. In this he does not dissent from or say anything contrary to the other authorities.

1853.
Feb. 22—28.
March 1.
Aug. 9.

Hofmeyr, Neethling's Curator,vs.
De Wet, Neethling's Executor.

The *Censura Forensis* and *Grotius*, then, are confirmed not only by the *Roman-Dutch Law* and *Van der Keessel*, but also by *Peckius*, in laying down that adiation by a survivor of two spouses, of benefits given by them reciprocally to each other in their joint will, will deprive the survivor of the power to alter the will, even as to her or his own share of the joint estate.

In giving his reasons why a will in favour of children, made by the predeceaser, with the consent of the survivor, could not be revoked by the survivor, *Peckius* stated that the disposition on the part of the survivor or "spouse consenting" passed into a contract. This reason the *Censura Forensis* adopts for the more favourable case, for revocation, of a will in favour of strangers, almost in the very words of *Peckius*, " because the one has, with the consent of the other, made a will of the goods of both, and the disposition, which otherwise would be revocable on the part of the testator, passes into a contract on the part of the one consenting to it, and becomes irrevocable." It would appear, therefore, that *Van Leeuwen* and *Peckius* considered in both cases that the instrument became a contract immediately on the occurrence of the death of the predecessor. This is the view which occurred to myself at an early stage of the case, and I have neither heard from the Bar, nor found from the books, anything to disturb it. These authorities, on the contrary, expressly confirm it.

The *Censura* says, no doubt, in the passage to which I have before referred, that if the consent of the survivor be doubtful, then, in favour of intention, the survivor may revoke, and he gives, as one instance of what would raise such a doubt, the circumstance that the will is so framed that the estate " must come to the relations of both in equal moieties." He does not say that, even in such a case, revocation would be competent. He only gives it as an instance for doubt as to consent, on which to found revocation. And it obviously does furnish such an instance ; for, if the estate is to go by will in equal moieties, exactly as it would have gone without the will, there is no benefit to the predeceaser for which he can be supposed to have contracted, in return for giving to the survivor the usufruct for life of the whole estate. It is only in this view that the leaning in favour of revocation where the will gives the estate to the relatives of the two, equally, seems to be intelligible.

Voet, in the passage relied on by the defendants, deals with this very matter, though a little differently. He does not give the case put as an instance merely of evidence of want of consent to the mutual will, but he says broadly that "if the spouses contract that after the death of the survivor the goods shall *go equally to the relatives of the two*," the survivor may revoke. Now, it is to be observed in this passage, that it regards simply a mutual will by which two spouses give their estates to their relatives equally, after the death of the survivor. It makes no express mention of reciprocal benefits, as do the other authorities; though it leaves a usufruct by the survivor to be inferred,—and it says nothing about adiation by the survivor, nor about consent given by the predeceaser to the survivor to make his will. These are cases with which that passage does not at all deal. Yet, with these omissions, *Voet* says, lower down, that the will will not be revocable by the survivor, "if the spouses acted together, testing the one upon the goods of the other, and each giving to the other the power of so doing ;" for it is to this case, he says, the words of *Grotius* only can apply, when he speaks of the will not being revocable.

Voet is supported in this doctrine, that the will is not revocable in such a case as that last supposed, by the *Censura Forensis*, in the passage before referred to, where it is said that revocation is prevented in the case in which two (especially spouses), testing together, the one institutes the other heir, on condition and under the burden that all the estate which should remain to the survivor out of the mutual estate should go to A or B, and the survivor should afterwards adiate the inheritance of the predeceaser ; because by their consent the estate had been consolidated and reduced into one patrimony. Reciprocal benefit and adiation of these benefits no doubt enter into the doctrine here stated, while they are omitted in *Voet*, but that only shows that *Voet* is less in favour of revocation than the *Censura*. For if, according to *Voet*, revocation be not competent, if the spouses "test the one upon the goods of the other, each giving the other the power of so doing," it will not be more competent,—but, on the contrary, will be less competent—if to that circumstance be added these others, that the spouses reciprocally benefited each other, and that the survivor has adiated these benefits.

1858.
Feb. 22—28.
March 1.
Aug. 9.
Hofmeyr, Neethling's Curator,rs.
De Wet, Neethling's Executor.

There is one other authority referred to by the defendants, *Boel on Loenius*, case 137. That commentator, in a passage not referred to from the Bar, says that revocation by a surviving spouse is competent when the two spouses have by will (of which he gives an instance pretty much in the terms of the one now in question) given their estate to their common children "*vel hinc inde proximioribus consanguineis et hæredibus,*" to the nearest relatives or heirs on both sides. Possibly this passage might bear out the defendant's case to the extent of showing that a will to that effect, without more, would be revocable. I say only *possibly*, for even then it would have to be considered whether his authority could be good without any specification whether the gift is to the relations on either side equally or disproportionately. But there is more in the present case—there are reciprocal benefits and adiation of these benefits, neither of which circumstances, in the number of cases he puts, he at all refers to.

The passages relied on by the defendants were to the effect that *revocation* is *not competent* when either spouse, with mutual consent, disposes of his or her own and the other's goods *among children*, a case which, he says, neither *Faber, Peckius,* nor *Everardus* had dealt with. This may be true enough, but *Van Leeuwen* had distinctly done so to the effect of saying that such a will, *i. e.*, a will by one of the goods of both, made with the consent of the other, would, without specifying who it might be in favour of, *be irrevocable*, unless the fact of consent should be doubtful, of which he said the fact of the gift being to the children would be some evidence.

The use which the defendants apparently wished to derive from this was negative—to show that if the will was irrevocable when made in favour of children, it was revocable when made in favour of strangers. This I cannot concede to them. *Van Leeuwen* gives his reason for saying why the will is irrevocable, because it has, by the death of the predeceaser, become a contract on behalf of those who are to take; but he says, as I have explained in words, this may be, so far, done away with, if the will is for the benefit of the relations of both in equal moieties; because, seeing they would by law take this way at any rate, there is no reason to presume a contract to obtain that which the law would give without it. I must hold, therefore, that if, according to *Boel*, a will by one of the goods of both, made by mutual consent, would not be revocable when in favour

A A

1863.
Feb. 22—28.
March 1.
Aug. 9.

Hofmeyr, Neethling's Curator. vs.
De Wet, Neethling's Executor.

of children, *multo fortiori* would it not be revocable if made in favour of strangers.

Another reference to the same commentator, as to a passage in which he says that a will is not revocable when the spouses, testing confusedly upon the goods of both, either in favour of children or of strangers, declare that the disposition is to be entirely that of the predeceaser, either expressly or tacitly, by taking away all power from the survivor, of changing or revoking the conjugal testament.

That may very well be, and yet the passage is no authority for saying that the will must be revocable where neither of these declarations is to be found, nor yet for overthrowing those authorities to which I have already referred, which show that such a will will not be revocable if there have been reciprocal benefits, and the survivor have adiated them, though there should not be any such express or tacit declaration.

The fair result of the investigation, then, is " that, " according to *Grotius, Perhius, Van Leeuwen,* and *V. d. Keessel,* " if the spouses have reciprocally benefited each other, by giving the survivor the usufruct of the *estate for life,* or any other benefit, and under this condition have, with the consent of each other, both dealt with the estate by their joint will as if the whole belonged to each, the survivor, if he adiate the benefits, cannot revoke the joint will, even as to his or her own share, because, by the death of the predeceaser, the will has become a contract, and that, according to *Van Leeuwen,* if the estate go by the will to the relatives of both, in equal moieties, that will be a circumstance to render it doubtful whether the will was made by consent, as to make it irrevocable, and incline a Court to hold it to be revocable ;" whereas, according to *Voet,* even if the mutual will gives the estate *equally to the relatives of the two,* and have the inference against contract yielded by that circumstance, still it will not be revocable, provided the spouses acted together in making the will, testing the one upon the goods of the other, and each giving to the other the power of so doing—without regard to the questions whether there were any reciprocal benefits, or any adiation of these benefits.

Now, beyond all controversy, the mutual will in the present case did not give the estate equally to the relatives of the two spouses—it gave it only to such of the members of either or both families as might be poor—not even at the time of the death of the survivor, or at any other single given period, but in all time to come. The qualification of poverty, therefore, might at one time belong to two members of one family and to five of other, and at another to ten members of the one family and none of the other, or in any other conceivable disproportion. As the only case—equality of bequest—to which the reference to *Voet* applies, does not exist here, the reference may be dismissed from consideration, reserving observation on the concluding part of the reference until I come to speak of the other authorities.

1853.
Feb. 22—23.
March 1.
Aug. 9.
Hofmeyr, Neethling's Curator, *vs.*
De Wet, Neethling's Executor

In order to see how far the other authorities govern the case, let me consider whether there were any reciprocal benefits given by the spouses, and whether the survivor adiated these benefits,—and, finally, what were the terms or form of expression by which the spouses made their testamentary dispositions.

Now the will, of whatever documents it may be held to c nsist, instituted the spouses, reciprocally, heirs to each other, and gave the survivor the usufruct of the whole for life. The widow was the survivor. She was admitted to possession of the whole estate, and enjoyed it up to the day of her death, which happened twelve *years* after that of her husband. By law the widow was entitled absolutely to half the estate; beyond that she had no right. The usufruct, therefore, of the other half, which she could have taken only under the will, was a benefit given to her by her husband, and her enjoyment of that usufruct for twelve years was as complete adiation as could well be imagined.

Then as to the mode in which the spouses dealt with the joint estate. By the will of 18th March, 1794, they institute " each other" and the children of the marriage " heirs *to all the property* which they may leave." The survivor to remain in the full and undisturbed possession of the estate," and they reserve to themselves power " to make such alterations or additional arrangements in this their last will as they shall think fit." There is no appearance here of anything like two wills written on one paper.

By the codicil of 17th August, 1826, the *two spouses together* give to Anna C. Neethling the interest of 60,000 guilders, part of it to consist of the interest of 30.000 guilders, which her husband owed to the testator, and the other half, being the usufruct of a house belonging to the testator, " unless " as to the half " the survivor of the donors shall direct otherwise."

By the codicil of 17th April, 1836, the spouses " *agreed with each other* and declared " that " *all debts* which *our* brothers, sisters, and their children of the first degree on both sides are indebted *to us* " are by virtue of the will assigned to them " as a poor fund *jointly* for the poor in one of these degrees of relationship *of one or of both sides*," and they directed that the executors should get in only the interest of the debts, " whilst the *further disposal* of the capital and the interest of that fund is left *to the first undersigned spouse, with which the second undersigned declares nunc pro tunc to be satisfied.*

The will of 27th April, 1836, states itself to be " relative to that which, after the death of both, shall be done with the estate *possessed by them* in community." It speaks of the spouses being childless, and their desire, after the enjoyment of the property " *amassed together by our* own industry," of " *directing jointly* " in what manner the remaining property should devolve. It then directs that the "*joint estate remaining*" with the survivor should be ascertained and be invested " *in immovable property.*" It then says, " *We* bequeath " to A. C. Neethling " an annual sum of 1,200 Rds." Then, " *we* bequeath " to H. J. Neethling " a sum of 300 Rds. per annum." Then follow three gifts of annuities, each of which are accomplished by the words, " *we* bequeath."

There then follows, first, an individual bequest by the testator of all Free-masonry articles, of his clothes and ornaments, and his law books. And another individual bequest by the testatrix of all her clothes and personal ornaments.

The will then resumes the plural: " *We* declare that *our* estate shall never be alienated or diminished," but that after compliance " *with our* " hereunder following usufructuary dispositions shall serve for the support of the poor, " limited to the *own descendants of one of our deceased fathers,* bearing the name of *Neethling or Smuts.*" " *We* appoint as heirs of the interest, *our* three living brothers, &c., as also *our* godchildren *on both sides, share and share alike.*" " *We* appoint as heir of the capital of *our* estate, H. J. Neethling," &c., who is to be content with his share, according to the will, and to renounce the Falcidian portion, and is to consider himself a *fidei-commissary on behalf of the next heir,* and so long as six of the *joint heirs* of the interest are alive, is to allow the executors to manage the capital. For that purpose " *we* appoint as executors of this *joint estate,*" the Association, &c., *i.e.,* the present defendants.

The will of the 13th June, 1836, directs the survivor to have an inventory made out, but declares that it need not be filed or exhibited to the Master of this Court or any other functionary. And says that the survivor shall be the executor or executrix respectively.

The only appearance in any of these testamentary papers of anything like the *separate* exercise of testamentary power is the trifling bequest, by the testator, of the Free-masonry articles, his clothes, and ornaments, and by the testatrix of her clothes and ornaments. All the rest is so completely within the authorities, which make revocation incompetent, as to justify one in thinking that the testator, who was a professional person, and drew some of these wills and codicils himself, had the authorities in view at the time. It is impossible to read the phrases I have extracted without saying the spouses "disposed reciprocally of the joint estate," and "made one disposition of the single joint patrimony, consolidated by mutual mixture," in the words of *Van Leeuwen*; —that they "disposed by mutual consent of the joint estate in the words of *Van der Keessel*;—and that "the spouses acted together, testing the one spouse upon the goods of the other, each giving to the other the power of so doing," in the words of *Voet*.

1853.
Feb. 22—28.
March 1.
Aug. 9,
Hofmeyr, Neethling's Curator, *vs.*
De Wer, Neethling's Executor.

I can have no doubt, theretore, whatever might have been the effect, had there been *no* reciprocal benefits, and no adiation of them by the survivor, that there having been both, the mutual will was not revocable by the survivor.

There are several other points of law raised, which I do not think it necessary to notice at any greater length than to satisfy the parties that I have not overlooked them.

It was said that the will of 27th April, 1836, could not take effect as a codicil, because it instituted heirs, and disposed of the whole estate, which a codicil could not do,— neither could it take effect as a will, because it was revoked by the codicil of 2nd June, 1838.

I am of opinion that neither of these positions will avail the defendants, for the testamentary paper of 27th April must take effect, if at all, neither as a codicil nor as a will, but *as a part* of the will composed of it and all the other testamentary papers enclosed within the deed of superscription; and I am of opinion that it must take effect, because the omission in the codicil of 2nd June, 1838, to enumerate it among those that were confirmed could not have the effect, *per se*, to revoke it; and even if it could do so, that would be done away with by the subsequent act of the testators, in delivering it to the notary to be enclosed along with the other papers, as part of their "last will and desire."

It was also argued that the will of 1794, having made a direct institution of the widow, as heir to the mutual estates. to be enjoyed as "her own property," and the codicil of 2nd June, 1838, having set up and confirmed the will of 1794, the effect is to destroy the paper of 27th April, 1838, so far as it infringes upon the absolute right given by the will of 1794.

To that doctrine I cannot accede. The will of 1794 expressly reserved power to make "such alterations and arrangements in this their last will as the parties should think fit." And the paper of the 27th April being to be read as part of the will, is to be regarded as such "altera-

1858.
Feb. 22—28.
March 1.
Aug. 9.

Hofmeyr Neeth-
ling's Curator, vs.
De Wet, Neeth-
ling's Executor.

tion or additional arrangement," and, viewed as such, produces no difficulty or confusion ;—all that it does is to make that institution fidei-commissary, which, by the will of 1794, had hitherto been direct and absolute.

It was also argued that the testamentary paper of the 27th April, because it had been written by the testator himself, was void, so far as it interfered with the testatrix's share. But I am satisfied, on examination of the authorities, that they only apply to make void gifts in favour of the writer of the will himself, or of those who substantially are the same as himself, viz., children not yet forisfamiliated, slaves and the like; but such gifts are not at all in question here.

There was a good deal of argument, also, and some reference made to authorities, to show that inheritance cannot go by contract, but must go by last will or by intestacy, and that a man cannot deprive himself of the power of testing— all of which positions may be true enough in cases to which they apply, but they have no application here, for the reasons, among others, which will be found in 2 *Consult.*, 275, but which I need not go through here.

Upon all these grounds I am of opinion that judgment must be given for the plaintiff in the terms asked by the declaration, to the effect of declaring that the only authority under which the defendants can act, in administering the joint estate of the spouses, is all the papers found within the deed of superscription of the 2nd June, 1838, including that of the 27th April, 1836.

Judgment for plaintiff accordingly.

[Plaintiff's Attorney, *J. C. Berrange*.
Defendant's Attorneys, *Redelinghuys & Wessels*.]

SAUL SOLOMON AND CO., PRINTERS, CAPE TOWN.

www.ingramcontent.com/pod-product-compliance
Lightning Source LLC
Chambersburg PA
CBHW031419230426
43668CB00007B/362